The Bible, the School, and the Constitution

The Bible, the School, and the Constitution

The Clash that Shaped Modern Church-State Doctrine

STEVEN K. GREEN

OXFORD
UNIVERSITY PRESS

OXFORD
UNIVERSITY PRESS

Oxford University Press, Inc., publishes works that further
Oxford University's objective of excellence
in research, scholarship, and education.

Oxford   New York
Auckland   Cape Town   Dar es Salaam   Hong Kong   Karachi
Kuala Lumpur   Madrid   Melbourne   Mexico City   Nairobi
New Delhi   Shanghai   Taipei   Toronto

With offices in
Argentina   Austria   Brazil   Chile   Czech Republic   France   Greece
Guatemala   Hungary   Italy   Japan   Poland   Portugal   Singapore
South Korea   Switzerland   Thailand   Turkey   Ukraine   Vietnam

Published by Oxford University Press, Inc.
198 Madison Avenue, New York, New York 10016

www.oup.com

Oxford is a registered trademark of Oxford University Press

Library of Congress Cataloging-in-Publication Data
Green, Steven K. (Steven Keith), 1955–
The Bible, the School, and the Constitution: the clash that shaped the
modern church-state doctrine / Steven K. Green,
p.   cm.
ISBN 978-0-19-982790-9 (hardcover: alk. paper)—ISBN 978-0-19-982791-6 (ebook)
1. Religion in the public schools—Law and legislation—United States—Cases.
2. Freedom of religion—United States—Cases.   3. Church and state—United States—Cases.
4. Religion in the public schools—Law and legislation—United States—History.
5. United States. Supreme Court—History.   I. Title
KF4162.G74 2012
344.73'0796—dc23   2011018787

1 3 5 7 9 8 6 4 2

Printed in the United States of America
on acid-free paper

CONTENTS

PREFACE

The genesis of this book goes back many years to my interest in the origins of the legal conflict surrounding prayer and Bible reading in the public schools. Early in my research, I quickly realized the interconnectedness of that issue with the controversy over public funding of religious education. Research into the origins and evolution of the nineteenth-century School Question, as it was called, led me to the apex of that conflict following the Civil War, a particularly active period in which people from many walks of life debated the role of religion not solely in education but as part of the nation's identity. This very public discussion took place in Congress, the courts, and in the press, and it inspired several attempts to amend the language of the religion clauses to the Constitution. In one of my first writings on this period, "The Blaine Amendment Reconsidered" (*American Journal of Legal History*, 1992), I explored the recurrent claim that the near passage of the Blaine Amendment in 1876—which would have applied the religion clauses to the states, among other things—undermined the legitimacy of the later incorporation of the Bill of Rights pursuant to the Due Process Clause of the Fourteenth Amendment. To my surprise and pleasure, that article has been cited over the years as a leading analysis of the Blaine Amendment, though commonly not for its primary thesis but for its documentation of the religious (anti-Catholic) impulse in the events surrounding the amendment. Courts also, including the Supreme Court in 2000, have cited that article for that latter theme in evaluating the historical basis for the rule against funding religious education. Those citations, while always gratifying to receive, have often failed to appreciate the limited scope of the latter discussion and the larger context of the "great church-state debate" of the mid-nineteenth century.

In this book I explore the development of the nineteenth-century School Question to its culmination in the Blaine Amendment, but on a more comprehensive level. I hope to elucidate the variety of impulses and attitudes that informed both aspects of the School Question and how that controversy impacted modern Supreme Court doctrine. I build on themes contained in more recent articles and in part of my book *The Second Disestablishment* (2010), but here present a complete argument. [Portions of Chapter Six previously appeared in "The Insignificance of the Blaine Amendment," *Brigham Young University Law Review* (2008:295–333) and is reprinted with permission.]

In a project with such long roots, it is impossible to name all who have provided substantive insight. Over the years, I have benefitted from helpful comments from Fred Gedicks, Derek Davis, Frank Kemerer, Steven Gey, Tom Berg, Rick Garnett, Paul Finkelman, and Noah Feldman, among others. I also wish to thank my editor at Oxford University Press, Theo Calderara, my assistant Reyna Meyers, and the staff at the Willamette University libraries, particularly Galin Brown. As always, I could not have accomplished this work without the love, support, and patience of my wife, Cindy, who never tires of hearing about church-state history. This book is dedicated to my mother, Pauline, and my mother-in-law, Betty, whose devotions to their Protestant and Catholic faiths and commitments to interfaith respect were a model for us all. We miss them dearly.

The Bible, the School, and the Constitution

Introduction

On June 17, 1963, the United States Supreme Court announced its decisions in *Abington School District v. Schempp* and *Murray v. Curlett*, companion cases involving the constitutionality of Bible reading in public schools. The outcomes of both cases were eagerly anticipated. Only a year earlier, the Court had struck down, 8-1, a New York law that had required the daily recitation of a prayer in public schools. Reaction to the "Regent's Prayer" case (*Engel v. Vitale*) had been swift and decidedly negative. Religious leaders—ranging from Cardinal Francis Spellman and Episcopal Bishop James A. Pike to evangelist Billy Graham—had condemned the ruling. "God pity our country when we can no longer appeal to God for help," Graham declared. Politicians joined in as well. North Carolina Senator Sam Ervin, a self-described constitutional expert who would later gain fame during the Watergate hearings, insisted that "the Supreme Court has made God unconstitutional." Despite the widespread public condemnation of *Engel*, the justices did not retreat. By the same 8-1 margin, they found that readings from the Bible and recitations of the Lord's Prayer, conducted as part of daily opening exercises, violated religious neutrality as required by the Establishment Clause of the Constitution.[1]

The public outcry over the *Schempp* and *Murray* decisions was even louder than the one over *Engel*. Because *Engel* had involved a prayer drafted by a state agency, some religious leaders were ambivalent about the outcome. In contrast, *Schempp* and *Murray* involved informal practices of prayer and Bible reading that were common throughout the nation's public schools. Politicians and religious conservatives roundly condemned the decisions, with South Carolina Senator Strom Thurmond calling the holdings "another major triumph of secularism and atheism which are bent on throwing God completely out of our national life." Billy Graham claimed that the decisions outlawed practices that stretched back to the time of the Pilgrims, and Alabama Governor George Wallace, repeating an earlier act of defiance, challenged the justices to stop him from going into the schools and reading from the Bible to students.[2]

The public interest in the cases reached a magnitude rarely seen in American constitutional history. Only the desegregation holding in *Brown v. Board of*

Education (1954) had garnered similar media attention and engendered a public debate over the meaning of a constitutional principle. *Christianity Today* reported that while the cases were being decided the Supreme Court received as many as fifty letters a day in favor of prayer and Bible reading, and Congress twice held hearings on the issue. Newspapers, popular magazines, and religious and scholarly journals critiqued the controversy for weeks following the decisions, and the CBS television network produced a widely watched program: "Storm Over the Supreme Court." Responding to the decisions, Congressman Frank Becker of New York introduced a proposed constitutional amendment to bar schools or other government institutions from prohibiting public prayers or Bible readings. When congressional hearings on the proposed amendment were held in the spring of 1964, more than one hundred people testified, most favoring the amendment. Overall, the Bible reading controversy "attracted the widest attention and the largest following," asserted a religious magazine, and for many people it represented "America's greatest battle." But more was at stake than mere Bible reading; as one religious leader remarked, the controversy raised the "greater question" of "whether the United States will continue to give honor and respect to God in national life." The fight dragged on until Congress narrowly voted down the proposed amendment in 1971. The high court would reaffirm the substance of the 1963 decisions in later rulings, but some would say the issue was never resolved, at least in the court of public opinion.[3]

The attention given to the 1962–1963 prayer and Bible reading decisions was not unprecedented, however. Little noticed in Justice Tom Clark's majority opinion in *Schempp* and in Justice William Brennan's lengthy concurrence were references to a similar controversy that had erupted following the Civil War. As precedent for their opinions, Clark and Brennan relied on an 1873 decision of the Ohio Supreme Court which had similarly ruled against Bible reading in the schools. That decision had been part of a much larger controversy over public school religious exercises and the funding of religious education, the justices noted, one that had also embroiled the nation. That controversy, too, had resulted in a proposal to amend the Constitution to resolve the interrelated religious issues. The parallels, while not exact, were striking. And as Justices Clark and Brennan surmised, the Court's current foray into the thicket of religion and public education was unlikely to be any more successful in resolving the thorny issues than the earlier episode.[4]

The United States Supreme Court first asserted authority over these issues in the 1940s when it ruled that the Bill of Rights applied to the states. In 1947, a slim Court majority upheld minor forms of public financial assistance for children attending parochial schools, while suggesting that more significant aid would violate church-state separation. The following year the Court struck down a program of religious instruction in the public schools, declaring that "a state cannot consistently with the First [Amendment] utilize its public school system to aid any or all religious faiths or sects in the dissemination of their doctrines." These rulings, too, were highly controversial, not just because of the outcomes but because the Court was exercising jurisdiction over local school policies. Just as significant as the decisions themselves was their suggestion of a particular ordering of the nation's sacred and temporal realms, one, which many critics insisted, renounced the nation's religious heritage.[5]

These school decisions became the source of the Court's leading standards (or "tests") for adjudicating religion clause controversies generally.[6] For much of the latter twentieth century, the Court applied what some termed a "strict separationist" approach to church-state issues, one that prohibited most forms of government support for religion, including both financial and symbolic support. Despite ongoing criticism from religious and political conservatives, the Court held its ground; in later holdings, the justices forbade the posting of the Ten Commandments in schoolrooms while they affirmed the teaching of evolution, to the exclusion of "creation science." On the funding side, the Court rejected most legislative efforts to provide financial assistance to religious schools. By the close of the century, few areas of constitutional law were more highly charged or socially divisive. The high court's rulings on religion and education became part of the nation's modern "culture wars."[7]

Critics of the Court's church-state jurisprudence have charged that the education decisions fail to respect the nation's religious heritage and long-held traditions, resulting in a "naked public square," if not a "culture of disbelief."[8] More recently, criticism of the Court's Bible reading and funding decisions has come from within. In the early 1990s, the Court narrowed its earlier holdings prohibiting Bible reading in schools by allowing student-led devotional activities in extracurricular clubs. Then, in 2001, the Court opened the door to in-school religious instruction by holding that officials must allow religious groups access to school facilities—and to school children (with parental permission)—based on free speech grounds. All but reversing the Court's own 1948 decision prohibiting religious instruction in school buildings, Justice Clarence Thomas wrote that where "the school facilities are being used for a nonschool function and there is no government sponsorship of the [group's] activities, the impressionability of students would not be relevant to the Establishment Clause." To ban the religious group would constitute discrimination against its religious expression.[9]

The most significant criticism of the Court's own jurisprudence came in a 2000 case, *Mitchell v. Helms*, involving federal educational assistance (library books, instructional materials, computers, and multimedia equipment) provided to religious schools. Speaking again for a plurality of justices, Justice Thomas rejected the Court-created presumption that financial aid given directly to religious institutions necessarily advanced their religious missions and thus violated the Establishment Clause.[10] Thomas also refuted the long-held assumption that some institutions were so religious—"pervasively sectarian" in character—that they were ineligible to receive (or appropriately use) public funds for instructional purposes. Not only was this exclusionary rule not required by the First

Amendment, Thomas argued, it undermined those very principles by forcing government to discriminate against religion. Delving into the same history Justices Clark and Brennan had explored in 1963, Thomas wrote that longstanding "hostility to [providing] aid to pervasively sectarian schools has a shameful pedigree."

> Opposition to aid to "sectarian" schools acquired prominence in the 1870s with Congress's consideration (and near passage) of the Blaine Amendment, which would have amended the Constitution to bar any aid to sectarian institutions. Consideration of the amendment arose at a time of pervasive hostility to the Catholic Church and to Catholics in general, and it was an open secret that "Sectarian" was code for "Catholic."

In short, Thomas concluded that nothing in the Establishment Clause required government to exclude religious schools from receiving public funds. The "no aid" principle and the pervasively sectarian doctrine were "born of bigotry, [and] should be buried now."[11]

Justice Thomas's harsh condemnation of doctrine the Court had itself promulgated was remarkable, and it signaled that an important shift in perspective had taken place in church-state jurisprudence. Thomas's opinions did not merely indicate that the Court plurality had changed its mind on whether religious activities in the public schools or discrete forms of public assistance to religious schooling violated the Establishment Clause. Nor did his opinions simply discount the concerns expressed by Thomas Jefferson and James Madison that public involvement in religion was a first step toward an oppressive religious establishment.[12] Rather, Thomas insisted that the rules against funding religious institutions generally, and parochial schools in particular—provisions that are contained in the majority of state constitutions—advance a corrupt constitutional principle. The claim, as was elaborated in Philip Hamburger's influential book, *Separation of Church and State*, is that the no-funding rule of separation of church and state is an erroneous if not profane doctrine, one that is not based on broad-minded principles but rather on religious bigotry. In essence, to exclude religious groups from access to public benefits or public schools, even when the benefit or access is used for religious activity, is a form of religious discrimination.[13]

Whether or not one agrees with this assessment, this is a significant reaccounting of the development of separation of church and state in America. Essentially, this view declares that the ideological basis for fifty years of modern church-state doctrine was based not on noble principles espoused by Jefferson and Madison, but on bias and suspicion arising a half-century later by those who sought to maintain a Protestant stranglehold on the culture by subjugating all religious competition—particularly the Catholic Church. And it characterizes the nineteenth century debate over religious school funding—and the related controversy over religious activities in the public schools—as being motivated primarily by anti-Catholic animus. It challenges standard interpretations of nineteenth century legal and educational history and calls for a reevaluation of those historical developments.

Since the 1940s the Court's holdings on religion and education have fit neatly into two distinct categories: religious activities in the public schools (e.g., prayer, Bible reading, posting of the Ten Commandments, the teaching of religious alternatives to evolution), and the public funding of religious (parochial) schools. But this categorization obscures the fact that these issues are, and have long been, interrelated. For the nation's first 150 years, controversies over school prayer and school funding were inseparable. Comprehensive public education arose in the early nineteenth century chiefly as an alternative to private religious schooling. Early reformers believed the new nation required a system of "common" schools to educate the great mass of American children in the rudiments of knowledge and the values of republicanism. To accomplish this goal, the common schools had to be controlled by public officials, not religious agencies. Another way early common schools distinguished themselves from the array of church-run schools was to assert their accessibility to children of all social classes and religious faiths. To further that distinctiveness and attract a broad array of children, common schools emphasized their own form of religious instruction: "nonsectarian" education. Though defying a single model, nonsectarian education involved instruction in widely held Protestant beliefs, in contrast to the more doctrinal instruction common in private religious schools. As the nineteenth century progressed, external and internal pressures forced the religious character of nonsectarian instruction to evolve, such that over time it became less devotional and more rote. Despite this gradual transformation, Catholics, Jews, and religious nonconformists still objected to the residual Protestant character of the public schools. At the same time, conservative Protestants complained that the public schools were becoming secularized and "godless," an assessment shared by Catholics. The controversy over whether schools should inculcate moral and/or religious values, and the content of that instruction, would embroil public schools throughout the century.

A chief hallmark of nonsectarian education was its purported appeal to children of all religious faiths. Public school funds could pay only for this "universal" nonsectarian education, not for the more sectarian education of private religious schools. This "no-funding" principle arose out of several reinforcing objectives: an effort to limit competition for common schooling; a belief in the indispensable assimilating role of a common "public" education, which must take place under the control of public officials; a concern for ensuring educational standards and public accountability; and a desire to avoid religious dissension, competition, and control over access to public monies. Protestant antipathy toward the Catholic Church was, indisputably, a factor as well. Public school educators, themselves overwhelmingly Protestant, associated Protestantism with republican values and

Catholicism with authoritarianism. At times, this last basis for prohibiting the funding of religious education overshadowed the other rationales.

Ironically, nonsectarianism and the no-funding principle worked at cross purposes. The Protestant character of nonsectarianism was a leading impetus for Catholics to create a system of parochial schooling, which in turn undermined claims about common school universality. The symbiotic tension between Bible reading and school funding only increased once Catholic officials began appealing to state officials for a share of the public school funds for their schools. The conflicts generated by these Janus-like issues evolved into the most contentious church-state controversy of the nineteenth century, the Mormon question notwithstanding. The controversy was so prominent that it acquired its own name: the "School Question."

One cannot appreciate the Supreme Court's modern church-state jurisprudence without understanding the development of the School Question during the nineteenth century. Although the controversy raged in towns and cities across America throughout the nineteenth century, it reached its zenith in the years immediately following the Civil War. For approximately a decade, the inter-related controversies over Bible reading in the schools and the funding of parochial schools captured public attention to a degree that had never happened before. As the *Schempp* justices noted, during this period a state supreme court struck down the practice of nonsectarian prayer and Bible reading in the public schools for the first time. At the same time, Protestant conservatives and religious skeptics proposed competing amendments to the United States Constitution to guarantee, respectively, that America was a Christian nation or a secular republic. Finally, leading politicians proposed their own amendments to the Constitution, putatively designed to resolve the School Question but chiefly for political gain. This latter amendment drive evolved into what became known as the "Blaine Amendment."

The issues of Bible reading and school funding engaged Protestants and Catholics, skeptics and theocrats, nativists and immigrants, educators and politicians. At times, the debate devolved into religious and ethnic dispersions designed to appeal to the baser fears and prejudices of people. At other times, the controversy engendered thoughtful discussion about the appropriate role of religion in public education. Most significant was that the debate was not restricted to the particulars of Bible reading or parochial school funding. The controversy subsumed issues of greater import: the promise of universal public education; the duty of government to promote religious values; the connection between moral virtue and civic participation; the role of religious institutions in civil society; and the compatibility of religious diversity with a republican system that had arisen in a nation with a relatively common Protestant stock. The School Question became a proxy for a debate over America's cultural and religious identity at a crucial time. Participants in the debate appreciated that larger issues were at stake. One contemporary remarked that although "the subject of Bible-reading and religious worship [in the public schools was] one of the sharpest issues between the Catholic and the Protestant...it manifestly does not cover the whole question in controversy." Rather, "the great principles involved" brought "to the surface the whole subject of Church and State, civil government and religion, in their relations to each other."[14]

The events of the period thus provided Americans the opportunity to engage in a grand—and sometimes not so grand—public debate over the meaning of separation of church and state in a democratic society. Rarely in the nation's history have people of different social standings and from various walks of life engaged in a national discussion over the meaning of a constitutional principle. This was one of those rare moments, though reasoned discussion was at times eclipsed by inflamed rhetoric. Yet modern critics of church-state separation have been quick to simplify the passions of the period and condemn the rhetoric while ignoring the substantive discussions that took place. Critics have also lost sight of the fact that hyperbole and impassioned argument are often part of democratic discourse. This public discussion on the meaning of Church and State, both base and profound, laid the foundation for future church-state controversies and the resulting decisions of the Supreme Court.

This book analyzes the events surrounding the School Question chiefly from 1869 through 1876. It examines the myriad factors that informed the controversy, including contemporary understandings of nonsectarianism and the no-funding rule. It places the school controversy within its context to see whether contemporary understandings of nonsectarianism and no-funding were based chiefly on religious bigotry. To be sure, this "decade" encompassed neither the beginning nor end of the School Question controversy. If rioting and arson are any indication, the decades preceding this period were more epic. The controversy also continued at a heightened level for at least a quarter century beyond 1876.[15] But these years were the fulcrum of the controversy, setting out the constitutional arguments governing both school prayer and the public funding of religion, arguments that have remained relatively unchanged. The controversy laid the foundation for modern church-state doctrine.

1

The Rise of Nonsectarian
Public Education

The history of nonsectarian education and its corollary, the no-funding principle, is inseparable from the rise of public schooling during the early nineteenth century. For much of the twentieth century historians embraced the accomplishments of the common school movement and praised the goals and commitments of educational reformers such as Horace Mann, Henry Barnard, and Samuel Lewis. These education pioneers battled suspicion about universal education and resistance to taxation, professionalization, and standardization to fashion an educational system that became the nation's most important and enduring civic institution.[1] More recently, the rationales for the antebellum common school movement have come under close scrutiny. A new generation of scholars, along with a bevy of commentators, have challenged assumptions about the necessity of a universal state-controlled education system. In particular, they have repudiated early efforts to assimilate immigrant children into a system that reflected a Protestant vision of America.[2]

Aspects of this latter critique are well-deserved. Early public education relied on assumptions of an inherent relationship between Protestantism and republicanism that denied the legitimacy of alternative models. Often, assimilation meant a form of conformity that abjured ethnic and religious differences. Yet the story of the rise of American public schooling is complex. Recent scholarship has tended to view the rationales for and effects of nonsectarian common schooling through a modern lens, colored by current notions of religious pluralism and respect for ethnic differences. By today's standards, the concerns and aspirations of many early education leaders appear misguided at best, elitist and xenophobic at worst. But at the time, most education leaders—many trained as Protestant clergy and others with close ties to Protestant institutions—worked tirelessly to create an education system that would acculturate children from diverse social, religious, and national backgrounds and assimilate them into the unfolding republican experience. Central to those efforts was the widespread belief that instilling moral virtue in children was indispensable for perpetuating the nation and its republican system of government. The way to inculcate those necessary civic values was to instruct in the indisputable source of virtue, Christianity. For at least the first half of the nineteenth century, no one—not religious liberals such as Unitarian Horace Mann or ultramontane Catholics such as Bishop John Hughes—disputed the importance of religion for developing moral character in children or the role of education in that endeavor. "In the nineteenth century," education historian Lawrence Cremin once observed, "the moral good was so intimately bound up with religious faith that the two were practically inseparable in the minds of the people." The point of departure was whether those Christian virtues should reflect an evangelical, Catholic, or nominal Protestant perspective.[3]

Some scholars have assigned the disreputable motivations of Protestant nativists to those educators who were in charge of developing and operating America's early public schools. To be sure, both nativists and educators were stalwart Protestants, both believed that the promise of America was intertwined with its Protestant character, and both saw public schooling as indispensable for attaining that national promise. However, to tar them with the same brush is to ignore the complexity of contemporary attitudes over matters of immigration, assimilation, cultural uniformity, and national allegiance, as well as the diverse forces and ideologies that informed common schooling.[4]

A final problem in recent scholarship has been to view nonsectarianism and the no-funding principle as relatively static. Nonsectarianism was a dynamic concept during the century, varying in content and application depending on time and place. Though nonsectarianism was based on shared assumptions about the indispensability of moral and civic education and the interconnectedness of Protestantism and republicanism, there was no single model that all public schools followed, notwithstanding the commanding influence of reformers such as Horace Mann and Henry Barnard. Local control over education and varying degrees of religious homogeneity ensured that the patterns differed from one decade to another and one city to the next. And the principle and practice of nonsectarianism evolved over time.[5] By the time of the Blaine Amendment (1876), nonsectarian education was being transformed from a curriculum that emphasized moral values by teaching "universal" Christian principles to one that was increasingly secular with perfunctory reliance on religion.[6]

A similar development was also taking place with respect to the public funding of religious schools. For the first third of the century, private religious schools regularly received financial assistance from state and local governments, as did the variety of early common schools and religiously unaffiliated charity schools. By mid-century that practice had effectively ended, a casualty of concerns about accountability, security of the school fund, and notions of church-state separation, including fears about ecclesiastical control of public monies. Initially, most people did not view the funding question in constitutional terms, focusing instead on pragmatic considerations. By the late 1820s, however, common school advocates began to argue that the funding of religious schools was inconsistent with the "political" principles underlying republican government. State legislatures enacted laws and constitutional provisions prohibiting public funding of sectarian institutions. In some instances, these express no-funding provisions complemented existing "no compelled support" clauses that, at least on paper, also restricted the government support of religion. This developing no-funding rule applied not only to Catholic schools but also to the plethora of Protestant schools (Episcopal, Methodist, Presbyterian, Lutheran, Dutch Reformed) and was responsible for a decline in the latter. Neither nonsectarian instruction nor no-funding was initially viewed as a constitutional issue. But as common schooling developed, constitutional considerations became an integral part of the discussion.

The Origins of Nonsectarian Education

Nonsectarian education arose out of a general movement to establish a system of publicly operated schools that would be accessible to children of all economic, ethnic, and religious groups. At the time of the nation's founding, the limited educational opportunities for children turned generally on income or geography. Children of the wealthy and merchant classes received education through private tutors or in private academies, some of which were religiously affiliated. By the mid-eighteenth century, a loose system of town or "district" primary schools had been established in New England and in a handful of seaboard cities. These district schools, serving local children, were not "public" in the modern sense. They commonly involved a hybrid of public and private-religious cooperation, with the established or "settled" town minister frequently serving as the teacher. The early district schools relied on a combination of "rates" (tuition charges to parents) and local taxes for support, though poorer parents could apply for rate exemptions.[7] Aside from the New England district schools, "public education"—in the sense of schools that were open and free to children of all classes—was otherwise nonexistent. Finally, in a handful of cities denominational "charity" schools provided a basic education to poorer children. Philadelphia had ten such schools at the turn of the nineteenth century, and New York City six, operated by Presbyterian, Episcopalian, Methodist, Quaker, and Lutheran groups. Whether children received their instruction from tutors, academies, district schools, or charity schools, it was predominately religious (i.e., Protestant), with a heavy emphasis on reading religious texts and memorizing religious doctrine. Texts such as the strongly Calvinist *New England Primer* were common.[8] Under these early arrangements, no schooling was entirely tax-supported, universally available to all children, or secular in content.[9]

Following the Revolution, some political leaders began to advocate for a system of public education, one that was free and open to children of all classes and potentially funded by public taxation. Those who argued for public education had several interrelated goals. One was a desire to expand the availability of schooling for poor children who did not attend charity schools and for the larger number of children from working families who fell through the gaps. Thomas Jefferson encouraged his former professor George Wythe to "Preach, my dear Sir, a crusade against ignorance; establish and improve the law for educating the common people." Other political leaders echoed these sentiments; John Adams, writing in his influential *Thoughts on Government* (1776), urged the new states to provide for a "liberal education of youth, especially of the lower class of people."[10] Closely related to the desire to expand the availability of schooling was the belief that education would act as an important sedative on the potentially unruly lower classes, instilling the virtue and self-discipline that did not come naturally. As David Nasaw has described this perspective, a "common school education would be a moral education. By making the population more moral, the common schools would also make it more docile, more tractable, less given to social discord, disruption and disobedience." Despite the paternalism behind using moral instruction to control the lower classes, artisans and craftspeople generally supported the push for expanding educational opportunities as a means of financial advancement and social mobility. From its inception, public education had a strong character-enhancing and acculturating aspect, a goal that remained throughout the century. "[E]ducation and intelligence not only insure order, quiet, and peace," wrote one journal in 1870, "but add immeasurably to the material wealth, civilization, and well-being of the community."[11]

A final impetus for the interest in public education was the belief that the future of the Republic depended on the nation's ability to transmit skills of democratic governance to current and future generations. Many in the founding generation embraced this belief. They feared the new nation was susceptible to those threats that had doomed earlier republics: self-interestedness and factionalism. Echoing this pessimistic view of human nature, James Madison wrote in Federalist 51 that structural checks on the accumulation and exercise of power were necessary because people were human and "not angels." Instruction of children in republican skills and civic virtue was indispensable for the stability and ultimate success of the new republic; education, Noah Webster insisted, was "essential to the continuance of republican governments." Thus a chief goal of education was to "convert men into republican machines," as Benjamin Rush wrote. This was necessary, Rush continued, if "we expect them to perform their parts properly in the great machine of the government of the state." For the next generation to assume this role in participatory governance, two acquired talents were necessary: knowledge and civic virtue.[12]

Education historian Carl Kaestle has argued that this latter impulse was less important to early schoolmen than they professed. "Training for a job or for intelligent voting were subordinate to the goal of character building. . . . public schools' dominant purpose . . . was to produce industrious, sober, punctual, God-fearing citizens."[13] To be sure, not until the 1830s did many states extended suffrage and other citizenship rights to laborers and the landless. However, concerns about the fragility of republican government and the necessity of an educated citizenry for its security cannot be discounted. Henry Barnard, a leading education reformer of the antebellum period, would write in 1838 that the object of common schooling was "to make these [children] intelligent and virtuous men, that they may be intelligent and virtuous citizens; to fit them, in other words, for the faithful and competent discharge of their political, social and public duties."[14] Universal education, under the control of public authorities, would encourage knowledge, break down class differences, and train children in the essential skills for the still unfolding republican society. This central mission of public education did not dissipate; in 1875 the *New York Times* would maintain that public "schools are the nursery of the Republic." Even at the century's end people still expressed concern about the fragility of republican government and that the skills of self-governance were not innate but had to be taught.[15]

As they were promoting universal public schooling, early education reformers began questioning the pedagogical value of religious instruction. Most schooling of the time—private academies, church charity schools, and even district schools—relied extensively on Bible readings and religious catechisms from the *New England Primer* to teach reading and writing (exclusive Latin or English grammar schools were possible exceptions). A common attitude, as expressed by the overseers of one Connecticut town, was that schools must teach children "to honour and obey their parents," "to revere the ministers of the gospel...[and] the sabbath," and to remember "their dependence on God, of their accountability to him, of their mortality, and of the importance of religion both as a preparation for death, and the only means of true peace, comfort, and usefulness in this world."[16] On one extreme of the reformers stood Jefferson, who in 1779 had drafted a plan for establishing public elementary schools in Virginia. Jefferson proposed that "instead of putting the Bible and Testament it the hands of children at an age when their judgments are not sufficiently matured for religious inquiries, their minds may here be stored with the most useful facts from Grecian, Roman, European and American History."[17] Other reformers agreed with Jefferson only partially. Rush and Webster also criticized the extensive use of religious texts and sectarian instruction common in much schooling, arguing that the repetitive reading of scripture led pupils to disrespect its precepts and inhibited their ability to think critically. Yet like most early reformers, Rush and Webster did not advocate removing religious texts from the schools entirely; rather, they believed in the value of religion for teaching moral virtue and obedience. The "only foundation for a useful education in a republic is to be laid in Religion," Rush asserted. Without this, there could be "no virtue, and without virtue, there can be no liberty," which was "the object and life of all republican governments." While Rush and Webster encouraged using secular subjects such as geography, economics, law, and government for teaching moral character, they also supported the reading of selective passages of the Bible in the schools. Their wish was "not to see the Bible excluded from schools but to see it is used as a system of religion and morality." Despite such conceptual distinctions, the lines between religious and secular instruction remained blurred; Webster's own popular *Speller* made liberal use of scriptural references for teaching writing skills.[18]

Whereas Rush and Webster urged a curriculum that was predominately secular, a more comprehensive argument for nonsectarian education came from Maryland clergyman Samuel Knox. In 1799, Knox submitted an entry in an American Philosophical Society competition for the best design for a public education curriculum. Knox proposed a program of secular liberal study, one "confined to a proper knowledge of the English language, writing, arithmetic, and practical mathematics, completed by some approved compend of history and geography." In a break from the common practice, Knox advocated removing all religious instruction other than the teaching of "a reverence of the Deity, a sense of His government of the world, and a regard for morals." Still, Knox did not object to a "short and suitable" nondenominational prayer each day addressed "to the great source of all knowledge and instruction," and advocated the use of a "well-digested, concise moral catechism" for teaching ethics. The distinction between Knox's proposal and the status quo was subtle but significant. Though eschewing religious indoctrination, Knox insisted that schools could "present the most sublime ideas of the Deity" to teach morals and "to excite to the love and study of science." An additional distinction for Knox was that religious ideas and texts were to be used to achieve chiefly secular goals.[19]

At this early stage, neither Knox, Rush, nor Webster tied their aversion to religious indoctrination to constitutional principles. Neither did they seem aware of any tension between such principles and their own advocacy of using "sublime" (i.e., universal) religious ideas to instruct moral character. Hinting at constitutional questions to come, however, Knox argued that his system of "secular" education was the only means of "preserving that liberty of conscience in religious matters which various denominations of Christians in these states justly claim." Knox's emphasis on practical subjects and his concern for the sensibilities of children from various religious backgrounds helped lay the foundation for a concept of nonsectarian instruction divorced from most doctrinal influences and control.[20]

One of the first attempts at a nonsectarian educational program was the Free School Society of New York City, founded in 1805.[21] At the time, New York City had a variety of private "pay-schools" and a handful of charity schools run by Episcopalian, Lutheran, Presbyterian, and Dutch Reformed groups. Prior to 1795, most private and charity schools received limited public support, so access to primary education may have been relatively widespread. In 1795 the state legislature enacted a law that defunded private pay-schools, though it continued to fund charity schools. At the same time, the city's population was rapidly expanding, partially through immigration, which created new demographic and economic pressures on the city. By 1805, the number of unschooled children had increased, with many poorer children being excluded from the charity schools because of insufficient space and religious membership requirements.[22] In response, Quaker philanthropists and civic leaders organized the Free School Society to provide schooling for all poor children. As a way to distinguish its charity schools from denominational schools, the Society stressed the nondenominational character of its curriculum, which, its announcement asserted, made its schools accessible to children of all religious faiths. Society schools would teach the "common rudiments of learning" while instructing in only "the fundamental principles of the Christian religion, free from all sectarian bias, and also those general and special articles of the moral code, upon which the good order and welfare of society are based." Picking up on a theme advanced by Rush, Webster, and Knox, the Society asserted that its nonsectarian curriculum would allow children of all faiths to learn free of the stupefying effects of sectarianism.[23] The Free School Society found support for its program of nonsectarian instruction from the newly developed British Lancasterian education method, which, in addition to using student monitors as instructors, employed a nonsectarian moral curriculum designed to transcend denominational boundaries.[24]

The officials of the Free School Society attempted to walk a narrow line. At the same time that Society officials were championing its nonsectarian curriculum to city and state officials, they were busily convincing local clergy that its system of nonsectarianism did not mean secularism. From its inception, the Society promoted its schools as *distinctly* Protestant, declaring that one of its "primary object[s], without observing the particular forms of any religious society, [will be] to inculcate the sublime truths of religion and morality contained in the Holy Scriptures." Beginning in its first school, directors instituted a practice of daily readings from the King James Bible, followed with the reciting of the Lord's Prayer and the singing of Protestant hymns.[25] Society teachers also relied on religiously infused catechisms—said to be "free from sectarian principles"—to teach arithmetic, the alphabet and for general character education:

> teacher: Children, who is good?
> answer: the Lord is good.
> teacher: To whom should we be thankful?
> answer: Be thankful unto Him.[26]

In addition to the religious exercises and catechisms, Society teachers used readers and spellers developed by Protestant educators and benevolent societies. These early texts, as Ruth Miller Elson has documented, strongly emphasized religious themes and lessons: "a sense of God permeate[d] all books as surely as a sense of nationalism."[27] Religious exercises and the use of religiously oriented texts continued even after their merger with the public Board of Education in 1853. Beginning in 1838, however, the Society started eliminating the more devotional qualities of its program, following the model being developed in Massachusetts by Horace Mann.[28]

To deflect criticism of its "unsectarian" approach, Society officials organized "Sunday Schools" to supplement the nonsectarian curriculum with more devotional instruction. The nondenominational Sunday or "First Day" Schools, an innovation also brought over from England, reinforced the nonsectarian approach by teaching universal (i.e., Protestant) religious doctrines. At first, Sunday Schools were yet another educational offering, providing basic secular and religious instruction for nonschooled poor children who worked six days a week. With their expansion in America, Sunday Schools turned chiefly to religious instruction and Bible memorization.[29] During its early years, the Society required students to assemble at their respective schools on Sunday mornings so that monitors could lead them to local church services or Sunday Schools. When the number of students became too large to supervise at Sunday services, teachers took roll on Monday mornings to determine "the number of scholars who attend[ed] at the various Sunday schools or places of worship on the Sabbath." Finally, for those students who desired sectarian instruction, Society teachers dismissed scholars once a week to attend catechisms conducted by representatives of the various churches, an early form of "released time" instruction.[30] This array of activities allowed the Society to promote the Christian character of its schools while eschewing instruction into the tenets of particular denominations:

> Special care must be taken to avoid any instruction of a sectarian character; but the teachers shall embrace every opportunity of inculcating the general truths of Christianity, and the primary importance of practical religious and moral duty, as founded on the precepts of the Holy Scriptures.[31]

In retrospect, the Society's nonsectarian program, with readings from the Protestant King James Bible, hymns, Calvinist catechisms, and religiously oriented texts, appears highly devotional if not sectarian, as it did at the time to Catholic and Jewish parents.[32] But the "nonsectarian" programs must be viewed from the perspective of the early 1800s, when most Americans, Protestant and Catholic alike, believed that civic education could not be divorced from instruction into religious and moral values. For the first half of the century, the point of disagreement was not whether public schooling should be religious or secular, but how religious that education should be. The only alternative to the emergent nonsectarian schools was a denominational school with a curriculum that emphasized instruction in particular doctrines. In the early 1800s, the nonsectarian emphasis on a liberal curriculum infused with commonly shared religious values represented a break from the status quo.[33]

In another departure from denominational schools, early nonsectarian instruction eschewed the goal of converting children to Protestantism. Though the distinction between instruction and conversion is a fine one, the aim of nonsectarianism was to instill a reverence for the Deity and the sublime truths of the Bible while teaching the necessary morality and virtue upon which republicanism depended. Attempts to convert children to any denomination would have caused discord and undermined the ideal of universality that nonsectarian republicanism sought to achieve. As the Society declared, the primary object of its program was "to form habits of virtue and industry, and to inculcate the general principles of Christianity." Such instruction would prepare the children from the lower classes for their participatory role in republican society. "Early instruction and fixed habits of industry, decency, and order, are the surest safeguards of virtuous conduct." But Society officials made clear that responsibility for ensuring a child's salvation lay with his parents.[34] Thus at this time, the Protestantism taught in the common schools was not a tool of conversion or a stopgap against a growing Catholicism. Before the mid-1830s, the nation's Catholic population was relatively small and was not viewed as a threat to Protestant culture.[35] Rather, the early nonsectarian programs, and those later developed by Horace Mann, were designed to diffuse conflict among Protestant sects and to attract children excluded from Protestant denominational schools. Noah Feldman has written:

> the theorists of the common schools thought that the schools must impart some foundational moral values to promote civic virtues and believed that those moral values must derive in some way from Christian religion.... Non-sectarianism, it was thought, would keep the state out of bitter inter-denominational disputes, enable the flourishing of diverse voluntary, private churches, and simultaneously enable the state to take a stance in favor of broadly shared, foundational Christian virtues.[36]

Seen in this light, nonsectarian education was not chiefly an effort by dominant Protestant groups to maintain theological control over public education at the expense of Catholics, Jews, and other religious minorities. That the common schools were consciously Protestant was not denied; however, the Protestant complexion of early common schooling reflected the belief that the schools could promote commonly shared beliefs and practices without reverting to denominationalism. Reformers viewed the Protestantism found in schools as inclusive, rather than exclusive; what nonsectarianism excluded were those sectarian differences that separated the various Protestant bodies.[37] Only in mid-century, as nonsectarian instruction became less doctrinal and Catholic immigration increased, did Protestant tract societies seek to turn religious exercises into modes of conversion.[38] Equally important, education leaders understood the complexion of common schools to be "American" as much as they were "Protestant." Protestantism was such a part of the national identity in the early nineteenth century that educators had difficulty distinguishing between it and republican values; they "assumed that Americanism and Protestantism were synonyms and that education and Protestantism were allies."[39] To these reformers, and for many educators later in the century, religious instruction was inseparable from the civic values necessary to sustain America's political society.[40]

Attendance at the Free School Society increased, and its number of schools grew, in part due to its nonsectarian emphasis and a board of trustees that comprised New York's leading citizens. Still, it was essentially a charity school and represented only one of several educational options in the city. The Society's 1825 Annual Report noted that although its schools had "conferred the blessings of education upon a large number of [poor] children," it was "to be lamented that a description of public school is wanting amongst us, where the rich and the poor may meet together; where the wall of partition, which now seems to be raised between them, may be removed." In 1826 the Society changed its name to the New York Public School Society, in part to attract children from other schools and social classes, but also to secure its financial position with the common council and the state legislature as the city's default public school.[41] Over time, its nonsectarian program became the model for other evolving public schools in northeastern cities, though the degree of religious instruction varied greatly, particularly in smaller town and district schools in areas with greater religious homogeneity. Like the expanding urban free charity schools, these quasi-free district schools served as the nucleus for the common school movement that emerged in the 1830s.[42]

Between 1800 and 1835 nonsectarian free charity schools were established in Philadelphia, Boston, and Baltimore, among other places. Gradually, they consolidated with denominational charity schools or drove them out of business. In the process, the unaffiliated charity schools secured an increasing share of local and state school monies. At the same time they were consolidating and expanding, the nonsectarian charity schools sought to extend their presence by appealing to children from working-class families. Throughout the 1820s and 1830s, schools like the now—Public School Society worked to shed their stigma as pauper schools and become known as free public schools open to all children.[43]

The Impact of Horace Mann

In 1827, Massachusetts became the first state to enact a statewide law aimed at standardizing education. Disparities in resources and educational quality among town schools fueled the movement for greater state control. The desire for standardization was also attributed "to increased urbanization and industrial development and to insecurity about the capacities of republicanism to cope with the apparently imminent decline of a rural and agricultural society to which republicanism was thought to be intimately connected."[44] An important section of the law forbade teaching doctrines of particular sects or using sectarian textbooks in the state's common schools, including those located in otherwise religiously homogenous rural districts. At the same time, the law reiterated a provision of an earlier law that required instruction in "the principles of piety, justice, and a sacred regard for truth, love to their country, etc." This section of the 1827 law, enacted before significant Catholic immigration to Massachusetts, was directed at diffusing the growing intra-Protestant conflict that would lead to disestablishment in the state six years later. In his later reports as Board Secretary, Horace Mann complained about the difficulty he encountered eradicating school books that taught doctrines particular to one or another Protestant denomination. Entrenched practices were hard to change; ten years after the law's enactment Mann wrote that he still "found books in schools, as strictly and exclusively *doctrinal* as any on the shelves of a theological library."[45]

The 1827 law also created a state board of education, which appointed Horace Mann as its first Secretary in 1836 (figure 1.1). In his twelve-year tenure, Mann became the nation's most visible and forceful advocate for nonsectarian education. Under his leadership, nonsectarian education evolved away from the early Protestant curriculum of the New York Free School Society. Mann set out to change both the assumptions and applications of nonsectarian education by eradicating its remaining doctrinal character and any possible evangelizing goals. As Mann reported following his initial inspections of district schools, he "heard teachers giving oral instruction, as strictly and exclusively *doctrinal*, as ever heard from the pulpit."[46] Mann quickly ordered the removal of Calvinist catechisms and Biblical instruction. Rather than teaching those common *doctrines* shared by orthodox Protestants, such as punishment for sin after death, Mann urged public schools to emphasize universal religious *values*. "The diversity of religious doctrines, prevalent in our community, would render it difficult to inculcate any religious truths," Mann wrote.[47] Instruction in universal religious values would allow children to develop the moral character and civic virtue necessary to operate in republican society. Yet Mann insisted that schools retain the Bible as the sourcebook for those universal religious truths. Relying on his Unitarian belief in the unmediated power of Bible reading, Mann argued that schools should teach the "fundamental principles of Christianity," but that the school's obligations stopped there out of respect for freedom of conscience:

> [A nonsectarian system] earnestly inculcates all Christian morals; it founds its morals on the basis of religion; it welcomes the religion of the Bible; and, in receiving the Bible, it allows it to do what it is allowed to do in no other system,—*to speak for itself*. But here it stops, not because it claims to have compassed all truth, but because it disclaims to act as an umpire between hostile religious opinions.[48]

An inherent tension existed within Mann's ideal of nonsectarian instruction. On one hand, he eschewed the teaching of shared religious *doctrines*, insisting that the goal of Bible reading was to further religious knowledge and moral values. Yet Mann also promoted Bible reading for the purpose of instilling religious *devotion*.

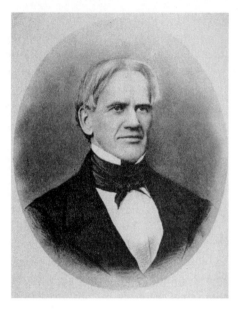

Figure 1.1 Horace Mann. The Granger Collection, New York.

One goal of his system was "to make the perfect example of Jesus Christ lovely in [the children's] eyes." Mann believed that the "germs of morality must be planted in the moral nature of children, at an early period in their life." But only by relying on the sublime truths of the Bible rather than engaging in religious indoctrination would children naturally and freely discover their faith.[49] Nonsectarian instruction was not imparted "for the purpose of making him join this or that denomination...but for the purpose of enabling him to judge for himself, according to the dictates of his own reason and conscience...his religious obligations." In his later reports to the Board, Mann responded to evangelical critics by emphasizing the widespread use of the Bible in Massachusetts schools:[50]

> In every course of studies, all the practical and perceptive parts of the
> Gospel should have been sacredly included; and all dogmatical theology
> and sectarianism sacredly excluded. In no school should the Bible have
> been opened to reveal the sword of the polemic, but to unloose the dove
> of peace.[51]

Still, Bible reading, and the goal of instilling general religious fealty, were chiefly means to an end: the building of moral character. Mann had no interest in converting children. Religious instruction was about furthering moral education and religious inquiry. Mann's numerous writings and reports reveal this fine distinction. Through the use of universal religious truths, common schools would instill moral character and implant the desire for greater religious devotion, which would be attained in the home and church. Although moral education had been the overriding goal of early reformers such as Benjamin Rush and a stated goal of early nonsectarian education, it was often inseparable from instruction into shared Protestant doctrines. Mann more clearly separated religious and moral education.[52]

Though Mann differed from his evangelical counterparts as to the underlying purpose and manner of religious instruction, he accepted, if not embraced, the underlying premise of nonsectarianism: that all Christians could agree on certain uncontroversial, universal religious truths that could be taught in the schools. He essentially saw that agreement as existing on a more general level. "[T]he points on which different portions of a Christian community differ ... are far less numerous than those on which they agree," Mann wrote. These points were universal because, in Mann's mind, they "constituted the best possible preparation for each to proceed in adding those distinctive particulars, deemed necessary to a complete and perfect faith." Under the same logic, a curriculum "which did not recognize the truth that we were created to be religious beings, would be as though we were to form a human body forgetting to put in a heart."[53] This unfailing belief in universality was a blind spot for common school educators when they encountered complaints from Catholics and Jews. But at least initially, educators believed they had settled on a system that would appeal to all well-meaning Christians, including Catholics. "Protestants like Mann sincerely believed that their nonsectarianism was capacious enough to include Catholics, who were Christians like themselves," Noah Feldman writes. Mann argued that common schools "should do all they could to make themselves acceptable to Catholics; in return, Catholics ought to participate in the venture of common schools rather than form schools of their own."[54]

Although Mann receives credit for this refinement in nonsectarian instruction, the ideas were not unique to him. Many at the forefront of establishing public schooling in other states—Henry Barnard, Samuel Lewis, and Calvin Stowe, among others—advocated similar reforms. On one hand, the reformers concurred that religion must remain at the center of public education, that schools had an obligation to teach character and moral virtue that was derived from the scriptures. Where a biblical standard of morality is taught, asserted Barnard's *Connecticut Common School Journal* in 1841, "there will be more order and quietness; the children will be more easily governed, and will make greater proficiency in their studies." But at the same time, public schools must abandon the teaching of Protestant doctrines: "Instruction in those points which divide the sects from each other, must be confined to the family and the Sunday school," Calvin Stowe exclaimed. Rather, "[t]he Bible, the whole Bible, and nothing but the Bible, without note or comment, must be taken as the text-book of religious instruction." Teachers should emphasize principles of God's love and sovereignty and those virtues of duty and honesty which all Christians shared, ideals found in the books of Psalms, Proverbs, and the Gospel of Matthew. This material would awaken curiosity in children and inspire them to lead virtuous lives: "those divine sentences will be in his mind forever after, read to be called up to check him when any temptation assails his heart."[55]

These refinements to nonsectarian education were not without controversy. Throughout Mann's tenure, evangelicals, Catholics, and religious liberals assailed Mann and his system. "Mann's brand seemed to many evangelical Protestants to be suspiciously 'Unitarian,'" wrote religious historian Sidney Mead, and "what passed as 'nonsectarian' religious teaching seemed to many Unitarians, Roman Catholics, and others to be evangelical Protestantism." Evangelicals labeled the Massachusetts schools "Godless," while New York Catholic Bishop John Hughes charged Mann's system amounted to "the sectarianism of infidelity."[56]

Throughout much of 1838, Mann engaged in an ongoing dispute with Frederick A. Packard of the American Sunday School Union over Mann's refusal to approve a Union-promoted reader for school libraries. Disagreement centered on the 1827 law that prohibited the use of sectarian texts in public schools. Mann maintained that the reader's references to a retributive God and a future state of judgments and rewards made it sectarian; the book "would shock the moral & religious feelings of a large portion of our community," Universalists in particular. Even though the book taught doctrines that many Protestants embraced, Mann insisted it was still sectarian and inappropriate for a public school education.[57] Defending the reader, Packard also cited the 1827 law, relying on it's injunction that schools instruct children in "piety." Mann could not have it both ways, Packard argued, using the "character & government of God" to teach piety

> without "favoring some particular religious tenet" which is expressly forbidden by the Statute of 1826 [sic] ... The very definition of piety is "discharge the duty to God," and how can the principles of piety be taught intelligibly without constant reference to the character of God & to the provisions & sanctions of his law as revealed in the Holy Scriptures?

Packard insisted that the 1827 law, as he interpreted it, was thus "wise, wholesome, [and] necessary," whereas Mann's "monstrous construction" of the statute was "mischievous" and "absurd." Over the course of a dozen letters, the dispute became acrimonious. Packard charged that Mann's system would "exclude all religious teaching" about "revealed religion," substituting instead Mann's own views of "natural religion & ethics." This version of nonsectarianism was "a grand instrument in the hands of freethinkers, atheists & infidels," Packard accused. "They [like Mann] would shut out every ray of light from the Bible."[58] Later attacks on Mann's system came from Congregationalist, Presbyterian, and Episcopalian journals. The common thread in the charges, as represented by Reverend Mathew Hale Smith, was that schools should teach "the whole Bible: the Law, the Prophets, the Psalms, the New Testament" without omitting the "truths and sanctions which nine tenths of professing Christians believe essential to sound morals and an honest life, no less that the salvation of the soul." Like other evangelical critics, Smith charged that Mann's selective use of the Bible was as sectarian as the alternatives he condemned.[59]

One other critic of Mann's reforms is worthy of note, chiefly because he would become a leading commentator on the School Question in the ensuing decades. Orestes A. Brownson was a Boston intellectual, an acquaintance of Emerson, Thoreau, and Channing, and a prolific commentator on religion and culture for the *Boston Quarterly Review* and his own *Brownson's Quarterly Review* (figure 1.2). In his youth, Brownson had been a religious wanderer. By the late 1830s he had tried Presbyterianism, Transcendentalism, Universalism, and Unitarianism; his religious journey would lead him to embrace Catholicism in 1844, where he would emerge as that faith's leading intellectual voice. Even before his conversion, Brownson stressed the importance of religious obligation and the reality of God's authority. He criticized Mann's "whole theory of education as founded in error." Mann's efforts to refine the essential principles of Christianity were "doomed to disappointment," Brownson insisted, because there was "no common ground between all the various religious denominations"; the difference between Unitarians and Calvinists was "fundamental." "All, who attempt to proceed on the principle here laid down, will find their Christianity ending in nothingness. . . . No sect will be satisfied; all sects will be dissatisfied." Brownson's pessimism was his own, but

Figure 1.2 Orestes Brownson. The Granger Collection, New York.

his critique that schools could not teach Christianity half way would haunt non-sectarianism for the remainder of the century.[60]

Mann and his system weathered Packard, Smith, and Brownson's attacks, as well as later critiques. His responses to the criticisms took seemingly contradictory tracks, however. Mann defended his system as teaching the most sublime religious values and as being consistent with Christianity. This defense appeared time and again in his letters and annual reports of the Board of Education.[61] In response to Smith, Mann insisted that the "whole influence of the Board of Education, from the day of its organization to the present time, has been to promote and encourage...and to direct the daily use of the Bible in the schools." Mann was making an astute argument, relying on Protestant belief in the clarity of the scriptures to deflect more specific complaints that notions of sin and salvation were not being taught.[62] But Mann stuck to his position, arguing that relying on more specific Protestant doctrine would create dissention that would destroy the public schools: "sectarian books, and sectarian instruction ... [will] prove the overthrow of the schools." This latter argument led Mann to raise a third point seemingly at tension with his first. Any greater reliance on religion, and particularly a goal of instilling religious faith, would violate rights of religious conscience. Teaching only universal religious truths, however, respected those rights.[63]

In refining his responses, Mann, a lawyer by training, began developing arguments that his system of nonsectarianism, and not the devotional instruction promoted by his critics, was necessitated by the religious liberty provisions of the Massachusetts Constitution. At this nascent stage, Mann did not argue that devotional exercises were necessarily unconstitutional, only that his approach was more consistent with constitutional principles. Implicit, though, was the argument that greater state support for religion violated rights of religious conscience and undermined notions of religious equality essential to a republican government. Also, Mann emphasized that governmental favoring of or identification with particular creeds would create dissention among faiths that the founders both feared and abjured. For Mann, these principles had a constitutional grounding, even if he would not have conceived of them as legal prohibitions.[64]

In his concluding Twelfth Report, Mann included an extended defense of his system and a final rebuttal to criticism that his version of religious education was un-Christian. Mann had made similar defenses in his correspondence and earlier annual reports, but this final response was more extensive—some forty-six pages—and more retrospective. The argument reveals Mann's systematic thinking about nonsectarian education and how it fit with broader concepts of republican democracy and religious liberty. It lays out several arguments for the virtues, if not the indispensability, of separation of church and state, and his points sound as if they could have been written one hundred years later during the modern Supreme Court's first forays into religion and education issues. Significantly, Mann anchored his arguments not solely in the requirements of the 1827 law but also in the mandates of the Massachusetts Constitution.[65]

Mann claimed that all arrangements between governments and religion fell into one of two systems. The first system, common throughout history and still prevalent in Europe, held that "the regulation and control of the religious belief of the people [is] one of the functions of government." Under "the other system, religious belief is a matter of individual and parental concern; and, while the government furnishes all practicable facilities for the independent formation of that belief, it exercises no authority to prescribe, or coercion to enforce it." Mann left no doubt as to which system was superior. American government was the "solitary example" of this latter system, one "where freedom of opinion, and the inviolability of conscience, have been even theoretically recognized by law."[66] Not only did the American system promote freedom on conscience, it limited the state's ability to act on matters of religion. Mann argued that "Every intelligent man understands, that there are some things which are within the jurisdiction of government, and other things which are not within it." Rights "which are strictly religious lie out of, and beyond the jurisdiction of civil government." Here Mann echoed the arguments of James Madison, who sixty years earlier had written that "in matters of religion, no man's right is abridged by the institution of civil society; and that religion is wholly exempt from its cognizance."[67] Paralleling Madison's point, Mann wrote that "[p]rimarily, religious rights embrace the relations between the creature and the Creator, just as political rights embrace the relations between subject and sovereign, or between a free citizen and the government of his choice; and just as parental rights embrace the relation between parent and child." Not only did each entity operate in separate spheres, with civil government lacking authority over religious matters; for government to legislate in those areas violated the rights associated with the creature-Creator relationship. Again, echoing Madison, Mann wrote:

> the relation of man to his Maker never changes. Its object and its obligations are immutable. The jurisdiction which God exercises over religious obligations which his rational and accountable offspring owe to Him, excludes human jurisdiction. And, hence, it is that religious rights are inalienable rights.[68]

In arguing that the state had no interest in religious opinions, Mann realized he was undermining his claim that the state had a duty to teach moral education based on religious principles. Mann sought to reconcile this by insisting that the connection between morals and religion was inviolable: "Practical Morality...can never be obtained without Religion." This was because "the whole frame and constitution of human soul" showed that he is a "religious being." The state could not fulfill its duty to advance morals divorced from instruction into religion.[69] Mann acknowledged the tension in his theory: if "religion is absolutely essential to the stability of the State, as well as to the present and future [success of education]; why, it is naturally asked, should not the government enforce it." The problem was that in order to enforce religion, the state would first be required to define it. Not only was this outside the authority of the state, but more troubling, "if government begins to define religion, it must define what it is not, as well as what it is; and while it upholds whatever is included in the definition, it must suppress and abolish whatever is excluded from it." This brought Mann to his defense of his nonsectarian system. Because his system abjured all use of creeds and doctrines, it freed the state from defining religion. While his system "welcomed the religion of the Bible," it allowed it *to speak for itself.* Still, Mann acknowledged that there were constitutional limitations to his approach; his system used only as much religion as was "essential to the vitality of moral education," which was consistent with what "the constitution and laws of the State allowed and prescribed."[70]

Mann believed other constitutional principles supported his version of nonsectarianism. Mann insisted that an essential principle of the Massachusetts Constitution was the legal equality of all sects. More than tolerance of minority beliefs was required. "Men have become tolerant of intolerance, and among many nations of Christendom the common idea of Religious Freedom is satisfied by an exemption from fine and imprisonment for religious belief. They have not yet reached the conception of equal privileges and franchises for all."[71] Although he was ambiguous on this point, Mann implied that full religious equality had not yet been achieved in Massachusetts, despite the state constitution's edict of equal protection and nonsubordination of any religious sect.[72] Only with the recent state disestablishment (1833), Mann noted, had the requirement of "absolute equality" had been made law. Achieving that equality in practice was more difficult. There was an "energetic tendency of men's minds to continue in a course to which long habit has accustomed them."

> Doubtless the time will come when any interference, either by positive infliction or by legal disability, with another man's conscience in religious concernments, so long as he molests no one by the exercise of his faith, will be regarded as the crowing and supereminent act of guilt which one human being can perpetrate against another.[73]

Mann thus believed his system of nonsectarian education was indispensable to achieving the ultimate goal of religious equality. It would protect rights of conscience and prevent any means for proselytizing. Mann was so convinced as to the ultimate universal appeal of his system—and of its constitutional grounding—that he could not conceive that it could violate the conscience rights of Catholics and other religious minorities.

Finally, Mann used his exegesis to consider the question of using tax funds to pay for religious education, an issue that was becoming more contentious nationally with Catholic appeals for shares of school funds for parochial education. Like the other issues, the funding question also took on constitutional dimensions for Mann. While acknowledging the religious quality in his education system, he argued that if people were taxed to support the schools as "religious institutions . . . it would satisfy, at once, the largest definition of a Religious Establishment." That was why people were not taxed to support the public schools as "special religious institutions," but for the purpose of "developing and training those powers and faculties of a child." For this reason, the public schools could not be more religious, lest they violate the religious conscience of dissenters, including Catholics.[74]

> [I]f a man is taxed to support a school, where religious doctrines are inculcated which he believes to be false, and which he believes that God condemns; then he is excluded from the school by the Divine law, at the same time that he is compelled too support it by the human law. This is a double wrong . . . because he is constrained, by human power, to promote what he believes the Divine Power forbids. The principle involved in such a course is pregnant with all tyrannical consequences. It is broad enough to sustain any claim of ecclesiastical domination, ever made in the darkest ages of the world.[75]

Mann's strong condemnation of public financing of religious education was not directed at the developing Catholic parochial system and its early requests for public funding. Rather, it was aimed at his evangelical critics who wanted the common schools to teach Protestant doctrines. Mann was blind to the fact that his same critique could be leveled at his use of religion to teach morality. Mann's myopia is explained in part by the fact that at this time, Catholics complained that his system promoted secularism. Only later did Catholics complain that Bible reading without note or comment favored Protestant views of perspicuity of scripture and was in fact sectarian. What is significant, however, is that Mann identified a constitutional principle against the public funding of religious education. In so doing, Mann laid the groundwork for Protestant arguments against funding Catholic parochial schools and, ironically, later arguments by Protestant liberals, skeptics, and Jews that any use of the Bible in the public schools violated the conscience of taxpaying non-Protestants. Even though Catholic leaders would raise similar arguments, they maintained that the constitutional offense would be mediated by sharing the tax funds among all religious and public schools.[76]

That Mann thought about his system in constitutional terms at this early stage is remarkable. The bulk of his writings reflect practical considerations: ensuring the future and stability of the common schools; providing a moral based education necessary for the advance of the republic. Still, Mann believed that his system of universal nonsectarian education reinforced constitutional principles and, in a sense, was mandated by them. For Mann, this was not a convenient afterthought or an opportunistic embrace of principle. Rather, the compatibility of nonsectarianism with constitutionalism was central to his endeavor.

The Protestant "Settlement"

Mann's system created a dilemma for evangelical and mainstream Protestant leaders. On one hand, Mann had placed the Bible at the center of his program, and he likewise emphasized the importance of Christian morals in common education. On the other hand, his system eschewed Protestant doctrines (such as the substitutional atonement of Jesus) that many thought essential and noncontroversial. Equally troubling for Protestants, Mann's emphasis on universal religious truths at a general level implied an impending separation of education from religion. Congregational theologian Horace Bushnell expressed the frustration of many Protestants that they were witnessing a "general estrangement" of religion from public education: people "have come to look upon the interest of public education as a matter entirely apart from religion," he lamented in 1839. This trend had to be avoided. "Education without religion, is education without virtue. Religion without education, or apart from it, is a cold, unpaternal principle, dying without propagation." Yet Bushnell recognized that in order to preserve its role in the common schools, religious instruction had to adapt:

> The great point with all Christians must be to secure the bible in its proper place. To this as a sacred duty all sectarian aims must be sacrificed. Nothing is more certain than that no such thing as a sectarian religion is to find a place in our schools. It must be enough to find a place for the bible as a book of principles, as containing the true standards of character and the best motives and aids to virtue.... To insist that the state shall teach the rival opinions of sects and risk the loss of all instruction for that, would be folly and wickedness together.[77]

Over time, most educators and Protestant leaders embraced the Massachusetts model, abandoning their initial misgivings about Mann's refinements to nonsectarian education. With its emphasis on moral instruction based on the Bible and shared religious principles, nonsectarianism attracted an increasing number of Protestants who were willing to put aside their theological differences for the greater good. If there was "any one point on which the public mind is entirely united," wrote Reverend B. P. Aydelott of Cincinnati in 1837, is "that education to be useful, or even safe, must be *Christian*."[78] The loss of doctrinal purity was offset by the certainty that core religious principles would continue to be taught in the schools. "[A]ll who are Christians profess to adopt these great cardinal principles and precepts as the rule of their lives, no matter by what name they are known," declared a contributor to the *American Journal of Education*.[79] Protestants might disagree over the intensiveness of religious instruction in the public schools, but all agreed on the centrality of prayer and Bible reading. More important, Mann's system was sufficiently capacious to allow moderate evangelicals like Aydelott and Bushnell to embrace a system of unmediated Bible reading without necessarily accepting the full complement of Mann's ideology. Being, perhaps, more candid than Mann, Bushnell insisted that despite the innovations to nonsectarianism, the common schools were still Christian, if not Protestant, and still provided "a sound Christian training."[80]

No doubt, many Protestants were also looking over their shoulders—if not forward—to the growing number of Catholic complaints about the more doctrinal aspects of nonsectarianism, and they saw Mann's half-loaf as a way to preserve the essence of a Protestant-based education while deflecting the more damning Catholic charges. In addition, by relying chiefly on unmediated Bible reading rather than evangelical-slanted texts, Protestant educators could counter that Catholic attacks were directed at the use of the Bible itself. Cincinnati's Aydelott publicly embraced the Mann system early on, criticizing the use of denominational readers in the schools, arguing that the Bible—"no selection from the Bible—but the Bible *itself, ought to constitute the class book in our common schools. Only the Bible can spread over the whole ground.*"[81]

The ultimate success of Mann's model is difficult to assess. Many school boards probably embraced Mann's theory of nonsectarian education more than the actual practices it encouraged. With its reliance on the Bible and emphasis on teaching morals, Mann's nonsectarianism legitimated distinctly Protestant activities that he abjured. Whereas Mann had acknowledged a vague religious rationale for his system, evangelicals frequently kept religious inculcation as a primary emphasis. Education, wrote Reverend George Burgess in the 1856 *American Journal of Education*, "must be religious, and must include religious instruction in all necessary knowledge of the truths of divine revelation." Evangelicals like Burgess persisted in their belief that doctrinal consensus could be achieved at a more particular level, although they would have avoided calling it "doctrine." Religious "truths" were not "doctrine." Based on this distinction, Burgess insisted that public schools:

> can inculcate the whole moral code of the Gospel...It can exclude and counteract every influence of infidelity. It can, in many instances, with the universal consent of the community, affix a more decidedly religious character to the school duties of each day, by the observance of daily prayers...[and] introduce the Bible, and promote, by daily reading, the familiar knowledge of its contents, not as if it were a mere reading book, though the best, but as the generally acknowledged word of God.... [And, it] can...impress, as occasion is offered, all that great and priceless mass of truth in which all Christians are substantially united.[82]

One way that evangelicals used the nonsectarian model to their advantage—besides encouraging schools to use "good moral class-books" for "great effect"—was to insist upon hiring "competent" (i.e., evangelical) teachers who would, by example and emphasis, "inculcat[e] moral truth and Christian virtues in our common schools." When the teacher "reads the Sacred Scripture each morning (and no school should ever be opened without reading them), he will select those parts which will most readily attract juvenile curiosity and most seriously impress youthful hearts," proposed one Protestant commentator. Moreover, when the teacher

> leads in their devotions (and this service should always follow the reading of God's holy word), he will take great pains to pray like a child, . . . moved by brevity and humiliation, by earnestness and simplicity to touch the deepest fountain of feeling in his pupils. By this reading of Scriptures and offerings of prayer he will teach them that they should begin every thing with God. . . . Thus he would make morality permeate all true culture, and seize every little incident whereby he could expand the idea of right or deepen the love of truth.[83]

Nonsectarianism, in essence, offered a model that readily lent itself to adaptation. By mid-century, most public schools had acceded to Mann's innovations to some degree. In some locales, those accessions resulted in few changes to the prevailing practices that favored the dominant Protestant denomination; in others places, particularly in cities with more religiously diverse populations, the religious exercises were conducted without comment, though the prayers and Bible readings still retained a distinctive Protestant quality. Practices with respect to Protestant-oriented textbooks also varied widely, depending frequently on the availability of a text. In many cases, antebellum textbooks still espoused a Protestant bias and worldview; some were merely more overt in their Protestantism and in their disparagement of Catholicism than others. [84]

Whatever the true quality of nonsectarianism, the changes afforded greater immunity from charges that the schools were teaching doctrinal Protestantism. As an example, in 1838 a committee of the New York Legislature responded to a petition seeking to prohibit all religious exercises on the ground that they "enforce[d] peculiar religious opinions at the public expense . . . leading to, if not actually forming, a union of church and state." The legislative report, written by Henry Barnard, acknowledged the likelihood that many teachers and students welcomed the exercises because of their devotional quality. But the *object* of the exercises, Barnard insisted, was to teach morals and virtue, to ensure that children "may be[come] intelligent and virtuous citizens." No one doubted that "the best code of morals known" was contained in the Bible. "Children must be instructed in moral truth and be taught to feel habitually the force of moral obligation; and to do this according to the best standard, the use of the Bible for that purpose cannot be dispensed with." In essence, Barnard insisted, "[t]o teach christian morals, referring to the Bible both for the principles and for their illustrations, is a widely different thing from teaching what is understood to be a christian religion." The burden was on those who wished to exclude religious exercises to "show that this religion, by its necessary operation, is pernicious in its effect on the mind and morals." With these changes, some substantive and others cosmetic, most Protestants had signed on to the new version of nonsectarianism by mid-century.[85]

Catholic Resistance to Nonsectarianism

The development of common schooling between 1820 and 1850, and the Protestant settlement over nonsectarian religious instruction, did not occur in a static religious environment. It coincided with a proliferation of new religious movements (e.g., restorationists, Campbellites, Mormons, Adventists) and, more important, a rise in foreign immigration. As nonsectarian schooling expanded, common schools integrated the growing population of immigrant children, an increasing number of whom were Catholic. Initially, many Catholic leaders supported the common free schools and recommended attendance by Catholic children. In a handful of religiously diverse cities, such as Philadelphia and Cincinnati, public school officials dropped (or did not initiate) the Protestant catechisms or required that Bible readings be conducted without commentary by teachers.[86] At first, Catholic officials raised few objections to such use of the Protestant Bible. The Philadelphia *Catholic Herald* in 1834 affirmed that "religion must be the foundation and the topstone of education" and recommended that "the Bible should be studied more diligently than any other volume, and . . . the spirit of religion should pervade even the common school."[87] Indeed, even modern critics of nonsectarian education have noted that "[p]rior to 1840, there was no strong Catholic protest against the Common School Movement. On the contrary, many Catholic leaders were at first sympathetic to the movement and indeed participants in it."[88]

That amicable situation deteriorated with the influx of Catholic immigrants after the 1830s, with Catholic leaders increasing their attacks on the Bible readings, prayers, and other nonsectarian practices. Several factors led to the deterioration of relations between Protestants and Catholics in the common schools. First, with the dramatic increase in Catholic immigration, initially from Ireland but later from Germany and Italy, Protestant leaders became alarmed that foreign "Romanism" posed a threat to public education and republican government. This development, coinciding with the rise of mid-century nativism, hardened Protestant positions and perspectives, making them less willing to accommodate Catholic requests. During this same period, America was emerging from the great spiritual awakening of the previous decades, a phenomenon that established evangelical Protestantism as the de facto cultural ethic. One by-product of evangelicalism had been the rise of interdenominational reform societies, ranging from temperance and Sabbath organizations to domestic mission and Bible societies. A chief objective of these latter societies was to evangelize nominal

Protestants and Catholic immigrants, and they frequently directed their efforts at the public schools. In addition to urging devotional instruction, groups such as the American Bible Society, the American Sunday School Union, and the American Home Missionary Society promoted school textbooks that emphasized moral virtue and religious obedience, all from a Protestant perspective. These books praised the virtues of Protestant culture while they disparaged Catholic culture and faith, either overtly or by innuendo. Protestantism was identified with progress, republicanism, and individual conscience, whereas Catholicism was commonly associated with superstition, despotism, and mindless obedience to authority.[89] From the beginning, Catholic leaders denounced the numerous "misrepresentations of the tenets, the principles and the practices of our church" that occurred in the public schools. One could "scarcely find a book in which some one or more of our institutions or practices is not exhibited far otherwise than it really is, and greatly to our disadvantage," charged an 1829 pastoral letter; "the entire system of education is thus tinged throughout its whole course; and history itself has been distorted to our serious injury."[90]

Increasingly, Catholic leaders asserted the culprit was not simply Bible reading or biased reading materials but the overall Protestant orientation of the schools. In 1834, Cincinnati Bishop John Purcell referred to the newly established public schools as "*sectarian* free-schools" where "children of poor Catholics frequent for the purpose of learning to read" but where "under the pretext of Charity and to the grievous abuse of that sacred virtue and name, the fountains of spiritual life are poisoned and those unsuspecting children have tracts placed in their hands."[91] In turn, Protestants interpreted Catholic complaints about nonsectarian curriculum and readings from the King James Bible as attacks on Christianity and the scriptures themselves. This doctrinal misunderstanding, fueling intransigence and suspicion on both sides, would engender Protestant-Catholic conflicts over the public schools for the remainder of the century.

That many Protestants believed they had recently made concessions on the religious exercises to satisfy each other and, secondarily, Catholic concerns, made them resist these criticisms. Bible reading and nondenominational prayers were increasingly conducted without comment or instruction by teachers; excluding even these practices would deny Protestant children their right to moral training, educators insisted.[92] Some schools instituted policies that excused Catholic children from participating in the daily exercises or allowed readings from the Douay Bible, though the effectiveness of such policies varied widely. And a handful of public schools in religiously heterogeneous cities never instituted or later rescinded requirements of daily religious exercises, Bible reading included. St. Louis, with its large German Catholic population, never adopted a practice of prayer and Bible reading, and in 1844 the Detroit Board of Education voted down a modest resolution by one of its members to allow the Douay or King James versions to be read, without note or comment, according to the wishes of the parents. Despite the insistence of several Protestant leaders that the "Bible itself is no Sectarian Book," the Detroit Board reaffirmed its policy from previous years. It was true, the Board wrote in a report, that it had "not reported the Bible as a school book" and had not "directed the teachers . . . to impart religious instruction to their children, by reading the Bible." But, the Board continued:

> Does a man evince disrespect for the Bible by sometimes laying it aside for other books, or to pursue other studies and avocations; and does it follow that because we have provided that the scholars and teacher of our schools, should spend the time prescribed for school hours, in other studies, not embracing religion as such, as part of our system, that we intend to case reproach upon it? . . . If [we] have not adopted the Bible as a school book, neither have [we] sought to interfere with any individual right.[93]

The Board insisted its action was necessary to ensure that the city's Catholic population stood "in this latter respect, at least, upon an equal footing with the protestant population." Of equal concern for the Board was the potential for religious conflict over this "much agitated subject," as the board members were very aware of the bloody riots over Bible reading that had occurred in Philadelphia only six months earlier. The Board did not want its actions to "engender bickering and bad passions which would eventually mix themselves up with party strife and the clamor of demagogues." Unrelenting Protestant opposition to the Bible ban finally forced the Detroit Board to authorize the reading of alternative scriptural versions, but it resisted additional efforts to expand the policy.[94]

Accommodations of non-Protestants in other public schools were often more limited, particularly once a school board had adopted unmediated Bible reading as its practice. This meant that Catholic and Jewish children were frequently subjected to the Protestant exercises and sometimes punished for refusing to participate. In some places, Catholic and Jewish children also faced proselytizing by Protestant bible, tract, and missionary societies, usually with the complicity of school officials. Catholic leaders objected strenuously to the practices, which only provided fodder for Protestant claims that Catholic officials desired to keep their children in ignorance and away from the "light" of the Bible. In October 1842, a frustrated priest in upstate New York publicly burned several King James Bibles that had been distributed in Catholic communities by tract societies. The event, sensationalized by Protestant and nativist newspapers, only reinforced Protestants' belief about Catholic hostility toward the Bible, with nativists emphasizing that the priest was a foreigner from Quebec acting under the direction of the Bishop of Montreal.[95] Two years later, a more notable—and violent—conflict between Protestants and Catholics erupted in Philadelphia, ostensibly over the decision of the school board to excuse Catholic children from reading the King James Bible. The ensuing "Bible riots" resulted in approximately thirty deaths and the destruction of several Catholic churches.[96] These events only hardened the intransigence of both sides.

Nonsectarianism in the Courts

Eventually, Catholic resistance to Protestant exercises ended up in court. In November, 1853, public school officials in Ellsworth, Maine, expelled fifteen-year-old Bridget Donahoe from school after she refused to read from the King James Bible as required by school policy. The Ellsworth policy was relatively moderate, similar to the model advocated by Horace Mann: the Bible was used as a reader without teacher elaboration, not as part of a devotional exercise. The policy lacked an excusal provision, however, so Bridget and her father sued, asserting that requiring her to read the Protestant Bible infringed on her right of religious conscience. According to their attorney, James Rowe, Bridget "was required to take part in a religious exercise from which her conscience shrunk, because, as she believed, God's word was perverted in its meaning." School officials could not require a student to sacrifice "any portion of the constitutional right of liberty of conscience, in order to secure her right to a common school education." Rowe also claimed that the practice of Bible reading violated the Maine Constitution by preferring Protestantism over Catholicism, effectively excluding "a whole class of our citizens from the enjoyment of the schools." Leaving no constitutional claim unused, Bridget's attorneys finally argued that punishing her for refusing to read from the Bible constituted a religious test for the receipt of a public benefit.[97]

The Ellsworth practice put the plaintiffs in a bind, as they knew that school officials would justify the Bible reading on grounds it was nonsectarian; even the plaintiffs acknowledged that the exercises were not devotional in nature. Appreciating that this defense could undermine claims of religious preference and violations of religious conscience, Rowe made a gamble. He attacked the underlying premise of nonsectarianism, charging that the practice of Bible reading without note or comment was sectarian. School officials knew that "all persons of a certain religious denomination are unable to comply with" the reading of the King James Bible, Rowe argued. This made the schools "exclusive and sectarian" and "no longer public," rather than nonsectarian and truly universal. The Donahoes' suit thus went beyond merely challenging devotional Bible reading to attacking the notion of nonsectarianism itself.[98]

As anticipated, attorneys for the school defended the school policy on the ground that Bible reading was nonsectarian: it was not used "as an act of religious worship" or for conveying "impressions favorable to the particular tenets of any sect or denomination of Christians." Rather, stated counsel Richard Dana, the school board had chosen the Bible as a text for its historical, poetic, literary, and moral qualities: "[f]rom the common English Bible, too, we derive our household words, our phrases and illustrations, the familiar speech of the people." At the same time, Dana insisted that the Bible was not simply any book but that its readings served a higher purpose. The Bible not only represented the "noblest monument of style, of thought, of beauty, of sublimity, of moral teaching, or pathetic narrative, [and] the richest treasury of household words," Dana argued; only the Bible could teach morality. "How can the principles of morality be taught except on the basis of religion? A system of morality not founded on religion, is not morality, but only enlightened self-interest." Although Dana's second argument was in tension with the first, it was consistent with the prevailing view that the Bible could be used not only for its secular qualities but for its religious aspects as well. Schools had the duty to "preoccupy the minds of the young with the tender, the beautiful, the rhythmical, and magnificent, the sublime, which God in his bounty, the wisdom, too, has poured out so profusely into the minds of his evangelists and prophets." Using the "common English Bible" to teach morality and these universal religious truths could not infringe on Bridget's rights of conscience, Dana claimed; after all, school officials had excluded those "passages in which the two [Protestant and Catholic] translations differ."[99]

Dana's defense of Bible reading could have rested there. But Dana could not resist insinuating that something sinister was at work behind the lawsuit. Moral education, and the Bible itself, were under siege. State law required school officials to teach morality and virtue, and they had discretion to choose the best source. "If the Bible is not read, where so well can 'the principles of morality and all the virtues' be taught?" Dana charged that Bridget and her father were not motivated by conscience but were acting under the direction of Catholic officials eager to expel the Bible from the schools. "Can anyone doubt that the real question is not whether each child shall choose its version, but whether the Bible shall be read at all?" School officials had worked diligently to ensure that the use of the Bible was "not perverted to sectarian purposes," and until recently neither Catholic parents nor anyone else had objected to the practices. Dana pleaded with the Donahoes "to make sure that they are acting on their own convictions, and not under the influence of men whose office gives them great power to direct and lead," and who "cut[] them off from the best means of acquaintance and sympathy with the nature of our institutions, and the habits and feelings of our people." The goal of these "men" (i.e., priests) was to overthrow "the entire system of common public secular education by the State," he insisted. Dana's accusation of Catholic designs, coinciding at a time of rising anti-Catholicism, was gaining in popularity among educators and nativists. Catholic parents did not object to Bible reading, the argument went; hostility came from the Catholic clergy, which feared a loss of control over their followers when they were exposed to the light of the scriptures.[100]

The trial judge upheld Bridget's expulsion, and her father appealed the case to the Maine Supreme Judicial Court. Before the high court, the case became a referendum on the practice of Bible reading rather than on the authority of school officials to dismiss Bridget. That issue constituted the bulk of the supreme court's opinion. The court affirmed the lower holding, adopting the school attorneys' arguments that the readings were nonsectarian and did not violate the state constitution's prohibitions on religious preferences and subordination of sects. Most important, the court endorsed the notion of nonsectarianism. Justice John Appleton conceded that the exercises could not be sustained if the purpose was to instruct "in the theological doctrines of any religion, or of any religious sect." But he denied that readings from the King James Bible contravened that rule. The parties had agreed that there had been no instruction into "articles of faith." Because "[n]o theological doctrines were taught," nor creed "affirmed or denied," the readings were nonsectarian and could not infringe upon a child's rights of conscience.[101]

Like the arguments of the school attorneys, Justice Appleton's opinion was at tension with itself. Appleton went further than the school attorneys to minimize the religious significance of the exercises, asserting that the Bible was "used merely as a reading book," the use of which no more promoted Christianity "than would reading the mythology of Greece or Rome be regarded as...affirmance of the pagan creeds." At the same time, he embraced the singular importance of Bible reading for transmitting morality. The Bible "is best fitted to strengthen the morals and promote the virtues which adorn and dignify social life," he wrote, and recognized for "the sublime morality of its teachings." Again demonstrating uncertainty over the function of the Bible, Appleton wrote that the Board had not indicated an "authoritative sanction of [the] purity of text or accuracy of translation" in adopting the King James version but had merely stated its preference, which could be "expressed and acted upon without infringing upon the just rights of others." To grant the Donahoes their relief would thus empower "any sect the right to annul any regulation" of the constituted authorities, and make schools subordinate "to the decrees and the teachings of any and all sects, when their members conscientiously believe such teachings." Ultimately, the court held that the school committee had the authority to select the version it felt was best suited for the task of teaching morality.[102]

In the *Donahoe* decision, Justice Appleton steered clear of the more nativist-leaning arguments of the school attorneys. He acknowledged the growing sectarian conflict surrounding religious exercises in the public schools. Appleton pleaded to both sides to practice "mutual charity and forbearance" and engage in "mutual concession and compromise" to diffuse the festering conflict. Still, blame lay chiefly upon the "[l]arge masses of foreign population" who resisted assimilation into American culture. Only "through the medium of the public schools" could "the process of assimilation be so readily and thoroughly accomplished," Appleton insisted. He urged immigrants to "imbibe the liberal spirit of our laws and institutions" so as to become "citizens in fact as well as in name."[103]

By embracing the concept of nonsectarianism, the *Donahoe* court set the pattern that state courts would follow throughout the remainder of the nineteenth century. Provided that public schools used those portions of the Bible upon which there was little dispute or disagreement—at least among Protestants—and instructed in "universal principles" of religion and morality, the use of the King James Bible was legally supportable. Also, because the Bible was unobjectionable and necessary for instilling moral values, its use could not infringe on an objector's religious conscience. Still, future courts would struggle with the tension present in "nondevotional" religious exercises, as had Justice Appleton. If readings from the Bible were chiefly to fulfill a secular purpose—instilling morality and virtue—was the Bible indispensable, or were those goals inherently religious? How were courts to acknowledge the unique nature of the Bible readings without confirming the religious objections of Catholics, Jews, and other nonconformists? And finally, how would it affect a school's ability to teach morality if a court found that the indisputably religious school practices—prayers, Bible readings, and hymn singing—still common in many locales, were impermissible? Courts would struggle to reconcile these issues throughout the nineteenth century and into the next.

The most significant aspect of the Maine court's emphasis on the secular quality of the religious exercise was that it aligned the doctrine of nonsectarianism with still-developing constitutional principles. The court distanced itself from the school board's argument that an affirmation in the state constitution of "the Sovereign Ruler of the Universe" implied "the [legal] superiority of any form of religion or of any sect or denomination." Nonsectarian exercises were permissible not because Maine was a Christian state but because their minimal religious quality was consistent with the constitution's nonsubordination and no-preference clauses. The constitution, Appleton insisted, recognized "no ecclesiastical or other organization as having power over its citizens" and "no religion, nor any form of religion as such, as having any binding force over its citizens."[104] Appleton's linking of nonsectarian Bible reading to constitutional law had two contradictory effects. Initially, it affirmed a narrow view of church-state separation by keeping a preferential and overtly religious practice within its scope. Nonsectarianism was constitutional despite its religious character, provided that was not its purpose. Yet by minimizing both the religious nature and purpose of the exercises, the holding instituted that requirement as a constitutional standard for future legal conflicts. Although the *Donahoe* decision preserved nonsectarian exercises as they currently existed, it laid the constitutional foundation for their ultimate demise.

The *Donahoe* holding, with its generally cautious approach, was followed shortly by a more sensational Bible reading case. Five years after the Maine decision, a conflict over Bible reading erupted in Boston, home to an expanding Catholic immigrant population. Unlike the more reflective *Donahoe* decision, the holding in *Commonwealth v. Cooke*, like the controversy itself, fell victim to the religious and ethnic tensions between Catholic immigrants and Protestant natives. During the period between the *Donahoe* and *Cooke* trials, the nativist Know-Nothing party had risen and fallen in Massachusetts, but relations between Protestants and Catholics remained tense. Even more than with *Donahoe*, the events and legal proceedings in *Cooke* demonstrated how the controversy over nonsectarianism was evolving into a Protestant-Catholic conflict.[105]

In March 1859, Catholic students in a handful of Boston public schools began protesting the daily religious exercises, reputedly encouraged to do so by a local Jesuit priest, Father Bernardine Wiget. Disturbances quickly spread throughout schools in the Irish wards. In one school, officials expelled more than 100 Catholic students for refusing to repeat the Lord's Prayer and the Ten Commandments; expulsions citywide grew to as many as 400 in one week.[106] Tensions ran high; the Boston *Daily Evening Telegraph* claimed the disturbances threatened "to unsettle the school system and to turn the school house into an arena for settling disputed religious dogmas instead of a structure devoted to educational purposes." While calling for calm, the *Evening Telegraph* laid blame for the trouble on the Catholic priest, remarking that no person can "be regarded as a good citizen who would inflame the differences between races and religions in this community."[107]

At the height of the protests, McLaurin F. Cooke, a master at a particularly hard-hit school, the Eliot grammar school, ordered a defiant student, Thomas Wall, to repeat the Ten Commandments. Wall refused, stating that his father had told him "not to be a coward for his religion, and not for his life to say the [Protestant] commandments." Cooke then beat Wall on his hands with a cane until the boy relented. Newspapers sensationalized the incident, reporting that the whipping continued for thirty minutes, inflicting wounds and swelling on Wall's hands. Wall's injuries were apparently not serious, but his father filed a criminal complaint for assault and battery and had Cooke arrested.[108]

By the time Cooke came to trial in municipal police court in April, religious and ethnic tensions were at their apex. The case became the *cause célèbre*, with newspapers throughout the northeast reporting on the proceedings. The legal issue was whether Cooke was justified in punishing those students who refused to participate in the required religious exercises. However, the trial quickly turned into a referendum on Bible reading in the public schools and the legitimacy of Catholic objections thereto. Father Wiget, the Catholic priest behind the disturbances, became, as much as Cooke, the subject of the trial. Defense witnesses testified that Wiget had orchestrated the outbreaks against the wishes of many Catholic parents. In an organizational meeting at St. Mary's Church, Wiget had reputedly ordered 900 children to resist repeating the Commandments; after the incident, he had awarded the wounded Wall a silver-dipped medal for heroism. The allegations against Wiget were not without merit. A Swiss Jesuit who had fled Switzerland after the civil war of 1847, Wiget was part of the conservative ultramontane Catholic revival that sought to reassert the primacy of the church. By urging Catholic parents and students to assert their rights and not acquiesce to nonsectarian instruction, Wiget represented a more assertive style that clashed with the Protestant establishment.[109]

Cooke's attorney, Henry F. Durant, exploited the prevailing nativist sentiment, eagerly painting the foreign-born priest as the instigator of the disturbances and the true villain in the case. Durant praised the public schools as places where "the children of the emigrant and the alien sat side by side with the son of the free born American," learning the same values and being "free and equal under the law." However, a "dark" and "fearfully dangerous power" from a "foreign land" had launched an "attack upon our laws and our institutions." Durant claimed that Wiget and other priests sought to undermine American principles by instructing Catholic parents to "separate their children from those free schools where all meet beneath the same roof, speak the same language...and enter together the great republic of letters." No one "had the right to instruct children to violate the rules and regulations of our public schools," Durant insisted, particularly a conniving, foreign Jesuit.[110]

In less hyperbolic moments, Durant argued that the Eliot school exercises were consistent with an 1855 statute that required the daily reading of the Bible in the schools without note or comment. School officials had to select some version of the Bible for the task, Durant told the court, and the King James Bible was "accepted by all sects of Christians but one who speaks the English tongue as a translation sufficiently correct." Children "learn piety from it, not sectarianism, not creed; but pure religion, undefiled before God," Durant asserted, adding that "Our Bible never had been, never can be sectarian." Merely reading the Bible could never violate a child's religious conscience, Durant argued; in fact, unmediated Bible reading *encouraged* freedom of conscience and furthered "the true principles of religious liberty and toleration." In contrast, the Catholic Douay Bible, with its marginal notations, was "avowedly a sectarian book, written and published with that acknowledged object."[111] With this argument Durant sought to recast the nature of Wall's underlying claim. It was Father Wiget and his "bogus bread and butter saint and martyr"—"little Saint Tom"—who threatened to undermine freedom on conscience in the schools by excluding the Bible, not its enforced reading and recitation. Durant closed by suggesting that a nefarious plot was at work, one in which Wiget had ordered children to resist in hope that they might be whipped, "in order that the Jesuits might raise the cry of religious persecution [and] might under that cry arouse public feeling, and drive the Bible from the schools." In this recasting of facts, the Jesuit priest, not the defendant, was the villain.[112]

The prosecutor, Sidney Webster, appeared unprepared for Durant's aggressive defense. He fumbled through an unenviable argument that forced him to defend the reputed Catholic intransigence while disputing the value of Bible reading: "Our schools are maintained, or should be maintained, to teach secular subjects....We do not send children to public schools to learn Biblical doctrines." Even under different circumstances, Webster was making a losing argument; during this period, few people challenged the importance of religious instruction for teaching morals, or of the authority of public school officials to do so.[113]

The outcome of the trial was not a surprise. The court held that Cooke's actions were justified and dismissed the charges. Rather than simply holding that Cooke had acted to enforce a school policy, Judge Maine eagerly validated Bible reading and nonsectarian instruction. Maine insisted that "our fathers" had placed the Bible in the public schools, "not for the purpose of teaching sectarian religion," but as "the best book to teach children and youth the principles of piety, justice, and a sacred regard to truth, love of their country, humanity." These and other virtues were "the ornaments of human society, and the basis upon which a republican constitution is founded." Because the religious exercises were required by state law, Cooke was authorized to require Wall's compliance, Maine declared. Wall "was punished for insubordination, and a determination to stand out against the lawful commands of the school. Every blow was for a continued resistance and a new offense."[114]

Judge Maine's finding that Bible reading was nonsectarian served two interrelated functions. By justifying Bible reading on secular, pedagogical grounds, the court buttressed the school's authority to engage in such practices. At the same time, Judge Maine was more willing than the Donahoe court to affirm that a secondary purpose of the exercises was to instill "knowledge of God and of his will." Second, finding the exercises to be nonsectarian allowed Maine to reject Wall's claim that the policy violated his rights of conscience. Because Bible reading served the secular function of instilling important virtues, "[t]o read the Bible for these and like purposes, or to require it to be read without sectarian explanations, is no interference with religious liberty." If courts recognized Wall's claim, then "every denomination may object for conscience sake," Maine asserted, resulting in "a war upon the Bible and its use in common schools."[115]

As a result of the Donahoe and Cooke holdings, nonsectarianism made the transition from an educational concept to a legal doctrine. Despite the Protestant bias of each decision, both courts essentially used secular rationales to uphold the distinctly religious practices. On one level, this may indicate little more than a transparent attempt to couch a religious bias in more acceptable terms. But the language in the Donahoe opinion, and even in Judge Maine's decision, reveal that both judges had purchased the theory of nonsectarianism. In their minds, the underlying purpose of the exercises was chiefly secular, making reliance on religious rationales unnecessary. Accepting the premise of nonsectarianism also permitted both courts to reject claims that forced participation in the practices violated Catholic rights of conscience. If the practices were ostensibly secular and for the purpose of instilling morality and virtue, the conscience claims of students were not legitimate. Through such reasoning, the courts had legalized nonsectarianism and ensured the continuation of the practices. Neither court seemed aware, however, that their rationales would eventually lead to demise of nonsectarian prayer and Bible reading; the more that the purposes of instilling morality and virtue were shorn from their religious roots, the less necessary the religious practices became.

Following the reasoning of the two decisions, in July 1859 the New York City Board of Education amended its policy of ward-optional Bible reading to one of mandatory daily Bible reading in all its schools. This change elicited accusations from Board members representing Catholic wards that the move was "clearly an act of aggression" designed "to force [Protestant] views and practices upon others." The dissenters claimed Protestant members of the Board were "eager for a crusade in behalf of the Bible."

> When religious matters are degraded from their high and holy sphere to the uses of partisanship of any kind, it is too often found that those who are loudest in their professed advocacy, are not always, either in their language or conduct, the most consistent with religious purity or principle.[116]

The Board of Education stuck with its new policy, although it was enforced only sparingly in Catholic wards.

As the New York incident indicates, that courts had now weighed in on behalf of nonsectarianism did little to resolve the controversy. Catholic leaders still objected that Bible reading without note or comment reflected a Protestant theological belief in unmediated scriptural inspiration and was inherently sectarian. At the same time, Catholic clergy insisted that the purging of Christian doctrine from education rendered the public schools secular, if not infidel. "Listen not to those who would persuade you that religion can be separated from secular education," instructed the American hierarchy in their 1852 Pastoral Letter.[117] Though separated from the Catholic leadership by a chasm, many Protestant clergy were similarly troubled at the loss of a religious justification for Bible reading; they sensed that the trend toward readings without note or comment might not be the final step. "[W]hile it is essential to forbid sectarianism in the public schools, it is as essential to bring them under the teachings and power of true religion," insisted Reverend George Cheever in 1854. "[R]eligion should not be driven out under cover of repealing sectarianism," Cheever wrote; "it is as clearly the right and duty of the State to instruct the children in religious, as it is secular truth." Protestants questioned whether they had conceded too much for too little gain, particularly since those concessions had not brokered an armistice from Catholics. On the contrary, Catholics were beginning to amass support from Jews and secularists who met them half-way on their complaints about the Protestant bias of public education. The holdings in *Donahoe* and *Cooke* did little to ease Protestant insecurities.[118]

Following the *Donahoe* and *Cooke* cases, the Massachusetts legislature enacted a new law in 1862 reaffirming that Bible reading without note or comment was to be conducted in the public schools, but that no student should be forced to participate in the exercises. The purpose of the law was "to impress on the minds of children and youth . . . the principles of piety and justice, and a sacred regard for truth." The new law did little to prevent abuses or ameliorate Catholic complaints. In 1866 a Catholic student challenged the law after she was expelled for refusing to bow her head during a prayer. The Massachusetts Supreme Judicial Court upheld the expulsion and new law. The justices agreed that school officials could not require students "to conform to any religious rite or observance" that conflicted with their beliefs. But the Court found the law did not compel students to join in prayer, only requiring them to observe "quiet and decorum during the religious service."[119] Since many Massachusetts schools had dropped forced recitations of the Bible during Mann's administration, the new law probably changed little in the way of prevailing practices. As important, the 1862 law affirmed the view that Bible reading was not sectarian in character. And most significant, the new law reaffirmed Protestant belief that nonsectarianism provided a workable solution to the School Question while adequately addressing all Catholic complaints.

By mid-century, the Protestant acceptance of Mann's system of nonsectarianism, and its early sanction by courts, created the impression—or at least the hope—that the School Question had been settled. But no sooner had that consensus been achieved than it began to crumble. People began to question the role of public schools in teaching fealty to any religious principles, universal or otherwise. A new generation of education reformers, led by William Torrey Harris, Superintendent of the St. Louis public schools and later U.S. Commissioner of Education, would take nonsectarianism into its third phase, one that made a greater distinction between character education and religious instruction. Harris, joined by religious liberals like Henry Ward Beecher and Samuel T. Spear, would advocate removing all religious practices in the public schools, not solely to appease Catholic complaints but also out of a conviction that rote Bible reading did little good, while it presumed an authority over religion that the state did not possess.[120] Some within the secular press would shortly reach the same conclusion. A March, 1860 article in *Harper's New Monthly Magazine* urged a reevaluation of the Bible's use in the schools, though it stopped short of calling for its abolition. "The Bible question will cease to make difficulty, if the great majority who . . . insist upon having it in the schools, will give practical proof of their freedom from bigotry, and their desire to make the book a manual of piety and charity, instead of dogmatic theology or priestly ritualism." This marked a significant advance for the magazine, which had historically supported nonsectarian education. For the time being, however, the illusory belief that the controversy over religious exercises had been settled, and the impending crisis over secession and civil war, allowed the issue of Bible reading in the schools to subside temporarily. To the dismay of many observers, Protestant and Catholic alike, the controversy would reemerge in the late 1860s with a renewed vengeance.[121]

2

The Development of the "No-Funding Principle"

The corollary to nonsectarianism, the prohibition on the public funding of religious schools, shared a common history with the former principle. Like the notion of nonsectarian education, the no-funding rule was a dynamic principle, evolving throughout the first half of the century. Initially, as communities established their first schools in the late eighteenth and early nineteenth centuries, there was little distinction between "public" and "private" schooling. Early schooling was commonly a joint endeavor among local officials, businessmen, and religious leaders. Many early schools—town or district, private-pay secular, private-pay religious, and denominational charity schools—received a share of whatever public support was available, though most schools other than charity schools also charged students a tuition or "rate." Once states and locales embraced the idea of universal common schooling under the nominal supervision of public authorities, the logical step was to grant public schools exclusive control over public school funds. By the second third of the nineteenth century, the dominant practice was to restrict public funding to education under the control of public officials. By that time, a clearer division between public and private schooling had emerged; the majority of private schools were religiously run and, increasingly, Catholic in orientation.

The no-funding rule arose out of several complementary rationales. Like nonsectarianism, the rule initially reflected practical considerations; only later did the principle take on legal or constitutional dimensions. Foremost, public school officials opposed dividing school funds as a way to secure the financial stability of the nascent common schools. In the early nineteenth century, public commitment to a system of public education did not come naturally and had to be earned. Competing educational options stood in the way of gaining this public commitment, and private schooling challenged the ideological argument for a system of universal, common schooling that acculturated children into republic society. Second, once public officials embraced universal common schooling, education—and its funding source—had to be controlled by public authorities to ensure its success. The editors of *Harper's New Monthly Magazine* insisted in mid-century that "state education can be rightly meant nothing else than a governmental control—having the charge and supervision of the very purposes, and all the purposes, for which the funds are bestowed."[1] Closely related to this last impulse, public officials increasingly viewed the no-funding principle as a means to standardize education and ensure its financial accountability. And over time, schoolmen and public officials came to identify the no-funding rule with constitutional principles of religious nonestablishment. Funding religious education violated this last principle in three ways, according to contemporaries: it violated rights of conscience to force one person to pay for another's religious instruction; it produced religious dissension through the competition for funds; and it resulted in ecclesiastical control over public monies. All of these concerns, while standing on an independent footing, were reinforced by Protestant perspectives toward Catholic parochial schooling. On one level, educators and Protestant leaders firmly believed that public funding of Catholic schools would undermine all of these considerations. Further coloring this perspective was the widespread belief among Protestants that Catholic schooling was antagonistic to republican values, an attitude reinforced by anti-Catholic animus. The no-funding rule thus found its most common application in the debate over the funding of Catholic schools.[2]

The Early Development of the No-Funding Rule

The idea of public financial support for education arose during the nation's early years, coinciding with the formation of state governments. Several states enacted laws or constitutional provisions that laid the foundation for public schooling; Massachusetts passed the first statewide school law in 1789, requiring communities to establish elementary schools. In time, northern and midwestern states replicated this pattern. Following on these provisions, states shortly enacted laws authorizing communities to impose taxes to support public schooling and later, many established statewide school accounts or "School Funds." Initially, public funding subsidized existing local schools, which, as discussed, were frequently a hybrid of private-religious-public endeavors. In the nascent stages of publicly supported education, the lines between public and private schooling were frequently indistinct.[3]

The development of practical and legal rationales for the no-funding rule can again be seen in the early experience in New York. As discussed in the previous chapter, schooling in New York City and upstate during the late 1700s took on several forms: exclusive academies and boarding schools, private-pay schools (both religious and entrepreneurial), denominational charity schools, and town-operated "district schools." All but the first would have been considered "common" in the sense they offered a similar rudimentary education of reading and character instruction for children of the middle and lower classes. And all but the first may have received some local public support, however small. In 1795 the New York

Legislature enacted an "act for the encouragement of schools," which appropriated $50,000 annually for five years to the city and towns to support existing schooling, though one goal of the legislation was to encourage communities to establish new common schools based on the New England district school model. The law did not distinguish between privately and publicly operated schools, as that line was often illusive. The distribution of the funds was left to local officials, and in New York City, the Common Council voted in 1796 to limit the state funding to denominational charity schools, excluding the private-pay schools, both secular and religiously affiliated. The New York Legislature declined to reauthorize funding between 1800 and 1805, even though it had established a state common school fund out of proceeds from state lotteries in 1801. The Common Council's decision to limit public funding to charity schools meant that common "free" schooling in the city would arise out of these religiously affiliated schools, and not through a separate "publicly" created school system.[4]

As discussed in the previous chapter, after it was established in 1805, the Free School Society grew at the expense of the other charity schools. Over time, it gained an increasing share of the available public funding, due in part to the attraction of its nonsectarian program, but also because of political connections with the mayor and Common Council. By 1825 the Society operated eleven elementary schools and claimed that it had taught 20,000 children in its twenty-year existence. Despite its growing prominence, Society schools still competed with the denominational charity schools and private-pay schools, some of which also admitted poor children for little or no tuition. The directors of the Society viewed this disaggregated state of affairs as inimical to its goal of universal education; despite its efforts, at least one quarter of the poor children in the City still went unschooled, Society officials claimed. Society officials also maintained that the instruction and facilities of the charity and private-pay schools were often substandard. The Society's 1825 Annual Report summed up these concerns:

> Our free schools have conferred the blessings of education upon a large number of children of the poor, but still it is to be lamented that a description of public school is wanting amongst us, where the rich and poor may meet together; where the wall of partition, which now seems to be raised between them, may be removed; [and] where kindler feelings between the children of these respective classes may be begotten.[5]

One factor absent from the report was that the Society viewed other charity and private-pay schools as competitors for public school funds. After twenty years of operation, the Free School Society was refining its mission and positioning itself to become the City's *de facto* common school.[6]

That goal, and the Society's favored financial position, encountered a challenge in 1822. In 1820 Bethel Baptist Church had established a charity school in its church basement and began receiving appropriations from the common school fund. Two years later the church secured a state grant from surplus school funds to construct a school building—with the possibility of opening additional charity schools—a privilege that had heretofore been afforded only to the Free School Society.[7] Viewing the grant as a threat to its financial well-being, the nonsectarian model, and its long-range goals, the Society submitted a memorial to the state legislature urging its repeal. The memorial touted the uniqueness of the Society's program, asserting that only it was equipped to provide schooling to the growing number of poor and vagrant children. Unless the Society was financially able to "embrace and relieve their condition," these children would be "exposed to temptations of the most pernicious kind," eventually "swell[ing] the list of crimes on the records of criminal courts, fill the penitentiaries with convicts, and subsist by committing depredations on the property of their fellow citizens." (The memorial noted that only one out of 14,000 Society students had ever been arraigned in criminal court.) It made little sense to divide the scarce school funds, the memorial asserted, particularly when need was growing and when disbursement would encourage the creation of additional ill-equipped charity schools.[8]

In addition to making pragmatic and self-interested points, the Society raised what can best be described as an early church-state argument. It emphasized that its nonsectarian program was available to children of all faiths and backgrounds (no "distinction of sect or name is known in admitting scholars"), a practice it insisted was consistent with republican principles.[9] The Society also made several points that would serve as the basis of an emergent no-funding principle: funding of religious schools would cause competition and rivalry among faiths; the grant "impose[d] a direct tax on our citizens for the support of religion" in violation of rights of conscience; and the school fund was "purely of a civil character," not to be under the control of a religious institution. "[T]he proposition that such a fund should never go into the hands of an ecclesiastical body or religious society, is presumed to be incontrovertible upon any political principle approved or established in this country.... that church and state shall not be united," asserted the memorial. In raising this last argument, the Society introduced a new distinction between "civil" and "religious" purposes for the school fund, suggesting that the ongoing funding of denominational charity schools did not meet that "civil" purpose. The memorial closed by asserting that a central principle of republican government was "to let religion support itself." The "experience of this country [had] show[n]—what appears problematical in the eyes of Europe—that religion requires no aid from the civil arm." The memorial did not allude to any provision in the New York Constitution; rather, the Society characterized its church-state arguments as arising out of "political" principles, required by the nature of republican institutions. However, it is apparent that the Society trustees viewed these principles as having a general constitutional basis.[10]

The mayor and Common Council filed a memorial supporting the Society's position. It too commended the Society's inclusive program, noting that the Society was "allied to no sect or party" but open to children of all faiths. The memorial cautioned that the "future establishment of sectarian schools" receiving public dollars would work to the detriment of a uniform common education as was offered in the Society's schools. Finally, the City memorial also raised a church-state argument, expressing concern that funding sectarian education would enlist a "spirit of rivalry . . . between different sects," which would "disturb the harmony of society" and "infuse strong prejudices in the minds of children taught in the different schools." Drawing the same bright-line distinction as the Society, the City insisted that the school fund was "purely of a civil character, designed for a civil purpose," intimating that education in a sectarian school would not satisfy that purpose, even though denominational schools had been serving that civil purpose for thirty years. But beyond arguing that the funding of religious education was *ultra vires*, the City also described the prohibition in quasiconstitutional terms, asking rhetorically whether entrusting the fund "to religious or ecclesiastical bodies is not a violation of an elementary principle in the politics of the State and country."[11]

The legislative Committee on Colleges, Academies, and Common Schools considered the various memorials, and in 1824 recommended the Legislature discontinue funding for religious charity schools. Unlike the memorials, its report relied chiefly on church-state grounds, declaring that it would be "a violation of a fundamental principle . . . to allow the funds of the State, raised by a tax on the citizens, designed for civil purposes, to be subject to the control of any religious corporation."[12] The Legislature, though, opted for a more politically expedient course, voting to authorize the City Common Council to make all future allotments of the school fund in the city. The following year, after additional lobbying by the Society, the Common Council voted to end the funding of religious charity schools. After 1825, only those schools of the Society and the handful of nondenominational charity schools were eligible to receive public school funds. Although the decision turned chiefly on the superiority of the Society's program and facilities, the Council also expressed hope that its action would remove "causes of disagreement" between and produce "harmony . . . among religious sects." The following year the Society further secured its position as the *de facto* common school by changing its name to the "New York Public School Society" and restructuring its program to appeal to paying students.[13]

The Bethel Baptist episode confirmed the public funding of religious schooling as a church-state issue. Henceforth, the two issues would be intertwined. Even though the Society's church-state appeals represented a secondary attack on the Bethel Baptist Church petition, those arguments do not appear to have been an afterthought. From its inception, the Society had considered the religious universality of its nonsectarian program to be one of its superior assets. The Society still viewed its instruction as religious, but in a general sense rather than being sectarian. The purpose of its religious program was to instill moral character and religious devotion, not for proselytizing sectarian doctrines. Character education was a public purpose whereas doctrinal instruction was not. The Society abjured the deleterious affects of religious competition and dissent, and not simply to pre-serve its favored position over the school fund. Avoiding sectarian divisiveness was at the core of nonsectarian theory. It was a small step to translate these con-cerns into constitutional terms.

The Bethel Baptist episode also indicates that people viewed the emerging idea of a constitutional bar to funding sectarian schools in denominationally neutral terms. The Society and City had raised church-state arguments in response to a funding request made by a Protestant school. The Baptist school, like other Protestant charity schools, was sectarian in character, the Society asserted in one of its resolutions: funding the Baptist school "promot[ed] . . . private and *sectarian* interests." The City's memorial concurred that the Baptist school was sectarian, and it warned that to approve the request would encourage similar applications from other "sectarian societies."[14] Here, "sectarian" was equated with "denomina-tional," and the term was used in a generic manner not reserved for Catholic schools. Nothing in the memorials or reports indicates that Society and public officials were thinking about the funding of Catholic parochial schools when they were crafting their arguments. At that time, any religious school that instructed in particular doctrines was sectarian. Protestant charity schools were sectarian whereas the Society's nonsectarian schools were not. It was within this context that the rule emerged that public funds should not pay for religious education.[15]

Like the church-state arguments raised by the Society, City, and legislative committee, the Common Council's decision to defund the denominational schools did not rest on an interpretation of an express constitutional provision. Rather, the decision referred to "fundamental" or "political" principles of government. The same could be said for the action by the state legislature. Fifteen years later Catholic Bishop John Hughes would emphasize this point in his petitions for a share of the school fund for Catholic parochial schools. The extent to which the events of 1824–1825 established a *constitutional* precedent remained unclear.[16]

That people were coming to view the funding issue in constitutional terms is demonstrated by a second incident that arose some six years later. In 1831 the Roman Catholic Orphan Asylum and the Methodist Charity School petitioned the Common Council for a share of the school fund to support their programs. As before, the Public School Society resisted the challenges to its favored position by submitting memorials opposing the requests. This time, the Society placed greater emphasis on church-state grounds, tying the notion directly to the constitution. Funding of sectarian education was "contrary to the fundamental principles of liberty and equal rights, [contained in] the Constitution of the State," the Society asserted. The memorials borrowed several arguments from James Madison: that the funding of religious instruction violated rights of conscience; and the purpose of the ban was to protect people "of every persuasion, who have conscientious scruples about paying their money for the support of any particular faith." The Society also argued that public funding of religious education was indistinguish-able from paying for worship or the construction of religious edifices. Revealing a further development in its thinking, the Society asserted that the constitutional principles were not merely aspirational, they represented a legal mandate: public money could not "be diverted from support of the common schools without a *violation* of the Constitution." Finally, the Society raised an early argument about the *pervasively sectarian* character of the schools, noting that "one of the objects aimed at in all such schools is to inculcate the particular doctrines and opinions of the sect having the management of them." Employing language similar to that used by the United States Supreme Court some 150 years later, the Society insisted that the education provided in the two schools was "so combined with religious instruction" that it was impossible to separate the various functions. In characterizing the sectarian schools, the Society did not distinguish between Catholic and Methodist programs.[17]

The petitions and memorials were submitted to the Council's law committee. After a four month delay, the law committee issued a report on the Catholic Orphan Asylum that affirmed the Society arguments. The report emphasized that the school fund had to remain "inviolable" for the benefit of common schools and be accountable to civil authorities. Even though the Public School Society was also a private charity like the Catholic asylum, its public charter and open enrollment distinguished it from the denominational charity schools. The report related this evolution in the Society's character, stating that its schools "may be emphatically called common schools, and [they] have a just and legal claim to a portion of the school fund." In contrast, religious schools were not common:

> A school, to be common, ought to be open to all.... If religion be taught in a school, it strips it of one of the characteristics of a common school, as all religious and sectarian studies have a direct reference to a future state, and are not necessary to prepare a child for the mechanical or any other business.[18]

As significant for the no-funding rule was the committee's statement of the church-state question: "Can we, without violating the Constitution, appropriate any of the public funds to the support of those schools or institutions in which children are taught the doctrines and tenets of religious sectarianism?" By phrasing the question this way, the committee had answered itself: "to raise a fund by taxation, for the support of a particular sect, or every sect of Christians...would unhesitatingly be declared an infringement of the Constitution, and a violation of our chartered rights."[19] Like the Society, the Council now characterized the rule as constitutionally mandated. The committee agreed with the Society that the prohibition applied with equal force to the funding of religious education as it did to the funding of religious worship, declaring it could not "perceive any marked difference in principle, whether a fund be raised for the support of a particular church, or whether it be raised for the support of a school in which the doctrines of that church are taught as a part of the system of education."[20] Other considerations were also on the committee's collective mind. If the Council were to approve the Catholic petition, then

> Methodist, Episcopalian, Baptist, and every other sectarian school, [would] come in for a share of this fund.... If all sectarian schools be admitted to the receipt of a portion of a fund sacredly appropriated to the support of common schools, it will give rise to a religious and anti-religious party, which will call into active exercise the passions and prejudices of men. A fierce and uncompromising hostility will ensue, which will pave the way for the predominance of religion in political contests. The unnatural union of Church and State will then be easily accomplished—a union destructive of human happiness and subversive of civil liberty.

****

> It would be an incipient step toward engrafting in our institutions a system not less odious and oppressive, not less fatal in its consequences to the liberties and happiness of our country, to place the interest of the school fund at the disposal of sectarians. It is to tax the people for the support of religion, contrary to the Constitution, and in violation of their conscientious scruples.[21]

The law committee's report related only to the Catholic request, though its language indicated that the legal rationales applied equally to the Methodist petition. Perhaps anticipating the arguments of the Society and law committee, the Methodist Free School in the interim had sent a letter clarifying that it admitted non-Methodist children when space was available and that all children were "educated upon general [religious] principles, without reference to sectarianism," obviously seeking align its program with that of the Society. The move did not appease the Society, which claimed that granting the Methodist request would open the door to funding other denominational schools. Determining which programs were truly sectarian would be illusive, the Society suggested, and the "distinction between the Methodist and other churches, if it now exists, will be shortly removed by sectarian zeal." For some reason, the Methodist petition was referred to a different committee, the Committee of Arts, Sciences, and Schools. That committee accepted the Methodist's assurances that its program was not sectarian and recommended that it "be admitted to a participation of the fund."[22]

This presented the Common Council with two seemingly contradictory recommendations from two different committees. On one level, the reports were consistent in that each distinguished between sectarian and nonsectarian education, whether the facts truly supported that distinction. The different analysis in the two reports could possibly be an example of the evolving bias that Catholic education was always considered "sectarian," whereas Protestant-oriented programs were presumed to be nonsectarian until proven otherwise. However, the law committee's strong report had also criticized the funding of the Methodist school. As it turned out, the Common Council surprised everyone by approving the payment to the Catholic Orphan Asylum while denying the request of the Methodist Charity School. Apparently, the decision to fund the Orphan Asylum was based on the theory that the public money primarily supported the care of the orphans, not their education. The sole ground for rejecting the Methodist petition, however, was that its program was sectarian and thus ineligible for public support, as the law committee report had maintained.[23]

This episode was significant for the development of the no-funding rule in at least two respects. First, more than with the controversy over the funding of the Bethel Baptist schools, the various parties perceived the no-funding principle in constitutional terms. Funding of sectarian education was not merely in tension with general republican values but represented "a violation of the Constitution." As the Council's law committee commented, public funding of sectarianism was "a violation of the constitutional rights and conscientious scruples of the people." But the bar not only prevented infringements upon religious conscience, it also reinforced a broader principle that lay at the heart of republican values. Official support of religion had led to preferential treatment of the dominant faith, to the exclusion of others, resulting in religious conflict and dissent. Such a system had no place in a nation committed to democratic principles. Public funding of religion would result, in the words of the law committee, in the "unnatural union of Church and State...a union destructive of human happiness and subversive to civil liberty." The 1831 episode also reinforced the understanding from the Bethel Baptist controversy that the bar on funding sectarian education applied to all religious schools. Sectarianism was viewed in generic terms, not as something peculiar to the various functions of the Catholic Church. In this instance, because the Catholic Orphan Asylum was providing chiefly a benevolent service rather than sectarian education, it was eligible for public support, much to the chagrin of the Methodist parochial school. This decision, with its distinction, established a precedent in New York for the funding of some, but not other, religious institutions. Based on a distinction between care and education and the source of public funding—the school fund versus charitable grants—Catholic and other religious orphanages would receive public monies through the remainder of the century, in contrast to parochial schools. Such funding occurred even though the denominational orphanages also instructed their wards.[24]

New York school officials and politicians could have been forgiven for thinking that the Common Council's second decision had resolved the issue about funding sectarian schools. The Society, with its nonsectarian program, expanded its schools and consolidated power, such that by 1840 it held a near monopoly on the school fund. With Protestant charity schools now excluded from receiving public support, they gradually shuttered their doors, reconciling themselves that their goals of moral and religious instruction could be achieved through the Society's nonsectarian program as supplemented through Sunday schools and the activities of Protestant

Bible and tract societies (at that time, the American Bible Society pledged to ensure that the King James Bible was read in every common school classroom). The evangelical Protestant acquiescence to nonsectarian instruction, discussed in the previous chapter, was the leading factor in the demise of most Protestant schools, outside of the Lutheran community. This settlement over nonsectarianism was, of course insecure, as it excluded Catholics and the small community of Jews.[25]

The "Great Debate" of the 1840s

The early episodes in the development of the no-funding rule did not occur in an environment that was culturally or religiously static. Over the period just discussed, New York City underwent an extraordinary social and religious transformation. Between 1830 and 1850, the city, and America in general, experienced a significant rise in the number of Catholics, mostly attributable to immigration from Ireland and Germany. In the city, the Catholic population grew from approximately 1,300 in 1800 to between 60,000 and 80,000 in 1840, out of a total population of slightly more than 300,000.[26] By that year, the number of Catholic schools had risen from one, established at St. Peter's Church in 1801, to eight charity "free-schools," not counting a handful of private-pay Catholic schools. Still, three-quarters of Catholic immigrant children received their schooling through Society schools, if they received schooling at all.[27] Over time, Catholic leaders grew frustrated at the religious exercises, the Protestant-oriented texts, and the general disparagement of Catholicism in the public schools. American bishops, through a progression of Pastoral Letters of 1829, 1833, and 1840, increasingly criticized the hostility and misrepresentation that Catholicism regularly received in the common schools: through both instruction and school texts, "covert and insidious efforts are made to misrepresent our principles, to distort our tenets, to vilify our practices, and to bring contempt upon our Church and its members." As early as 1833 the bishops had recommended establishing parochial schools as an alternative to common schools, but adequate resources were wanting, particularly within a denomination of poorer workers and laborers.[28]

Until the Bethel Baptist school decision of 1824, the handful of Catholic charity schools had received money from the school fund along with the other denominational charity schools. Thus public financial support had already vanished before the rise in Catholic immigration and the subsequent need for parochial schooling as more Catholics became alienated from the public schools. This dilemma for Catholics called for a champion; they found one in New York Bishop John Hughes (figure 2.1).

John Hughes was one of the more important and controversial religious figures of the mid-nineteenth century. As a result, he has received mixed treatment from historians. Critics have labeled him militant, abrasive, and uncompromising whereas admirers have described him as astute, forceful, and indefatigable.[29] It is likely that there is some truth to all of these characterizations. Born in Ireland, the son of a poor farmer, Hughes immigrated to America in 1817 at the age of twenty and shortly entered the seminary in Emmitsburg, Maryland. Ordained a priest in 1826, Hughes served parishes in Philadelphia until he was appointed coadjutor bishop of New York in 1838 to assist the ailing Bishop John Dubois. With his Irish immigrant background, Hughes identified closely with the plight of the newly arriving immigrants from his native land. He viewed the American Protestant establishment through the experience of the Anglican-Catholic conflict that had engulfed Ireland for centuries. Hughes was also fiercely loyal to his church and its doctrines, aligning himself with the conservative ultramontane movement that resisted Catholic accommodations with liberalism in Europe and America. One way to protect the faith and its institutions, and maintain the fealty of Catholic immigrants, was to resist assimilation into American culture.[30]

Some have argued that this background and perspective ill-suited Hughes to lead American Catholics on the School Question—that his defiant faith and combativeness unnecessarily alienated education reformers and Protestant leaders at a time when compromise may have been possible. Vincent Lannie has written:

> Hughes did not adequately understand the Protestant tenor of his adopted country and its deep suspicion of Catholicism. For his was the "true" faith, and Protestant "heresy" was its deadly enemy. Catholic

Figure 2.1 Bishop John Hughes. The Granger Collection, New York.

newcomers to the United States especially had to be protected from an active Protestant proselytism and insulated against a pervasive Protestant environment if they were to retain their traditional faith. Because of a fundamental suspicion of an unsympathetic and often hostile majority, Hughes unfortunately, though perhaps understandable, adopted a defensive mentality and never seriously attempted to integrate his predominately immigrant flock into the mainstream of American life.[31]

Even Catholic historians acknowledge that Hughes's aggressive style contributed to the nativist backlash against Catholicism. Hughes "did little to assist his immigrant followers to understand their surroundings and to live in peace with their neighbors," writes David O'Brien. "He taught them that a strong, militant, and a politically united Catholic bloc could defend its interests, but he neglected to instruct them in the requirements of the common good."[32] Others have insisted that Hughes accurately perceived that Protestants would never surrender their control over public education, such that a separate system of publicly funded Catholic schooling was the only faithful solution. Admirers and critics concur that, at a minimum, Hughes contrasted starkly to the more quiescent and accommodating style that had marked the Catholic hierarchy up to that time.[33]

In the late 1830s the nation experienced the first significant outbreak of nativist sentiment in response to the surge in immigration from Ireland and Germany. Various nativist books and newspapers appeared, all designed to call attention to the growing Catholic-immigrant threat to a republican society that most Americans equated with Protestantism. The largely negative native American response relied on a combination of factors: Protestant aversion to Catholicism; republican fears of papal political designs in America; Anglo-American disdain for the Irish; and worker concerns about economic dislocation resulting from the infusion of a large laboring class. As addressed more fully below, the nativist response defies a simple characterization, but ethnic and religious bigotry played a large role. One vivid description is found in an 1838 entry in the diary of social critic George Templeton Strong:

> It was enough to turn a man's stomach—to make a man adjure republicanism forever—to see the way they were naturalizing this morning at the Hall. Wretched, filthy, bestial-looking Italians and Irish...; in short, the very scum and dregs of human nature filled the clerk of the C[ommon] P[leas] office so completely that I was almost afraid of being poisoned by going in. A dirty Irishman is bad enough, but he's nothing comparable to. a nasty French or Italian loafer.[34]

In New York and elsewhere, the newly arrived Irish affiliated themselves chiefly with the more populist policies of the Jacksonian Democrats. In contrast, the emerging Whig party with its evangelical Protestant base began to court those Americans with anti-Irish or anti-Catholic sentiments. The New York Whig party divided over the immigrant issue, however, with leaders William Henry Seward and Thurlow Weed reputedly eager to attract the foreign-born to their party. In 1838 Seward was elected governor, benefitting from voters blaming Democrats for the economic Panic of 1837. Hoping to entice immigrant support for his party, and his reelection,[35] Seward broached the School Question in his annual message to the legislature in January, 1840:

> The children of foreigners, found in great numbers in our populous cities and towns...are too often deprived of the advantages of our system of public education, in consequence of prejudices arising from differences in language or religion. It ought never to be forgotten that the public welfare is as deeply concerned in their education as in that of our own children. I do not hesitate, therefore, to recommend the establishment of schools in which they may be instructed by teachers speaking the same language with themselves and professing the same faith.[36]

Contemporary and later critics charged that Seward's support for Catholic schooling was politically motivated. Vincent Lannie insists, however, that Seward "did not suddenly become interested in educational matters" for political reasons; he sincerely sought to extend educational opportunities to the children of the poor and foreign born. Seward apparently disdained the educational and social inequality that existed in New York and believed in the importance of extending the benefits of a republican education to immigrant and working class children.[37] At the same time, Seward's desire to further educational opportunities to immigrants did not conflict with his desire to expand the constituency of the Whig party. In any case, if Seward was motivated primarily by political considerations, he miscalculated, as his proposal alienated him from many in the Whig party and Protestant establishment. Seward "underrated the power of nativism in his own party," John Pratt writes, "as well as the durability of the Irish-Democratic alliance."[38]

Seward was vague, possibly purposefully, as to his proposal. It lent itself to several possible interpretations: hire Catholic teachers and allow Catholic instruction in those public schools in Catholic wards; integrate existing Catholic parochial schools into the public school system; or provide public funding for freestanding Catholic schools. As it stood, there were few enclaves—chiefly German—where foreign language was the issue. Regardless of his meaning, the City's Catholic leadership took Seward's message as an invitation to share in the public school fund, and it quickly filed a petition with the Common Council requesting that a portion of the school monies be allocated to its eight charity schools.[39] Shortly thereafter, in March, a Scotch Presbyterian Church and two Jewish congregations also filed petitions with the Council asking for a similar pro rata share of the school fund. The petitions brought about the expected opposition from the Public School Society and Protestant churches. In its March 29 memorial, the Society again raised legal objections, arguing the requests would be "Unconstitutional— because it is utterly at variance with the letter and spirit of our chartered rights, and with the genius of our political institutions, that the community should be taxed to support an establishment in which sectarian dogmas are inculcated, whether that establishment be a church or a school." Dividing the school fund would also be "Inexpedient," the memorial continued, in that more good was accomplished by concentrating the money "in one channel" rather than apportioning it among many, which would undermine that "great principle of non-sectarianism." Memorials by Protestant churches echoed the Society's points, with the Methodists adding that if the petitions were approved, it too would request an equitable proportion of the school fund so it could "resuscitate [its] former school and erect others," a not too subtle threat to the integrity of the school fund.[40]

The responses caught the Catholics off guard; the petition, prepared in Bishop Hughes's absence in Europe, had emphasized the dire financial situation of the Catholic schools and not anticipated the objections from the Society and Protestants. In April, the Board of Assistant Aldermen, acting as a committee on school money, voted to deny the Catholic, Presbyterian, and Jewish petitions. The Aldermen's report chiefly echoed the Society's practical objections to the request. However, the report also offered constitutional rationales for its decision, points that Vincent Lannie describes as "sophisticated and remarkably contemporary in [their] analysis."[41] Responding to the claim that Catholics were taxed to support schools from which they were unable to benefit, the committee replied that Catholics were "taxed not as members of the Roman Catholic Church, but as citizens of the State of New York; and not for the purposes of religion, but for the support of civil government." That response relied on two implicit assumptions: that the effect of any school tax was religiously neutral; and that the nonsectarian program in the common schools did not exist for religious purposes. The committee insisted that if the Catholic argument about taxation was accepted, and Catholics received a pro rata share of the fund, then all people would be taxed "for the support of some one or other of our numerous religious denominations." By "granting a portion of the School Fund to one sect, to the exclusion of others, a 'preference' is at once created, a 'discrimination' is made, and the object of this great Constitutional guarantee is defeated," the report stated. The committee also disclaimed that the problem would be ameliorated by allowing all religions to participate equally in the school fund, a concept that would later be known as "nonpreferentialism." Such a solution would be "equally . . . repugnant to the principles of the Constitution," the report replied. Even if public funds paid for the teaching of the doctrines of all denominations, "there would still be a legal religious establishment, not confined to one or a few sects, it is true, but covering many." Taxes "would still be raised for religious purposes." The Aldermen adopted the committee report by a vote of 16 to 1.[42]

The Catholic petition and Council action reignited the School Question by exposing the potential consequences of Seward's recommendation. The Catholics, with a returned Bishop Hughes now leading the charge, vowed to press their claim, believing they had the governor's support. Hughes held several mass meetings over the summer and spared little in his condemnation of the public schools, alleging that nonsectarianism promoted sectarian Protestantism and infidelity at the same time. For Hughes, the Catholic claim was supported by right and justice, and he intimated that Catholics should take political action by not voting for any office holder who opposed a division of the school fund.[43] Hughes's statements and aggressive style elicited outrage from the mainstream and nativist press, the latter led by the *New York Observer*. Directing attention away from the merits of the Catholic claim, the *Observer* charged that Catholics opposed Bible reading, expanding on one of Hughes's earlier statements that "certain books of the Old Testament [are] not proper to be read by children even from the Catholic Bible, much less from a Bible which our church condemns as imperfect and corrupt." "What better evidence than the above, can be given, that this church seeks to shut out the light of divine revelation from the minds of its members?" the *Observer* railed. Catholic criticism of Bible reading was also a ploy for securing funding for its own schools, the *Observer* warned. Catholic designs "to a portion of the School Fund, for sectarian purposes" would "cost millions of treasure and streams of blood," and "can never be allowed." Nativists also expressed outrage at the Catholic threat to organize politically, which validated their rhetorical claims of papal intrigue. Hughes's call for political activism provided ammunition for the Protestant charges: "Here is an offer, publicly made under the sanction of the priests of this sect, to support that party in politics which will vote the public money for the support of the Roman Catholic religion. It is the most monstrous attempt at the union of Church and State that we have ever seen."[44]

In September, 1840, Hughes submitted a detailed petition to the Common Council requesting a share of the school fund for Catholic schools. The Public School Society filed a memorial in opposition, as did representatives of the Methodist Episcopal Church. In late October, a special committee of the Council held a public meeting on the petition and memorials, providing an opportunity for representatives from all sides to present arguments.[45]

The transcript of the meeting contains the most comprehensive arguments to date about the role of religion and education and its relation to church-state principles. Hughes spoke on behalf of the Catholics, directing his remarks at refuting the Protestant memorialists while complaining about the anti-Catholic bias of the public schools. Unfortunately for Hughes and the Catholics, his argument was often contradictory, which his opponents used to their advantage. Hughes denied he had ever claimed that pubic schools actively taught infidelity, only that such was the result of nonsectarianism. At the same time, Hughes insisted that the religion taught in the schools *was* sectarian in its Protestantism—in fact, he asserted, all religious instruction was necessarily sectarian. For Hughes, "nonsectarian" education was an impossibility. "They say their instruction is not sectarianism; but it is; and of what kind? The sectarianism of infidelity in its every feature." While insisting that the 1824 law had not forbidden public funding of sectarian schools, he claimed that Catholics had never requested funds for sectarian purposes: "The remonstrants warn you, gentlemen, against giving money for sectarian purposes. We join them in that admonition." (In his petition, Hughes had offered to restrict Catholic instruction at funded parochial schools until the end of the school day.) Although he generally avoided legal arguments, Hughes voiced agreement with the Society that religious establishments were to be abjured. But Hughes also declared that he did not want a "country of atheism." All Catholics wanted was "equality to all, protection to all, preference to none.... We want that the public money shall not be employed to sap religion in the minds of our children."[46]

Overall, Hughes's presentation offered the most thorough account to date of the Catholic position on the School Question. The nuances of the Catholic position were lost on most Protestants: nonsectarianism was inherently sectarian (i.e., Protestant), but education should necessarily be religious (i.e., Catholic); otherwise it promoted atheism. Hughes might have scored points by emphasizing that nonsectarianism was built on Protestant theological assumptions and was inherently religious, but he undermined his own argument by also insisting it was atheistical by failing to teach Christian doctrines. In that he was speaking to an audience already hostile to his arguments, his condemnation of the Protestant Bible and of public education failed to win converts to his position.[47]

The Society was represented by two attorneys who chiefly raised legal arguments against religious school funding. Pointing to the development of the previous two decades, they insisted that the no-funding rule was now "well-established public policy." That principle mandated that "not one cent, raised by public taxation, can go to support a religious institution—can go in payment for an education purely religious in its character," declared Hiram Ketchem, who was also a member of the Society board. This last statement was key for Ketchum; while he acknowledged that religion was taught in the Society schools, he insisted it was used only for the teaching of morals. "Religion is the foundation of sound morals," Ketchum asserted, and if "[s]ound morals are essential to the preservation of the community; why, therefore, shall not the city be taxed for that which is essential to her preservation?" Ketchum disputed Hughes's claim that if children "are not taught the doctrines of some known sect, there is no religion." The Society had "taught sound morals in all our schools." As for Catholic objections to textbooks, Ketchum and his colleague, Theodore Sedgwick, noted that the Society had sought out Catholic assistance in purging offending textbooks, but that the church leadership had not responded. Even then, Ketchum asserted that it was "impossible to have a public system to which some may not have scruples and objections."[48]

The Society lawyers also mounted a spirited defense of nonsectarianism as taught in the Society schools. Sedgwick insisted there were three alternatives for public education: to be "purely secular," moral, or sectarian. The state had chosen the middle course in order to imbue the "fundamental principles of morals about which there is no dispute." Yet Sedgwick's argument revealed how understandings of nonsectarian education had already evolved by the 1840s. In contrast to the Society's earlier program that had asserted the teaching of common Protestant principles as its "primary object," the Society now characterized its curriculum as being chiefly "'secular' and moral." Sedgwick insisted that "[s]o long as you give a secular education combined with moral instruction alone, and steer entirely clear of all doctrinal or sectarian principles, all are satisfied." For this reason, the attorneys insisted that common schools were not hostile to Catholicism, but being secular and moral institutions, they maintained "a perfect impartiality among all sects." Employing terminology that would become popular a century later, the attorneys claimed that the public school was a "neutral institution" when it came to religion.[49] Responding to Hughes's main argument, Sedgwick charged that it was at "variance and incompatible" with itself. "One is, that the dogmas of religion, or religion properly so called, is not taught in these schools, but . . . the sectarianism of infidelity. . . . Another objection to the system is, that the children are made Protestants: in other words, that religion *is* taught to them." This argument was irreconcilable, Sedgwick insisted: "a child cannot well grow up a Protestant and an infidel at the same time." Yet by asserting that the Society schools were chiefly secular, the attorneys confirmed part of Hughes's accusation about the irreligious nature of nonsectarianism. Although characterizations of secularism were doubtful at this time, it foreshadowed the secularizing trend that would accelerate following the Civil War.[50]

The two-day hearing concluded with a response by Hughes and statements by Protestant clergy, who unlike the Society attorneys, criticized not only the Catholic petition but also Catholic doctrines and practices. Methodist minister Thomas Bond defended the Protestant-oriented textbooks as reporting only "faithful history." If the bishop wanted the histories to discuss the "good of Catholics," then they "must record the evil also, or they are not histories at all." The most strident attack came from Presbyterian minister Gardiner Spring, who with nativist flourishes asked the Council to "look upon this application with suspicion and fear" as "Americans." Spring charged that Hughes's antipathy toward moral education was revealed in his condemnations of the Protestant Bible. In that the Protestant clergy willingly denounced Catholicism in a public setting demonstrated the growing division between Protestant and Catholic stalwarts. Were he given the "alternative between infidelity and the dogmas of the Catholic Church," Spring asserted, he would choose "to be an infidel tomorrow."[51]

Newspapers called the hearing "the great debate." Whether the label fit, it represented one of the earlier and more comprehensive public airings of Catholic complaints about nonsectarian education, Catholic claims for public financial support, and the legal and policy defenses of nonsectarianism. Much of the debate centered on charges and countercharges, about competing definitions of moral, religious, and sectarian education. In many respects, Hughes and his opponents were arguing past each other. Hughes never adequately explained how the common schools could be both sectarian and infidel at the same time, whereas the ministers and Society attorneys never comprehended Hughes's assertion that all religious instruction was inherently "sectarian" if it was to be religious. Other than claiming that the 1824 law had not prohibited the public funding of religious schools, Hughes never challenged his opponents' legal arguments that rested more on conclusions than on constitutional analysis. To his credit, Ketchum briefly asserted that funding of religious education violated rights of conscience and that religious piety and liberty were enhanced when left to "voluntary support."[52] But the respondents largely assumed that it was already settled constitutional doctrine that public monies could not pay for religious schooling. On its own, this certitude among the Protestants about a constitutional basis for the no-funding rule reveals how quickly legal attitudes had developed. And aside from a handful of derisive comments about Catholicism by the Protestant ministers, the debate was generally bereft of nativist vituperation. Although it was not a "great debate" in substance, it was a spirited and thorough account of each side's understanding of the School Question.

The special committee reported to the entire Council on January 11, 1841, recommending that the Council reject the Catholic petition. Largely adopting the arguments of the Society lawyers, the committee expressed confidence in the Society's sincere effort to provide a moral-based education free from "sectarian dogmas and peculiarities." It commended the Society's willingness to remove objectionable books and passages from its curriculum, noting that while some Catholics still felt excluded by the program, "[n]o school system can be perfect."[53] On the funding issue, the committee wrote that distributing money to religious institutions would threaten the integrity of the school fund: "if one religious sect should obtain a portion of the school fund, every other one would present a similar claim, and it would be a signal for the total demolition of the system." Granting the Catholics their request would result in religious dissension, the report speculated; it "would most probably be followed by a counteraction in the public mind . . . and the awakening of a spirit of intolerance." This was to be avoided.

> So long as Government refuses to recognize religious sectarian differences, no danger need be apprehended from this source; but when it begins to legislate with particular reference to any particular denomination of Christians, in any manner which recognizes their religious peculiarities, it oversteps a boundary which public opinion has established, violates a principle which breathes in all our constitutions, and opens a door to that unholy connection of politics with religion which has so often cursed and desolated Europe.[54]

After receiving the report, the Council voted 15 to 1 for its adoption, and the Catholics had lost a second round in their efforts to obtain public support for their schools.[55]

The committee's recommendation turned chiefly on its understanding of constitutional principles, though the committee also saw no reason to upset the existing system that, in its view, worked as well as could be expected. In his study of antebellum nativism, Ray Billington attributes the committee's recommendation, and the ultimate vote of the Council, to the growing anti-Catholic sentiment in New York stirred up by Protestant clergy and the nativist press. With his public condemnation of Bible reading and public schooling, and his unabashed effort to secure public funds for Catholic education, Hughes was an easy target for vilification if not demonization. Minor rioting and other disorder between rival religious gangs occurred in various wards during the council's deliberations.[56] But the impact of these common occurrences on the Council's decision is difficult to gauge. In contrast to Billington, Vincent Lannie maintains that "nativist hostility alone did not defeat the Catholic petition"—that regardless of "the defects of the public schools and the validity of certain Catholic charges, the Catholic solution [of public funding] seemed sectarian, unconstitutional, and un-American to the majority of the citizens of that day."[57] Authorizing any denomination to receive public aid for their religion, or to "introduce sectarian peculiarities of any kind into a public school," as the committee reported, "would very clearly constitute such school a sectarian school, and its support at public expense would, in the opinion of the committee, be a trespass upon the conscientious rights of every taxpayer." Nativist sentiment certainly made Hughes's job of convincing people about the merits of funding more difficult, but he was also working against a growing consensus opposed to funding sectarian enterprises.[58]

Following the Council's decision, the *New York Observer* extolled that "the union of church and state has been prevented." But the *Observer* predicted that the issue "had been put to rest for the present... [but] only for the present. The spirit that has made this attempt on the integrity of our institutions, by seeking to divert monies designed for the benefit of all, to the promotion of private sectarian interests, is a spirit that never slumbers."[59] The *Observer's* prophesy was true, though not because the newspaper possessed particular foresight. A week before the Council decision, Governor Seward had delivered his annual address to the Legislature, where he again pleaded for a solution to the School Question that included Catholic schools. Seward had barely been reelected in the 1840 election, even though William Henry Harrison and the Whigs had otherwise done well in New York. Many people, Seward included, attributed his near defeat to his support of the Catholic cause, which was unpopular within his own party. It was a "well known fact," wrote the *Observer*, that "Seward's partiality to the Roman Catholic pretensions nearly lost him his election."[60] As a result, Seward was more guarded in his 1841 address, in which he apparently retreated from his earlier proposal to fund Catholic schools or integrate them into the public system (as well as to support instruction in foreign languages). Still criticizing the public school system for failing to educate foreign-born children, Seward now called upon the legacy of Thomas Jefferson, commending a system of classless, universal education that assimilated all children into the republican polity.

> I desire the education of the entire rising generation in all the elements of knowledge we possess, and in that tongue which is the universal language of our countrymen. To me that most interesting of all our republican institution is the common school. I seek not to disturb, in any manner, its peaceful and assiduous exercises, and least of all with contentions about faith or forms. I desire the education of all the children in the commonwealth in morality and virtue, leaving matters of conscience where, according to the principles of civil and religious liberty established by our constitution and laws, they rightfully belong.[61]

Seward reaffirmed the right of immigrant Catholic children to receive a public education in a nonhostile environment, but he now more clearly embraced the singular role of the common schools and their role in instructing morality and virtue. He expressed naïve hope that a solution to the Catholic dilemma could be found within the public education system short of Catholic schools receiving any public funds. Seward sought to find a middle ground, though it was not one likely to satisfy either side.[62]

Hughes would not let up in his quest, and he drafted a memorial and organized a petition drive to the state legislature. At the same time, Seward continued with private overtures to Hughes and his assistants to find a solution, while seeking to endear himself to Catholic voters.[63] The state senate referred the memorial and petitions to Secretary of State John C. Spenser, a Whig ally of Seward's and the ex officio superintendent of common schools. Spenser drafted a report and proposed a bill that generally supported the Catholic position. Spenser criticized the monopoly of the Public School Society and that 8,000 children were excluded from the schools because of religious scruples. He recommended that education commissioners be elected for each city ward, who would then control the distribution of public school funds. Under the plan, the Society's schools would be integrated into a ward-administered system of district schools. More significant, all people recognized that the plan placed some common schools under the control of local officials in Catholic dominated wards. As for the issue of religious instruction, Spenser offered a seemingly contradictory solution. He asserted that the federal and state constitutions required the government to act neutrally toward the religious inclinations of its citizens. The Constitution's prohibition on enacting any law "respecting an establishment of religion or prohibiting the free exercise thereof" meant that the state must take a position of "absolute nonintervention" toward religion, Spenser wrote. No public official "has the authority to determine whether the religious doctrines and sentiments of any class of our citizens be right or wrong." Yet Spenser also insisted that "public sentiment would be shocked by the attempt to exclude all instruction of a religious nature from the public schools; and that any plan or scheme of education, in which no reference whatever was had to moral principles founded on these truths, would be abandoned by all." The solution, therefore, was for the legislature to leave the matter of religious instruction to each set of ward commissioners—a form of local option on the content of any religious training. Spenser rejected the idea of nonsectarian education as an alternative, concurring with Bishop Hughes that all religious instruction was inherently sectarian. Criticizing the Society's program of nonsectarian instruction, Spenser remarked that "it is impossible to conceive how even those principles can be taught, so as to be of any value, without inculcating what is peculiar to some one or more denominations, and denied by others." Spenser thus rejected the underlying theory of nonsectarianism: "[e]ven the moderate degree of religious instruction which the Public School Society imparts" was "sectarian." This finding was a major affirmation of the Catholic position, one that the Common Council had denied. Spenser acknowledged that his principle of "absolute non-intervention" would permit sectarian religious instruction "consonant to the views" of citizens who made up each ward. In fact, it had to be: if "some degree of religious instruction is indispensable . . . it cannot be imparted without partaking, to some extent, of a sectarian character." "The practical consequence is," Spenser admitted, "that each [school] district suits itself, by having such religious instruction in its school as is congenial to the opinions of its inhabitants."[64]

Spenser grounded his solution on his interpretation of the federal and state constitutions and notions of equal treatment of all citizens. These constitutional principles required, in Spenser's view, that the state remain hands-off on religious matters, not legislating one way or another. This left religious matters "to the free and unrestricted action of the people themselves." In a sense, Spencer was proposing an early version of "school choice," a legal concept the Supreme Court would struggle with 160 years later.[65] As he stated, his proposal would "leave such parents as desire to exercise any control over the amount and description of religious instruction which shall be given to their children, the opportunity of doing so." One can only speculate how the history of church-state law would have differed if Spenser's early "choice" program had been ratified at this stage. Yet Spenser did not consider whether people, acting collectively through their elected school representatives, were bound by the same requirement of "absolute non-intervention" in their official decision making about religious instruction. He apparently did not understand the constitutional mandate of neutrality toward religion to control such low-level collective actions. His report was also unclear whether local ward commissioners could designate existing Catholic schools to receive the public aid. Some people interpreted his proposal to allow this possibility, but all understood the proposal to create new district public schools which would, pursuant to

"absolute non-intervention" into religion, permit those schools to be administered by Catholics. The practical effect would be that Protestants could continue
to have their schools, probably administered by the Public School Society, while
Catholics would have their publicly funded schools in wards where they were in a
majority. And everyone agreed that Spenser's proposal would break the funding
monopoly of the Society and end its status as the de facto provider of public
schooling.[66]

Predictably, Protestant leaders, nativist groups, and the Public School Society
railed against Spenser's proposed bill.[67] The Society dispatched Hiram Ketchum to
Albany to address the legislative committee. His testimony included many of the
same legal and practical arguments he had made before the Common Council the
previous year. Central to his argument was that Spenser's bill would authorize the
funding of sectarian education, either in public schools or Catholic parochial
schools. He put the matter in clear and stark terms: "It [is] the union of Church
and State, which the laws and the institutions of this country abhor." Ketchum
asserted the bill violated a core constitutional principle: it would take "the tax
received out of the pockets of the people—and apply[] it to the establishment and
promotion of religious societies." But now that he had to defeat a bill recommending sectarian funding, Ketchum raised a new constitutional argument about
minority religious rights. "The Secretary admits that a majority of the people, in
a given district, has a right to indicate what religion shall be taught in the district
school; and to that religion, or that form whatever it may be, the minority must
submit." This situation, Ketchum insisted, would result in "tyranny of the
majority." The irony of this last argument was apparently lost on Ketchum, as
he had long since disabused himself of the notion that the nonsectarian
Protestantism of the Society's schools implicated rights of conscience of any religious minority.[68]

The New York Senate remained divided over Spenser's bill and adjourned in
May before it was able to act. This left the bill to be considered after a new legislature was elected in the fall of 1841. Both sides rallied their forces. Protestant nativists formed the American Protestant Union, headed by the inventor Samuel F. B.
Morse, who was also a noted anti-Catholic commentator, to oppose pro-Catholic
school candidates. The Protestants' political organizing received less attention—
or at least less public condemnation—than that of Bishop Hughes and the Catholic
leadership. Hughes sensed correctly that the Democratic Party would not take a
firm stand on the Spenser bill out of fear of alienating either Protestant or Catholic
supporters. Hughes held a series of meetings at Carroll Hall where, in what
Andrew Greely described as "a number of fiercely demagogic orations," he railed
against the public schools and political system. The Catholic leadership then
announced an independent slate of candidates for the city delegation to Albany.
Ten of the thirteen names on the ticket were trusted Democratic nominees, but
the remaining three differed from the Tammany Hall ticket.[69] When news of the
Catholic endorsements became known, Whig and nativist newspapers assailed

the new Catholic "Church and State" party. For Protestant natives, the Catholic action confirmed their long-ignored warnings about the political goals of the Roman Church. An independent electorate, and republican liberties, were under assault. "The foot of the Beast was trampling on the elective franchise, and His High Priest was standing before the ballot box, the citadel of American liberties, dictating to his obedient followers the ticket they must vote," railed the *Observer*. When the election was held, the ten Democratic candidates from the "Carroll Hall ticket," had won, but the three remaining Democrats without Catholic support had lost to Whigs.[70]

The election spurred action when the legislature reconvened in Albany in 1842. In the Democratic controlled Assembly, a bill was drafted along the lines of Spencer's recommendation, and it passed easily by a vote of 64 to 16. In the more evenly divided Senate, the bill was opposed by the Whigs and two Democratic senators from the city. Upon a motion by an up-state Democrat, the Senate amended the bill to prohibit granting public funds to any school in which "any religious sectarian doctrine or tenet shall be taught, inculcated, or practiced." The amended bill passed the Senate and then was accepted by the Assembly as a compromise.[71] The new law satisfied few people, though all sides claimed some victory. Bishop Hughes applauded the effective dismantling of the Society monopoly over public education and new administration of schools by elected officials. In Catholic wards, this meant public schools would be sympathetic to Catholic concerns. But the law also expressly prohibited the public funding of any Catholic or other denominational school, and forbade sectarian instruction in any publicly funded school. It was a dramatic reversal of Spenser's principle of "absolute non-intervention" of the state in matters concerning religious instruction. In the long run Hughes and the Catholics had lost more than they had gained. Though the law cut back on the overt Protestant instruction in some Society schools—and ensured its elimination in public schools in Catholic wards—Hughes had lost on his mission of public funding for education that conformed to Catholic doctrine.[72] Critics of Hughes contend that his combative and uncompromising style throughout the episode guaranteed the eventual outcome. Others insist that Hughes was never sanguine about succeeding on the funding issue—that the dye had already been cast—but that his chief goal was to dismantle the Public School Society. "The Bishop's actions and words indicate the he was skeptical of the possibility of receiving aid," writes David O'Brien. Rather, Hughes "wished to destroy the Public School Society and replace it with a less objectionable school system and in the process, to build up Catholic support for parochial schools by emphasizing the dangers of nonsectarian education." This approach reinforced Hughes's larger goal of forestalling the assimilation of his immigrant flock into the larger Protestant culture.[73]

To make the Catholic defeat worse, after some uncertainty about the meaning of the anti-sectarian clause, the legislature amended the law in 1843 to prohibit public funds from going to schools "in which any book or books containing sectarian compositions shall be used," thus indirectly reaffirming the notion of nonsectarian education. The amendment technically forbade the use of Protestant-biased texts in the public schools, but the Society already insisted that such books had been purged. To ensure that the new law was not misinterpreted, the following year the legislature ruled that Bible reading without note or comment did not fit within the new prohibition on sectarian education. The upside for Catholics was that this law would be interpreted as granting local school boards the discretion to choose which version of the Bible to be used.[74]

The true impact of the law on the no-funding principle shortly became known. In 1851, the New York Supreme Court (at that time an intermediate appellate court) implicitly addressed both aspects of the 1842 law in *People ex rel. Roman Catholic Orphan Asylum Soc. v. Board of Education*.[75] Citing to an 1848 law that allowed private orphanages to be reimbursed from public funds for the care of their wards, the Roman Catholic Orphan Asylum of Brooklyn requested a proportional share of the common school fund from the Brooklyn school board to pay for its educational expenses. On appeal, the supreme court held that the 1848 law's reimbursement provision was never intended to allow religious asylums to participate in the common school fund. A provision of the 1846 constitution limited application of the common school fund to "common schools." Relying on the 1842 law, the court held that asylums run by religious organizations were analogous to parochial schools and as such, were not "common schools" eligible to receive monies from the school fund. Common schools, the court wrote, were "not confined to a class, but are open to all... They are bound to instruct all the children... without regard to their social relations, their station in life or their religious faith." The ruling that the Asylum was not a common school affected monies received only from the state, however; the court upheld a separate distribution made from city funds. What is curious is that despite the latter ruling, the court affirmed the no-funding principle generally, stating that publicly funded schools must be "kept free from every thing savoring of sectarian influence or control." If the purpose of a school was to furnish instruction "of a partial or sectarian character, the state ought not, and cannot constitutionally, contribute to such a purpose." The court did not explain why this principle did not extend to all public monies allocated to religious asylums. The possible unstated assumption may have been that, consistent with the 1831 episode involving the Catholic Orphan Asylum, allocations to orphanages from non–school funds were considered to be for the care of the inmates, not for their education. This would be consistent with the court's broad language. Also, by distinguishing the Brooklyn Asylum's education program from that of the common schools, the court implicitly validated the Protestant nonsectarianism promoted by the Society's schools. With this decision, nonsectarianism and the no-funding rule received judicial sanction to match that from the legislature. No-funding was a legal concept.[76]

Expansion of the No-Funding Rule

The events that precipitated the rise of the no-funding rule in New York were particular to that state. Still, other states followed suit by consolidating educational funding to "common" free schools that were under the control of publicly elected officials and were nonsectarian in orientation. The timing and particularities of this transition varied from state to state and depended on the preexisting educational setting and emerging educational infrastructures.[77] According to educational historian Carl Kaestle, in more religiously homogenous settlements, as in the still-developing Midwest, religious schools received public assistance as late as the 1850s. The no-funding rule "was a public policy [that] developed gradually and unevenly at the local level during the nineteenth century."[78] Yet despite the fluidity in education that existed from the 1820s through the 1840s, a discernable trend was under way.

As influential as the New York laws of 1842–1843 were in the development of the no-funding principle, they were not the first of their kind. A common provision found in many early state constitutions were "no-compelled support" clauses, modeled after the 1776 Pennsylvania Constitution, which provided that no person could be compelled to attend, erect, or support any place of worship or to pay taxes to support any teacher of religion. Assuming that religious instruction was comparable to religious worship—as the New York City legislative committee determined in 1831—these clauses could have been interpreted to bar funding of parochial schools. However, there is little evidence that contemporaries understood these clauses in this manner, at least as representing an express constitutional bar. A lesser number of state constitutions contained their own "establishment clauses" modeled after the federal provision. Although such provisions arguably provided a firmer basis for the no-funding rule, early common school advocates usually relied on general constitutional or "political" notions for legal basis against religious school funding, as had been the case in New York, rather than on any express provisions.[79]

A third type of provision was represented by the 1827 Massachusetts law, which was the first of its kind to prohibit allocating funds for any school that taught sectarian doctrines.[80] Horace Mann relied on this law, and on his understanding of general constitutional principles, to argue that nonsectarian education was consistent with, if not required by, religious disestablishment. Mann asserted that if people were taxed to support religious schools, "it would satisfy, at once, the largest definition of a Religious Establishment." Following on the lead of Massachusetts, state legislatures began to enact laws and adopt constitutional provisions that expressly prohibited the expenditure of public funds for religious education or the benefit of religious societies.[81]

The first express educational no-funding constitutional provision appeared in the Michigan Constitution of 1835. In addition to including a no-compelled support clause, the drafters of the state constitution added a separate clause stating: "No money shall be draw from the treasury for the benefit of religious societies, or theological or religious seminaries."[82] The Michigan Constitution served as the model for no-funding constitutional provisions throughout the Midwest: Wisconsin (1848); Indiana (1851); Ohio (1851); and Minnesota (1857).[83] The Ohio Constitution in turn was the model for the no-funding provision of the Kansas Constitution, adopted in 1858, and the Indiana Constitution served as the basis for a similar provision in the 1857 Oregon Constitution. The legislative histories for these clauses are all but silent as to rationales for their adoption. One has to surmise the motivation for including these more specific clauses—likely in part to ensure the security of the school fund—but it is safe to assume that legislators were aware of Catholic challenges to public school funding in other states (see discussion below). Irrespective of the motivations, the understanding that public funds should pay only for schools under the control of public officials and not for religiously run schools gained momentum throughout the 1840s and 1850s. And increasingly, people associated these rules with constitutional principles.[84]

The number of judicial cases interpreting constitutional and statutory bars to the funding of religious schools and institutions is exceedingly small, particularly prior to 1870. The 1851 decision concerning the Brooklyn orphan asylum stands as the most detailed judicial consideration of the rule prior to the Civil War. A handful of later decisions indicate a developing judicial understanding of the no-funding rule. In 1858, the Connecticut Supreme Court of Errors held that directors of a common school were prohibited from permitting the school building to be used for regular worship services or a Sunday school. "No school district would undertake, by a direct vote, to tax its inhabitants to build a church, nor would it devote its school-house to the general purposes of a church edifice," the court held. Despite the question of religious use of a public school being distinct from the issue of public funding of religious education, the Connecticut court perceived the questions were interrelated and controlled by the same principle. It could "not be denied," the court wrote, that a school "under the supervision and entire control of the religious teachers of an ecclesiastical society is an entirely different institution from our statutory common school."[85] Eleven years later the Massachusetts Supreme Judicial Court applied similar principles to hold that public school monies could not be used to maintain a private school, created by an 1850 bequest, despite its having served as a town common school in lieu of publicly controlled school. The bequest required that the school trustees were to include the clergy and members of three local Congregational churches. The court held that this requirement, and the arrangement itself, violated the state constitution's prohibition on appropriating school funds to any school controlled by "any religious sect," which covered the Congregational "public" school.[86]

In contrast to those holdings, in 1867 the New York Supreme Court held that a Catholic orphan asylum in Rochester could receive a share of city tax monies raised for the education and care of orphan and indigent children. The court—constituting a different division from the court in the earlier Brooklyn case—interpreted the 1851 *Orphan Asylum* decision to prohibit only the appropriation of *state* monies to religious schools from the *common school fund*, and not from other sources. Unlike that earlier decision, the Rochester court did not discuss the no-funding rule or whether any constitutional issue was at stake. By claiming that the two orphan asylum holdings were consistent, the Rochester court implicitly reaffirmed the rule against funding religious schools when the monies were derived from the state education fund. However, the Rochester holding broadened the exception to the no-funding rule that emphasized the *source* of the public funds and the primary function of the recipient, care versus education. This is because an 1850 law expressly authorized allocations for charities from local *school* funds, with the court acknowledging that the monies would pay for "children educated in the orphan asylums." The decision was technically consistent with the 1832 ruling of the New York Common Council that had distinguished between funding the care of children in religious asylums and the education of children in parochial schools. Yet the Rochester ruling perpetuated a legal fiction that funding religious education conducted in orphanages was different from funding the same in parochial schools, with only the latter being prohibited by the no-funding principle. In New York, and in a handful of other states, courts would read an asylum exception into the no-funding rule into the early twentieth century.[87]

These decisions constitute the bulk of judicial commentary on the no-funding rule before the controversy reignited in the 1870s. They, along with the constitutional and statutory provisions, indicate an emerging—though uneven—pattern by the end of the antebellum period against the public funding of sectarian education. They also indicate a growing view that the no-funding rule represented not simply a policy decision but a legal mandate based on general, if not express, constitutional principles.

The Impact of Nativism on the Development of Nonsectarianism

Any study of the School Question would be incomplete without examining the role of nativism and anti-Catholicism in the development of nonsectarianism and the no-funding rule. Historians have long sought to explain the phenomenon of nineteenth century nativism, and several studies, some of which have been referenced, provide extensive treatment of this episode. The purpose of this section is not to offer a comprehensive account of the rise and impact of nativism during the century. Rather, consideration here is limited to exploring the way in which nativism and anti-Catholicism impacted the development of a constitutional doctrine.[88]

Critiques of nonsectarianism and the no-funding principle frequently associate the development of both doctrines with the nativist/anti-Catholic impulse of the nineteenth century. Some critics claim that the underlying basis for nonsectarianism was Protestant enmity toward the Catholic religion, its institutions and leaders, and its foreign-born adherents. Catholic bigotry was the fuel that drove Protestants to embrace and defend nonsectarian public education, and religious animus informed the legal doctrines that kept it in place. "The [common] school movement and nativism were not only contemporaneous," Lloyd Jorgenson writes, "they were...inextricably bound up with one another." For Jorgenson and other critics, the emerging rule against funding religious education was "a doctrine largely born of bigotry," which brought about "the disinheritance of the church-related schools."[89] In 2000, United States Supreme Court Justice Clarence Thomas employed similar phrasing in criticizing the Court's own rule prohibiting public funding of "pervasively sectarian" institutions, calling it a "doctrine, born of bigotry, [that] should be buried now."[90] Philip Hamburger has made the same argument in his book *Separation of Church and State*, though on an expanded level: separation of church and state, with the no-funding rule as its central tenet, would never have become a popular American creed or constitutional rule had it not been for anti-Catholicism. While Hamburger acknowledges that "not all Americans who supported [church-state] separation were anti-Catholic," he asserts that "nativist anti-Catholicism gave respectability and popular strength to their suspicions." As a result, Hamburger writes, because of "its lack of constitutional authority and its development in response to prejudice—the idea of separation should, at best, be viewed with suspicion."[91]

This accounting of the impact of nativism on constitutional doctrine has appeal for its simplicity, but it is incomplete in the end. What unifies these accounts are generalizations about the causes and meanings of nativist activity during the nineteenth century. If, as John Higham once remarked, "Nativism has been hard for historians to define," then Supreme Court justices and legal scholars possess no greater insight. At its core, nativism encompassed an intense prejudice and hatred of foreigners and accompanying efforts to use intimidation, force, or corrupt authority to subjugate immigrants and deny them equal status under the law. On a more general level, nativism represented an antipathy for things foreign—of foreign peoples, their institutions and ideas—in contradistinction with a strong affinity for national character and identity. Nativism was a popular and resilient force in large part because it identified with patriotism and love of country.[92] Hardly a defender of nativists, Orestes Brownson acknowledged that:

> Nativism is a component part of patriotism, and that it is the chief element in that complex thing which is called nationality.... Patriotism involves a preference; it is consequently a preference of one's country and one's fellow citizens over all foreign countries and citizens....[93]

The problem, according to Higham, is that nativism has had "a penumbra of meaning so broad and indefinite that sometimes it seems to refer to [little more] than a perennial human experience" of suspicion of things foreign. Another historian has described mid-century nativism as a movement of "the dedicated few and the casual many." Yet reducing nativism to little more that "a general ethnocentric habit of mind, blurs its historical significance."[94] Its manifestations, causes, and appeals were complex and do not lend themselves to a simple accounting.

As suggested by the title to his seminal study of antebellum nativism, *The Protestant Crusade*, Ray Billington attributed the phenomena primarily if not exclusively to longstanding anti-Catholic prejudice among Protestants. Billington claimed that the nativist upsurge of the 1840s and 1850s would not have occurred "had not the American people been so steeped in antipapal prejudice that they were unable to resist the nativistic forces of their day." Other possible explanations for native-born antipathy toward immigrants—economic, ethnic, cultural, or class factors—were "to a considerable extent rationalization[s] of previously existing [religious] prejudices."[95] Later critiques seeking a connection between nativism and nonsectarianism have made similar claims.[96]

Modern historians have generally rejected this "narrowly religious interpretation of nativism." Establishing a tie between nativism and anti-Catholicism only begins the inquiry.[97] The anti-Catholic impulse of the midnineteenth century was not new but built on a 200-year-old legacy of interdenominational antipathy (much longer if one includes the 400-year European conflict between Protestantism and Catholicism). Both the self-conscious Protestants who settled the colonies and the rationalist statesmen who founded the nation associated the Catholic Church with religious intolerance and political autocracy. Anti-Catholicism, already ingrained in colonial Protestantism with its closer temporal tie to the Protestant-Catholic conflicts of sixteenth and seventh century England, was reignited during the French and Indian War with colonists perceiving a threat presented by a Catholic France. Aversion to the Roman Church and the Catholic religion was so pervasive in early America that it was unremarkable. Read in isolation, the anti-Catholic statements of enlightened men like John Adams and Thomas Jefferson are shocking and discomforting. Yet most scholarship has demonstrated that anti-Catholicism, however that specific impulse is defined, was only one aspect of nineteenth century nativism and was less of a cause of nativism than it was its effect.[98]

Most modern scholars view nativism as an ideological and social movement, one with strong class and economic overlays.[99] Though commonly seen as a reaction to perceived foreign threats, the nativist impulse was as much a phenomena involving affirmative conceptions about nationality and nationhood. Whereas proto-nativist ideas and impulses existed during the national era, early antebellum nativism arose chiefly out of a desire to understand and define what it meant to be an American. Despite sharing a common language and a generally common ethnic stock (British), Americans of the second generation struggled with what were the indicia of national identity and citizenship. With the revolution against England, Americans had severed their ethnic allegiance with the mother country and resisted assigning British traits to "Americanism." Lacking an ethnic bond that defined the national identity of most peoples, Americans came to define themselves by their political values and institutions. (The association of being an American with Anglo-Saxon stock arose later in the nineteenth century.) Those values were the principles expressed in the Declaration of Independence and the preambles to the various constitutions, while the overarching institution was republican government. The most common element that tied together all nativist lodges and associations was their sense of patriotism. Patriotism, or love of country, was their greatest appeal. [100]

This association of Americanism with republican values meant two things: that to be American was an ideological condition rather than one that came naturally by birth or ethnicity; and, related, by relying on an ideological basis Americans lacked those common, natural characteristics that tied a people together. To be an American thus did not come naturally (or passively) but could be achieved only through effort and commitment—a commitment to republican principles. For generations schooled in classical republican thought—which taught the fragility of republics and their susceptibility to internal factions—this reliance on an ideological basis for Americanism seemed particularly tenuous. As a result, to be an American necessitated several things. First, Americans needed to be able to participate in republican government. This required that they possessed the intelligence and moral virtue to exercise their political rights. Closely related, individuals could be "partakers" of republicanism only if they exercised independence of thought and freedom from coercion. Those who were controlled or manipulated by others could not be effective citizens and, in fact, that condition threatened the individual autonomy central to republican citizenship. This concern about manipulation existed at the particular and general levels: citizens must be free from local dependencies and free from foreign loyalties. Third, many believed that to be American also depended on all people holding commonly shared values of republicanism. Alexander Hamilton asserted that "the safety of a republic depends essentially on the habits of a common national sentiment; on a uniformity of principles and habits." The prosperity and perpetuation of the nation relied on "render[ing] the people...as homogeneous as possible." The early interest in universal common schooling fit neatly with these concerns. Virtue and intelligence were essential for one's ability to act as an independent citizen and participate in self-governance. And for the republic to succeed, all people needed to be assimilated into the greater society that reaffirmed those essential values.[101]

Because nativists were committed to identifying and promoting national character, it followed that they would be suspicious of people with foreign values and allegiances. This meant two things. On the more obvious level, it meant vigilance to threats to republican values and institutions that came from foreign sources. According to David Brion Davis, a persistent theme in nineteenth century

America was a fear of subversion of American values and institutions by alien and secret organizations that demanded complete loyalty from their members.[102] One of those chief institutions was, of course, the emerging common school. Native-born Americans naturally interpreted criticism of public schooling, particularly by foreign-born clerics, and resistance to its assimilating practices, as efforts to subvert republican society. On a more immediate level, however, fear of subversion also required attentiveness to potential corruption within American institutions that would undermine republican values. This apprehension led nativists to be on guard for political corruption, particularly when public officials abandoned republican values by appeasing foreigners and their institutions for political gain. The chief explanation for the meteoric rise of the Know-Nothing Party in the mid-1850s was voter belief that the Democratic and Whig parties were unwilling to deal with the social and economic displacement of the period while their leaders were capitulating to the very forces that were responsible for the erosion of the American way of life.[103] An early example of this internal/external tension in nativist thought is the proto-nativist reaction of the late 1790s. At the same time Federalists apprehended a foreign threat represented by the revolutionary French republic and its agents, thus leading to the enactment of the Alien Act, they were distressed at the homegrown attraction to radical ideas that they believed threatened the fragile American government, leading in turn to the Sedition Act. The point is that the nativist impulse, and popular attraction thereto, had as much to do with the inherent insecurities present in establishing a national identity as it did with reacting to foreign forces and threats.[104]

As can be seen, nativism embodied a general concern of how people with foreign ideas and allegiances were to be assimilated into a nation that required an allegiance to uniform republican values. On an immediate level, native-born Americans reacted to the Irish and German immigration of the antebellum period for several reasons. One was economic. America experienced an economic recession in 1837 that lasted for five years. The "Panic of '37" came at a period of economic and industrial transformation and dislocation of workers and artisans. Craftspeople and artisans saw their economic well-being threatened by the rise of factories that relied increasingly on an unskilled labor force. Competition arose between the skilled native workers and the unskilled immigrants who worked for less money. According to Michael Feldberg, "skilled craftsmen resisted their economic displacement and exploitation by whatever means were available, and nativist politics was just one method of resistance."[105] Not only did the unskilled immigrant worker threaten the native workers' economic well-being; in the minds of many, the former lacked the independence and autonomy of the latter that was essential to republican participation.[106] Related to economic insecurity and concerns about occupational displacement was the sense that the majority of Irish immigrants in particular were paupers—"the very scum and dregs of human nature"—who would overburden the limited public welfare system and resort to begging and crime.[107] At least initially, such fears were based chiefly on prejudice and stereotypes; the majority of Irish and German immigrants during the 1830s were not impoverished peasants but came from middle and working classes. Still, the number of foreign-born paupers in the almshouses of New York, Boston, Philadelphia, and Baltimore increased in the mid-1830s, only to skyrocket as a result of the famine-produced immigration during the next decade. Also, throughout the 1840s and 1850s, the percentage of emigrants in American jails increased at a disproportionate and troubling rate compared to the native-born.[108] Many Americans doubted whether the nation could assume the economic and social costs of assimilating such a large number of destitute foreigners. Others suspected that the autocratic governments of Europe were unloading their most undesirable denizens on America's shores, in part to undermine the nation's republican institutions.[109]

Another factor that elicited a nativist reaction to immigration was ethnicity, in particular, a pervasive Anglo-Saxon antipathy for the Irish. In his important study of Irish immigration and American nationality, Dale Knobel argues that disdain for Irish emigrants was primarily a matter of ethnicity: "that a standardized image of the Irish—distinct from images of immigrants, naturalized voters, or even Roman Catholics—circulated widely in antebellum society." Knobel notes that there was "a specifically anti-Irish sentiment—differentiable from anti-Catholicism, anti-foreignism, or anti-monarchicalism—which grew from what may have been a half-conscious but surely was a widely shared sense that American republicanism could only be sustained by a people who possessed a particular innate ethnic character."[110] Early Americans shared with their British cousins the general view of Irish as servile, undisciplined, self-indulgent, and subject to rebelliousness. Other objections to early Irish immigration centered on Irish radicalism, reflecting the common nativist fear that foreign-born might entangle the nation in European intrigue and conflict.[111] Beyond the pervasive belief in Irish radicalism, and their unwillingness to adhere to democratic means to achieve political change, much prejudice was based on the class and ethnic differences. Finally, Irish and German emigrants generally resisted assimilating into the greater society, settling in Irish or German wards and establishing their own social and benevolent societies, fire companies, and militias as a way of maintaining their solidarity. The clannishness of the foreign-born particularly irked the native-born; they interpreted efforts at preserving ethnic self-identity as a rejection of republican values and a desire to transplant foreign values onto the American culture.[112] Orestes Brownson, often an irritant to the Catholic hierarchy, sensed the significance of this factor for native-born Americans, and he criticized Irish and German immigrants for insisting on remaining "foreigners in feeling and character." Catholic immigrants must assimilate into the American culture for the church to prosper, Brownson insisted.

> Other races, as long as they remain distinct and separate, remain foreigners in regard to American nationality, and they do and can partici-

pate in that nationality only as they flow in and lose themselves in the main current of Anglo-American life.[113]

A final factor in mid-century nativism was, unquestionably, the long-standing American strain of anti-Catholicism. The Protestant settlers of British North America had brought with them their cultural antipathy toward Catholicism and the Roman church. American colonists of the seventeenth and eighteenth centuries were well-versed in the intractable European struggle between Protestantism and Catholicism. Protestant Americans could recite page and verse the oppression of Protestants at the hands of Catholic officials and their temporal surrogates (at the same time forgetting or justifying similar Protestant outrages). In addition, Protestants considered the Catholic Church autocratic and opposed to enlightenment and republican principles. The Catholic Church "claims infallibility for itself [but] denies Spiritual Freedom, Liberty of Mind or Conscience, to its members," wrote the liberal Theodore Parker. It was the "natural ally of tyrants, and the irreconcilable enemy of Freedom." Protestant suppression of Catholics in Britain under measures such as the Test and Corporations acts were not simply pay-back or acts of religious intolerance—many saw them as insurance against future Catholic domination. For the colonists, this religious conflict was recent history, a history that had not been resolved. It should not be surprising that all of the founders expressed either subtle or overt anti-Catholic sentiments. Such attitudes were ingrained in the Protestant psyche and a pervasive part of American thought throughout the founding period into the nineteenth century.[114]

The anti-Catholicism of the antebellum period was thus not a new phenomenon, though there is little question that it increased in response to the Irish, German, and Italian immigration of mid-century. "Anti-Catholicism," however, is an imprecise term that may encompass multiple motivations. As Philip Hamburger also acknowledges, "[m]uch anti-Catholicism had little to do with religion."[115] Much enmity toward the Catholic Church was directed at the institution and its hierarchy rather than at the rank-and file-Catholic. As mentioned, for many Americans the Catholic Church represented the antithesis of republican values. Authoritarian and autocratic, the Catholic Church looked "dangerously un-American partly because [it] did not harmonize easily with the concept of individual freedom imbedded in the national culture." In contrast to the Catholic Church's hierarchical interpretation of doctrine, Protestantism relied on a system of unmediated interpretation of scriptures which, Protestants asserted, was consistent with freedom of conscience. It was the Catholic clergy, with their teaching of Catholic doctrine, that interfered with the ability of rank-and-file Catholics to develop that independence of thought necessary to participate in republican governance.[116]

Closely related to its doctrinal authoritarianism were native-born concerns about the political nature of the church. The Catholic Church's close association with monarchial governments, particularly the Austrian government of Prince Metternich during the 1830s, raised alarms about Papal designs in America.

Although such anxieties seem far-fetched today, many Americans of the 1830s felt that the national boundaries were less than secure, that foreign powers still had territorial designs in continental America. Both Samuel F. B. Morse and Lyman Beecher in their 1835 writings expressed this general theme of foreign intrigue.[117] The despotic governments of Europe, aligned with the Catholic hierarchy in Rome, had suppressed democratic movements in Europe and were now exporting their "anti-republican tenets" in America through foreign-born priests, Catholic orders, and the Leopoldine and Ludwig Missionsverein Foundations that supported establishing Catholic churches and schools in America. That the majority of priests were ultramontanists in their fealty to the papacy and opposed to liberal trends in Europe only added credence to such claims.[118] In their screeds, Morse and Beecher distinguished their vilification of the Catholic hierarchy from rank-and-file Catholics, and both purported even to distinguish disdain for the papacy from Catholic theology. "The great body of emigrants to this country are the hard-working mentally neglected poor of Catholic countries in Europe, who have left a land where they were enslaved, for one of freedom," Morse insisted. Catholic adherents may be ignorant and pliable, but they were not necessarily evil. "I have no fear of the Catholics, considered simply as a religious denomination, and unallied to the church and state establishments of the European governments hostile to republican institutions," Beecher claimed. The threat came from the bishops and priests, most being foreign born, who swore allegiance to a foreign potentate who was aligned with, if not controlled by, despotic governments. "They are Jesuits in the pay and employ of a *despotic* government," Morse insisted; "they are *foreigners*, who have been schooled in foreign seminaries in the doctrine of passive obedience."[119] According to David Brion Davis, it was no accident that Morse's mid-1830s analyses of the Catholic threat to America used essentially the same terms as his father, Reverend Jedediah Morse, had used when he was exposing the dangers of the Bavarian Illuminati some forty years earlier.[120]

Inevitably, antipathy for the Church hierarchy and its clergy trickled down to Catholic adherents, particularly new Catholic immigrants who arrived with no previous experience in self-governance. Immigrants, and Catholic immigrants in particular, lacked the skills and independence of thought to participate in republican society. "Most of them are too ignorant to act at all for themselves, and expect to be guided wholly by others," Morse warned. And those others were "of course their priests."[121] If Catholic immigrants were not controlled by the priests, then they were controlled by the corrupt politicians and ward bosses who bought their political support. For native-born Americans who celebrated the ideal of the selfless independent voter, "immigrants seemed to pervert the democratic process by voting in blocks that were easily manipulated by ward bosses and party wirepullers who appealed to ethnic and religious identity."[122]

It should come as no surprise, therefore, that nativist and nonnativist Protestants viewed a common American education as essential to assimilate Catholic children into the American culture and instill those values of self governance—to "impregnate their minds" in "the republican atmosphere" of the common schools. "Let the Catholics mingle with us as Americans," Beecher pleaded, "and come with their children under the full action of our common schools and republican institutions, and the various powers of assimilation, and we are cheerfully to abide the consequences." Equally unsurprising is that Protestants and nativists interpreted Catholic complaints about Bible reading and the Protestant complexion of the common schools as attacks on the schools themselves and the republican values at the core of nonsectarian education.[123]

The 1830s jeremiads of Morse and Beecher appealed chiefly to "muscular" Protestants and xenophobic partisans but had little impact on the views of most native-born. According to Michael Holt, those nativist patriotic organizations that did exist were "small and relatively apolitical" until the mid-1840s.[124] But it did not take much to arouse the dormant strain of suspicion toward Catholicism and transform it into active feelings of anti-Catholicism. The threats of economic competition and dislocation presented by the Catholic immigrants were one factor, particularly following the Panic of 1837. In addition, anti-Catholic sentiment increased through the 1830s and 1840s, brought about by the advent of several anti-Catholic newspapers and the sensational accounts of Catholic debauchery and corruption contained in fictional works such as *Awful Disclosures of the Hotel Dieu Nunnery* by Maria Monk. Victorian Americans lapped up the lurid tales of priestly abuses of victimized and enslaved females in confessionals and nunneries. One study of the period has noted that even as early as 1835, anti-Catholic narratives "had become [such] a moneymaking venture that many entered into [it] with entrepreneurial gusto. 'The abuse of the Catholics,' noted one magazine, 'is a regular trade, and the compilation of anti-Catholic books . . . has become a part of the regular industry of the country, as much as . . . the construction of clocks.'"[125] Evidence suggests that public outrage over such sordid "exposes" led to the 1834 burning of an Ursuline convent and girls school in Charleston, Massachusetts, by a Protestant mob. The *Catholic Telegraph* blamed the arson on those authors who "pander[ed] to the ferocious passions of the mob" by publishing "calumnies . . . against the religion, the persons and the institutions of their Catholic neighbors."[126] Even with such occurrences, Jean Baker writes, there "was nothing new about Catholic-bating ministers, titillating nativist literature, and mysterious secret societies," during the 1830s and 1840s. During this period, "nativism remained emotional, rhetorical, and spasmodic. Generally hostility to Catholics and immigrants for their suspected foreign connections was limited to special occasions and was neither widely pervasive nor greatly attended." Despite increased anti-Catholic sentiment, there was no organized nativist movement in America until the mid-1840s. Rather, nativism was represented chiefly through a hodge-podge of small patriotic groups that served as local fraternal and benevolent societies.[127]

A perfect storm was brewing, however. In mid-decade immigration skyrocketed, occasioned first by the Irish famine and then by the failed republican revolutions in Germany and Italy. The arrival of now disproportionately poor immigrants coincided with renewed economic dislocations, leading to native-immigrant tensions and conflicts. The most infamous outbreak between Protestant nativists and Catholic immigrants occurred in Philadelphia in 1844 and arose ostensibly over the issue of Bible reading in the public schools. Philadelphia was prime for such an outburst. Over the previous decade the city had witnessed a rise in economic and cultural tensions between Irish and native workers, with the latter seeing the influx of unskilled immigrant laborers as a threat to their jobs and wages. Class and ethnic conflict was not new to the city, or to most cities on the east coast, and that conflict frequently manifested itself in gang rioting and public disorder.[128]

Controversy over religious exercises in the public schools was also not new to Philadelphia, although an accord between Catholics and Protestants had generally been reached by the early 1840s. Philadelphia established its public schools in 1834, building on an existing system of tax-supported charity schools that had used the nonsectarian Lancasterian program as its model. Under the prevailing practice, teachers daily read the King James Bible, usually without note or comment, possibly followed by a prayer or hymn. At the urging of Catholic Bishop Francis Kendrick, the Board of School Controllers in 1834 forbade the use of unauthorized textbooks that disparaged Catholicism. Four years later, the state legislature enacted a law that clarified the status of religious exercises, essentially memorializing the existing practice of nonsectarian exercises. While declaring that the Bible contained "the best extant code of morality," the law provided that the Bible "shall be used as a school book for Reading, without comment by the Teacher, but not as a textbook for religious discussion." Though the law was silent about the version, the assumption and practice was that schools used the King James translation of the Bible. Despite this preferential use of the Protestant Bible—and the ongoing efforts of Protestant tract societies to promote biased texts in classrooms—the city's Catholic leadership acceded to the arrangement.[129]

The groundwork for the riots took place in 1842 when the school directors in a Catholic working class neighborhood fired a Catholic teacher for refusing to lead her students in readings from the King James Bible. Around the same time several Catholic children at other schools were punished by school authorities for refusing to read from the King James Bible. Bishop Kendrick protested the teacher's dismissal and other actions with the Board of Controllers and requested that "Catholic children be not required to join in the singing of hymns or other religious exercises." Kendrick, like Protestant leaders of the city, was very aware of the school controversy taking place in New York at the time. Kendrick was less of a firebrand than New York's Bishop Hughes, however, and he refrained from attacking the King James version or the school curriculum generally. Instead, he asked that Catholic children simply be allowed to read from the Douay version of the Bible or be excused from participating in the Protestant readings.[130]

In January, 1843, the school board adopted two resolutions: the first ordered that no child be required "to attend or united in the reading of the Bible" if her parents conscientiously objected; the second provided that any consciously objecting child could read from that version of the scriptures that she preferred, and that readings were to be conducted without note or comment.[131] The action was only a partial victory for Kendrick. Catholic children were now excused from participating in the Protestant exercises, but the requirement that Bible reading be conducted without note or comment excluded many uses of the Catholic Douay version, which contained marginal comments and notations. Most important, the resolutions did not prohibit the schools from conducting religious exercises for Protestant children. Despite the modest concessions to the Catholics, Protestant clergy and newspapers roundly condemned the decision, with many falsely claiming that the bishop had orchestrated removing the Bible from the schools. In a widely circulated pamphlet, Reverend Walter Colton railed that Kendrick sought "to cast the Bible out of the public schools, and to suppress all religious exercises." The charge had just enough truth to it, as the board's decision effectively eliminated Bible reading in those schools in Catholic dominated wards.[132]

Even before the board announced its decision, eighty Protestant clergy representing a cross-section of local churches formed the American Protestant Association (A.P.A.) to rally support for Bible reading and inform Protestants of the theological and social threats presented by the growing Catholic menace. Their memorials raised familiar nativistic themes. A "foreign priesthood" was segregating its adherents into "a distinct body" that was "alien in sympathy and interest from the mass of the American people." Not only were the Romanists "direct[ly] interfer[ing] with our political elections," the Association wrote in an address to the school board, they were "directing efforts to destroy the religious character and influence of public Protestant education." The Protestant clergy were not reacting solely to the Catholic requests but also against the trend occurring in nonsectarian education championed by Horace Mann; after all, the Board's resolutions tracked the provisions of the 1838 law. Protestants were experiencing a loss of certainty that the daily exercises would retain a distinctive Protestant hue. The nativist *North American* summed up the concern in remarking how for years, "the schools have been in operation, planned by Protestants, founded by Protestants, directed by Protestants, and almost wholly supported by Protestants." Protestants were losing control, and Catholics were the convenient scapegoat.[133]

Following the Board's resolutions in January 1843, local nativists organized the American Republican Party to prepare for upcoming elections in which Irish were expected to vote in a block for sympathetic candidates. Initially, the American Republicans did not make religious appeals, preferring to emphasize patriotism and economic security issues among native-born workers. With the Bible issue now at the forefront, the American Republicans adopted it as part of their mantel. Through pamphlets, newspapers, speeches, and sermons, the American Republicans and A.P.A. kept Bible reading in the public mind, while stoking anti-Catholic sentiment. "[E]very man who loves his country, his Bible, his God, is bound by all lawful and honorable means to resist every attempt to banish the Bible from our public institutions," asserted the speaker at one Protestant rally.[134]

Not all Protestants joined in the frenzy. In March 1844, William Furness of the city's First Congregational Unitarian Church characterized the Catholic grievance as supported by "perfect justice." Catholics simply requested that they be relieved "of having views of Religion, which they do not believe, favoured in schools which they are required to support," Furness wrote in a sermon.[135] Furness also cast the controversy in larger, church-state terms. Readings of the King James Bible preferred one body of Christians over another, while they violated the latter's rights of conscience. To Furness, Bible reading, even when conducted without note or comment, violated constitutional principles:

> It is our perpetual boast that in this country we have no one form of Religion established by law. But we do virtually have a Religion established by law, when we insist that a Version of the Scriptures, the correctness of which is disputed by a large and respectable portion of the Christian community, shall be used in our places of public education.

If then, "there is any just idea of religious liberty among us," Furness pleaded, "[t]he practice of reading the Bible in the Public Schools, as a religious service will be given up."[136] What further distinguishes Furness's discourse is that it was one of the first to equate public school Bible reading with a religious establishment, an idea that judges in Ohio would expand on twenty-five years later. At this time, only Catholics characterized the issue in church-state terms, and then that Bible reading infringed on religious conscience. Although Protestants were increasingly likely to view funding of sectarian schools as a church-state violation, they were oblivious that nonsectarian Bible reading could raise a constitutional issue. On the contrary, they were prone to argue that excluding Bible reading violated the conscience rights of the Protestant majority. As one Protestant would remark in the 1854 book, *Right of the Bible in Our Public Schools*, "To deprive me of one of these benefits [of education], upon the ground of religion, is an outrage upon my conscience, and upon the principles of religious liberty. . . . My scruples in favor of the Bible are at least as sacred, and as worth of regard, as the scruples of any other man against the Bible."[137]

Matters simmered until May 3, when the American Republicans tried to hold a rally in the heavily Irish-Catholic working class suburb of Kensington. After the natives were disbursed by a Catholic mob, the American Republicans threw down a gauntlet by announcing a larger meeting in Kensington on May 6. That day, several thousand Protestants, primarily young workingmen and boys, marched down the street to the center of the ward where they encountered a Catholic mob. Fighting broke out. At some point shots were fired, allegedly from the windows of a Catholic fire company, the Hibernia Hose House, and a Protestant boy lay dead. In the ensuing melee more shots were fired as nativists attacked Catholic homes, resulting in more Protestants dead and injured. The nativists retreated, but over the following two days larger mobs of Protestants and Catholics battled in the Kensington streets with clubs, knives, and guns. This time the nativists got the upper hand, burning two Catholic churches, a seminary, the Hibernia Hose House Company, and some thirty Catholic homes. Rioting finally ended when a contingent of U.S. Marines, reinforcing the ineffective militia and police, forced the mobs to disburse.[138]

A shaky peace ensued for two months. Each side buried its dead—at least six killed and twenty wounded—proclaiming them martyrs to their respective faiths. Recriminations abounded, with Protestant newspapers assigning blame to foreign priests who were attempting to sow religious discord by excluding the Bible from the public schools. A handful of secular newspapers, though, placed blame on the "inflammatory appeals" of Protestant clergy and nativist agitators. A Grand Jury investigated the riots and in June concluded that Catholics had instigated the conflict, not only by introducing deadly force, but by seeking to remove the Bible from the schools, thereby inflaming the Protestants. Essentially vindicated, the emboldened American Republicans organized a new rally to be held on Independence Day.[139]

Concerned that the upcoming nativist rally might invite new violence, Catholics in the Southwark suburb convinced the priest of St. Philip de Neri to permit them to store weapons in the church, to be guarded by an Irish militia. News of the action reached the nativists, and a large number assembled outside the church on July 5 to demand the sheriff and state militia search the church. The search produced close to 100 muskets stored in the church. For the next three days, mobs milled about, challenging the state militia guarding the church while engaging in scuffles with Catholic gangs. After several nativists were arrested and placed in the church under the guard of the Irish militia, rioting ensued. In addition to fighting between Catholics and nativists, the latter exchanged fire with the military who were seeking to protect the church and other Catholic property. When the violence finally subsided, thirteen people lay dead and more than fifty wounded. A second Grand Jury laid blame for the Southwark riots on the Catholics for storing weapons in the church. This time Catholic designs on the public schools received less condemnation; rather, the events demonstrated the threat to public safety and democratic institutions represented by the growing foreign presence in the nation. Following the second wave of riots, Bishop Kendrick gave up seeking to resolve the Bible reading issue in the public schools. Like his counterparts in other dioceses, he turned his attention to creating parochial schools to serve the growing number of Catholic children.[140]

The Philadelphia "Bible Riots" were a sad chapter in Protestant-Catholic relations and in American history generally. They revealed how simmering ethnic and economic conflict could erupt over a secondary issue, such as Bible reading in the schools. Michael Feldberg argues that for most economically threatened artisan and working class Protestants, the decision to align with the nativists lay chiefly with economic, ethnic, and class factors, and not with the issue of Bible reading. The causes of economic and social fragmentation were complex, however, whereas the religious issue was easy to manipulate to inflame anti-immigrant sentiment. "For the working class nativists," Feldberg writes, "the Bible issue was just one more in a series of challenges that the immigrants had been raising since the late 1830s." Artisan and working class native-born were also drawn to Protestant causes—temperance, Sabbath observance, and the School Question—as a way to distinguish themselves from the Catholic immigrants. Bible reading thus took on symbolic importance. The accommodation of Catholic religious interests in the public schools indicated to the Protestant artisans and working class that the same Irish Catholic immigrants who threatened their economic well-being were their cultural equals. The issue of Bible reading in the schools, of particular interest to stalwart Protestants, was chiefly a proxy for the larger economic and ethnic issues that concerned the rank-and-file-native-born.[141]

Still, the Philadelphia Bible riots demonstrated to nativists that the School Question could be a rallying cry for carrying out their general goal of suppressing immigrants. The controversy succinctly embodied many elements at the heart of the nativist ideology: a foreign controlled authority (priests); an already despised, insular and nonassimilating ethnic group (Irish) lacking the skills and autonomy to participate in self-governance; an alien ideology (Catholicism) that competed with Protestant republicanism; and a challenge to a central civic institution (public schools). It is of little surprise that later nativist groups, including the Know-Nothings, adopted both the School Question and separation of church and state as platforms in their anti-immigrant campaigns. The year following the Philadelphia riots, the American Republicans (soon to dissolve as a political party) would declare:

> Our sole object is to form a barrier high and eternal as the Andes, which shall forever separate the Church from the State. While we regard the religion of the Bible as the only legitimate element of civilized society, and the single basis of all good government, we are greatly opposed to the introduction of sectarian dogmas into the science of our civil institutions, or the incorporation of Church creeds into the political compact with our government.[142]

Yet an Andean barrier did not prevent nonsectarian religious exercises in the public schools. On the contrary, American Republicans believed "the Holy Bible, without note or comment, to be the most proper and necessary book, as well for our children as ourselves, and we are determined that they shall not be deprived of it, either in, or out of school." After the mid-1840s, nativist groups would become some of the more vocal proponents for nonsectarian education and the principle of separation of church and state.[143]

With people diverted by the annexation of Texas and the subsequent war with Mexico, organized nativism subsided during the second half of the decade. It reemerged with a vengeance in the 1850s, however, primarily through the efforts of the Know-Nothing Party. The resurgence of 1850s nativism is attributable to several factors. First, immigration continued to rise, spurred by ongoing economic and political upheavals in Europe. The destitute Irish Catholics, who crowded the eastern cities, and the radical Germans, who settled in the upper midwest, represented a renewed threat to Protestant republican values. Native-born also grew distressed that earlier immigrants were now eligible to vote in elections and were exercising their political muscle. Whigs and Protestants attributed the 1852 election of Democrat Franklin Pierce to the rise in Catholic immigrant votes.[144] Adding to the reminders by nativists and Protestant stalwarts of a Catholic-immigrant threat, native-born artisans, craftsmen, and laborers faced ongoing economic and social dislocation that many attributed to competition from lower-wage immigrant workers. Finally, native-born voters grew increasingly dissatisfied with the corruption and ineffectiveness of the existing political parties.[145] In contrast to the major parties, nativist groups reinforced a sense of patriotism, fraternity, and control over one's life. And immigrants, primarily Catholic, represented the greatest threat to American values and economic security. Michael Holt writes that by the mid-1850s, "what Catholic immigrants represented menaced the dearest values of Americans: social order, political democracy, public education, and social mobility."[146]

Foreign and domestic events involving the Catholic Church between 1848 and 1853 also contributed to the growing religious discord and fueled fears of native-born Americans. Following the failed 1848 republican revolution in Italy that temporarily sent Pope Pius IX into exile, the papacy adopted a discernibly hostile attitude toward European liberalism. The previously "liberal" Pius aligned himself with the conservative ultramontanists and Jesuits, and church leaders elevated their condemnation of the republican movements sweeping Europe while they praised monarchists. Americans followed the events in Europe closely, sympathizing with the republicans and lionizing their leaders: Hungarian Louis Kossuth and Giuseppe Mazzini and Giuseppe Garibaldi of Italy. For many, Catholic opposition to liberalism and democracy, while chiefly in response to European events, substantiated nativist claims that the church was autocratic, despotic, and a threat to American values.[147]

At the same time, the increasingly ultramontane American hierarchy, led by Archbishop John Hughes, adopted a more critical stance toward American institutions, one matched by a more aggressive style. Most American bishops supported the new papal conservatism, with Hughes praising the church's condemnation of liberalism by publicly criticizing Louis Kossuth during his popular American tour. Hughes also set out to challenge Protestantism's claim to cultural dominance, a tactic Orestes Brownson described as "carrying the war into the enemy's country, and compelling Protestantism to defend itself." In November,

1850, Hughes gave a highly publicized but ill-timed speech attacking Protestantism as corrupt and in decline. Catholics had a "mission to convert the world, including the inhabitants of the United States, the people of the cities, the people of the country, the officers of the Navy and the Marines, the commanders of the Army, the legislatures, the Senate, the Cabinet, the President, and all." Hughes's speech and other pronouncements by the hierarchy "indicate[d] the commencement of a new era in the controversy between Catholics and Protestants," Brownson wrote in his *Review*. "Catholics are beginning to shake off their timidity, to assume in controversy their legitimate position, and to speak in bold and energetic tones which become them." For Protestants and nativists, however, the new style only confirmed their apprehensions about the Catholic threat to America and its institutions.[148]

As part of this new aggressive style, Catholic leaders increased pressure on the School Question. While still seeking accommodation on Bible reading in the schools, the bishops turned their attention to acquiring public funding for their parochial schools. In 1852, the Plenary Council of Catholic Bishops, chastened by the school conflicts in New York, Philadelphia, and elsewhere, delivered its clearest call for a system of parochial schools, asking Catholics to "make every sacrifice which may be necessary" for "the establishment and support of Catholic schools." Led by Archbishop Hughes's *Freeman's Journal*, Catholic newspapers urged the faithful to renew demands for public funding for Catholic schools and to seek laws restricting Bible reading in the public schools. Catholic officials doubled their efforts to secure funds from state and local authorities, though usually with little success. More than anything, the renewed Catholic activity allowed Protestants and nativists to raise the hue and cry over papal designs.[149] Protestants also reacted to the *Donahoe* Bible reading case from Maine (1853), which received national attention. Even though the court upheld Bible reading over the Catholic complaints, the case demonstrated Catholic intransigence on the issue. Finally, Protestants saw Catholic overreaching in a controversy over lay-trustee control of local parish property. In 1852, American bishops sought to exert ecclesiastical authority over lay-controlled church property, but their efforts backfired when the Pope sent a special nuncio, Gaetano Bedini, to mediate the conflict. Protestants interpreted the mission as papal disregard for ideals of democratic self-governance and American property law. The pope had also selected the worst emissary. Bedini had allegedly participated in the brutal suppression of Italian republicans in 1849 while serving as the civil governor of Bologna. Italian expatriates and German freethinkers protested "the Butcher" Bedini's trip with deadly riots occurring in several cities. Nativist press characterized the episode as additional evidence of papal authoritarianism and another sign of the church's wider political agenda in America. All of these events drew renewed public attention to the "Catholic problem" and the School Question in particular.[150]

These factors, coming together in the early 1850s, created an environment that gave rise to the nation's most significant nativist movement: the Know-

Nothings. As with other nativist groups, the School Question was not the main cause of the Know-Nothings; they were more concerned with stemming the political power of immigrants and Catholics through measures such as instituting a twenty-one year residency for voting. Still, a strong system of nonsectarian common schools represented a way to assimilate immigrants and curtail Catholic power while promoting republican values. The Know-Nothings thus seized on the issue in the mid-1850s as a means of garnering support and advancing their overall agenda; once in power, they sought to pass laws to protect nonsectarian public education at the expense of Catholics, among other measures. For a while, Know-Nothings and other nativists were the loudest proponents of nonsectarian common schooling. Yet despite embracing the School Question and the notion of church-state separation generally, the Know-Nothings were relatively ineffective in advancing those principles on a legislative level. With one possible exception, there is little evidence that the Know-Nothings or other nativist groups contributed in a meaningful way to evolving constitutional ideas about church-state relations.[151]

As already discussed briefly, from the 1830s through the 1850s a handful of states enacted laws or constitutional provisions prohibiting public financing of religious or sectarian institutions. Michigan was the first state to enact an express no-funding provision in its 1835 constitution, providing that "no money shall be drawn from the treasury for the benefit of religious societies, or theological or religious seminaries." Over the next decade, Ohio (1851) and Indiana (1851) added express no-funding provisions to their constitutions, while several new states—Wisconsin (1847), Minnesota (1857), Oregon (1857), and Kansas (1858)—included no-funding provisions in their initial constitutions. The timing and content of these constitutional and statutory revisions are undoubtedly connected to the heightened awareness of the School Question and Catholic immigration in the 1840s and 1850s, if not to agitation by Protestants and nativist groups. Whether these provisions are attributable to anti-Catholicism and nativist activity is more difficult to assess.[152]

In the case of Michigan, anti-Catholicism does not appear to be a leading cause for the enactment of its initial no-funding provision. In the 1830s, the state had few parochial schools and the enactment came before the wave of Catholic immigration. Ray Billington notes that at the time that Michigan was drafting its initial constitution, the Protestant Home Missionary Society reported little concern over Catholic activity in the upper Midwest. Both Catholic and Presbyterian clergy were involved in the movement to establish nonsectarian schooling at the collegiate and common school levels.[153] As the Irish-Catholic population in Michigan grew over the next decade, with immigrants drawn to construction work in canals and railroads, Catholic-Protestant tensions increased. One controversy erupted in the Detroit public schools in the mid-1840s over whether to require the reading of the Douay or Protestant version of the Bible in the schools. For three years, the School Board rebuffed the Protestant-led measure, demurring that it possessed authority over religious matters. Catholics, the board noted, had been "equally active and ardent in obtaining the passage of [the public school] law" and deserved to stand "upon an equal footing with the protestant population." Finally, in 1845, the Detroit School Board yielded to the pressure and approved the reading of either version of the Bible without note or comment, effectively giving preference to the King James Bible.[154]

That controversy may have affected attitudes. In 1850 the Michigan legislature revised the state's no-funding provision as part of a constitutional revision, strengthening the existing language by adding that no public monies or state property could be appropriated or drawn for the benefit of a "religious sect or society" or "for any such purpose."[155] Whether the revised provision is attributable chiefly to anti-Catholicism is unclear. Professor Fromisano argues that controversy over the School Question did not reemerge in Michigan until late-1852 after Bishop Peter Lefevre revived Catholic requests for a share of the school fund. Organized political nativism, in the form of an alliance between Fusion/Independents and Know-Nothings, arose during 1853–1854, at least three years after constitutional revision. That alliance produced a nativist-leaning legislature in 1855 which succeeded in enacting a prohibition law and a measure affirming the legal authority of lay trustees over church property. The extent to which anti-Catholicism was responsible for the 1850 no-funding provision is more difficult to gauge.[156]

A clear connection between anti-Catholicism and constitutional formation is lacking in several other states, as well. In Wisconsin, the common school movement predated the establishment of a Catholic parochial school system, as did the enactment of its constitutional no-funding provision. As in other parts of the country, reformers emphasized that Wisconsin public schools would infuse republican values in children from both native stock and immigrant backgrounds while "fus[ing] them into a 'homogeneous whole.'" One study finds "no evidence that the [Wisconsin] lawmakers and constitution makers were anti-religious in making the [no-funding] requirements, or that they harbored a prejudice against any sect," despite growing tensions between native Protestants and German Catholic and Lutheran immigrants during the late territorial period. Professor Jorgenson, a critic of the common school movement, also documented no anti-Catholic animus in his study of the creation of the Wisconsin public education system.[157] Similarly, at the time of Indiana's constitutional revision in 1851, less than 6 percent of Indiana inhabitants were immigrants and fewer still were Catholics. One study of the rise of Indiana educational policy asserts that the no-funding provision was not "a remnant of nineteenth century religious bigotry promulgated by nativist political leaders who were alarmed by the growth of immigrant populations and who had a particular disdain for Catholics."[158]

Finally, there is no evidence of anti-Catholic sentiment in the enactment of the Oregon Constitution in 1857. The minutes of the Oregon constitutional convention lack any statements that indicate a controversy over religious school funding. The only religious issues were whether to allow for legislative chaplains or acknowledge the deity in the constitution preamble, both proposals being rejected.[159] During the debates, one Oregon delegate articulated his understanding of the constitutional basis for the no-funding provision, stating he did not

> believe that congress had any right to take the public money, contributed by the people, of all creeds and faith [sic], to pay for religious teachings. It was a violent stretch of power, and an unauthorized one. A man in this country had a right to be a Methodist, Baptist, Roman Catholic, or what else he chose, but no government had the moral right to tax all of these creeds and classes to inculcate directly or indirectly the tenets of any one of them.[160]

Another Oregon delegate remarked that it was true that "this constitution goes a step further than other constitutions on this subject, but if that step is in the right direction, and consistent with the proper development of our institutions, I see no weight in the objection that it is new. Let us take the step farther, and declare a complete divorce of church and state."[161]

This cursory review is far from conclusive and does not negate the possibility that constitution drafters in some states held anti-immigrant, anti-Irish, or anti-Catholic sentiments. In Ohio, Illinois, and Minnesota, for example, Protestant bodies were instrumental in defeating legislative proposals to extend school funds to Catholic schools. What it does suggest is that such prejudices may not have been the dominant motivation for the enactment of many no-funding provisions.[162]

This is not to discount the *efforts* of nativists to enact anti-Catholic legislation or otherwise subordinate Catholics and immigrants generally. Wherever they had political strength—primarily Massachusetts, Maryland, New York, and Pennsylvania—Know-Nothings attempted to advance their agenda through legislative measures to investigate Catholic convents, impose a twenty-one year residency for voting, and protect Bible reading while prohibiting the public funding of parochial schools. Yet most studies of antebellum nativism indicate that the Know-Nothings were relatively ineffective in enacting anti-Catholic legislation, even in those states where they briefly held clear majorities. Oscar Handlin maintained that overall the "party's anti-foreign accomplishments were quite insignificant."[163]

Massachusetts stands as one state with a clear tie between anti-Catholic sentiment and the enactment of a no-funding provision. In 1853, Massachusetts held a referendum on a new constitution that would have included a no-funding provision. The reform-oriented constitution failed by 52 percent of the vote, though the no-funding provision came closest to passing.[164] Populist reaction to the constitution's defeat was partially responsible for the electoral success of the Know-Nothings the following year, with the party sweeping the legislature and governor's office. Once in power, the Know-Nothing legislature pushed several measures aimed at Catholics and Irish, including disbanding Irish militias, excluding Irish from state jobs and Catholics from public office-holding, extending the residency for naturalization to twenty-one years, and establishing a committee to investigate nunneries and convents. The legislature also mandated the reading of the King James Bible in the public schools (amended in 1862) and enacted a constitutional amendment restricting state funding for common schools and prohibiting the appropriation of any monies for schools of "any religious sect."[165]

No one disputes that these discriminatory measures were directed at Catholics and Irish, but the question remains why so many legislators concurred in these actions. Professors Handlin, Formisano, and Mulkern, among others, argue that people were attracted to the nativist and Know-Nothing movements for many reasons, anti-Catholic and anti-Irish sentiments being only one element. Many people supported the Know-Nothings for their stance on political reform and anti-corruption, rather than for their religious agenda: "Know-Nothingism wore many faces, as befit a populist movement." In contrast to their nativist proposals, Know-Nothings were more successful in enacting a host of progressive legislation, including providing property rights to married women, establishing a board of insurance commissioners, increasing the homestead exemption, and desegregating the public schools. Handlin probably overstated matters by describing the Know-Nothing administration as "progressive and fruitful," but many supporters regarded it as such. Historians have also recognized the complexity of the Know-Nothing agenda, which, according to Formisano, "was populist *and* progressive *and* reactionary." Legislators may have viewed efforts to strengthen the common school system by eliminating its perceived threats as a positive achievement, not simply as a mean spirited swipe at Catholics.[166] The point is that the motivations for supporting the nativist agenda were varied and complex. As Professor Mulkern has written:

> Ultranativism was the dark side of Know-Nothing populism. Meanspirited and cruel, it was subversive of the rights of minorities.... Hostility toward the Irish Catholic minority, however, was not the *sine qua non* of Know-Nothingism. Paddy and the Pope were not the only common enemies. [Know-Nothingism] had risen to power on the strength of the people's desire to shake off the incubus of all corrupt and domineering cliques and parties.... If the Know-Nothing government fell short in its efforts to meet the highest standards of republicanism, it was not the first to falter.[167]

In the final analysis, the Know-Nothings and other nativists saw the common schools as an indispensable instrument for advancing republican ideals, if not to maintain an American identity. Already predisposed in their bigotry toward Catholics and immigrants, they viewed parochial schools as a threat to that most important of American institutions. Their embrace of the School Question and church-state separation was thus both genuine and opportunistic. The nativist impulse, and their stance on the School Question, no doubt influenced attitudes of other Americans who otherwise did not embrace the overall nativist agenda. That Protestant attitudes toward the School Question were chiefly attributable to that impulse, however, remains in doubt.

Nationally, the Know-Nothing party fell from favor as quickly as it had arisen, losing out to an insurgent Republican Party and increasing tensions between the North and South. Concerns about foreign threats—religious, ethnic, or economic—receded to the more pressing issues of slavery, secession and possible civil war. Nativism and anti-Catholicism did not disappear during the Civil War years, but it subsided as a national issue. So, too, did public controversy over the School Question. Both issues would reappear with a renewed vigor in the late 1860s.

3

The Cincinnati "Bible War" of 1869–1873

The early controversies over nonsectarian Bible reading in the schools and the funding of religious schooling set the stage for most significant church-state case of the nineteenth century, *Minor v. Board of Education*, otherwise known as the Cincinnati "Bible War" of 1869. When the controversy finally was resolved, Ohio would become the first state to authorize the banning of unmediated Bible reading from the public schools, the practice at the heart of nonsectarian education. The decision of the Ohio Supreme Court, though ostensibly vesting discretion with local school boards over the issue of Bible reading, pierced the façade of religious universality that had insulated the nonsectarian practices for seventy years. Bible reading, the justices held, even when conducted without note or comment and conducted for the purpose of instilling morality rather than religious devotion, was a religious exercise and inconsistent with constitutional principles. *Minor v. Board of Education* is arguably the most important church-state holding that precedes the incorporation of the First Amendment by the United States Supreme Court in the 1940s.[1]

That said, the political and social ramifications of the Cincinnati Bible War were as important as the ultimate judicial holding. The controversy refocused national attention to the twin issues of nonsectarian religious exercises and the public funding of parochial schooling, issues that had been hibernating since the Civil War. The events in Cincinnati broke open the floodgates, ushering in a national discussion about the meaning of separation of church and state and religious pluralism in a democratic society. The questions were specific and general, mundane and of great consequence. Was Bible reading inherently sectarian? Did its reading, even without note or comment, violate rights of conscience of religious dissenters? For that matter, were Catholics and other religious minorities entitled to equal regard by the government, one that many people still assumed was grounded on Protestant values? Should public education to be secular, Protestant, or generically religious? Could public schools fulfill their mission of instilling morals without teaching religion? Did government have an obligation—or the underlying authority—to ensure the religious well-being of its citizenry? Did government have *any* role in religious matters? And if the Bible was excluded from the schools, would that action satiate Catholic claims for a share of the public school fund? These were the heady questions that emerged from Cincinnati Bible controversy, questions that would be debated at a heightened level for the next eight years, while setting the parameters for such discussions for years to come.

That the catalyst for this great national debate about church and state arose in Cincinnati is not surprising. In many respects, Cincinnati, as the commercial and transportation center for the upper Mississippi Valley, had been at ground-zero for religious controversies for years. By the mid-nineteenth century, Cincinnati was one of the larger and more important cities in what was still considered the western United States. Like both New Orleans and St. Louis, it had a vibrant religious diversity, and since the 1830s the city had served as a magnet for foreign immigration. Although Irish Catholics began settling in the Cincinnati region in the late 1830s, the majority of immigrants were Germans, encouraged to migrate to the Mississippi Valley by German and Catholic associations. Most German immigrants to Cincinnati were Catholic, although German Lutherans also migrated during the 1840s, to be followed by another wave of Germans after 1848, this time liberals and freethinkers fleeing the failed revolution of that year. In addition to having more than twenty Catholic parishes, both German and Irish, mid-century Cincinnati had a smattering of Presbyterian, Methodist, Disciples of Christ, and Baptist churches, as well as German Lutheran and Jewish congregations. Two of the nation's leading Jewish leaders—rabbis Max Lilienthal and Isaac Mayer Wise—resided in the city. Cincinnati was one of the more religiously heterogeneous cities in the United States.[2]

Foreign interest in settling the Mississippi Valley caught the attention of Protestants and nativists. In the early 1830s, the American Home and Foreign Missions Society directed resources to combat the foreign immigration to the region, expressing concern that the Valley could become predominately Catholic. Provoking particular alarm was the fact that the immigration was not merely happenstance but encouraged by German and Austrian Catholic societies, such as the Leopodine Foundation, which provided assistance for the building of Catholic churches and schools.[3] Lyman Beecher, the indefatigable leader of evangelical Calvinism, became the chief spokesperson for the Protestant phalanx. Moving to Cincinnati in 1832 to lead the Presbyterian Lane Seminary, Beecher quickly recognized the dire situation at hand. After completing a fundraising and speaking tour of the east coast, Beecher organized his remarks into a widely circulated tract, *A Plea for the West*, published in 1835. In it, Beecher raised a hue and cry for Protestant action to stem the immigrant Catholic tide into the Midwest. Beecher insisted that the "world has never witnessed such a rush of dark-minded population from one country to another, as is now leaving Europe and dashing upon our shores." While the influx of individual Irish and German immigrants was of concern, Beecher was most distressed by the elements that were facilitating the mass migration. The Catholic Church, with its Austrian and German allies, had a goal of dominating the Mississippi Valley, Beecher warned. The threat lay in "the political claims and character of the Catholic religion, and its church and state alliance with the political and ecclesiastical governments of Europe hostile to liberty.... Their policy points them to the West, the destined centre of civilization and political power they once had." Beecher's alarmist claims held an element of truth, as two Catholic sponsoring organizations, the Leopoldine Foundation and Ludwig Missionsverein, received the patronage of the Austrian and Bavarian governments. The potential of a Catholic-dominated Midwest appeared quite real to Protestant leaders who had only to point to the Catholic populations in Canada to the north and to those in Texas and the Mexican territories in the southwest. Protestant America would be relegated to that region east of the Appalachian Mountains, and future power in America would rest in a Catholic-dominated heartland. Plainly, "the political destiny of our nation will be decided in the West," Beecher declared. For Beecher and other concerned Protestants, the common schools would be an impediment to the ascension of Catholic power in the West. Hope for not only the West, but for the nation as a whole, depended on a vibrant system of common schooling—one that promoted Protestant-republican values—to assimilate immigrant children into American culture.[4]

Public schooling came to Cincinnati in 1829 when the city amended its charter to create a system of free, tax supported common schools. Earlier schooling had been provided by a handful of private academies operated chiefly by Protestant clergy, a Lancasterian seminary associated with a Presbyterian church, and a Catholic charity free-school established in 1829. With many of the city's civic and religious leaders hailing from New England, the early common schools reflected a decided Protestant hue, though of a nondenominational quality. Protestant-oriented religious exercises—prayer, Bible reading, catechisms—and textbooks reflecting a Protestant bias were common in the early days.[5] The state's first superintendent of schools, Samuel Lewis, an associate of Horace Mann, led the drive for a less doctrinaire form of nonsectarian Protestantism, which slowly took root in Ohio's public schools. Lewis received support from Calvin Stowe, Beecher's son-in-law, who agreed that "the whole Bible, and nothing but the Bible, without note or comment, must be taken as the text-book of religious instruction." Pressure to moderate the religious exercises also came from the growing Catholic population, led by Cincinnati Bishop John Purcell. Writing in the *Catholic Telegraph* in 1834, Purcell criticized not simply the Protestant exercises but the overall Protestant character of the schools themselves, calling them *"sectarian* free-schools."

> [T]he children of poor Catholics frequent [the public schools] for the purpose of learning to read, [but] where, under the pretext of Charity and the grievous abuse of that sacred virtue and name, the foundations of spiritual life are poisoned and those unsuspecting children have tracts placed in their hands, insinuating the vilest and most malicious slander of our real principles....[6]

The city school board reacted to criticisms about the Protestant complexion of the public schools, insisting that the religious exercises were conducted for the purpose of instilling morals and good behavior, not religious devotion. To placate Catholic concerns, however, the board in 1839 directed that the Bible would be read without note or comment and that sectarian teachings were to be prohibited. Despite this action, Catholic children were still exposed to readings from the King James Bible and to textbooks containing anti-Catholic passages. In 1842, at the request of Purcell, the board modified its policy to excuse Catholic students from participating in the religious exercises, establishing a rule that "no pupil should be required to read the Testament or Bible against the wishes of parents or guardians." The board also invited Purcell to inspect the textbooks for any offensive passages. Even though the King James Bible continued to be read in the classrooms and instruction was "still far from being... without any sectarian bias [as] we should wish [it] to be," the *Catholic Telegraph* wrote following the changes, "half a loaf is better than no bread."[7] Catholic leaders still objected that Catholic children were being exposed to the Protestant exercises, so in 1852 the school board again expanded the policy to permit dissenting students to "read such version of the sacred scriptures as their parents or guardians may prefer." The provision came with the condition that all scripture readings were to be made without marginal readings or comments by the teachers, which often barred readings from the Catholic Douay version. Again, the *Catholic Telegraph* praised the tolerance and "liberality which characterize[d] the Cincinnati [School] Board" and its policies, though the Purcell and other Catholics still objected to the Protestant bias of the curriculum. Additional complaints produced no further accommodations, and after 1852 Purcell set out to establish a system of Catholic private schools in Cincinnati.[8]

A competing system of Catholic schools was already well under way. By 1848, nine or ten parish schools already existed in Cincinnati, educating over 2,000 students. Twenty years later, by the time of the Bible War, the number of children in Catholic schools had grown by sixfold to sevenfold. Following the pronouncement from the national Plenary Council of 1852, Bishop Purcell became more insistent about the necessity of Catholic-based schooling for Catholic children. He also increased his efforts to obtain public financial assistance for his parochial schools, though to little avail. The specter of Catholic demands for a share of the school fund would haunt the events of 1869–1870, even though that issue was not part of controversy. That fact would not prevent Protestant and nativist agitators from linking the two issues in their campaign to retain Bible readings in the Cincinnati schools.[9]

The Controversy

In the years following the Civil War, Cincinnati's population had risen to approximately a quarter million, with half of its residents being either foreign-born or children of foreign-born. By 1869 the number of Catholic children being educated in area parochial schools had risen to between 12,000 to 15,000, whereas the public schools enrolled only 19,000. Continuing Catholic immigration to Cincinnati meant that the parochial school enrollment would soon surpass that of the public schools. That summer, a newly elected Catholic member of the school board, F.W. Rauch, opened discussions with Catholic officials, including Father Edward Purcell, Vicar General of the archdiocese and brother of now-Archbishop John Purcell. Rauch and other board members proposed folding the Catholic schools into the public school system, with the former restricting themselves to teaching only secular subjects, with no teaching of religious subjects or from religious texts. Father Purcell responded favorably to the merger idea, counter-proposing that Catholic teachers be allowed to teach in their old schools and that the formally Catholic schools, most located on the grounds of Catholic churches, be available for religious instruction on weekends. With both sides in apparent agreement, Rauch introduced a resolution at the September 6 board meeting to establish a committee to proceed with consolidation. At the same meeting, a non-Catholic board member, lawyer Samuel A. Miller, proposed a separate resolution to prohibit "religious instruction and the reading of religious books including the Holy Bible" in the Cincinnati schools. Miller stated that his proposal was intended "to allow the children of parents of all sects and opinions, in matters of faith and worship to enjoy alike the benefit of the school fund." Apparently the Miller resolution had not been part of the negotiations but was added as a way to facilitate the agreement. The two resolutions nonetheless became intertwined, particularly in the public mind, with the dominant perception being that Catholic officials had demanded the exclusion of the Bible as a *quid pro quo* for agreeing to consolidation.[10]

The announcement of both resolutions generated a fury of opposition from Protestants as well as many rank-and-file Catholics. The nativist *Cincinnati Gazette* howled that a "Jesuitical scheme was afoot," while the Methodist *Christian Advocate* claimed that the actions would not only endanger the moral and intellectual development of youth, but also would foretell "the ruin of the Republic." For many Protestants, the resolutions confirmed an evil conspiracy: the board had been in secret negotiations with the Archbishop to give up Bible reading in order to fold in the Catholic schools, which critics argued would remain Catholic but in name only. At the same time, the Holy Bible and all texts with religious references would be expelled. The only religion that would remain in some public schools would be Catholic! The resolutions were but a nefarious Catholic plot to undermine public education.[11]

Father Edward Purcell, and his brother the Archbishop, had also misjudged the level of opposition, this time among German priests who saw their schools as a way to maintain German-Catholic traditions and a sense of community. Despite efforts of the *Catholic Telegraph*—edited by Father Purcell—to assuage German-Catholic concerns, the damage had been done; the Purcells were forced to back down. After a contentious meeting between the merger committee and Catholic leaders, the Archbishop released a letter to the board on September 18 withdrawing Catholic support for the consolidation plan. Although his brother publicly blamed the retraction on the outcry from the nativist press, the Archbishop implied that consolidation would never have been possible. "The entire government of public schools in which Catholic youth are to be educated cannot be given over to the civil power," Purcell wrote. "We, as Catholics, cannot approve of that system of education for youth which is apart from instruction in the Catholic faith and the teachings of the church." Purcell's letter was silent as to the Bible reading resolution, but its contents indicated that the church also would never endorse a system of secular education. With his rejection of Rauch's merger plan, Purcell had little interest in joining in the debate over Bible reading.[12]

Purcell's letter was the death-nail to the consolidation proposal. Yet despite the Catholics' withdrawal from the school merger, the Bible reading resolution remained on the table. A vote on that resolution was delayed until November 1, which provided time for pro- and anti-Bible reading forces to rally their troops. Pro-Bible reading forces quickly organized a "Friends of the Bible" committee, while Protestant clergy and newspapers thundered their opposition to the resolution. One of the leading opponents was Reverend Amory D. Mayo, a member of the school board and minister of the city's conservative Unitarian church. That fall, Mayo delivered a series of public lectures where he foretold the "instantaneous destruction of our public schools" if the Bible was excluded. Catholics and "an Atheistic sect [had] joined hands to divide, distract, and wholly change that great institution," the public schools, Mayo charged.[13] Mayo's own position on Bible reading reveals the complexity of views among its supporters. As a theological liberal, Mayo championed unmediated Bible reading for its "unrivaled precepts of virtue and wisdom and its inspiring ideals of character." This perspective differed little from that of Horace Mann, Calvin Stowe, and the host of Protestant educators who embraced Bible reading chiefly for its universal moral precepts and as an instrument for character building. Americans "believe in the Bible because it is the best guide to morals and religion," Mayo insisted, and "they support the [nonsectarian] common school because it is the best way to educate the mass of American youth," including immigrant children. On a different level, Mayo shared the uneasiness that many Protestants still harbored about nonsectarian instruction. He concurred with his evangelical counterparts that Bible reading was also necessary to instill religious devotion in children. The Bible was indispensible—it was not merely a moral textbook; it was holy, the unique source of divine, eternal truths. "We place the Bible in the school without note or comment, or explanation, because no book or teacher so well enforces the universal religion of love," Mayo declared. "When a child reads the Ten Commandments and the Sermon on the Mount, repeats the Lord's Prayer and beholds the character of Jesus, he does not need to be told; there is religion and morality at their fountain head."[14] Mayo's own views reflected the tension that existed within Protestantism:

was the Bible merely a source-book for teaching morals—and thus something that could be replaced by a less objectionable work—or was the Bible indispensible for its moral and religious qualities and to be used to guide children in their own spiritual development? Although both perspectives acknowledged the value of Bible reading, the former was willing to yield on the issue for the good of the common schools. This distinction represented the emerging battle-line within Protestantism.

The variance in Protestant perspectives did not matter for the immediate controversy, as both views clung to the importance of Bible reading. The stakes were high, and supporters like Mayo were not beyond exaggerating for the sake of the cause. As a school board member, Mayo knew that the archdiocese no longer supported either resolution, but he alleged that the Catholic Church was behind the effort to remove Bible reading. Mayo's rhetoric in his first lecture was generally restrained, and he concentrated on the necessity of Bible reading and the government's duty to promote religion in general. His more reflective observations about the relationship between church and state—"every modern government has declared that it contains the divine law from which all authority on earth is derived"—were overshadowed by later remarks, which took on a nativist tone. Referring to the Pope's 1864 Syllabus, which had condemned the separation of church and state and education apart from the Catholic Church, Mayo charged that "the priesthood had always been hostile to American ideas and institutions." Not only were priests "moving to gather the Catholic children into sectarian Romish schools" where they would be denied the skills of American citizenship, they were seeking to deny that source of republican ideals, the Bible, from Protestant children as well. A "black brigade of the Catholic priesthood" (Jesuits) was behind the resolutions and was seeking nothing less than "to knock out [the Republic's] underpinning, to poison the very wells of its water of life... and [to] darken the very light by which it lives and breathes." United with skeptics, Catholic priests would "banish the Bible from the schools" and "plunge [the nation] into the bottomless pit of Atheism."[15] Mayo was not alone in his incendiary rhetoric. Employing similar hyperbole, the Methodist *Christian Advocate* declared that Catholic opposition to Bible reading was part of a "Romanist policy" that sought "the overthrow, the abolition, of the whole American scheme of Common School Education." And the demise of public education would "mean ultimately the ruin of the Republic," the *Christian Advocate* claimed. The *Cincinnati Gazette* and other Protestant newspapers made comparable claims.[16]

Although local sentiment generally opposed the resolution, a handful of people rallied support for the resolution, led by liberal Unitarian minister Thomas Vickers. Vickers, like his foil Mayo, was also a school board member but unlike Mayo supported Miller's resolution. Vickers and freethinking lawyer Johann B. Stallo organized a pro-resolution rally on September 26, but the event was disorderly and poorly attended. With Catholics not engaged, support came chiefly from a handful of religious liberals, freethinkers, and the small Jewish community led by rabbis Max Lilienthal and Isaac Mayer Wise.[17]

The Friends of the Bible committee also sponsored a rally, coming two days after the pro-resolution group. In contrast to that earlier event, the Friends of the Bible meeting on September 28 drew a "very large and enthusiastic assembly of earnest people," reputedly 3,000 in number, according to one newspaper. As another newspaper reported, "Pike's Music Hall was literally jammed with citizens last night anxious to add their influence to that of the friends of the Bible to prevent the abolishment of that book from the public schools."[18] In addition to hearing from local Protestant leaders, the assemblage heard from three prominent lawyers who would represent the plaintiffs in the upcoming litigation: Rufus King, William M. Ramsey, and George R. Sage. King, whose grandfather and namesake was a signer of the federal Constitution, was the former president of the School Board and current dean of the Cincinnati Law School. King's remarks were brief and predictable, in which he declared the Bible to be "the corner-stone of our American institutions." The other two lawyers offered previews of their legal arguments to come. Both men affirmed that America was founded as a Christian nation, such that the government had responsibility to promote Christian values—here, Protestant values—particularly in the public schools. "This is a Christian land; ours is a Christian civilization," Ramsey declared. Thus "the hour that shall witness the final banishment of the Bible from the public schools—if such an hour shall come—will also witness the end of the [education] system itself."[19]

Ramsey and Sage's less hyperbolic remarks revealed that they were already preparing for the legal battle to come. Both attorneys understood that the issue of Bible reading presented a constitutional question, and both men proffered narrow views of the constitutional protections and proscriptions concerning religion. Neither Bible reading nor the Protestant complexion of the public schools constituted an establishment of religion under their interpretation of the law. The framers were concerned only about "the evil of an established church," Ramsey asserted. For there to be a religious establishment, Sage echoed, the state must promote creeds, doctrines, and penalties for nonconformists. Nonsectarian Bible reading and exercises, because of their universality, could never rise to such a level. Both attorneys also disputed the validity of complaints by Catholics, Jews, and freethinkers that Bible reading infringed on their rights of conscience. Because "no evil proceeds from reading the Bible...no question of conscience [was] involved." Even if such a claim could be made, it was not entitled to constitutional protection. The "free exercise of religion," Sage insisted, "was inspired by reverence for the Christian religion and the Holy Bible upon which it rests." It was "simply a barrier against infidelity and intolerance," not a ground for protecting the same. Under this view, only claims grounded on Christianity or its sacred text were entitled to religious protection.[20]

The legal arguments were but previews; the purpose of the meeting was to rally support for the cause, which meant offering red meat to the audience. Ramsey and Sage did not disappoint. Surprising the audience, Ramsey blamed atheists and infidels for seeking to expel the Bible from the schools, not the Catholics. "No my friends, this proposition does not come from the Catholics." Rather, "the source from whence the proposition to exclude the Bible from the schools . . . [came] from the infidels" who sought to tear down Christian civilization. In contrast, Sage laid blame squarely at the foot of the Catholic hierarchy, based on its long history of antagonism toward religious liberty and republican institutions. Despite this difference of opinion, both men concurred that Catholic efforts to obtain a share of the school fund were at the root of the Bible controversy and had to be resisted. The funding issue, again, lurked beneath the controversy. The immediate concern, however, was the survival of Bible reading and the common schools.[21]

The controversy over the Bible resolution percolated throughout the fall, garnering national attention. On November 1, the school board met and, after hours of acrimonious debate, voted 22 to 15 to approve the resolution to exclude the Bible from the schools. All ten Catholic board members voted for the resolution, as did one of the two Jewish members. But an additional eleven votes came from Protestant and nonreligious members of the board, indicating that not all people were swayed by the anti-Catholic rhetoric surrounding the controversy.[22] This wider support for the resolutions did nothing to quell the dissent, and two days later representatives of the Friends of the Bible obtained a preliminary injunction from Superior Court Judge Bellamy Storer, halting implementation of the Bible reading ban. The matter was then set for a hearing on the merits later in November.[23]

Even before the resolution had been adopted, newspapers from across the nation had joined in the debate. Protestant journals and newspapers, particularly those of Methodists and Presbyterians, lashed out at the resolution, assigning blame to the Catholic Church. The proposal was the clearest example of "the conspiracy formed by the American papal hierarchy against our Public School system," charged one journal, while another screamed in a headline: "Shall the Bible or the Pope be Schoolmaster!" "Romanists" would not "rest until our whole system of common school education is utterly overthrown," wrote *Zion's Herald*.[24] In their condemnations, evangelicals generally ignored that the archdiocese had not supported the resolution or that half of the board members who voted for the measure were not Catholic. That every Catholic school board member had voted against Bible reading sufficiently demonstrated Catholic antipathy toward public schooling, the *Christian Advocate* charged. "It was simply another step . . . toward the entire destruction of the school system, and the division of the public money among sectarian institutions." Because the common schools relied on the same moral foundations as the democratic state, they could no more dispose of the Bible, that "great foundation of morals," than they could books on literature and mathematics. But more was at stake than simply Bible reading or even the survival of the common schools. At risk was the nation's ability to sustain itself by ensuring that its citizens acquired those virtues and skills necessary to operate the republic. As another newspaper put the matter succinctly, few issues could be more important to a nation that was a "Republic of the Bible."[25]

If the *Christian Advocate* reflected the perspective of most evangelicals, it did not represent the views of all Protestants. Even before the controversy had erupted, a small but growing number of educators and Protestant leaders had begun to argue that public schools should be free of all religious instruction, including nondevotional Bible readings. Bible reading, prayer, and hymn singing, even when conducted in a nonsectarian manner, were exclusive, divisive, and inconsistent with the goal of universal education. On Thanksgiving Day, 1869, Henry Ward Beecher, the influential pastor of the Brooklyn Pilgrim Congregational Church (and, ironically, the son of Lyman Beecher), delivered a sermon supporting the Cincinnati school board decision. Beecher asserted that public schools should "not only be free and common, but they should be *unsectarian*." What Beecher meant by the term was something different from the common understanding of nonsectarian education. Beecher did not seek a curriculum that was completely bereft of religious elements. At this time, few people advocated for an educational program that was totally secular, however they would have defined that term. But if Bible reading had to be banned to preserve the universality of public schooling, Beecher announced, then "I vote to exclude it." And "if the reading of the Bible obliges us to forego our principles of toleration, I shall maintain our principles of toleration." A few weeks later, Beecher wrote an opinion piece for the *New York Tribune* which reaffirmed his stance against Bible reading in the schools. While declaring that Bible reading "would do a world of good and no harm" in most contexts, Beecher insisted that compelling schoolchildren of other faiths "to read it, or to hear it read" amounted to "religious compulsion." Catholic and Jewish complaints about the Protestant character of public schooling were not only valid, "we join with them in thinking this to be wrong." Significantly, Beecher not only viewed the issue in egalitarian terms but in constitutional terms as well. Compulsory Bible reading in the schools was "not in accordance with American doctrine of the liberty of conscience" and should be abolished, he stated: "It is too late to adopt the church-state doctrine." In constitutional matters, the preferences of the religious majority should never prevail over the rights of religious minorities: "That would be giving the charter of universal tyranny to power." Thus while Beecher stopped short of advocating that public schooling should essentially be secular, his sentiments came close to that point. For Beecher, the state "ha[d] no business to teach religion, or to show partiality to one or another sect in religion."[26] In addition to Beecher, support for the Board's resolution came from Rev. Joseph Thompson of New York's Broadway Tabernacle and William Lloyd Garrison. Thompson urged "an impartial system of education...free from all religious and sectarian bias" which occurred with Bible reading. Garrison defended the Board's action chiefly on constitutional grounds: the resolution "plac[ed] all the people on the same plane of natural and constitutional rights...while leaving them free to propagate their own religious and political views in their own way." Responding to evangelical claims about the necessity of Bible reading, Garrison charged that "Bigoted sectarism is ever ready to use the arm of secular power to authenticate its creed." The removal of the Bible did not indicate "religious degeneracy, but rather [the] growth in popular enlightenment and the recognition of equal rights."[27]

The sentiments of Beecher, Thompson, and Garrison were echoed in the columns of *The Independent*, the nation's leading Protestant newspaper, and in several lesser religious journals. Editorials commonly took two forms. Some Protestant leaders and journals grudgingly endorsed the removal of religious exercises as a compromise for preserving the public schools. "If we are to be forced to divorce religious from secular education, in order to preserve the public schools," wrote the *Living Church*, "we will preserve them at that price, and believe it is better for both sorts of education." Just as moderate evangelicals had once defended nonsectarianism as a way of ensuring the Protestant character of public education, some were now abandoning its most notable feature in order to hold onto a semblance of Protestant control of the schools. For other Protestants, it was less a choice between two evils than a recognition that Bible reading conflicted with rights of conscience and other church-state principles. The Episcopalian *American Churchman* insisted that Bible reading undermined the responsibility of parents and the church to teach religious devotion. Because the common school was an arm of the state, the *Churchman* wrote, "it has nothing to do with the Bible, religion, or morals, the state having no religion." The American Revolution had forever altered church-state relations, and the "functions of the two bodies were separated." Under the Constitution, continued the *Churchman*, the "state declared itself incompetent to deal with religion." Even Protestant journals in the former category acknowledged the legitimate "conscientious scruples" of those who objected to the exercises. As one Presbyterian chastised his fellow evangelicals, shall we "render our common school system secure, by waiving the reading of the Bible in our schools; or shall we bigotedly insist upon its continuance and *risk all the consequences*?" Although these Protestants may have initially supported removing the Bible out of desperation, they were beginning to see the merits in the Catholic complaints.[28]

Finally, support for the board's resolution came from mainstream newspapers and periodicals, with favorable editorials appearing in *Atlantic Monthly*, *The Nation*, and *Harper's Weekly*, among others. *Harper's* position is notable in that only a decade earlier it had embraced Bible reading as the means of ensuring evangelical dominance of the public schools. Following the trial in December, the magazine called for removing the Bible from the common schools. In addition to restating Beecher's concerns about religious conscience, *Harper's* challenged the underlying premise of nonsectarianism, declaring that time had come for Protestants to recognize that not all Christians agreed on the same "great general truths" of the Bible. Consensus over even basic theological teachings was not possible, so public schools should be restricted to secular education solely and "should have nothing to do with any religious tenets whatever." The *Harper's* article also disputed the spiritual value of rote prayer and Bible reading, stating that the great lessons of Christian charity and love of God "do not appear in a ceremonial and hollow reading to a chapter in the Bible." These views, while representing the minority perspective among Protestant and secular newspapers, revealed nonetheless how attitudes were evolving toward nonsectarian instruction and toleration of Catholic claims.[29]

Harper's Weekly's position toward nonsectarian instruction had progressed significantly over a short period; however, it was far from embracing the Catholic position. *Harper's* shared a general concern with the mainstream press that Bible reading and biased texts provided Catholics with ammunition in their ongoing battle for a share of the common school fund. Ironically, at the same time that the magazine was calling for religious respect and toleration over the Bible reading issue, it was running scurrilous anti-Catholic cartoons by Thomas Nast which portrayed Catholic clergy as bent on uniting church and state while destroying public education. Bible reading "furnish[ed] a weapon for the enemy" in their campaign to destroy the public schools, *Harper's* argued. "Do not leave them an honest sectarian objection." "Free the schools of every thing against which this kind of opposition may be fairly urged, and then stand fast upon the principle that the public money shall not educate the people in the private religious faith of the teachers."[30] The growing division within Protestantism over the propriety of Bible reading had not dented the consensus against the funding of parochial schools.

The Trial

Trial on the Bible reading resolution had initially been set for November 15 in front of Judge Bellamy Storer, who had issued the injunction. In the interim, allegations arose that Storer, a Methodist layman and former president of the school board, had advised the plaintiffs on drafting their injunction petition. Embarrassed over the allegation of judicial bias, Storer delayed the trial until November 29 so it could be heard by all three judges of the Superior Court. In addition to Storer, the case was heard by Judge Marcellus B. Hagans, who was also an evangelical Methodist and a founder of the local Sunday School Union, and Judge Alphonso Taft, father of the future President and Chief Justice. Although Taft was a Republican and conservative politically, he was a member of Reverend Vicker's liberal Unitarian church.[31]

Six of Ohio's more prominent lawyers—three on each side—argued the case before the superior court. The plaintiffs' attorneys were the same who had participated in the mass rally against the board's action, and all were fervent advocates of Bible reading in the schools. In addition to Rufus King's legal pedigree, George

Sage was a former federal judge. The defense team, representing the school board, included Johann B. Stallo, George Hoadly, and Stanley Matthews. Johann Stallo was a German émigré who had taught college chemistry and physics and was widely regarded as a leading freethinker. In 1848 Stallo had written *The General Principles of the Philosophy of Nature*, a book that presaged many of Darwin's evolutionary theories. Stallo had not merely defended the board resolution in speeches and rallies, he had fueled the controversy by urging that public school curriculum should be bereft of all religious influences. George Hoadly, a Mason and liberal Unitarian, was a former superior court judge who was later elected governor of Ohio. Coincidentally, Hoadly was a descendent of eighteenth-century Calvinist giants Jonathan Edwards and Timothy Dwight. The third defense lawyer was Stanley Matthews. Matthews was also a former trial judge who would later serve in the United States Senate and eventually be appointed to the United States Supreme Court. Unlike his two colleagues, Mathews was a conventional Protestant, a respected elder of a Presbyterian church. Perhaps on purpose, the school board had not selected a Catholic attorney as counsel.[32]

The proceedings in *Minor v. Board of Education* contain the century's most comprehensive legal debate over the role of religion in public education and, more generally, over the relationship between church and state. The arguments in the trial—there were no contested facts—lasted five days and ranged from heated rhetoric to reasoned discussion about the significant constitutional issues at stake. What stands out in the exchanges among counsel is an awareness that the constitutional interpretations they were advancing transcended the instant controversy—that the issues implicated the nation's core republican values and would provide a foundation for church-state law for the future.[33]

Despite being able to rely on a forty-year practice of Bible reading—not to mention having the overwhelming support of Cincinnati's Protestant establishment—the plaintiffs' attorneys carried the heavier legal burden. Because the school board's action carried a presumption of validity, the attorneys had to convince the three-judge court that the board had exceeded its authority in prohibiting Bible reading. This necessitated the tenuous argument that the state constitution did not simply permit religious exercises in the public schools but actually obligated school boards to provide such instruction. To support this proposition, the plaintiffs' attorneys argued that a system of secular education that taught morals and good character was insufficient—that public education could not be divorced from religious instruction based on the Bible. The argument, in essence, was that nonsectarian instruction had a goal of promoting religious fealty among children, not simply morality, a charge Catholics had been making for years. Yet to make this argument, the plaintiffs had to reconcile language in the state constitution banning government preference for "any religious society" and prohibiting any religion or sect from controlling the public schools. Finally, the plaintiffs' attorneys had to distinguish two earlier Ohio Supreme Court decisions that, in interpreting a state Sunday law, had disputed that Christianity was entitled to any legal preference. As a counterweight to their myriad disadvantages, the plaintiffs' attorneys could count on the religious sympathies of two of the judges.[34]

Faced with adverse law and precedent, the plaintiffs' attorneys argued that broad principles underlying the Ohio Constitution presumed a close relationship between church and state, imposing an affirmative duty on the state to promote religion. They found support for their argument in Section 7 of the bill of rights which, incorporating language from the Northwest Ordinance of 1787, stated that "religion, morality and knowledge [were] essential for good government" and that the legislature was obligated to protect "the peaceable enjoyment . . . of public worship, and to encourage schools and the means of instruction." By reading the two passages together, they argued, the section required the state to teach religion and morality in the public schools. And that "'religion' to which the Constitution refers," attorney William Ramsey insisted, had to be "the religion of the Holy Bible." "The religion of the Bible is the only religion known to the Constitution and laws of the State of Ohio, and instruction in its elementary truths should be given in the schools."[35] Ramsey and his colleagues were making a leap in equating the constitution's reference to religion with Christianity, but they offered two supporting arguments. First, the overwhelming practice in Ohio schools, as well as in the common schools in other states, had been to teach general Christian principles, counsel claimed. Prior practice and majority preference suggested that Christianity was what was meant by "religion." But second, Rufus King asserted, the Ohio Constitution implicitly recognized Christianity. "This is beyond doubt or cavil, a Christian state. That is the general and prevailing religion of the people; and the courts are bound to notice and maintain it, just as they would any general custom of the State, whenever it is called in question." And the Bible, King continued, was "the foundation and the authoritative exponent of religion and morality so recognized by the Constitution as essential to government."[36]

King's argument implicated an earlier legal dispute over whether the common law, as adopted by the American states, incorporated Christian principles, such that courts were bound to recognize and enforce Christian practices. For the first half of the nineteenth century, courts had struggled with what was meant by the maxim that "Christianity is part of the law." Legal giants such as James Kent and Joseph Story had promoted the maxim, and antebellum judges had relied on it to uphold convictions for blasphemy and Sunday law violations. By mid-century judicial use of the maxim had become controversial, with some judges and lawyers asserting it was inconsistent with principles of religious equality and church-state separation. In 1853 the Ohio Supreme Court had been one of the first to expressly dispute that courts had authority to enforce Christian modes of conduct based on the maxim.[37] Rufus King acknowledged that the state supreme court had refuted that Christianity was part of the common law. He brushed aside those decisions, insisting that because they had involved a Sunday law, "all that is said in those cases concerning the relation between religion and the State, is simply *obiter dic-tum*—irrelevant to the matter [to be] decided" here. Christianity might not have the full force of law, but "its precepts and principles [still] enter[ed] largely into the formation of the common law," King declared. He invited the superior court judges "to make some sense" out of the constitution's language affirming the importance of religion for public education. Because the constitution obligated public schools to teach religion and morality, King asserted, that religion could only be the Christianity of the Bible.[38]

The judges and lawyers understood the far-reaching implications of King's interpretation for church-state relations. Seeking to clarify King's position about the law's obligation to promote Christianity, George Sage insisted that the plaintiffs were not asking the court to recognize that "Christianity is part of the law." The state supreme court had held otherwise, he acknowledged. Rather, the state constitution merely recognized religion as "the bond of society, the basis upon which our institutions rest, as essential to good government." It was Christianity in this broad sense—"propositions which are the foundation of and necessary to the constitution and the stability of society"—that the constitution recognized and, in turn, obligated public schools to encourage. Despite Sage's effort at reha-bilitation, the essence of the plaintiffs' case necessitated King's interpretation: that language in the constitution was not hortatory but created a legal obligation upon the state, and its public schools, to teach religion. And that religion could be none other than Christianity, "the religion of the Bible," which courts had histor-ically protected over other religions. Although the plaintiffs' attorneys were care-ful not to equate Christianity with Protestantism, and even asserted that "[t]he God of this Bible is the God of the Christian—be he Catholic or Protestant—of the Unitarian—of the Jew!", other parts of their argument made clear that the only bible was the Protestant King James Bible.[39]

In addition to making a mild "Christian nation" argument, the plaintiffs' attorneys embraced an older view of nonsectarianism, one that ran counter to the growing trend. By mid-century, the concept of nonsectarian instruction had evolved, such that the chief rationale of Bible reading was to teach morals, good character, and citizenship. Although Horace Mann believed that unmediated Bible reading would also expose children to those sublime, universal religious principles and create an awareness of God's love, religious devotion was a secondary objective, at least in theory. The state's duty was not to teach religious fealty, but only to demonstrate the connection between morality and religion and leave it to the child to take that step toward devotion if she so chose. While Mann's system promoted unmediated Bible reading to teach morals, it encour-aged schools to use the Bible in nondevotional ways, similar to what had been proposed in earlier negotiations between the Cincinnati school board and the Catholic leadership: to use those excerpts from the Bible that promoted morals and good character. Whether the board's resolution banning "religious instruction, and the reading of religious books, including the Holy Bible," prohibited this latter use was open to debate. The board's attorneys maintained that the resolution barred both devotional and ceremonial Bible reading but did not exclude readers that relied on biblical passages to teach morality. The plaintiffs' attorneys argued the opposite, that the resolution barred not only the Bible but all books with religious references. Chiefly, though, the plaintiffs argued something narrower: that the resolution forbade all teaching into *religious* principles, which the constitution required.[40]

Thus to prevail in their lawsuit—or at least under the legal theory they had selected—the plaintiffs' attorneys argued that the Cincinnati schools must use the Bible not merely to teach morality but to instill religious devotion. In parts of the nation this remained the prevailing practice, and many evangelical clergy urged that nonsectarian Bible reading lost all meaning if it was not devotional in character. But this practice was in decline, and fewer school districts justified their religious exercises on this ground. The plaintiffs therefore proposed more than a return to the legal status quo of Bible reading justified on moral grounds. As much as they cited to Mann for authority, the attorneys criticized rote Bible reading without note or comment that was increasingly common and central to Mann's system. Through Bible reading, a child should "comprehend that it teaches that he is an immortal being; that there is a Supreme being to whom he is accountable," Ramsey asserted. The moral truths found in the Bible will not only "qualify him for the various duties of society and citizenship" but also for "his spiritual welfare." Yet careful not to go too far, the plaintiffs insisted that this instruction could involve only those "elemental truths of religion that are common to all sects." The line that the plaintiffs sought to maintain was a difficult one indeed; it demonstrated the consternation among evangelicals that they were losing control over nonsectarian Bible reading.[41]

The practical implication of the plaintiffs' position was not lost on the school board attorneys, who used it to their advantage. George Hoadly argued that under the plaintiffs' interpretation of the state constitution, the prior practice of Bible reading in Cincinnati schools was likely insufficient. If the state had the duty to teach "little children...in religious truth, then it is the solemn duty of the State of Ohio to teach them all religious truth." The resulting exercises would be *more* sectarian, Hoadly insisted, rather than unsectarian, and they would violate the constitutional prohibition against sect preferences.[42] Chiefly, though, the board attorneys denied that the state constitution obligated schools to teach any form of religion. Stanley Matthews insisted the phrase from the Northwest Ordinance was hortatory and simply implied that "religion, morality, and knowledge" would be the outgrowth of an educated public. In contrast to the Ordinance, the board attorneys argued that the constitution's prohibition against religious preferences (and its declaration in Article VI, section 2, that no religious sect could control the public schools) meant that religious instruction was probably unconstitutional. Even if the judges were hesitant to reach that conclusion, Matthews asserted, "[t]here is nothing whatever to require, or even to justify the conclusion that any express instruction in religion should be given in the schools at all."[43]

As the plaintiffs' interpretation of "religion" had forced them to take a position beyond what was necessary to preserve Bible reading, the school board attorneys' interpretation of the constitution led them in the opposite direction: to challenge the notion of nonsectarian instruction itself. They knew that the court could find that Bible reading was indispensible for teaching morals without accepting the plaintiffs' broader religious argument. This led the board lawyers to argue that the reading of the Bible, even without note or comment was "an act of worship, precisely that; an act of Protestant worship." Even ceremonial religious exercises "no doubt teach[] to the child that the Holy Bible is a work *sui generis*, to be read only with a sense of awe and reverent devotion," George Hoadly claimed. The board attorneys also attacked the assumption underlying nonsectarianism: that school officials could identify and teach "precepts common to all Christian denominations." Because Protestants disagreed on matters of scriptural interpretation, there was no "residuum of a common factor" that was appropriate for the schools, Stanley Matthews asserted. Claims of a "broad Christianity" represented "an impossibility in fact as well as in law." Johann Stallo raised a related concern with nonsectarianism, that public school teachers "under whose direction the Bible is to be read, are not abstract, non-denominational Christians.... Each has his religious bias, of which he will find it difficult to divest himself when he comes to read the Bible." Stallo insisted that the inevitable "tendency of Bible reading, without note, [is] to lend itself to sectarian teaching."[44]

Paradoxically, the arguments of the plaintiffs' and board attorneys led them to the same conclusion: each side agreed that nonsectarianism, as it had developed by mid-century, was not workable. Both sides concurred that ceremonial reading of the Bible had to be devotional. For the plaintiffs, it was indispensible if it was to have meaning; for the defendants, it was inevitable. By so agreeing, both sides conceded that the concept of nondevotional Bible reading was a misnomer. And though the plaintiffs insisted that the absence of Bible reading would lead to infidelity, the board attorneys asserted that there was no reason why a "[school] system may not be purely secular." Accepted notions of nonsectarian instruction were caught in the middle.[45]

As for the broader constitutional question of the state's obligation to promote Christianity, the board attorneys did not rest on Stanley Matthews' argument that the language in the Northwest Ordinance was simply hortatory. They also disputed the plaintiffs' claims about the state's relationship to Christianity. Leaving no stone unturned, Stallo, the freethinker, equated the plaintiffs' claims with the horrors of the Inquisition and the colonial Blue Laws. "If Christianity is part of the common law," Stallo argued, "then, there must be certain duties enjoined upon the citizens, which are peculiarly Christian." Seemingly oblivious to the evangelical leanings of two of the judges, Stallo launched into a litany of how Christianity had historically persecuted dissent and stifled learning in order to perfect religious conformity. It was not true, he insisted, that Christianity "is the foundation of our republican institutions;" rather, it was at tension with those values. Stallo urged the judges not "[to] do violence to the spirit of our liberties, no less the words of our Constitution by deciding that Christianity—Protestant Christianity—being the law of the State, [that] the rights of Jews, Catholics, and freethinkers not be considered."[46]

In contrast to Stallo, Stanley Matthews offered a more restrained argument of why the state constitution prohibited a legal preference for Christianity. Matthews went line by line through the various provisions of the state constitution, demonstrating how they mandated no preference for one religious belief or for even religion over infidelity. More than mere toleration was required: "Every religious body and association, without respect to its name of faith, is included and all are expressly placed upon an equality as respects their civil rights," Matthews insisted. But Matthews went a step further, arguing that notions of religious freedom included also the right *not* to believe: the constitution protects "as a civil right, unbelief and disbelief—the neglect of worship and even the denial of worship." This was a novel argument for the time, one not required by the facts of the case. In his expansive view of church-state matters, requiring teachers to read from the Bible also amounted to a religious test as a qualification for office. Finally, Matthews maintained that the constitutional prohibition against any religion exercising control over the school fund—a provision that Protestants claimed barred funding of Catholic schools—applied with equal force to prohibit the Protestant domination of the public schools. In so doing, Matthews was one of the first non-Catholic lawyers to argue that the no-funding rule should be applied even-handedly. Matthews' overall view of church-state relations was distinctly Madisonian, one in which the state possessed secular duties and authority only. Neither the government nor the law was founded on Christian principles, and neither had a role in promoting religion in any form. Matthews did not expressly argue that Bible reading in the schools was akin to a religious establishment, likely because the state constitution did not contain a nonestablishment clause. But he was clear that the constitutional proscriptions were not limited to preventing religious coercion alone. They prohibited the state from exercising authority over religious matters in any form: the gravamen of the constitution was that "religion is a concern exclusively of the individual person—a matter between man and God—with which the State has no right whatever to interfere," Matthews stated. "No man can be treated as an outlaw because he is an infidel."[47]

The parties in *Minor v. Board of Education* offered starkly contrasting views about the relationship between church and state. While the plaintiffs sought to preserve nonsectarian instruction, their understanding of the practice—one that was justified by its religious goals and effects—was a version Horace Mann and other education reformers had renounced. In contrast, the school board attorneys' understanding of the state's educational duties repudiated Mann's benign brand of nonsectarianism as inherently sectarian. Not only did each side differ over the indispensability of religion for public education, they disagreed on the more fundamental issue of whether the government should promote religious fealty or protect religious customs. For the plaintiffs, the vague constitutional declarations, reinforced by majority religious preference and common law tradition, obligated the state to advance nonsectarian Christianity (i.e., Protestantism). This authority to promote Christianity was presumptive, limited only by the requirement that the state not prefer one denomination or violate rights of religious conscience. "For all purposes of the State and justice, the presumption in favor of the truth of the Bible, and of the religion of the Bible, is conclusive," George Sage argued. "[W]hatever the State can do in this regard without violating that right [of conscience], it not only may do, but is bound to do."[48] For the board attorneys, the presumption was reversed. Christianity held no special status, and the state lacked authority over religion: "I deny the proposition that the civil power had any authority in spiritual matters," Matthews argued, "or any right to found any civil enactments upon the ground that they are breaches of the Divine law."[49]

The counsel for the two sides had espoused distinctly contrasting views on religion and education, Christianity and the state. These were not merely legal arguments concocted by attorneys to advance their clients' interests. Rather, they represented two contrasting views about church and state that resonated with many people. The plaintiffs advocated an older, limited view of the effects of disestablishment, one that was losing sway in America. In contrast, the board attorneys promoted a more emergent perspective that sought to reconcile the nation's growing religious diversity with latent constitutional ideals that were only now being realized. Although each perspective had its own constituency, neither was representative of the nation as a whole. Whereas the average American might share aspects of both views on church and state, the point was that the nation was becoming too diverse for there to be an "average" American on religious issues. The arguments in *Minor* demonstrated the growing diversity of views among Americans about church-state matters.

Newspapers and journals from across the nation closely covered the trial. Protestant newspapers were chastened, but cautiously optimistic at the probable outcome. Protestants "should be thankful for the extreme course taken by the Cincinnati council," wrote the Methodist *Christian Advocate* upon the conclusion of the trial. "It will awaken a thousand pulpits, as it has the press of the land; and to be warned of approaching danger, among intelligent men is to be armed against it." The *New York Observer* concurred that the school board's action had renewed the public's interest in the issue of religious instruction: "the question of expelling the Bible from our common schools...is not going to be forgotten like a sensational event of a day. The principle involved is too grave and the results aimed at reach too far down into the life of our institutions."[50]

Although the court arguments concluded on December 3, the court took two months to render its decision. On February 15, 1870, by a vote of two-to-one with

Judge Alphonso Taft dissenting, the court enjoined the board's resolution removing Bible reading.[51]

Each of the judges wrote an opinion, and like the attorneys, they did not restrict themselves to the issue of the board's authority to exclude Bible reading but engaged in extensive discussions about the relationship between church and state. Also like the arguments of counsel, the judges offered widely divergent views of the state's authority or duty to promote Christianity generally and within the public schools in particular.

Overall, the court majority held that the board had exceeded its authority by enacting the resolution. That holding required the majority to consider the plaintiffs' central argument that the constitution obligated the state, and its public schools, to encourage religion. Judge Marcus Hagans, writing the lead opinion, acknowledged that a tension existed within the constitutional language: how could the state ensure that it did not prefer any religion but still fulfill the mandate that religion and morality was "essential to good government"? To resolve that dilemma, Hagans reached for a tie-breaker. Counsel had overlooked another constitutional provision directing the legislature to "pass suitable laws to protect every religious denomination in the peaceable enjoyment of its own mode of public worship." Even though the probable meaning of the provision was to allow churches to incorporate and prevent disturbances of their worship services, Hagans extrapolated that the clause constituted a "positive injunction" upon the state to do what it could to facilitate religious fealty generally. Since the same sentence expressly required the state "to encourage schools and the means of instruction," the injunction in the former clause must apply to the latter. After all, the legislature facilitated public worship in other ways that were not mandated by the constitution such as enacting Sunday laws and proclaiming days of thanksgiving. It could do no less with the public schools.[52]

Judge Hagans could have relied on his syllogism to resolve the case. Instead he, like the plaintiffs' attorneys, chose to explore the more fundamental relationship between Christianity and the state. Hagans concurred with the plaintiffs' underlying claim that the Bible reading ban conflicted with Ohio's status as a Christian state. Christianity was "the prevailing Religion in the State," Hagans wrote, and while the state could never establish any form of ecclesiasticism, "religion of some sort, was always a necessary adjunct of the State," especially among civilized nations.

> The framers of the Constitution felt that the moral sense must necessarily be regulated and controlled by the religious belief; and that whatever was opposed to religious belief, estimated by a Christian standard, and taking into consideration the welfare of the State, would be, in the highest degree, opposed to the general public sense, and have a direct tendency to undermine the moral support of the laws, and corrupt the community.

That indisputable fact, memorialized in the state constitution's declaration that "religion, morality and knowledge are essential to good government," did more than recognize the importance of religion; it obligated the state to teach children its "elementary principles." Without examining the effect of the board's resolutions, Hagans concluded that they "positively prohibit religious instruction, and...cut off the instrumentality by which those essentials to good government are cultivated." They had to be struck down.[53]

Judge Bellamy Storer, also writing an opinion for the majority, endorsed Hagans' discussion about Ohio's status as a "Christian state." He concurred that "society must be formed and sustained for a religious purpose." Yet Storer went further than Hagans to ground that purpose in evangelical Christianity. "Without the teachings of the Holy Scriptures there is, we believe, no unvarying standard of moral duty, no code of ethics which inculcates willing obedience to law, and establishes human governments upon the broad foundation of the will of God," Storer wrote. That certainty found confirmation in the constitution's declaration that religion was essential for good government. Based upon the traditions of the people, it was indisputable "that revealed religion, as it is made known in the Holy Scriptures, is that alone that is recognized by our Constitution." Because neither the state nor its auxiliaries could do anything that conflicted with the fundamental position of Christianity in republican society, the school board's decision was *ultra vires* and void.[54]

Storer also rejected Stanley Matthews' argument that reading from the King James Bible was necessarily sectarian. His response was two-fold. First, both Catholics and Jews recognized the Bible as the "Word of God," Storer retorted, so how could it be considered sectarian? "What we understand by sectarianism is the work of man, not of the Almighty." By arguing nothing in the Bible was sectarian, only the meanings people attributed to its passages, Storer fully embraced the notion of nonsectarianism, albeit of a more evangelical variety. Under this theory, the Bible readings could be used to teach children not simply morals but also "the idea of obedience to God." Storer also argued that the purpose of the religious exercises had been merely to "enlighten, if not improve, the moral faculties." Now down-playing the devotional quality of the Bible, Storer stated he could not accept that "the mere reading of the Scriptures without note or comment, ... [could] be deemed an act of worship." Although the two theories were at tension with each other, both supported the reading of Bible passages without infringing upon conscience rights of Catholic and Jewish students. And because Bible reading was inherently nonsectarian, it was consistent with the no-preference clause of the constitution.[55]

Judge Alphonso Taft (figure 3.1) dissented from the holding, voting that the school board had authority to exclude the Bible from the public schools. Quickly disposing with the merits of the case, Taft pointed out that state law awarded "complete discretionary power" to school boards to manage their schools. The court should overturn the school board's resolution only if contravened clear state law, Taft declared. He insisted that the constitutional references to "religion, morality and knowledge" did not mandate that schools teach religion but merely recognized that religion and morality "would be promoted by encouraging schools and the means of instruction generally." Interpreted in this manner, the declaration was consistent with the constitution's clause preventing religious preferences. Not only did the board's resolution not violate the constitution or evince hostility toward religion, Taft wrote, it indicated "rather a neutrality toward all sects, which would not be otherwise maintained, and which had become essential to religious peace."[56]

Like his colleagues, Taft could have written a short opinion, one that upheld the board's authority by reconciling the two seemingly contradictory constitutional provisions. But he also decided to offer his understanding of the state's relationship to Christianity. This held greater risks for Taft than it did for judges Hagans and Storer. After all, public opinion favored retaining the religious practices. Many Protestants, and even some Catholics, agreed with the majority's affirmation of a mutually reinforcing relationship between government and religion. For a religious liberal such as Taft to publicly dispute such views carried grave political risks. Taft, though, seemed drawn to the issue, if for no other reason than to rebut the broad claims of his fellow judges. But Taft also had something to say, and he knew that his opinion would be widely read and debated. He was correct, as it is one of the more remarkable judicial opinions of the nineteenth century.

Figure 3.1 Judge Alphonso Taft. The Ohio Historical Society.

Taft went directly to the heart of the plaintiffs' claim: the "idea that the Christian religion was entitled to any higher or other privileges, before the law." The state supreme court had held that Christianity was neither recognized nor specially protected by state law, Taft reminded his colleagues. Neither the plaintiffs nor the judges could "escape the force of the ... Bill of Rights by assuming that the Protestant Christian religion was intended in the Bill of Rights, and that the sects of Protestant Christians *only* were, therefore entitled to protection," Taft wrote. "Between all forms of religious belief the State knows no difference." Referring to the legacy of Roger Williams, Taft asserted that the constitutional "ideal is absolute equality before the law, of all religious opinions and sects." The notion that Christianity was somehow incorporated into the nation's legal system, and entitled to the state's patronage, was overridden by constitutional principles. Fully disposing of the Christian nation maxim, Taft concluded:

> It is, therefore, an entire mistake, in my opinion, to assert, that the Protestant Christian religion has been so identified with the history and government of our State or country ... or that when the Bill of Rights says that "religion, morality and knowledge being essential to good government," it means the Protestant Christian religion. That would be a preference, which the same section expressly disclaims, and emphatically forbids.[57]

Taft also denied that Protestantism was entitled to special treatment because it was the dominant faith: "No sect can, because it includes a majority of a community or a majority of the citizens of the State, claim any preference whatever." By protecting freedom of conscience and prohibiting religious preferences, the bill of rights required that the government be neutral toward religious matters: "while protecting all, it prefers none, and it disparages none." To hold that Protestants "are entitled to have their mode of worship and their bible used in the common schools," Taft concluded, "is to hold to the union of Church and State, however we may repudiate and reproach the name."[58]

Taft's understanding of constitutional principles led him to refute that ceremonial readings from the King James Bible were nonsectarian. Pursuant to the "no-compelled support" and "no-preference" clauses of the constitution, "[a]ll sectarian forms of sectarian worship are clearly excluded ... from the public school, which are maintained at the expense of all, and for the equal benefit of all," Taft wrote. "What then is the character of the morning exercise of reading the passage in the Bible, and appropriate singing in the schools daily?" Answering his own rhetorical question in a forceful passage, Taft wrote: "I think we are bound to regard it as both an act of worship, and a lesson of religious instruction.... I can not doubt, therefore, that the use of the Bible with the appropriate singing ... was and is sectarian. It is Protestant worship. And its use is a symbol of Protestant supremacy in the schools, and as such offensive to Catholics and to Jews."

Although Taft's references were to the religious exercises that had taken place in the Cincinnati schools, those practices had been some of the more permissive in the country, mandating the readings be without note or comment and allowing dissenting students to read their own religious texts or be excluded from the exercises. If Taft considered these exercises to be sectarian, then all readings from the King James Bible in the public schools were sectarian. But the implications of Taft's opinion went one step further: because Bible reading was inherently sectarian, not only was the school board correct in abolishing the religious exercises, their action was mandated by the state bill of rights. Probably giving the board members more credit than they deserved, Taft insisted that in enacting its resolution, the school board had "intended to carry out the constitutional ideas contained in the seventh section of the Bill of Rights." Taft left no doubt that he equated Bible reading with a constitutional violation, something that even the school attorneys had hesitated in doing.[59]

Taft's opinion was path-breaking for its time, though he had built on ideas that judges had been developing for decades. Taft's chief contribution was to articulate that government patronage of Christianity generally, and religious exercises in the public schools, raised constitutional questions. For Taft, both were inconsistent with separation of church and state. And Taft clearly indicated what that meant. Government was to be secular, and was obligated to promote religious equality over protecting the practices of the religious majority. This was a very modern notion of individual rights: that the constitution was to protect the rights of religious minorities over the preferences of the religious majority. "Absolute" religious equality was the ideal to strive toward. Taft also identified government neutrality toward religion as a constitutional principle: "The government is neutral, and, while protecting all, it prefers none, and *disparages* none." Finally, Taft affirmed that religious conscience was a distinct fundamental right protected by the constitution. Both Catholics and Jews had legitimate conscientious objections to the Protestant exercises. More important, those claims had to be viewed from the perspective of the dissenters, not from that of the religious majority that insisted that Bible reading was nonobjectionable. Taft sympathized with Catholics about being forced to support what "must be fairly held to be *Protestant schools*," yet he insisted that the solution was to make the schools fully secular. A distribution of taxes to support parochial schools "can not be done under the Constitution."[60]

Overall, Taft's opinion was the most comprehensive and articulate exposition of church-state principles to date. In it, he identified religious equality, neutrality, noncoercion, and nonsupport as distinct core principles underlying religious liberty and separation of church and state. He also asserted that these constitutional principles required the government and its institutions be secular, though not hostile to religious belief. His opinion, which the United States Supreme Court would quote in its seminal 1963 school prayer decision, laid the foundation for church-state jurisprudence for years to come.[61]

For the immediate time, thought, Taft's position had lost. Superior in its analysis, it failed to convince his colleagues who were wedded to the powerful presumptions that imbued nonsectarian education. The court majority made the injunction permanent, which prohibited the board from enforcing its resolutions. News reports overall applauded the majority holding. The *New York Tribune* called Judge Hagan's lead opinion "able," while the Methodist *Christian Advocate* extolled that Protestant Ohio was again "safe, for a while, at least." Taft, in contrast, was branded the "Unitarian Atheist" for his opinion, with newspapers foretelling the end of his political career.[62] Despite the sigh of relief from the Protestant and mainstream press, few observers believed that the Superior Court decision had resolved the contentious School Question, in Cincinnati or elsewhere. The Democratic-leaning *Tribune* expressed alarm that the nation could "soon be plunged into a whirlpool of fierce contention between zealous Catholics and equally zealous Protestants, regarding Schools and School Taxes." Its Republican counterpart, the *New York Times*, declared with bravado that "[i]f we must have this fight, by all means lets us have it quickly, and get done with it."[63] Other commentators put the issue in larger terms. The *New York Observer* speculated that "the question of expelling the Bible from our common schools . . . is not going to be forgotten like a sensational event of a day. The principle involved is too grave and the results aimed at reach too far down into the life of our institutions." *The Independent* concurred, noting that "[n]othing is more evident than that the school question is now fully launched upon the public." The controversy had now "become a living necessity of the times." Few believed that the battle for the soul of America's public schools had been resolved.[64]

The "Great Debate"

The controversy over Bible reading was, of course, far from being over. The school board appealed the decision to the Ohio Supreme Court which, after receiving briefing by the parties, sat on the case for three years. While people awaited the outcome of the Cincinnati decision, controversy over the School Question only intensified. Writing in January 1870, *Putman's Monthly Magazine* observed that "There seems to be dawning upon the country anew, a question that has more than once been furiously battled over already, that of the Bible in Public Schools." Skirmishes erupted throughout the Northeast and Midwest. In June 1872, the State Superintendent of the New York public schools ordered school boards on Long Island to suspend the practice of daily Bible readings and religious exercises in response to Catholic complaints. Similar moves were under way in Chicago, Buffalo, Rochester, and in other northern cities as more public schools dropped required religious exercises. Not all conflicts were resolved smoothly. In Philadelphia, the school board tabled a proposal to end religious exercises following a public outcry. And in 1873, several New Jersey schools expelled Catholic

students for refusing to take part in religious exercises, exacerbating tensions between Catholic parents and Protestant board members. At the same time, Catholic
officials in New York and Illinois, among other states, continued with their efforts
for state financial support for their orphanages and schools, further eliciting the
ire of evangelical Protestants. It was, as the *Atlantic Monthly* characterized, like a
"new storm is fairly upon us."[65]

Over the ensuing six years the nation engaged in what may rightly be called a
Great Church-State Debate. Initially, commentators focused on the Bible reading
issue at the expense of the funding question, a fact not surprising considering the
attention given to the Cincinnati case. Several aspects of this debate over the
School Question are significant. First, participants viewed the conflict not only in
religious terms but as implicating constitutional or legal issues as well. Also
significant was the variety of perspectives represented in the debate. Division did
not break down simply along Protestant, pro-Bible reading, and Catholic, anti-
Bible reading, lines. The Protestant position splintered into several camps,
although the divisions remained fluid: (1) evangelicals and nativists who insisted
on devotional instruction while they decried the machinations of the Catholic
Church; (2) moderate Protestants who sought to retain the status quo of unmediated Bible reading for the purpose of moral instruction; (3) moderate (and a few
evangelical) Protestants who called for expelling Bible reading primarily to silence
Catholic claims of Protestant bias in the schools; and (4) liberal and moderate
Protestants who sought to expel Bible reading on grounds of fairness for the
Catholic position or out of constitutional convictions. Catholic leaders, although
of one mind in opposing the Protestant exercises, varied in their condemnation of
public education and their willingness to support the assimilation of immigrants
into American culture. Then there was a cacophony of groups generally opposed
to religious exercises and, likely, all uses of the Bible: freethinkers, secular newspapers, professional educators, and Jews. Overlaying these divisions was a variety
of strange alignments on the various issues encompassed by the School Question.
As one journal noted, Catholics and freethinkers were united in banishing the
Bible, evangelicals and freethinkers were united in opposing Catholic power, and
Protestants and Catholics were united against freethinker efforts to secularize
education. "Seldom if ever, has any question arrayed the different classes of individuals so strangely as that which pertains to our common schools."[66]

The public debate over the School Question also revealed that people understood that the controversy was not limited to the immediate questions of Bible
reading or parochial school funding, but that it encompassed larger issues about
the role of public education and the proper relationship between religion and the
state in a republican society. *Putman's Magazine* noted that while Bible reading
was being played out on a local level, "it is really a national question." "Nor is the
mere question of the Bible in Schools the real one at issue." Rather, "the existence
of the American common school system" was at stake. Columnist Samuel T. Spear
of *The Independent* concurred, writing that the controversy "bring[s] to the sur-

face the whole subject of Church and State, civil government and religion, in their relations to each other."[67]

As would be expected, the bulk of commentary came from evangelical leaders who, in sermons and articles, defended Bible reading while they condemned the funding of religious schooling. This group differed from those Protestants who supported the status quo of unmediated Bible reading, and they insisted that Protestants had already surrendered too much ground on the issue. "The trouble plainly" with the status quo, wrote Reverend D. Gans, "lies with us Protestants. We want the Bible in the school, and yet we do not want it there. We want it as a book, but do not want it in its positive teaching, ... in its doctrine." These conservatives believed that the only way to retain nonsectarian public education and stave off Catholic challenges was to return the practices to their religious roots. Accommodating Catholics was not only fruitless, public education was already on the road to secularism and infidelity. Not surprising, much of this commentary was reactive, alarmist, and anti-Catholic in tone: America was founded as a Christian (i.e., Protestant) nation; Christianity and republicanism were mutually reinforcing and interdependent; the Bible (i.e., King James version) was the centerpiece of Christian culture and the foundation of morals; the public schools were Protestant institutions with a responsibility of instilling religious devotion and republican virtues in children; only Bible reading could achieve that level of religious devotion and civic morality upon which the nation's existence depended; and, Bible reading was under attack from a cabal of Jesuits, atheists, and foreigners.[68]

Much of this commentary relied on inflamed rhetoric and hyperbole. But occasionally, the sermons and articles placed the controversy in larger church-state terms that revealed evangelical attitudes about the nation's religious identity and its obligation to promote religion:

> Since this government is a Protestant Christian government, the law of self-preservation requires that it should recognize God, in its official acts and in its institutions, and see that the principles of its religion are in some way made known to all the subjects of the government.[69]

Other sermons and articles employed Christian nation rhetoric made popular over a generation earlier: the "Republic was founded by Protestants; its constitution and laws, its theory of government, are based on the principles of the Word of Truth." While most commentators breezed over constitutional questions about religious equality and nonestablishment, a handful sought to reconcile their views with constitutional language. Commonly, these evangelicals interpreted such provisions as forbidding only preferential treatment of one Christian or Protestant denomination over another. The "Constitution guards against any union of church and state, or any church establishment, dependent on the State," wrote Presbyterian minister Daniel Rice. This meant that the state "refuses to identify itself with any one sect or denomination more than another." But disestablishment "does not mean, and was never intended to mean, an expulsion of religion." Thus to promote Christianity generally, and nonsectarian religious principles in the public schools, did not cross that line into sect preference. "We cannot conceive it possible to establish a state religion," concurred Presbyterian George R. Rudd, "unless it be in connection with come creed, confession, sect or ecclesiastical organization." Essentially, because the nation was "built on the foundations of the Christian religion" (i.e., Protestantism), it was not required to cast aside its religious obligations simply because Catholics, Jews and infidels claimed that Bible reading contravened their rights of conscience. "If, just as the nation was established to be a Republican nation . . . *founded on Christianity*, then it is no more unconstitutional for it to teach Christianity in its schools . . . and [it] no more infringes liberty of conscience, than it does to teach its civil polity as a Republic."[70]

A common theme in these writings was that Bible reading, and the nation's reinforcing relationship between Protestantism and republicanism, were under attack by Catholics, infidels, and misguided liberal Protestants. "The objection to the use of the Bible in our schools comes from infidels and Roman Catholics," charged Harvard's Andrew P. Peabody in an 1870 sermon. Despite the two groups being at polar opposites, it was "a notorious fact that the infidel leaders and the free religionists on one hand, and the Romanists on the other, have acted together under the agreement that, if the latter would render their aid in excluding the Bible from the schools, the former would give their votes and influence in behalf of special appropriations for sectarian schools," Peabody claimed. To make matters worse, liberal Protestants now advocated the Bible's expulsion. "[D]oes it not stagger human belief that these same ministers join with Romanists and Atheists to purge our educational system of all moral and religious influences?" charged Presbyterian George Rudd. Not only was their complicity a "mournful, humiliating fact," liberal Protestants misled people with their "illogical inference: *that the reading of the Christian Scriptures in our public schools is equivalent to a state or established religion.*"[71]

Conservative evangelicals directed the bulk of their vitriol, however, toward the Catholic hierarchy for its "uncompromising hostility to public schools." "What the Catholic Church seeks is power," claimed Boston's Warren H. Cudworth. "Their Church condemns free schools, condemns the free press, condemns a free Bible . . . condemns free thought and free speech, and about everything else that is free, including railroads and telegraphs because they lessen papal power." The truth was, wrote another Protestant minister, is that a "system of public schools, under the control of the state, either with or without the Bible is an abomination to the Catholic authorities." And, it followed, if religious instruction did not constitute an establishment, then the "expulsion of the Bible at the demand of Romanism makes the schools a Roman Catholic establishment."[72]

At the end of the day, most evangelicals did not advocate returning to the status quo of rote, nondevotional Bible reading. Bible reading should be more than merely a means for instilling universal moral principles; the ends should be devotional, as well. "The Bible should be used devotionally, furnishing language for prayer and praise, responsive reading and singing." Exercises should "excite and stimulate the feelings of devotion and worship" in children, as well as the "righteous" and "great principles of self-government." Despite the emotionalism of the moment and the temptation to use inflamed rhetoric to capitalize on a highly charged issue, evangelicals appreciated that a much larger issue was at stake: the religious character of education and the religious soul of the nation.[73]

Not all evangelicals resorted to alarmist polemics when defending Bible reading. Three scholars with impeccable evangelical credentials, Tayler Lewis of Princeton, J. H. Seelye of *Bibliotheca Sacra*, and Lyman Atwater of the *Presbyterian Quarterly and Princeton Review* all offered reasoned commentary. All three were as committed to retaining devotional Bible reading as their evangelical colleagues. Education "divorced from morality and religion, becomes shrunken, distorted, and monstrous," remarked Atwater in April 1870. For Atwater and the others, it was "religious and moral truths, ideas of the infinite and perfect, God and eternity, that most quicken, expand, and sublime the human, especially the youthful, intellect." Although they agreed that Catholics and freethinkers posed a threat to religious-based education, they perceived the controversy as being more complex. A variety of challenges were bombarding America's institutions and its Protestant culture: Darwinism, biblical criticism, industrialization, urbanization, and a rapidly expanding foreign immigration. Compounding these factors, a growing secularism, brought on by the appeal of materialism, was making a serious challenge to religion, reinforcing a sense that religion was less relevant to modern society. Many evangelicals believed the nation was experiencing a "spiritual crisis;" the School Question was but a cause and effect of this greater threat. As a result, evangelical scholars directed much of their scorn toward liberal Protestants like Henry Ward Beecher and Samuel Spear who appeared ready to surrender on core principles. Their willingness to capitulate to Catholics on the School Question would bring about the total secularization of American education, which to evangelicals, would be catastrophic for the nation's future.[74]

At the crux of the School Question was whether the nation's institutions and functions should be secular. Could the state be nonreligious without being antireligious? Lewis, Seelye, and Atwater all answered "no." Claims that the state could be neutral toward religion were "false," "specious and misleading," Lewis insisted. The state was the aggregate of its citizens who were moral beings, Lewis maintained, so it "must have a theology—or it must favor atheism." Atwater echoed the belief that "[n]ot to give us any religion, or morality radicated in religious sanctions, is to give us immorality and irreligion. Here neutrality is impossible."[75] In making this argument, the scholars generally eschewed Christian nation hyperbole and proof-texting. For them, the relation of the state to Christianity was both derivative from individual believers and direct through a covenant between a Christian people and their God. In an article in *Bibliotheca*

Sacra, Seelye claimed that "[t]here is a spirituality which is the man; and it this same spirituality, in a broader sense, which is the State.... All this brings out the intimate and necessary connection of the State with religion: the two grow out of the same element in the human soul." What this meant for church-state purposes, was that:

> Public law, if it shall be established and defined, must spring from the same spirituality where religion itself has its seat. Religion, in order to its full exhibition, needs a social relation among men[,] and the State, in order to its valid existence, needs a religious condition in man. The state cannot be conceived without religion; for it is the essence of the State to be an arrangement and exposition of ethical principles.

This did not mean that religion was a proper end of the state, however. "Religion may be employed by the State as a means to secure the end of civilization and freedom," Seelye wrote, "but these latter may never be yielded to subserve any religious advancement." When the state acted with religious goals in mind, other than to support the spirituality of its citizens, then it "has gone beyond its true bounds, and altogether transcended its legitimate authority." At the same time, Lewis affirmed, the government "cannot treat Christianity as a nonentity. It cannot legislate for a Christian people as though it had no religion.... the state must be Christian or anti-Christian." Under this view, the state must recognize its Christian bonds and support an environment for churches to pursue their mission. But the state was not to advance religion itself.[76]

As for those constitutional provisions forbidding the state from supporting or preferring religion, they had to be read with an understanding of that "supreme element of the national life, lying deeper than [the] constitutions," Atwater wrote. The "unsectarian character of our civil constitutions does not mean atheism or infidelity, or the disowning of our common Christianity." Lewis agreed: the Constitution's authority was "divinely ordained." But he was more insistent about what should control in matters of apparent conflict: "No plea of the Constitution...can avail us here. God has established a higher law, a higher constitution of humanity, of society, of political life; and this constitution we must [obey]." In the end, this arrangement authorized, if not obligated, the state to support the peoples' spiritual needs through devotional religious exercises in its schools. "[W]hat we insist on first and last is, that the Bible, the Lord's Prayer, the recognition and assertion of fundamental moral and religious truth shall not be *prohibited* in our public schools on any pretext whatsoever."[77]

Offering a different perspective were moderate Protestants and educators who supported the status quo of unmediated Bible reading. These generally were disciples of Horace Mann and Henry Barnard who embraced "the American idea that unsectarian practical Christian education and morality [are] the corner-stone[s] of the true American education in the citizen and the State itself." These moderates supported religious exercises in the schools chiefly for instilling morals and for character development. They believed that the great universal moral principles were found in the Bible: "as a text-book in morals, the Bible is incomparable." They also embraced the Bible as an unsurpassed work of literature, history, and poetry. "The human race could better spare all other books than be deprived of the Bible." Despite their unflagging belief in nonsectarianism, advocates of unmediated Bible reading understood that the practices raised church-state issues. The "question how far the religious teaching of the Bible can be carried, consistently with the general principles of free government, presents some difficulties," acknowledged A. E. Rankin of the Vermont Board of Education. But because the Bible was not used to teach religious doctrine or impose devotion on children—at least in theory—most saw no constitutional conflict. Because the state was using the Bible to teach morals, it was not advancing religion: "Religious worship is but an incident to the school," Rankin asserted. This view, increasingly under siege from all sides, was still supported by a large number of Protestants and educators who put their faith in nonsectarianism as the solution to the School Question.[78]

A third Protestant perspective advocated abolishing all religious exercises in the public schools, including the nondevotional use of the Bible. Joined by an increasingly vocal secular press, this small but influential group of religious liberals was breaking with the status quo. Leading the way was Henry Ward Beecher, who had been out front as the controversy in Cincinnati unfolded in the fall of 1869. As discussed, Beecher advocated removing religious exercises chiefly on pragmatic grounds, but also out of empathy for Catholic conscience claims. Beecher called on the common school to be a "civil and not religious institution," though he stopped short of demanding that it should be "secular." Schools should be "free and common" and "unsectarian," Beecher claimed. Beecher also split from many Protestants by asserting that "[b]ecause the common school is not a religious institution, it is not therefore irreligious or unreligious." Merely because the schools did not teach children religion did not mean they would be "brought up infidels." Schools would continue to teach morals through readers, but leaving religious instruction to the family and the church. This was the only solution to the School Question and to resolving growing religious dissention. And, as Beecher's *Christian Union* insisted, it was the "Foolish Protestants" who had fallen into the Catholic trap by insisting on Bible reading. The "most extraordinary accession which the Roman party has received is that of the Protestant zealots who are determined to force the Bible into our schools, not perceiving that *that* gives up the whole question."[79]

If Beecher was the symbolic leader of Protestant liberals, Presbyterian minister Samuel Spear, a columnist for the *Independent*, was the most articulate advocate for removing religious exercises from the public schools. Like Beecher, Spear supported the Cincinnati school board's resolution. Also like Beecher, Spear viewed the issue as implicating matters of conscience, and he concurred that religious exercises gave Catholics an argument for sharing in the public school funds. Spear went further that Beecher, however, by articulating a comprehensive view of church-state relations, one that required both a secular state and a secular school system. The first and "fatal mistake consists in committing religion to the civil power at all," Spear remarked in a sermon on April 27, 1870. If Americans accepted "the democratic theory of the State," he insisted, then we must "confine its sphere exclusively to *secular* and *temporal* functions." Spear disputed that anything in the nation's history or founding documents had established a "*Christian* government." There was "not a single sentence in the Constitution to give the least countenance to the idea that Christianity or any other system of religion is any part of the law of this country," Spear asserted. Such claims by Bible reading advocates were "unsupported;" the federal and state governments were "neither Christian nor anti-Christian, but simply democratic and republican." The nation's expanding religious diversity, "all of whom stand, in legal estimation, on exactly the same basis...absolute *citizen-equality*," only reinforced the ideal of a secular state. Spear's understanding of the Constitution was sophisticated for the time. The document contained not merely *principles* upon which the nation operated; it also established constitutional *rights* that could enjoin the government when it acted in a religious manner. And these rights were superior to the democratic process: "The majority-conscience is as really bound by the end of civil government as the minority conscience."[80]

What this theory meant for Bible reading in the schools was that the state lacked authority to require its use. Not only did Bible reading violate rights of conscience and religious equality, it contravened the true role of the public school as a secular institution. Here, Spear went further than Beecher to call for the compete secularization of public education. "The impregnable ground is to make the Public School *wholly secular*, and remit to the Sabbath School, the Church, and the family, the specific work of religious education." (By 1875, Beecher came around to Spear's position, writing that the common school "is secular, it must be kept secular, and it must be guarded against anything that shall make it other than secular.")[81] Spear chastised Protestant moderates who insisted on nonsectarian religious instruction or the Bible's use as a "common reading book." They were being dishonest or insincere: "The theory of Bible reading in the Public School is founded upon the fact that it is a *religious* book." Here he agreed with conservative evangelicals:

> Why insist on the perfunctory form...Why call it religious teaching, and yet, as is confessedly the fact, restrict it within the narrowest limits possible, without abandoning the whole idea. Why so much zeal about the form and comparatively so little about the substance?[82]

Spear charged that Bible reading advocates were either "very poor reasoners" or simply "bigots." Spear also rejected using the Bible to teach morals, literature, grammar, or history; he disputed using readers comprised of Biblical passages.

Some public official would have to do "this work," which raised it own constitutional concern. "By what authority shall the selections be made, and from which of the two versions shall it be made? What part of the Bible shall thus be selected?" Spear asked. Spear thus offered multiple reasons that Bible reading violated constitutional norms. First, the government was secular, not aligned with Christianity or any other religion, and it lacked all authority over religious matters. The constitutions guaranteed religious equality, not preference for Christianity and toleration for the rest. Bible reading also violated the rights of conscience of Catholics, Jews, atheists, and other non-Christians. And Bible reading forced all Catholics and religious minorities to provide tax support for instruction in another faith, an additional violation of conscience rights. To use the Bible was to "create a religious establishment in these schools at public expense."[83]

As Spear's critique of Bible reading demonstrates, religious liberals were more willing than their Protestant counterparts to rely on both general constitutional principles and express constitutional provisions. They believed that the no-establishment and no-preference clauses contained in the various constitutions were dormant sources of expansive rights. Writing at the same time as Spear, Professor H. L. Wayland of Franklin College insisted that constitutional principles demanded "absolute religious equality" in the schools, while Indiana Unitarian minister Nathaniel Seaver argued that policies requiring Bible reading were laws "'respecting,' i.e., favoring or recognizing an 'establishment' of religion." Bible reading was "religious instruction," Seaver insisted, and because the state constitution also prohibited the compelled support of any minister or ministry, "[s]uch instruction is ministry and unconstitutional." Like Spear, Seaver believed that "Constitutionally the schools must be strictly secular." Thus Spear and other liberals opposed Bible reading not chiefly as a way to deflect Catholic claims to a share of the school fund; on the contrary, they believed that the rule against funding religious education applied equally to all schools, public and religious. Their commitment to church-state separation and secular education was based on principle: "the intention of the framers of the constitution evidently was to perpetuate through all time an impassable barrier between the union of Church and State," wrote attorney G. W. Collings. Because Bible reading constituted religious teaching and worship, it "is in violation of these Constitutional prohibitions in both their letter and spirit." In the end, the liberals viewed the controversy over Bible reading as implicating constitutional norms that transcended the immediate conflict.[84]

"Allied" with Beecher, Spear and other liberals were two disparate factions. The first were mainstream Protestants who, while supporting Bible reading in principle, were willing to forego the practices to protect the public schools. Representing this position was the Methodist *Christian Advocate*, which reaffirmed its conviction that unmediated Bible readings and "a brief, unsectarian, opening prayer, should certainly be inoffensive." But Protestants must be willing to "omit even these, rather than have the common-school system broken to pieces." The *Methodist* concurred that it "would rather omit these [practices] than endanger the system by farther intrusions of religious forms or lessons which might be obnoxious to honest religious prejudice." Holders of this perspective saw no constitutional bar to nonsectarian religious exercises, though they agreed the constitution constrained sectarian instruction, however that was to be defined. They also concurred generally with their conservative brethren that the state was not required to be neutral with respect to advancing religious principles, only that neutrality here made practical sense. Yet these Protestant pragmatists increasingly acknowledged Catholic claims of conscience. A satisfactory solution should have been to dismiss objecting students from participating in the exercises. But such accommodations had not quieted Catholic complaints, so in order to preserve the common schools and prevent a division of school funds, they were willing to exclude the Bible, hopefully to be replaced by character text books and supplemented by the church and Sunday schools. To not do so risked too much: "Shall we disarm our opponents, and render our common school system secure, by waiving the reading of the Bible in our schools," asked the Presbyterian *Herald*, "or shall we bigotedly insist upon its continuance and *risk all the consequences*?"[85]

A second allied faction, quite distant from the pragmatic Protestants, comprised Jews and committed secularists. Though distinct, the Jews and secularists—such as members of the emerging Liberal Leagues—also opposed nonsectarian Bible reading and the public funding of Catholic schools. In contrast to the pragmatic Protestants, they desired not only to diffuse the conscience claims of Catholics but also to protect the conscience rights of all religious dissenters, Jews and nonbelievers alike. "Equality and not simple toleration is the basis of all our republican institutions," declared the *Jewish Times*. "[H]ence no discrimination in favor of one and to the prejudice of another class should be suffered to continue." These principles required an entirely secular system of public education. "Our public schools are not intended for religious establishments. They are created for the specific purpose of diffusing among the people useful knowledge," stated the *Jewish Times*, though it agreed that schools should still teach moral values.[86] The growing community of freethinkers and religious skeptics concurred that religious and moral education could be separated. A system of secular schools did not mean that children could not be "morally educated," declared Damon Y. Kilgore of the Liberal League of Philadelphia. But moral instruction should never rely on the Bible, which was an "obstacle to the...intellectual progression of mankind." Like Spear and the religious liberals, Kilgore saw the issue in constitutional terms, asserting that Bible reading "violates the American idea of complete separation of Church and State, as well as the letter and spirit of our State Constitution." Because this was a constitutional matter, Kilgore stated, it was not "a question of expediency to be settled by majorities, but rather one of principle involving rights."[87]

The emergent secularist and skeptic community of the 1870s held diverse views, however. Some secularists went further than Kilgore, disclaiming that the state had any role in making its citizenry moral:

The state is not bound to provide its children with moral and religious principles. It is bound to provide them with just and equal laws, and to leave their moral and religious culture to the benign social atmosphere thus engendered. The state has absolutely no responsibility for the spiritual welfare of its subjects, but only for their material welfare.... The state is simply indifferent to the morals of its subjects, provided they do not result in any actual injury to person or property.[88]

In addition, secularists disagreed among themselves whether there was any role for the Bible in public school education. At times, this disagreement led to internal conflict. Octavius B. Frothingham had founded the Free Religious Association in 1867 to promote a form of theistic humanism and religious inquiry free from doctrinal constraints. Three years later, the Association established a journal, *The Index*, edited by Francis E. Abbot, which "quickly became the most distinguished heterodox paper in America."[89] In a June 17, 1875 article in *The Index*, Frothingham and A.W. Stevens, the paper's associate editor, advocated using the Bible as a textbook for literature and ancient history. In an editorial the following week Francis Abbot chastised his colleagues. To use the Bible as a textbook would satisfy no one while it would anger both Protestants and Catholics who perceive the scriptures as divine revelation, Abbot wrote. Abbot charged that his colleagues failed to see that "they propose to retain it on terms which are the greatest possible insult to the sincere faith of Christian believers." He insisted that "nothing less than a total exclusion of the Bible is what the 'absolute secularization of the schools' must mean."

> To use the Bible merely as a text-book would be to use it as the symbol of the political supremacy of religious rationalism. The principle of secular government condemns that supremacy just as much as it condemns the supremacy of Catholicism or Protestantism. The secular idea requires that just so long as the Bible is the subject of religious controversy among living sects or parties...it shall be totally excluded from the public schools.[90]

The disagreement among the freethinkers festered, and three months after the editorial appeared, Stevens resigned from his position at *The Index*. Consensus on the role of the Bible was even wanting among religious skeptics.[91]

Finally, standing at the opposite end of the spectrum from the skeptics were the Catholic hierarchy and Catholic press. Since the 1852 Plenary Council, the Catholics had been more united and defiant in their position, opposing all forms of Protestant religious exercises in the public schools while seeking a share of public school funds for their parochial schools. One Boston Catholic priest stated the position succinctly: "Catholics would not be satisfied with the public schools even if the Protestant Bible and every vestige of religious teaching were banished from them.... [Catholics] will not be taxed either for educating the children of Protestants, or for having their own children educated in schools under Protestant control."[92] This unequivocal stance belied the diversity of thought among Catholics in how best to achieve those goals. The conflicts of the 1840s–1850s had radicalized some Catholic clergy, such as Cincinnati Archbishop Purcell. They now argued there was no room for Catholic compromise and that further Protestant accommodation was not likely. They attacked the public schools as both godless and sectarian in their Protestantism. Striking at the heart of common schooling, they denied that the state had any role in the education of children. At times, their rhetoric inflamed the debate and, in so doing, encouraged Protestant recalcitrance and reinforced conspiracy theories. Following the Cincinnati court hearing, but before the decision, Archbishop John Hughes' *Freeman's Journal* issued a missive declaring that Catholics "do not want to be taxed for Protestant, or for godless schools. Let the public-school system go to where it came from—the devil." Using similarly incendiary language, Purcell's *Catholic Telegraph* asserted that: "It will be a glorious day for Catholics in this country when, under the laws of justice and morality, our school system shall be shivered to pieces. Until then, modern paganism will triumph." Such comments, while made within a particular context, only inflamed the debate. Protestant and nativist newspapers reprinted the remarks as evidence of Catholic enmity toward public education and their unwillingness to assimilate into American culture.[93]

Other Catholics viewed such rhetoric as counterproductive. Although Catholics had not participated actively in the events in Cincinnati, the church had endured much of the blame, and not solely from nativist and stalwart Protestant newspapers. In April, 1870, Orestes Brownson wrote a detailed exposition on the subject for the *Catholic World* in an effort to explain the Catholic position on the School Question. Catholics opposed Protestant exercises, Brownson wrote, not simply because they exposed Catholic children to alien religious doctrines and violated their conscience rights, but also because the exercises by necessity excluded Catholicism. Catholics valued "no education that is divorced from religion and religious culture." As a result, Catholics sincerely opposed efforts "to make the schools either purely Protestant or purely secular;" both were "hostile to our religion, and such as we cannot in conscience support [either option]." While some people pointed to the Cincinnati school board's action as a solution, excluding the Bible would "not help the matter," Brownson declared. It would "only make the schools purely secular, which were worse than making them purely Protestant." Brownson also described why Catholics refused to accept nonsectarian Bible reading as an option; like devotional Protestant exercises, it was still Protestant. Nonsectarianism for Catholics was an impossibility—everything religious was sectarian. The difference between Catholics and Protestants was thus "not a difference in details and particulars only, but a difference in principle," he wrote. "Catholicity must be taught as a whole, in its unity and its integrity." Catholic opposition to Bible reading was thus based on the fact that it was inherently Protestant and, even if it was not, it was incomplete.[94]

Ever the loyal Catholic, Brownson sought to rehabilitate the hyperbolic comments of Archbishops Hughes and Purcell, asserting that Catholics did not oppose public education, in a sense. Catholics, "of course, utterly repudiate the popular doctrine that so-called secular education is a function of the state," he reaffirmed. But Brownson declared Catholics were "decidedly in favor of free public schools for all the children of the land," and "that the property of the state should bear the burden of educating the children of the state." The nub was that Catholics opposed *secular* public education, which would make the schools "nurseries of infidelity and irreligion." Brownson had evolved from his more assimilationist days, fifteen years earlier, when he had endorsed secular education supplemented by instruction in the church. Now he insisted that education had to be religious (i.e., Catholic) throughout. The only solution was to "divid[e] the schools between Catholics and Protestants and assigning to each the number proportioned to the number of children each has to educate. This would leave Catholics free to teach their religion and . . . Protestants free to teach their religion and apply their discipline in the Protestant schools." Although Brownson called this system one "of free schools at the public expense," it was not public education in the sense that that term had evolved by 1870. It limited the government's role to that of a financier, not a provider or administrator. But Brownson was not engaging in wordplay. Even though his proposal went against the trend toward consolidation of state authority over education, it harkened back to earlier arrangements where religious schools had at times received public support to act in stead of a public common school. Brownson was resurrecting a more fluid notion of "public" education. But his proposal also assumed that with a division of the school funds, Protestants would be able to unite on the content of their religious instruction, a likelihood that most Protestants disputed.[95]

Brownson's comprehensive article also addressed constitutional issues. He asserted that rights of conscience protected Catholics in two ways: first, against exposure to Protestant exercises; and second, against being forced to support through taxation Protestant-oriented public schools. But the conscience claim went a step further. "Our conscience forbids us to support schools at the public expense from which *our religion is excluded*, and in which our children are taught either what we hold to be a false or mutilated religion, or no religion at all." Protestants, Brownson continued, possessed a similar conscience claim against supporting secular schools: "Neither Catholics nor Protestants who believe at all in religion will consent to be taxed to support infidel, pantheistic, or atheistic education; and so-called purely secular education is really nothing else." Here, Brownson hoped conservative Protestants would identify with Catholics' arguments about being forced to support secularism. The constitutional protection afforded religious conscience went only so far, however: it did "not guarantee[] to any one the freedom of not worshipping God, to deny his existence, to reject his revelation, or to worship a false God. The liberty guaranteed is the liberty of religion, not the liberty of infidelity."[96]

In contrast to his truncated understanding of conscience rights, Brownson's view of church-state relations imposed *greater* restrictions on the government's authority over religious matters than many evangelicals endorsed. The state should stay out of religious matters, he declared, it had "no right to make itself a proselytizing institution for or against Protestantism, for or against Catholicism." The state's role was "to protect us in the free and full enjoyment of our religion," not to make people more religious. In a sense, this was a minimalist view of state involvement in religion similar to what James Madison had advocated eighty years earlier. Religion, Brownson insisted, "is accountable to no civil tribunal." He thus denied that the Catholic Church opposed separation of church and state or that it could not coexist under the nation's constitutional system. Catholics could be loyal Americans and support essential republican principles. Brownson's article was nuanced, consistent with Catholic doctrine, but also approachable by Protestants. There is no evidence that it made any converts, however. Those most likely to find its religious arguments persuasive—evangelical Protestants—were too distrustful of Catholic ambitions and doctrine, whereas liberal Protestants and secularists, possibly more open to Catholic conscience claims, were repelled by the argument for a system of sectarian education.[97]

The following month, Brownson elaborated on his discussion of church-state matters in an article in *Catholic World*, aptly titled "Church and State." While speaking for only himself, Brownson expanded on Catholic understandings of church-state relations, highlighting points that his earlier article had skimmed over. One purpose of the article was to clarify the papacy's 1832 and 1864 encyclicals which had condemned liberty of conscience and church-state separation. But as he had long done, Brownson also sought to rectify Catholicism with the American situation. Employing an Augustinian model, Brownson insisted that humans existed in two distinct spheres, the spiritual and the temporal. The same moral order existed with society "which is not the state alone, not church alone, but the union of the two in reciprocal commerce. The two are distinct, each has its distinctive nature, laws, and functions, and neither can perform the functions of the other, or take the other's place." This suggested a regime of church-state separation, consistent with the earlier *World* article, with each entity maintaining its own sphere.[98] However, Brownson offered an additional wrinkle that likely confused and repelled any Protestant readers. Because both entities were equally subject to God's laws, Brownson wrote, "they cannot in the normal state be separated." A "separation of the state from the church destroys its moral life, and leaves society to become a mass of moral rottenness and corruption." This was what the 1864 syllabus had condemned: those efforts to secularize the state and separate it from its moral grounding and higher authority. American Protestants, Brownson insisted, did not fully understand the constitutional principle of church-state separation; both entities had separate functions but both were bound by God's laws.

And it was the duty of the church, as representing the spiritual order, to interpret that binding law.

> [I]t is for her in the moral order to direct and control civil society, by judicially declaring, and applying to its action, the law of God, of which she is, as we have just said, the guardian and judge, and to which it is bound by the Supreme Law-Giver to subordinate its entire official conduct.[99]

Seeking to assuage Protestant concerns of Catholic dominance, Brownson noted that the "church is not less bound by the law of God than is the state; for she does not, as we have said, make the law, she only administers it." What Brownson did not appreciate was that in seeking to make the Catholic position less threatening to Protestants, he was exacerbating their concerns by reaffirming Catholic authority over binding moral laws.[100]

More important for the larger debate, Brownson insisted that Catholics and the church could coexist in the American republican system. In other essays, Brownson chastised those in the hierarchy who discouraged Catholic assimilation into the culture. And Brownson insisted that the Catholic position on the School Question was consistent with constitutional principles. He affirmed the separate functions of the church and the state, and that both God's law and constitutional principle required "each to remain distance from the other, each with its own organization, organs, facilities, and sphere of action." However, Brownson ultimately believed that because both entities were subject to God's law, "American society is based on the principle of their union; and union, while it implies distinction, denies separation." Although this schema decried a temporal role for the church, a worry for all Protestants, it argued that the nation was bound by religious doctrine as interpreted by the church: "what [the church] declares to be the law of God is the law, which binds every conscience; and all sovereigns and subjects, states and citizens are alike bound to obey her." This was anathema for Protestants. Further alienating him from Protestants and secularists was Brownson's emphasis on the essential value of separation as protecting the church from the state, while omitting the opposite concern, and that conscience rights did not extend to heretical and schismatic sects. This provided little comfort to secularists and Protestants of all stripes.[101]

This public debate over Bible reading in the schools continued in the press and pulpits for several years. Various factors make the debate notable. First, the debate revealed a diversity of perspectives, not simply between Protestants and Catholics, but within those groups (and within other groups as well). The divisions did not break down along expected lines. Protestants divided over the propriety of Bible reading and, more significantly, over the state's role in religious matters. Many sought to find some accommodation for Catholic concerns. Others saw any accommodation as fruitless, as the Catholic position was too extreme and would lead to the dismantling of public education as it had developed over the previous seventy years. While Catholics were more unified in their positions, their points of emphasis varied widely. The only matter on which Protestants, Jews, and secularists agreed was their opposition to the funding of Catholic schools; however, that issue was not a major part of this phase of the debate. Second, the debate indicated that the participants appreciated the complexity of the competing ideological and constitutional issues. A majority of the contributors viewed the controversy in religious *and* constitutional terms. Although commentary reverted to common Catholic fear-mongering at times, much of it rose above such attacks to tackle the larger issues at stake. In so doing, it established the groundwork for the legal debates on religion and education for future generations.

The Holding

In the midst of this debate, the Ohio Supreme Court handed down its ruling in the Cincinnati Bible case. In a unanimous holding, the supreme court reversed the superior court, reinstating the school board's decision to exclude the Bible and other religious exercises.[102] The court held that the school board possessed the authority to decide whether to hold religious exercises. To reach that conclusion, the justices had to immerse themselves in the church-state issues. Writing for the court, Justice John Welch rejected the plaintiffs' argument that the religious acknowledgment in the Northwest Ordinance obligated public schools to teach religion. Siding with the board attorneys, Welsh wrote that the "fair interpretation of seems to be, that true 'religion' and 'morality' are aided and promoted by the increase and diffusion of 'knowledge.'" That provision did not require the teaching of religion any more than it directed the form of "knowledge" to be taught. Welch also disputed that the term "religion" contained in the constitution meant Christianity or that the state was obligated to support Christian principles, either generally or in the public schools. "We are told that this word 'religion' must mean 'Christian religion,' because Christianity is a part of the common law of the country," Welch wrote, responding to the plaintiffs' Christian nation argument.

> Those who make this assertion can hardly be serious, and intend the real import of their language. If Christianity is the law of the State, like every other law, it must have a sanction. Adequate penalties must be provided to enforce obedience to all its requirements and precepts. No one seriously contends for any such doctrine in this country, or, I might almost say, in this age of the world.

"*Legal* Christianity is a solecism," Welch asserted, "a contradiction of terms." Welch and his colleagues were not about to breathe life into an antiquated maxim, particularly one they considered to be inconsistent with constitutional norms.[103]

Having affirmed the school board's authority, Justice Welch could have ended the court's opinion there. Nonetheless, he proceeded to address the two larger issues presented by the case: the nature of Bible reading and the proper relationship between religion and government. On the first issue, Welch concurred with Judge Taft that Bible reading was inherently devotional and favored Protestantism. Pointing to the state constitution's no-preference clause, Welch intimated that the exercises were likely to be unconstitutional, though he stopped short of rejecting nonsectarianism outright. But Welch agreed with Taft that consensus could never be reached over what portions of the Bible to teach: "Suppose the state should undertake to teach Christianity in the broad sense in which counsel apply the term, or the 'religion of the Bible,' . . . which of the doctrines or truths claimed by each will be blurred over, and which taught in preference to those in conflict [will be included]?" The prospect of a state official making such determinations also troubled Welch. Whether agreement on religious principles could ever be achieved, Welch made clear that the state constitution did not require religious instruction, and the failure of schools to so provide did not evince hostility toward religion.[104]

Welch had already addressed the relationship between religion and government in refuting the plaintiffs' Christian nation argument. But he returned to what he called "the terrible enigma of 'church and state.'" As Supreme Court justices would do a century later, Welch embraced a Madisonian understanding of church-state relations, to whom he cited for authority. Religion was "eminently one of those interests, lying outside the true and legitimate province of government." The state "can have no religious opinions." Not only did government lack authority to act on behalf of religion, Welch declared, it was not "at all adapted for producing, perfecting, or propagating a good religion." For Welch, this meant a regime where each entity exercised its own authority and neither interfered in the affairs of the other.

> United with government, religion never rises above the merest superstition; united with religion, government never rises above the merest despotism; and all history shows us that the more widely and completely they are separated, the better it is for both.

Welch thus saw the principle of church-state separation as enforcing a two-way street: "Let the state not only keep its own hands off [religion], but let it also see to it that religious sects keep their hands of each other."[105]

Welch's understanding of disestablishment was quite broad, encompassing other principles: it ensured equality among faiths and guaranteed "a man's right to his own religious convictions," meaning a conscience right. Welch also asserted that constitutional interests operated in an anti-majoritarian way: "Constitutions are enacted for the very purpose of protecting the weak against the strong." Finally, Welch understood disestablishment to prohibit the government's financial support of religion. Here, Welch used the no-funding principle to affirm Catholic claims of rights of conscience; the state had "no right to tax [citizens] to support religious instructions" in public schools, Welch declared. To do so was "the very essence of tyranny" and the "first step in the direction of an 'establishment of religion.'"[106] Overall, Welch's opinion lacked some of the force of Taft's dissent, but it was no less sweeping in its embrace of First Amendment values. Although *Minor* was highly significant for being the first case to strike down nonsectarian Bible reading, the constitutional principles announced by the court were as important as the specific holding.

In contrast to the heightened attention given to the School Question following the trial in *Minor*, public reaction to the supreme court decision was relatively subdued. The conservative *Christian Statesman* warned that "a minority of unbelievers," now "[a]rmed with the judgment of the Supreme Court...will be able ultimately to drive the Bible out of the Schools." But most newspapers, including the *New York Times* and *New York Tribune*, made only passing references to the holding. In the three years since the trial the number of school boards excluding religious exercises had grown, thus making the decision less noteworthy. And in New York and elsewhere, revelations of public funding of Catholic orphanages and schools were diverting attention from the issue of Bible reading. Also, despite the broad affirmations in Welch's opinion, the ultimate holding vested broad discretion with local school boards to decide for themselves whether to allow religious instruction. Unlike Taft's opinion, the supreme court had not declared Bible reading to be unconstitutional, though it had suggested as much. The *Christian Advocate*, which had strenuously opposed the Cincinnati resolutions in 1869, put the best face on the decision by claiming that it "ordain[ed] a kind of 'local option,' not of the people directly, but of the Boards. Practically this may be a very good decision in most cases, for probably in the great majority of cases school boards will favor the continuance of the Bible reading where it is now practiced." But the *Advocate*'s stance on Bible reading had also evolved in the interim. The journal now suggested that a better solution might be "to make the public schools secular institutions" open to all religious groups and to "remand the giving of religious instruction to the Church and the family."[107]

Yet anyone who read Welch's opinion understood the significance of the holding. For the first time, judges had declared that Bible reading was not only unessential for a common education or republican society, it was inconsistent with the very principles upon which constitutional government was built. Welch and Taft had also repudiated nonsectarianism as a workable theory and had cast doubt on the constitutionality of Bible reading in the public schools. Although one could read the supreme court opinion as rejecting only the religious justifications for nonsectarianism that the plaintiffs had asserted at trial, on appeal, the plaintiffs had relied chiefly on secular rationales for the nonsectarian practices. Regardless of how critics might parse the holding, *Minor* was a watershed decision, and its repercussions would be felt throughout the remainder of the century and into the next. The decision forever changed the way people looked at nonsectarian Bible reading. It settled the question of whether nonsectarian instruction could ever reclaim its devotional roots or justifications. From this point forward, the question was whether *any* use of the Bible was constitutional. *Minor* had forever changed the focus of the debate.[108]

4

"The Amendmentists"

The actions of school boards in Cincinnati and elsewhere abolishing nonsectarian exercises, now sanctioned by the Ohio Supreme Court, signaled that educational and constitutional norms were in flux. For a half-century, nonsectarian instruction, emphasizing universal religious principles, had seemed a sensible solution to diffusing religious discord over educational content while enabling schools to teach religious devotion and morality. Nonsectarianism also reinforced republican values; in fact, most educators and Protestant leaders believed the nation's future depended on the ability of schools to instill a civic morality in children, one that was anchored in a common religion. Yet the public debate over the School Question that was taking place in school boards, newspapers, and the courts revealed that not all people shared those assumptions underlying nonsectarian education. On the contrary, Americans held contrastingly different understandings of the appropriate relationship between the government and religion. The school controversy was leading people to reconsider presumptions about the nation's obligation to support religious principles and institutions.

The speeches, articles and sermons of the period also demonstrate that people appreciated the larger significance of the School Question. The controversy revealed that the moral and religious values that defined the nation were not static but were up for grabs. In this dynamic environment, school boards and legislatures could bend to pressures of locally dominate religious groups. Courts could strike long-standing practices based on evolving interpretations of constitutional provisions. This new uncertainty alarmed no group more than evangelical Protestants. For them, the unfolding school controversy reflected a larger, disturbing trend. Compounding those events were other challenges to the dominant Protestant culture, some direct and others subtle: Darwinism, Biblical criticism, materialism, urbanization, industrialization, and, of course, immigration. Consensus on Christian values and the role they played in society could no longer be presumed. In contrast, religious liberals and secularists more readily embraced the modernizing trend while they touted the superiority of their interpretation of constitutional values. They remained very aware, however, that they were a distinct minority in a culture that was still ruled by an evangelical Protestant ethos, one that exerted significant influence on the nation's social, political, and legal institutions. And like their evangelical counterparts, liberals and secularists pondered the impact of Catholic immigration on the nation's values and institutions.

The hopes and fears of the 1870s would lead both religious conservatives and secularists to seize upon the idea of amending the Constitution as a way of consolidating their respective visions of America's religious or secular character. These "Amendmentists," to use *The Independent's* depreciatory term, understood the power of constitutional doctrine to influence cultural norms. They appreciated, in the words of one group, "how legislation moulds the character of a people, and especially how potent is the influence of the fundamental law of the government upon the views and conduct of the people of any nation." The most famous of these efforts was the failed Blaine Amendment of 1875–1876, which sought to apply the religion clauses of the Constitution to the states while expressly prohibiting the public funding of religious education. The idea of amending the Constitution to change—or reinforce—its religious balance was not original to James G. Blaine, however; other attempts at constitution-tinkering predated that amendment and laid precedent for that effort. Although these initial proposals were also unsuccessful, the cumulative effect was to reinvigorate the national debate over church-state relations in the 1870s. The School Question was a leading catalyst for these efforts, though it was not the sole cause for the various proposals. More accurately, the school controversy was the most prominent symptom of the larger concerns of people who believed they were about to become losers in a struggle to redefine the nation's religious character.[1]

Two proposed constitutional amendments are considered in this chapter: the Christian Amendment, and the Religious Freedom Amendment. (The Blaine Amendment is examined in the following chapter.) While neither proposal received serious consideration by Congress (the second measure never obtained a hearing), each influenced public attitudes toward the School Question and helped direct the debate about the nation's religious character.

The Christian Amendment

The events that produced the Christian Amendment preceded the decade of the 1870s and arose out of concerns that related to the School Question only tangentially. As suggested by its name, the measure involved a proposal to insert an affirmation of God's sovereignty in the United States Constitution. However, as the Christian Amendment movement gained momentum, the issue of strengthening the religious character of the public schools became one of the movement's chief goals.

The impetus for the Christian Amendment arose out of a spiritual malaise during the early days of the Civil War. With secession and early Northern losses on the battlefields, Protestant clergy questioned whether the war indicated God's displeasure with the nation. God was punishing America not only for the sin of slavery but also for its collective spiritual failings. The nation's "calamities... result[ed] from our forgetfulness of God, and from slavery, so long as our nation's reproach," wrote a report by the Northern Methodist Church, "and that it becomes us to humble ourselves and forsake our sins as a people, and hereafter, in our laws and acts, to honor God."[2] Other Protestants thought the problem was more systemic and required greater measures. Seeking to make sense of the early Union defeat at Manassas, theologian Horace Bushnell placed fault at the very foundation of American government, which he insisted had been established without a moral or religious basis. Because the Constitution failed to recognize that all power was derived from God, it generated "no feeling of authority, or even of respect" among the people. Even the Confederate constitution acknowledged the authority of "Almighty God." Time may have come to recognize the supremacy of God in the federal document.[3]

Many northern Protestants were drawn to Bushnell's suggestion, and the nation's leading religious journal, *The Independent*, initially endorsed the proposal. The Constitution "provides, as it should, against a religious establishment, religious tests, or any infringement upon the rights of conscience," stated a September 1861 editorial. But for too long, the nation had failed to distinguish between "*legislating* for a particular creed or form of religion, and *recognizing* the great foundation truth of all religion—the just authority of a Holy and Almighty God." *The Independent* shared Bushnell's regret that the Constitution

> does not even recognize the fact that it is an ordinance of God for the well-being of society that civil government shall exist; and that such government should be administered upon the principles of truth, justice, order, and beneficence set forth in the moral government of God.

The nation was suffering from its own hubris. The people and their leaders had engaged in a "godless habit of thought and action" by declaring that "'We, the people,' [are] the original source of all authority and power, and have worshiped the work of our own hands" rather than acknowledging the superior law of God, *The Independent* asserted.[4]

One group of Protestants was particularly attracted to Bushnell's proposal. The Reformed Presbyterian Church (Covenanters) had long criticized the lack of an affirmation of God's authority in the Constitution. Strict in their Calvinist beliefs, the Covenanters adhered closely to the Westminster Confession of Faith, which provided that civil magistrates held power only through God's authority and that officials were obligated to uphold the church through the suppression of all heresies and blasphemies. Covenanters believed that states, like individuals, were moral entities subject to God's laws. The only legitimate governments were those that acknowledged God's authority. Covenanters therefore denounced the political doctrines of popular government and state sovereignty. Because the national constitution lacked an affirmation of God, Covenanters refused to vote or hold public office.[5]

In 1861, members of a Covenanter synod met in Allegheny, Pennsylvania, to draft a petition deploring the absence of God and his laws in the Constitution. The petition received support initially from Senator Charles Sumner, and in 1862 two Covenanter ministers presented the document to President Lincoln. Lincoln was noncommittal, and in all likelihood placed little importance on the incident. For the first time, however, the Covenanters gained the attention of the highest levels of government, and they did not miss the significance of the event.[6]

Armed with their new sense of importance, Covenanters and other supporters of a constitutional amendment organized a conference in Xenia, Ohio, in February 1863. Representatives of eleven Protestant denominations from seven northern states attended the three-day conference, though it was dominated by various orthodox Presbyterian bodies. On the second day John Alexander, a Presbyterian attorney and wealthy industrialist, spoke of the "crowning, original sin" that had led the nation to war and of the need for repentance. That sin, rather than slavery, was "the neglect of God and His law, by omitting all acknowledgments of them in our Constitution." In order to regain God's favor, Alexander proposed that "the most important step remains yet to be taken—to amend the Constitution so as to acknowledge God and the authority of His law." Prepared for the occasion, Alexander read a draft of a proposed amendment to the Preamble to the Constitution (amendment language in italics): "We, the People of the United States *recognizing the being and attributes of Almighty God, the Divine Authority of the Holy Scriptures, the law of God as the paramount rule, and Jesus, the Messiah, the Savior and Lord of all*, in order to form a more perfect union...." The convention enthusiastically embraced Alexander's proposal, with delegates unanimously adopting a favorable committee report on the amendment the following day. The delegates disbanded, agreeing to meet again to promote their new cause.[7]

Unbeknownst to the Xenia delegates, a similar convention of Protestants met in Sparta, Illinois, the day after the first group had adjourned. Also expressing concerns about the need for national repentance, the Sparta group passed a resolution that called for the "faithful administration of the government according to the principles of the Word of God" and acknowledging Christ's authority in the political realm.[8] The following January, representatives from both conventions met in Allegheny, Pennsylvania, where they formed the Christian Amendment Movement, soon to be called the National Reform Association. At this early stage, the raison d'être for the Association was to secure an amendment to the national constitution that acknowledged the Lordship of God and Jesus Christ which, its members believed, would guarantee that America was Christian in appearance and in law.[9] Support for the measure, and the Association itself, came chiefly from the Reformed Presbyterians and other orthodox Calvinist bodies: the United Presbyterian and Associate Reformed churches. Later that same year, the Old

School Presbyterians and the northern Methodists endorsed the amendment, the latter being the largest Protestant denomination in the country. Presbyterian and Methodist support was significant because many of the Association's moderate leaders would come from these mainline denominations. Early on, the Episcopal Church and Dutch and German Reformed bodies also endorsed the Association's goal. Although the Association would tout the diversity of religious support for the measure, the movement remained under the control of orthodox Calvinists throughout its existence.[10]

The Allegheny convention elected John Alexander president and formally adopted his proposed amendment in the form of a memorial to Congress. To garner broader support, the memorial also recommended that "such changes with respect to the oath of officers, Slavery, and all other matters, should be introduced into the body of the Constitution as may be necessary to give effect to these amendments in the preamble." The memorial attracted support from Senators Charles Sumner, B. Gratz Brown, and John Sherman, brother of the famous Civil War general. *The Independent*, the nation's leading religious journal, also endorsed the memorial, as did the faculty of Princeton Theological Seminary. With the war raging and its outcome still in doubt, the idea of aligning the Constitution with God's favor carried a distinct appeal.[11]

Emboldened, Association leaders obtained a second audience with President Lincoln in February 1864. Lincoln, known for his religious convictions, had previously issued a Fast Proclamation calling for a national day of prayer and humiliation. He promised to give the proposal appropriate attention but was again noncommittal. "I will endeavor to do my duty to my God and to my country," Lincoln reportedly answered. Still, the Association representatives believed they had the president's unqualified support, later claiming that Lincoln had replied: "You got one of the things you asked for in my first administration (the emancipation of the slaves), and I hope you will get the second in my second administration." The Association would maintain that only the immediacy of the war and Lincoln's assassination prevented an early passage of the amendment. At the time, the National Reform Association felt that there was "no practical opposition" to the movement and that passage of their amendment was imminent.[12]

Despite the initial flurry of interest, widespread support for the amendment ran thin. Influential figures who had earlier championed the amendment balked at supporting it in practice. Lacking a leader of national stature, the Association approached Horace Bushnell. But by 1864 Bushnell's opinion of the nation's sinfulness had changed. Like many northern Protestants, his attitude toward the war had evolved with the successes of the Union army. No longer wayward, the nation had been sanctified through the blood of its casualties. Though still in sympathy with the motives of the Association's membership, Bushnell had adopted a different view of the Constitution: "Our whole civil order is the ordinance of God saturated all through with flavors of historic religion ... and sanctified by the indwelling concourse of God." The lack of an express acknowledgment of God in the

Constitution did not delimit "the good, great government our God has given us." Like most religious leaders, Bushnell now had little interest in the proposed amendment.[13]

Statesmen also rebuffed overtures from the N.R.A. for commitments of support. Charles Sumner, who had been one of the first to endorse the idea of an amendment, backtracked after Jewish constituents complained that it would amount to a religious establishment. Responding to a Jewish supporter in a December, 1864 letter, Sumner stated he was "astonished" by accusations that he "favor[ed] any proposition to disfranchise anybody...I have said that I should not object to a recognition of God by formal words in the Constitution....That is all; I take it no Hebrew would differ with me on this point." Sumner asked his supporter to "quiet your Hebrew associates with regard to me." An appeal to Supreme Court Justice Joseph Bradley, known for his piety, also received a snub. Bradley saw neither "the necessity [n]or the expediency" for "obtaining such an amendment," and he commended the "voluntary system" of church-state relations established by the founders. Finally, The Independent, which had eagerly embraced the idea three years earlier, came out against the amendment, now labeling N.R.A. members "fanatics" who sought "to engraft the Christian religion into the Constitution." Amendment proponents would have been satisfied if "in one pregnant sentence only, [the framers] had...recognized civil government as the ordinance of God," The Independent wrote caustically. But the journal did not take the effort lightly, speculating that the movement "bears the marks...the work of a calculating and interested party." Religious skeptics, it warned, "have ground for apprehending the formation of an ecclesiastical party to act distinctly in political affairs."[14]

Through the intervention of Senator John Sherman, the Association's proposed amendment was submitted to the Senate Judiciary Committee in late 1864. On March 2, 1865, the committee issued a short report requesting to be discharged from further consideration of the matter. The report, written by Senator Lyman Trumbull, was conciliatory, stating that the committee felt that it was "unnecessary and injudicious, at this time, to make such an amendment." Committee members believed that the Constitution already recognized "the existence of a Supreme Being" by requiring every officer to take an oath, Trumbull wrote; "and what is an oath but a promise corroborated or confirmed by an appeal to the Supreme Being?" The Constitution also "recognize[ed] the right of religion" through the protections of the Free Exercise Clause, Trumbull explained. How thoroughly the committee members endorsed the underlying concept of the memorial is in question. Trumbull's affirmations were partially motivated out of concern that newspapers were reporting that the committee had voted against recognizing God in the Constitution. "The Committee on the Judiciary reported no such thing," Trumbull wrote. Rather, the committee thought a formal acknowledgment was unnecessary, so it had "simply asked to be discharged from the consideration of the memorials." With the equivocal report, the matter was tabled.[15]

Trumbull's conciliatory language could not hide the fact that the Association had suffered its first major defeat. Interest in even a symbolic affirmation of the nation's dependence on God had waned with the impending Union victory. Congress had little reason to be reminded of America's spiritual waywardness now that the war was almost over. Also, like Bushnell, most northern evangelicals saw the victory of the Civil War as validation of America's chosen status and an affirmation of its manifest destiny. Even some southern Protestants were reinterpreting the war as an atonement for America's sins. Regaining God's favor through a formal affirmation no longer seemed important.[16]

With the rebuff by Congress and the war's end, Protestant support for a Christian Amendment evaporated. The Association barely survived, apparently holding no national conventions between 1866 and 1869. But interest in church-state matters was on the upswing, thanks to the unresolved School Question, which benefitted the N.R.A. Over a three-year period, the organization underwent an organizational and ideological restructuring that would direct its activities for the remainder of the century. Its rhetoric became less sectarian and dogmatic, while its agenda broadened and became more pragmatic in its approach. After 1868, the N.R.A. became a vocal advocate for stricter Sabbath enforcement, the rescission of permissive divorce laws, and for continuing Protestant religious exercises in the public schools. Although arguments about the theological necessity of a government based on Calvinist principles would appear in N.R.A. documents for years to come, the influence of the orthodox Calvinists became less noticeable.[17]

Most significant was the way in which the Association explained and promoted its Christian Amendment, which became less an end in itself than a means of accomplishing a broader agenda. When the Association was founded, supporters viewed the amendment as replete. In his address to the 1864 convention, John Alexander had insisted that the amendment was necessary for its own inherent reason: "We as a nation have thus forgotten Him—failed to acknowledge Him in our highest national act.... We do not affirm this to be our only national sin, but that it is our Original Sin against our Best Benefactor, and lies at the foundation of our numerous and individual transgressions." In contrast, four years later the Association's journal, *The Christian Statesman*, would write that "the Religious Amendment of the Constitution is not, in itself, the end we seek. It is but a means to an end, and that end is the arousing and combining of the Christian people of America in a compact, enthusiastic, determined movement to carry out the religious idea of government in all its practical applications." The shift in focus is evident in a later N.R.A. publication, *The National Reform Movement—Its History and Principles*, written in 1890 by the Association's long-time general secretary, David McAllister. In that official history, McAllister described the aims of the Association to be "the preservation of the Christian Institutions of this country," to wit: "our civil Sabbath; the Bible in the public schools; the securing of a uniform marriage and divorce law, conformed to the law of Christ; the retention of the oath in our courts; chaplains in our army and navy, etc." As almost an afterthought, McAllister added: "Also to secure an amendment to the Federal Constitution that would in suitable terms recognize the authority of Jesus Christ as the Governor of the Nation, thus placing the Nation in right relation with God and at the same time affording a legal basis for the Christian Institutions of our country." It would be through these more tangible issues, and not the amendment, the Association would exercise its greatest influence.[18]

This change in emphasis was reflected in a new leadership. Reformed Presbyterian minister T. P. Stevenson replaced Alexander as corresponding secretary (director) sometime after 1866. An indefatigable advocate and pragmatist, Stevenson worked hard to make the Association's agenda appear mainstream, albeit religiously conservative. In an 1874 address "The Ends We Seek," Stevenson downplayed the significance of the amendment, declaring "though it be [said] for the thousandth time, that we seek no union of Church and State." The Association proposed "nothing of a sectarian character," Stevenson asserted; in fact, religious liberals were "some of its ablest supporters." Rather, he claimed that "our movement aims [merely] to preserve the Christian institutions which have descended to us from our fathers." Those institutions—Bible reading, the oath, blasphemy laws, and "the Christian law of marriage"—were under attack by the forces of "infidelity and Romanism." But Stevenson was also candid that the Association was not engaging in a mere holding action. The organization "must do more than merely arrest the current which is bearing us away from God and religion. We must begin to make progress in the opposite direction . . . to attain a complete and consistent Christian character as a nation." For more than twenty-five years, Stevenson would lead the Association through its efforts to obtain socially conservative laws and secure a constitutional amendment.[19]

Another significant change in the leadership, though chiefly symbolic, was the election of William Strong, a justice on the Pennsylvania Supreme Court, as president in 1868. Strong was an interesting figure and deserves a complete biographical study. An Old School Presbyterian, Strong was raised in a conservative Congregationalist family in Connecticut. He graduated from Yale in 1828 and moved to Reading, Pennsylvania, where he opened a law practice in 1832. Politically ambitious as well as being religiously devout, Strong served in Congress before being appointed to the Pennsylvania Supreme Court in 1857. While sitting on that court, Strong relied on the maxim of the law's incorporation of Christianity to uphold a Sabbath law conviction. In 1870, President Ulysses S. Grant appointed him to the U. S. Supreme Court. Strong continued to serve as President of the N.R.A. until 1873, despite sitting on the very court that would have been called on to reconcile a Christian Amendment with the First Amendment had the former been ratified. Strong was known as an intellectual on the court, and like his colleagues, was business oriented and politically conservative. Strong resigned from the Court in 1880 at the height of his career to devote the remaining fifteen years of his life to the work of the N.R.A. and the American Bible Society.[20]

Strong's pragmatic approach is evinced in an early speech to the Association. Like Stevenson, Strong asserted that the goals of the Association "are not new in American politics." Parting from the hard-line position of the Covenanters, Strong stated, "We would cast no imputation on the well known Christian Character of many of the eminent men who framed the Federal Constitution." "We know that many who were foremost in its formation regarded their successes as owing only to the favor of God." Offering his own understanding of the nation's Christian character, Strong stated:

> Why then did the framers of this instrument not incorporate in it a distinct recognition of God and his law? [Alexander] Hamilton is said to have exclaimed, when asked the reason for this neglect: "I declare we forgot it." But the only satisfactory explanation is found in their known anxiety to avoid the unsound and hurtful union of Church and State, and in turn their conception of civil government merely as a social compact and not as the ordinance of God.

"Whatever explanation we put upon this unfortunate omission," Strong concluded, "it cannot be considered presumptuous, after the experience of nearly three quarters of a century, to propose amendments to any constitution, however admirable and beneficent." Or as Felix R. Brunot, who followed Strong as president of the N.R.A., stated more simply, "Our nation is Christian—the Constitution is unchristian."[21]

Beyond loaning his stature to the Association, Strong represented the new stance of the N.R.A. that appealed to many conservative Protestants. Unlike the orthodox Covenanters, Strong was willing to participate in the political system and saw the amendment as a means of facilitating a Protestant foundation for American culture. Like many Americans, Strong saw a threat in the growth of secularism, Catholicism, and Mormonism and was willing to speak out about these concerns while serving on the Court.

In a lecture to students of Union Theological Seminary in New York City in 1875, Strong affirmed the need for laws against blasphemy and Sabbath breaking to ensure "public decency, good order, and good morals—objects for which civil society exists." The laws and institutions "of all the States are built on the foundation of reverence for Christianity," Strong insisted, and "it must be settled, that the religion revealed in the Bible is not to be openly reviled or blasphemed, to the annoyance of sincere believers, without responsibility to the civil law." Acknowledging that the Constitution protected the freedom to practice one's religion, Strong argued it did not go so far as to allow those practices, such as Mormon polygamy, that undermined the foundations of a Christian society. To Strong, the protection of Christian morals and the preservation of Christian institutions would be the practical effect of the amendment.[22]

The emergence of leaders such as Strong, Stevenson, and McAllister thus reveals a shift in the theological basis of the movement. Initially under the control of ultra-Calvinists, the Association professed that the nation had never truly been Christian and that the Civil War was God's judgment for the lack of a covenantal relationship. Only an affirmation of Jesus Christ in the Constitution would put the nation in a correct alignment with God. Strong, Stevenson, and McAllister modified this stance, insisting that the nation had been founded upon Christian principles. The founding fathers simply had strayed from their duty of placing an affirmation in the Constitution. An amendment would make the Constitution reflect its historical origins, reminding people of its implicit religious covenant with God.

Chastened by its defeat in Congress in 1865, the Association set out to culti-vate the "right public sentiment on the relation of government to religion," T. P. Stevenson asserted, "without which the amendment would be as valueless as its adoption would be impossible." The Association printed a new version of its Memorial, containing the text of the amendment with supporting arguments. It distributed the Memorial to evangelical churches and sympathetic organizations, and called on people to form "auxiliary associations in your county or district; Sign the memorial of that association, or that is near you, that in due time it may be forwarded to Congress through your Representative." The Memorial carried the endorsement of William Strong, Senator B. Gratz Brown, and the faculties of Princeton and Western theological seminaries.[23]

The N.R.A. resumed holding national conventions in 1870, which it conducted chiefly to demonstrate its vitality to the mainstream press. Fortunately for the Association, they were relatively well attended. More crucial for advancing its agenda, the Association sponsored smaller meetings and lectures to build support for its cause and to solicit petitions to Congress.[24] It was through these lower-key events that the Association revealed its organizing talent. At every gathering its leaders asked ministers to encourage parishioners to write their representatives in Washington. In 1868, *The Christian Statesman* also put out a call for petitions, offering that "[f]orms of petitions have been prepared at this office and will be forwarded to any address on application." The announcement requested that sup-porters sign two copies of the petition, one for the Senate and one for the House. Later announcements urged signers to forward their petitions directly to Congress before its adjournment in March, 1869.[25]

By mid-1868, petitions began to flow into the offices of sympathetic repre-sentatives and senators who, in turn, submitted them in Congress.[26] At first, the number of petitions and memorials grew slowly. After January 1869, however, three to five petitions were being presented each day, with the number growing rapidly. Most of the petitions came from individuals and churches in the Northeast and Midwest, areas of Presbyterian and Reformed strength. For

example, on February 13, 1869, Senator Simon Cameron submitted nine petitions from Pennsylvania in the Senate. Six were presented from Ohio, one from
Michigan, and one from Vermont. On the same day, a memorial of over 3,000
citizens of the 16th Congressional District of Ohio was submitted in the House
of Representatives.[27]

Most petitions and memorials followed the format prepared by *The Christian
Statesman*. They asked Congress to amend the Constitution by acknowledging the
existence of "Almighty God as the source of all power and authority in civil
government" and "recognizing the obligations of the Christian religion" in
government. The similarity of the wording of petitions from different states indicates the degree of N.R.A. organizing; petitions from Kansas closely resembled
those from Pennsylvania. Rarely did the petitions provide information as to the
individual motivations behind the requests. But occasionally, a representative
elaborated on his personal feelings or the feelings of his constituents.[28]

On February 8, 1869, Senator John Sherman submitted a petition of 1,100
Ohio citizens praying for an amendment acknowledging "Almighty God as the
source of all power and authority in civil government." Long sympathetic to the
movement, Sherman had been instrumental in securing the Association's second
audience with Lincoln. He took a moment to express his feelings for the record.
"These are only a portion of a great many similar petitions that I have presented
from my constituents," Sherman said. He claimed they indicated a ground-swell
of "a common movement of the religious people of this country, looking to some
recognition in the Constitution of a Supreme Being."

> It has always seemed to me, in viewing the recent events, and the won-
> derful providences, I may say, that have transpired in the history of our
> country in the last few years, that it would be well, now that we are
> amending the Constitution and recognizing the logical consequences
> of those events, for us to place in that instrument some recognition of
> the Providence of Almighty God, and a recognition of the further fact
> that this nation and its institutions have been built upon Christian
> civilization.

Sherman saw "no reason why the proposed amendment should not be placed in
our fundamental law." Senators Richard Yates of Illinois and Simon Cameron of
Pennsylvania voiced similar support.[29]

Even before Sherman's speech the volume of petitions had begun to attract the
attention of the media. On January 13, 1869, the *New York Times* noted that a
"great number of petitions have been presented to Congress of late asking for an
amendment of the Constitution that will recognize the existence and authority of
Almighty God, and some of them ask for an acknowledgment of the Christian religion." Any such acknowledgment, "of course, is out of the question for many reasons," the newspaper editorialized. "As to the acknowledgement of the existence

and authority of Almighty God, the founders of the Government did not think it called for in a document of the nature of our political charter—the fundamental objects of which are the maintenance of civil order and the defense of the public liberties."[30] "'Order,'" retorted *The Christian Statesman* in response to the *Times'* criticism, "can only mean conformity to law—moral law—the law which God has revealed for the regulation of the lives of moral persons. If it is a fundamental object of the Constitution to maintain conformity among the members of society to the law of God, is it not most fitting that it should acknowledge the Lawgiver?" This propensity of the *Statesman* and N.R.A. spokesmen to react harshly to criticism only reinforced the impression that the group was possibly hiding a larger agenda.[31]

The petitions continued through the end of the session but both the Senate and House failed to act on the amendment. As Sherman indicated in his speech, Congress was engaged in the debates surrounding the passage of the Fifteenth Amendment. With members preoccupied with the suffrage amendment, no committee report was made on the Christian amendment before Congress adjourned in May of 1869.[32]

By the time Congress reconvened seven months later, whatever momentum supporters of the amendment had built was lost. The records of the 41st Congress from 1870–1871 are significant for the virtual lack of petitions or speeches in favor of the amendment. The few petitions submitted were forwarded to the respective judiciary committees with little comment. No reports, either favorable or negative, emerged from the committees. On January 10, 1871, Senator Richard Yates, one of the chief supporters of the amendment, took the floor of the Senate to introduce a petition from Illinois. Frustrated over Congress' inactivity on the amendment, Yates chastised the intransigence of the Senate Judiciary Committee. People had been submitting petitions for "some five or six sessions," he asserted, such that "stacks of petitions almost a mountain high must be in the rooms of that committee." Yates claimed that "nine tenths of the people of the State of Illinois believe that there should be in the Constitution of the United States, or at least in the preamble...a recognition of the supreme authority of God and the Christian religion." They did not intend "to be put off by the inaction of Congress, by the negligence of Congress."[33]

Even though Yates claimed overwhelming public support for the amendment— something impossible to verify—he was aware that some people were alarmed at the idea of a Christian acknowledgment in the Constitution:

[I]f there is anything in the subject matter prayed for inconsistent with the Constitution, as it at present exists, then it should be so stated. If there is any attempt in this movement, of any tendency to a church establishment in carrying out the object of these petitions, or any suppression of rights of individuals, let it be stated by the committee when their report is made.

Yates offered his own opinion on the matter, disclaiming that the amendment would "deprive a certain class of persons who do not believe in the Christian religion of their rights, and thus conflict with the Constitution." Rather, the amendment was fitting and long overdue; the nation "is too much indebted to the Christian religion for its national superiority for it to ignore Christianity." He called on Congress to act quickly.[34]

Yates' petition and motion were referred to the Senate Judiciary Committee where, most likely, they were lost in the mountain of other petitions. Congress took no action on the amendment in 1871 or 1872, and even though petitions in favor of the amendment continued to come in, their number was down to a trickle.

The reason for the decline in the number of petitions is more difficult to explain than the cause of Congressional inaction. Sherman's and Yates's exaggerations aside, a genuine outpouring of support for the amendment occurred throughout 1869. Debate over the School Question raged throughout 1869–1871, probably fueling interest in the need for an affirmation that would recognize the public role of religion. Also, through 1871, few opposing petitions were submitted, and but for Congress's preoccupation with Reconstruction and the passage of civil rights legislation, the Christian Amendment might have made it to a floor vote. But once the matter was put off it was difficult to regain the public interest that had been shown early on.

A second explanation for the lack of action on the amendment is mentioned in Yates's speech. Even strong proponents like Yates acknowledged that many people were concerned about the effect of a Christian Amendment on the conscience rights of non-Christians. And the N.R.A., though increasingly guarded in its statements, did not hide that they anticipated tangible benefits to flow from an amendment. This uncertainty—as to the practical effect of any amendment—was likely to have made some legislators hesitant to offer their support.

A growing choir of voices opposed to the amendment also stoked congressional concerns. News of the mounting petitions alarmed several groups, including Jews and Seventh-Day Adventists, the latter fearing the amendment would encourage the enforcement of rigid Sunday laws. Adventists also opposed the amendment on eschatological grounds, viewing it as a step toward aligning government with a false religion, a connection foretold in the book of Revelation related to the rise of the anti-Christ. That N.R.A. members had "convinced themselves that they are called by God to a mighty work" was only a greater cause for worry, wrote one Adventist.[35] As Jews and Adventists circulated a hue and cry among their members, criticism from the secular and mainstream Protestant press increased. In a January, 1871 editorial, the New York Times opined that the "sincerity and piety" of amendment supporters was "above suspicion." "Their wisdom, however, is not so apparent." The Times claimed the amendment would be "utterly ineffectual," and recommended that Congress leave religion to "voluntary agencies alone" and "leave the Constitution as it is." Other criticism came from The Independent, which, having once supported the idea, was increasingly critical of the effort. The amend-ment "might gratify the wishes of a certain class of the people," *The Independent* wrote, but it was "contrary to the convictions and wishes of a much larger class." In the end, "it would not make one Christian more or one sinner less."[36]

The Liberal Response

One other group was particularly alarmed by the potential threat presented by the Christian Amendment: religious freethinkers and skeptics. During the 1870s, religious freethought and skepticism experienced a resurgence, reviving an impulse that had been relatively dormant since the 1830s. With the creation of the Free Religious Association (F.R.A.) in 1867, liberal religionists and free-thinkers found a voice. Arising out of the liberal wing of Unitarianism, the free religion movement attracted people holding various theological heterodoxies— transcendentalism, spiritualism, scientific theism—but all being committed to religious and philosophical inquiry free from doctrinal constraints. Free religion-ists were not atheists. The F.R.A.'s founder, author and lecturer Octavius B. Frothingham, was a theistic humanist, denying God's transcendence but seeing the spirit of god working in and through nature. Frothingham and the F.R.A. advocated "the absolute supremacy of human reason in spiritual matters" and the marriage of modern science with religion. The chief feature of this reliance on reason was a belief in the perspicuity of truth through freedom of thought and practice. Free Religion preached that every person had a free consciousness, which drew inspiration from nature and through introspection. But free religionists also believed the "human race ought to be a religious unit, as a universal Brotherhood of Man based on faith in human nature and love for all human beings." As their name suggests, the F.R.A. was deeply concerned about the issue of religious freedom.[37]

Frothingham and Francis E. Abbot founded *The Index*, "A Weekly Paper Devoted to Free Religion," in 1870 to promote their cause but also to do battle with the N.R.A's amendment. Under Abbot's editorship, *The Index* became the leading voice against the Christian Amendment. On January 21, 1871, in an editorial titled "The Coming Conflict," Abbot accused amendment supporters of seeking to rob the nation of "its chief jewel, religious liberty." Abbot believed the nation was "on the eve of a great agitation of this question." There was no escaping the issue. "The present attempts will probably fail. But new ones, and more powerful ones, will be made," he predicted. The battle lines were clear: "Christianity is mustering its forces for open war against republican liberty, and the sooner the fact is recog-nized, the better."[38]

Abbot assumed responsibility for exposing the implications of a Christian Amendment, as well as the larger agenda of the N.R.A. For the next ten years, *The Index* and *The Christian Statesman* engaged in their own private war, with each journal criticizing the other organization while justifying its own existence by the presence of the other. Particularly disconcerting for Abbot was the tendency of the mainstream press to characterize the N.R.A. as well-meaning but misguided and ineffectual. One such critic of the amendment, *The Independent's* Samuel Spear, maintained that placing the acknowledgment in the Preamble would have no legal effect: it "makes no grants of power, imposed no restraints, and contains no provision for the organization and administration of government."[39] Such complacency among religious liberals only enhanced the potential for victory by the N.R.A., Abbot retorted. Abbot was also frustrated by N.R.A.'s success in explaining the amendment in moderate terms while downplaying its likely impact on religious pluralism. Back in 1868, in a less guarded editorial, "Is Our Movement Practical," *The Christian Statesman* had argued that the acknowledgment would have "the force of law," despite its placement in the Preamble. Congress would be legally bound to enact laws "purging national offices of all immoral and irreligious men" and to confine voting and elected office to "moral men" and "fearers of God." Laws ensuring "[s]ocial order and purity will come with them." Increasingly cognizant that such language was counterproductive, the Association reverted to speaking in generalities as to the likely effects of the amendment, insisting that it was proposing "nothing new." Abbot saw it as his calling to expose this hidden agenda.[40]

Abbot's frustration was evident when *The Index* reported on the Association's announcement for its 1872 national convention. The Association's goals, stated the announcement, were to ensure that "the government should be established on moral principles" while recognizing that "authority is derived from God." *The Index* fretted that the announcement was "prepared with consummate ability, and shows a thorough knowledge of the state of the average Protestant mind." "The singularity of the Call does not lie in its enunciation of any novel principles or ideas, but solely in the avowal of a purpose to carry old, universally accepted doctrines into practice." This "subterfuge" made Abbot's job of convincing the public of the dangers that much more difficult. *The Index* responded to N.R.A. propaganda in two ways, neither of which was particularly successful in currying public sentiment. First, Abbot tried to explain why the N.R.A.'s sanitized interpretation of a "moral government" was inconsistent with constitutional principles. This led Abbot to insist—though he needed little incentive to do so—that the Constitution required a "complete separation of church and state." For Abbot, a "complete separation" meant not merely the secularization of the nation's public institutions but of its culture as well. By 1875, Abbot would call for "active measures" to bring about "the immediate and absolute secularization of the state." Religious liberals like Samuel Spear might have concurred about the secularization of public institutions but would have resisted the latter sentiment. But Abbot's frustration in exposing the Association's extreme beliefs led *The Index* to advocate its own seemingly extreme positions, thus alienating potential support from religious liberals. Second, rather than challenging the N.R.A.'s claim that it represented the

Protestant conservative mainstream, *The Index* frequently resorted to exaggerated rhetoric that attacked Christianity generally. Christianity—not simply a reactionary faction—was "conspiring against the existence of the State." The amendment would lead to "the overthrown of the Free Republic and the creation of a Christian Theocracy in its stead." And it would lead, "sooner or later, [to] the destruction of the rights of free speech and a free press, in the interests of Orthodoxy" leading to "the return of the Dark Ages." Such hyperbole did little to convince mainstream Protestants and the secular press of the dangers inherent in the Christian Amendment.[41]

Most unfortunate, Abbot's polemical style hampered his ability to demonstrate that his positions on church and state were not simply reactive but comprehensive and progressive. Abbot believed strongly in his own cause of "liberalism," which extended beyond free religion. Theologically, Abbot was already drifting away from free-religious theism to a philosophy of religious skepticism, which became increasing apparent in the pages of *The Index*. He advocated rationalism and a universal brotherhood under a worldwide republic, while he criticized the spiritualism or "intuitionalism" that was prominent among many in the F.R.A., which Abbot viewed as the antithesis of a theism based on the scientific method. He criticized all religious orthodoxy and authoritarianism, Catholic and Protestant alike; as one Liberal document declared: "Catholic usurpation is no more treasonable than Protestant usurpation." On a practical level, Abbot spoke out against tax exempt status of churches and in favor of women's suffrage and the repeal of moralistic legislation proscribing blasphemy, drinking, and breaking the Sabbath. His goal was to create a "purely secular state," separate from all religious influences, a position he readily acknowledged.[42] Protestants, not solely of the N.R.A., used Abbot's statements to pronounce the threat free religion and "liberalism" presented to American society. One journal charged the "liberal" view on church-state was "identical with the Commune, the Red Republic and the political International in Europe." And Orestes Brownson, the consummate critic, claimed that Abbot and the Free Religionists exhibited "no great intellectual ability" but were "deplorably ignorant of the past and present, of the religions they believe they have outgrown, and especially of human nature."[43] Critics also pointed to Abbot's friendship with Charles Darwin to drive home their concerns. As the *Chicago Tribune* wrote, "Free Religion is no religion at all, but rather a theory or set of theories, based on a combination of morality and science.... It is not difficult to see why Mr. Darwin has accepted Mr. Abbot's creed, for Mr. Abbot's process is virtually the same as that of Mr. Darwin on science."[44]

Such criticisms did little to dissuade Abbot from advancing his vision of liberalism, including church-state separation. He genuinely believed that the majority of intellectuals, secularists, and liberal Christians would embrace liberalism in its various manifestations, including its understanding of the role of religion in a secular society. To further that cause, and make his position clear, Abbot published his most ambitious memorial, the "Nine Demands of Liberalism" in January

1873. The "Demands of Liberalism" left little in doubt, calling for the complete disassociation of government from religion through the abolition of tax exemptions for churches, courtroom oaths, Sunday laws, religious exercises in public schools, and chaplains for Congress and in the armed forces. The manifesto also called for prohibiting any public funding of "sectarian educational and charitable institutions." The ninth demand concluded with the appeal that "no privileges or advantage shall be conceded to Christianity or any other special religion; [and] that our entire political system shall be founded and administered on a purely secular basis." With its release, Abbot urged fellow secularists or "Liberals" to organize local "Liberal Leagues" to "lay the foundations of a great national party of freedom, which shall demand the entire secularization of out municipal, state, and national government." Despite the ill-chosen word "demands," the manifesto set out a comprehensive vision of separation of church and state, one that was broader than anything previously proposed.[45] Its understanding of separation would have excluded many church-state interactions that even religious liberals like Samuel Spear found acceptable. Most observers viewed it as calling for a completely secular culture, though Abbot insisted that his proposal would not encumber churches' internal religious functions. Despite Abbot's hope that all liberals could unite around his manifesto, the Demands of Liberalism backfired, alienating many liberal Protestants and Jews who viewed its calls as too extreme. For religious conservatives, its positions were even more alienating, and the N.R.A. used the Demands of Liberalism as evidence of the very assault on Christian institutions that necessitated a Christian Amendment.[46]

Despite his missteps, Abbot had one advantage over the Christian Amendment, which was time. Throughout 1872–1873 the proposed amendment languished in Congress. For over a year no congressman had risen to champion the proposal. Petitions in favor of the amendment continued to be submitted, but as a matter of course. The greater the Association's efforts at sounding moderate, the less the amendment seemed necessary. The conservative *Presbyterian Quarterly and Princeton Review* expressed "sympathy with our friends who . . . have organized to promote, the express recognition in our national constitution, of some belief in God and Christianity." But the journal refused to accept that "because [Christianity] not expressly mentioned, [it] is not in effect and substance the supreme element of the national life, lying deeper than constitutions. . . . [T]he unsectarian character of our civil constitutions does not mean atheism or infidelity, or the disowning of common Christianity." Even the militant *New York Observer* expressed regret at the movement's efforts. Not only was the amendment impracticable, it brought "the Christian religion into a conflict with the State, when the State is not in conflict with religion." The *Observer* feared that the proposal would "provoke[] hostility to Christian legislation" and thus endanger the gains Protestants had made to ensure that Christian morality existed within public institutions. With such ambivalence among allies, the Association faced a daunting task.[47]

Abbot went on the offensive in 1872. In January, he sent out a call to all who opposed the amendment to send him their names for a giant counterpetition to be sent to Congress to demonstrate that "this retrograde 'reform' will be met with prompt and vigorous protest." After identifying the Christian Amendment, the counterpetition stated: "We protest against such proposed amendments as an attempt to revolutionize the government of the United States, and to overthrow the great principles of complete religious liberty and the complete separation of Church and State on which it was established by its original founders." Abbot listed the counterpetition and the call for names on the front page of every issue of *The Index* for the next year.[48] *The Index* had learned from the N.R.A.'s example of grassroots organizing. On February 28, 1872, Senator Carl Schurz presented petitions with over 10,000 signatures from throughout the nation "asking Congress to preserve inviolate the great guarantees of religious liberty, and protesting against an amendment to the Constitution establishing religious tests." Two months later Charles Sumner introduced a similar petition from 6,300 citizens of Boston. The petition war remained a draw throughout most of 1872–1873, however.[49]

The Defeat of the Christian Amendment

In the interim, conflicts over the School Question kept church-state matters in the public spotlight. People on both sides of the Christian Amendment paid close attention to the outcome of the Cincinnati case. Even before the Ohio Supreme Court ruling, the N.R.A. highlighted the case as further proof of the need for the amendment. Speaking in New York in April of 1872, David McAllister decried the efforts of "opponents of Christianity" who sought to remove the Bible from public schools. "[I]f we had in our national Constitution that acknowledgement we had in nearly every State constitution, it would not only sustain the decision of the Ohio [Superior Court] judge, but would greatly strengthen the friends of our Christian system of education. And it is the aim of the association to have that undeniably legal basis in our Constitution, so that there will never be any question raised about the matter, and so that when men stand up to resist the Bible we may say, 'No; we recognize the Christian religion as a fundamental law of our Constitution.'" The Christian Amendment presented a solution to the School Question, or so McAllister claimed.[50]

Expectantly, the N.R.A. expressed outrage at the Ohio Supreme Court's decision in February 1873 upholding the Bible's removal from the Cincinnati schools. Aside from the holding, the Association objected to a passage in the court's opinion that appeared to chastise their efforts at securing a constitutional amendment. Justice Welch had written that "Religion is not—much less Christianity or any other particular system of religion—named in the preamble to the Constitution of the United States as one of the declared objects of government ... [or] as being essential to anything beyond mere human government." Even worse, Welch's sentiments had identified with the Liberals: "united with religion, government never rises above the merest despotism; and all history shows us that the more widely and completely they are separated, the better it is for both."[51] David McAllister threw down a gauntlet. If the constitution prohibits Bible reading in the public schools, he wrote, then "instead of expelling the Bible from our common schools, to make them conform to the fundamental law, which acknowledges neither God nor the Bible, we shall insert the acknowledgement of God and His law in the Constitution, and make it conform to our common schools."[52]

In actuality, the Ohio holding was a godsend for the Association, as it provided another rallying cry for their amendment. McAllister asserted that the issue was not one of conscience rights of non-Protestants but the perpetuation of the nation's moral structure. "The rights of society and of the nation [can] not, and must not, be passed over for the sake of granting individual requests...conforming to individual opinion or supposed rights." Recasting the religious liberty issue at stake, McAllister argued that religious dissenters "seem to regard their wants of more importance than the nation's rights, and [are] willing to crush out civil and religious liberty." In essence, the right of the majority of Americans to practice their religious beliefs was threatened through decisions such as the Ohio holding.[53]

The Association highlighted these threats in announcing its 1873 convention. "The question of the Bible in the Public Schools, of Sabbath Laws, and of many similar questions are now demanding attention and decisive settlement. Shall the Nation preserve the Christian features of its life? This is rapidly becoming the issue of our day." The question demanded an immediate answer. "Shall we obliterate every Christian feature from existing institutions? Or, shall we make the Constitution explicitly Christian? Shall we thrust the Bible from our schools to make them conform to the Constitution? Patriotism and true Statesmanship answer, No!" The Association hoped such calls would attract a large turnout of support at its convention.[54]

When the convention met in New York on February 26 and 27, 1873, the event received substantial coverage by the press. O. B. Frothingham covered the sessions for *The Index*, putting as negative a light as possible on the proceedings:

> The National Association for effecting a religious amendment to the Constitution of the United States held its long and loudly heralded Convention, in New York, on the 26th and 27th of February. The place appropriately selected was the vast subterranean Cave of the Cooper Union.... The hall was perhaps one-forth filled with hard-featured men and women evidently from the country round about.... The meetings were dull; no man of eminent name or of brilliant parts spoke. No letters from distinguished absentees were read. The statements were commonplace; the arguments were stale; the appeals were frigid. Those

present generally showed assent to the positions taken, but without enthusiasm, hardly with earnestness.[55]

The account by the *New York Times* was more generous. According to the *Times*, 385 delegates from nineteen states and one territory attended the convention. The sessions usually attracted 500 people, with one evening session drawing approximately 1,000. Although no one of national stature attended (Justice Strong having resigned the presidency), at least one governor, several judges, and numerous college presidents and deans appeared on the program. The convention adopted a new memorial asking Congress to pass a Christian Amendment that would "indicate that this is a Christian nation, and place all the Christian laws, institutions and usages of the Government on an undeniable legal basis in the fundamental law of the land."[56]

The convention was not the event hoped for, but it also was not the failure Frothingham depicted. The convention drew public attention to the Christian Amendment while people were still mindful of the Cincinnati Bible reading case. The Methodist *Christian Advocate* reported favorably on the convention, calling it "no small affair." The *Advocate* recommended its readers support the amendment. "The fundamental proposition on which this movement is based is the impossibility of state neutrality in religion and morals. Once grant this fundamental principle, and we see not how the object of this movement can be logically opposed or ignored."[57]

Hoping to win a small victory to regain the momentum, the Association turned its attention temporarily to Pennsylvania. In March, 1873, a convention assembled in Philadelphia to consider amendments and other changes to the Pennsylvania state constitution. Unlike many states, the existing Pennsylvania constitution contained no provision acknowledging the authority of God, declaring instead that "the people . . . ordain[ed] and establish[ed] this constitution." Leading up to the convention, religious conservatives had proposed to amend the preamble to acknowledge "Almighty God as the source of authority in civil government." Because Pennsylvania was a stronghold of N.R.A. support, the Association decided to lobby for the change but petition the convention for a more specific Christian acknowledgment. The state convention offered the N.R.A. the opportunity to test the strength of its arguments, while a victory would provide precedent for the battle at the federal level.[58]

On March 24, John Alexander and T. P. Stevenson appeared before the convention to plead their case. Their presentation, more than any other public statement, reveals how the N.R.A. understood the practical consequences of their amendment. Alexander told the delegates it was their imperative duty to go beyond making a simple affirmation of God to acknowledging "the Lord Jesus Christ as the Ruler of Nations, and the Bible as the supreme standard of righteous law, and by thus declaring that this is a Christian Commonwealth, place the Christian laws, institutions and usages of the state on an undeniable legal basis in our fundamental law."[59] Alexander and Stevenson offered two arguments in support of their proposal. First, they claimed their acknowledgment would affect no change but merely confirm existing understandings of the law. The state's test-oath for office holding already required a belief in God and a "future state of rewards and punishments." Also, in an 1823 blasphemy case the state supreme court had declared Christianity to be part of the common law. A declaration in the preamble would simply conform the document to the views of "the vast majority of the inhabitants of this State," Stevenson claimed. The argument that an official acknowledgment made no substantive change to the status quo always invited questions as to its necessity. Prepared for such responses, Alexander and Stevenson replied that an acknowledgment was necessary to remove any doubt as to the true source of political authority and the "binding force of the moral laws of the Christian Religion." Alexander and Stevenson sought to have it both ways, claiming that their proposal merely clarified current understandings while insisting that it would make Christian norms legally binding. In his remarks, Alexander revealed the transparency of the former claim by acknowledging their proposal would "create a constitutional presumption in favor of Christianity which is of use in the interpretation of law." It would "indicate that this is a Christian Commonwealth, and place all Christian law, institutions and usages on an undeniable legal basis in our fundamental law." Moreover, the change would correct an erroneous theory of popular government, the men insisted. Stevenson disputed that governments were created by social compacts with sovereignty resting in the people. Rather, the state should recognize "the divine origin of civil government.... There can be no truce between the true view of civil society and this false, pernicious, disorganizing, self-destructive theory" of popular sovereignty. As a final justification for their proposal, Alexander asserted that the state's Christian status was under attack from the disciples of Hobbs and Paine: "liberals" and forces of infidelity. Alexander read from Abbot's Demands of Liberalism and reminded the delegates that Bible reading had recently been expelled from the Cincinnati public schools. All public institutions that relied on Christian morals were in danger. The two men thus considered the Christian Amendment would have both symbolic effects and practical consequences for the law. It would recognize Christianity as the ultimate source of political authority while it would correct errant theories of government. And it would serve as a basis for proscriptive laws.[60]

The convention listened attentively, but in the end was unwilling to go as far as the N.R.A. requested. The constitution, ratified in December, 1873, contained no Christian affirmation. Delegates rewrote the preamble, but they substituted the proposed clause acknowledging "Almighty God as the source of all authority" with one simply thanking God "for the blessings of civil and religious liberty, and humbly invoking His guidance...." The document, however, retained the requirement that office holders acknowledge the existence of God and the future state of rewards and punishments. The constitution also preserved language affirming the peoples' "natural and indefeasible right to worship Almighty God according to the dictates of their own consciences."[61]

Even though the new constitution was hardly a victory for the N.R.A., Liberals complained the loudest. "The new Constitution," stated *The Index*, "disqualifies for office those who do not 'acknowledge the being of God and the future state of rewards and punishments,'—an outrage none the less heinous because it is but the reenactment of the same provision in the old Constitution." *The Index* attributed the acknowledgment to the N.R.A, despite the Association having failed to secure an express reference to God's sovereignty: "the Christian Amendment party have gained an important victory, accomplishing at least part of their purpose to 'put God into the Constitution.'"[62] The N.R.A., though, hesitated to claim victory. Too many omissions remained in the new document. It failed to provide for the Christian features of public education or guarantee the maintenance of Christian laws. And the sovereignty of God and Jesus were omitted from the Preamble. But overall, the N.R.A. was pleased with having secured any acknowledgment of God. "[A]lthough the vote which struck out the clause, originally reported by the Committee, acknowledging the 'sovereignty' of God, showed a singular ignorance of the subject with which they were dealing, yet we regard the Preamble as a notable gain to the cause of political Christianity," wrote *The Christian Statesman*. The N.R.A. also applauded the retention of the oath requirement for office holding. "In some respects, too, it must be admitted that the religious features of the new instrument are no worse, perhaps even better, than those of the existing Constitution." Most important for the N.R.A., however, was that the episode was "destined to play an important part in the controversies of the future."[63]

The success of a national Christian Amendment was still an open question. Francis Abbot feared the N.R.A. would use their victory in Pennsylvania as a springboard for the amendment. Moves were under way for securing similar acknowledgments in the Ohio and Michigan constitutions.[64] Abbot knew the time had come to give the movement a knock-out punch. For over a year *The Index* had been collecting signatures on a large counterpetition to Congress. As early as March 1873, Abbot had wanted to send the petition to Charles Sumner, who agreed to present it to Congress. Sumner, however, had been unable to submit the petition before the end of that session. Now, the counterpetition seemed all the more important. On January 7, 1874, Sumner finally presented the petition, which contained 35,179 names and was over 953 feet long. The event captured the attention of the press. The petition was so large, reported the newspapers, that it would have been more than a quarter mile long if it had not contained two names per line. "It is seldom that 35,000 people can be found to sign an appeal against a wise measure," wrote the *Boston Globe*, "and the 953 feet of the petition certainly go a great way in demonstrating the absurdity of the proposed constitutional plan of salvation." Abbot had secured a public relations coup.[65]

After Sumner's submission, Congress acted quickly. On February 18, the House Judiciary Committee issued a long-awaited report on the Christian Amendment. Benjamin Butler read the report of the Committee requesting that the Amendment be tabled indefinitely:

> That, upon examination even of the meager debates by the fathers of the Republic in the convention which framed the Constitution, they (the committee) find that the subject of this memorial was most fully and carefully considered, and then, in that convention, decided, after grave deliberation...that it was inexpedient to put anything into the constitution or frame a government which might be construed to be a reference to any religious creed or doctrine.
>
> And they further find that this decision was accepted by our Christian fathers with such great unanimity that in the amendments which were afterward proposed in order to make the Constitution most acceptable to the nation, none has ever been proposed to the States by which this wise determination of the fathers has been attempted to be changed. Wherefore, your committees report that it is inexpedient to legislate upon the subject of the above memorial, and ask that they be discharged from further consideration thereof, and that this report, together with the petition, be laid upon the table.[66]

With the negative report from the House, the amendment also died in the Senate. Unlike Trumbull's report nine years earlier, Butler's report contained no conciliatory language. This time, there was no statement that the Constitution already implicitly recognized God. According to the House committee, the founding fathers had explicitly intended the opposite. The framers were presented with the opportunity to acknowledge the existence of God and establish a religion in America, but had expressly declined to do so. Committee members were not prepared to go against what they viewed as clear direction from the framers. Furthermore, as the second paragraph of the report indicates, the committee was concerned that the proposed amendment would conflict with the no-establishment and free exercise clauses of the First Amendment. For these reasons, the committee requested that it be discharged from any further consideration of the amendment. The House approved the committee report, and in two short paragraphs, the Christian Amendment was dead.

The Christian Statesman sought to downplay the report as a minor setback. A February 28 editorial first attempted to disassociate the N.R.A. from the loss, claiming that the petitions which the judiciary committee considered had been submitted by a group of sympathizers rather than by the Association. Their lack of experience and poor timing were responsible for the disappointing showing by the amendment. The editorial failed to mention that the Association had orchestrated the petition drive among Protestant churches. The *Statesman* also insisted the report was inconclusive because the entire House had not had the opportunity to consider the merits of the amendment. "Heretofore, the only action has been (for the committee) to report adversely, and ask to be excused from further consideration of the subject," wrote the *Statesman*. The report did not represent the final word on the amendment, so far as the N.R.A. was concerned.[67]

After distancing itself from the report, *The Christian Statesman* proceeded to criticize the committee for its faulty historical analysis. "With all respect to the gentlemen composing this Committee we affirm that they have not examined carefully even the meager reports which are preserved of the debates in the Convention which framed the Constitution.... The omission of all religious acknowledgments from the instrument they framed may have been of deliberate intention in the minds of some; it certainly was not, so far as the evidence goes, the result of joint deliberation. Least of all did the nation understand that the new Constitution was a formal divorce of the government from the Christian religion."[68] The editorial concluded with a call for a renewed commitment to the Christian Amendment. "Shall the Christian features of our government be disparaged and assailed on every hand and secularism be allowed to work out the complete divorce of our government from every religious idea and institution [?]" No, responded the *Statesman*. "[T]he movement will survive this, as it has many another and more skillful blow."[69]

Despite the N.R.A.'s attempt to put the best face on the report, it was a stinging defeat, particularly considering its heroic efforts. Later N.R.A. histories would breeze over the episode, noting it was one of many legislative efforts of the Association. But the N.R.A. would never be stronger, or have greater support for its cause, than between 1870 and 1874. The episode was the closest the Association would come to achieving its goal of Christianizing the Constitution. Amendment supporters would continue to forward petitions to Congress over the coming years, where they were likely to have been added to that mountain on the committee-room shelf.[70]

The Religious Freedom Amendment

The defeat of the Christian Amendment in February 1874 signaled the death of any realistic prospect of inserting an acknowledgment of God's sovereignty in the Constitution. The N.R.A. would make another serious run at obtaining Congress' approval in 1896, following on the heels of a United States Supreme Court opinion declaring America to be a "Christian nation." But in 1874, no one knew that the future likelihood of securing an amendment was essentially nil. The N.R.A. still had a core of loyal followers and a larger number of sympathizers within the evangelical community. Although this latter group balked at supporting the Christian Amendment, they identified with the Association's call to reinforce the nation's Christian foundations through other moral reforms. Here, the N.R.A. would have its greatest influence. Over the succeeding twenty years, the N.R.A. would operate one of the more prominent and effective lobbying efforts in Washington, D.C., influencing moral legislation concerning Mormonism, temperance, obscenity, and Sabbath observance. The Association remained a force with which to be reckoned.[71]

No group was more responsible for the defeat of the Christian Amendment than the Liberals, led by Francis Abbot and *The Index*. Despite their victory, Abbot and the growing number of free religionists and skeptics, organizing into local Liberal Leagues, feared the residual power of the N.R.A. The day after the negative House report, *The Index* reported with horror that the N.R.A. had collected 54,228 signatures in favor of the amendment, 20,000 more than were on *The Index's* counterpetition, many of which had not been sent to Congress. "The whole energies of the Association are to be devoted to collecting further signatures," warned *The Index*. "They intend to have 2,000,000 names to present to Congress in 1876, the national centennial year, in favor of their movement. We consider it by no means improbable that they will succeed in this project. Whoever believes the Christian Amendment movement to be devoid of vitality, power, or other elements of a formidable agitation, will discover his mistake in due time."[72] Abbot and the Liberals were not about to write off zealots committed to ensuring that America was a Christian nation. "The stubborn fact is that 'the movement moves'" wrote a later editorial in *The Index*. "These persistent fanatics perfectly comprehend the situation; they perceive the necessity of making the national Constitution and the national administration harmonize; and they propose to do it by making the Constitution recognize Christianity."[73]

Another indication of the N.R.A.'s viability was the ongoing attention it received by the press. Two weeks before the House Judiciary Committee issued its report the N.R.A. had held its annual convention in Pittsburgh, the geographical center of its strength. The turnout emboldened the Association leaders. "An immense audience was present," reported the *New York Times*, "embracing delegates from almost every State in the Union and representatives of all Evangelical denominations." According to the *Pittsburgh Dispatch*, which provided a more detailed account of the proceedings, 1,063 delegates from eighteen states attended the sessions. "There was a large attendance and a decided enthusiasm on the subject as presented to the audience. There is scarcely a doubt that the cause for which such strenuous efforts are being put forth has gained ground in this community through the medium of the Convention."[74]

Not all observers were impressed. *The Independent* insisted that the large turnout indicated little as to the viability of the Association or its cause. An editorial charged the movement was still "intensely sectarian" despite of its claim of commanding mainstream support. Because the Association remained under the control of orthodox Calvinists, there would always be a limit to the movement's appeal. The absence of any prominent statesmen on the program merely confirmed this lack of appeal. "A large number of prominent names have been dropped [from the rolls], and quite a number of these, though continued as vice-presidents, seem to have sent no letters of endorsement," *The Independent* reported. "The session was enthusiastic and attended by over a thousand delegates; but, if we can judge from its adherents, it is losing strength."[75]

Despite *The Independent's* critique, the Association viewed its 1874 convention as a success. For nine years the Association had tried unsuccessfully to get its memorials considered by Congress. After the less than satisfactory victory in Pennsylvania, the embarrassment at the hands of *The Index's* counter-petition, and faced with the impending doom of the congressional report, the convention should have been the Association's last. Instead, the convention turnout was the largest and most enthusiastic to date, though it preceded the unfavorable House report. Although Justice Strong and several other public figures had resigned, the Association still claimed the support of at least three senators, a governor, and numerous judges and college presidents. It new president, Felix R. Brunot, served as President Grant's Commissioner of Indian Affairs. *The Independent* was likely correct that the intensity of support among notable figures was difficult to gage. But more important, the large attendance and generally favorable media coverage created the impression the N.R.A. was experiencing resurgence in the face of adversity. And when it came to motivating public opinion, appearances counted.[76]

The news accounts and minutes provide few clues for the "success" of the convention. Little, if anything new, was mentioned in the speeches. The threats of infidelity, Romanism, Mormonism, Sabbath desecration, and exclusion of the Bible from the public schools were all reemphasized in the same long talks.[77] As before, speakers portrayed the Association's goals in moderate terms. In his address, T. P. Stevenson insisted that the Association did not aim to create a union of church and state; rather, its goal was for the nation to "acknowledge and serve God for itself and not through the medium of church establishment." The amendment was simply "to express truly the actual character of the nation." Americans had nothing to fear from the movement. At the same time, however, the Association intended to go forward with its agenda of strengthening those laws and institutions that reinforced America's true Christian character.[78]

One other event helped reinvigorate Association members to their cause. Just prior to the N.R.A. convention, Francis Abbot published in *The Index* the first call for what became known as the Religious Freedom Amendment, intended as an alternative to the Christian Amendment. For the next three years, the front page of *The Index* contained the following proposed amendment to the United States Constitution:

ARTICLE I
Section 1. Congress shall make no law respecting an establishment of religion, or favoring any particular form of religion, or prohibit the free exercise thereof; or abridging the freedom of speech or of the press, or

the right of the people peacefully to assemble and to petition the Government for a redress of grievances.

Section 2. No State shall make any law respecting an establishment of religion or favoring any particular form of religion, or prohibit the free exercise thereof; or abridging the freedom of speech or of the press, or the right of the people peacefully to assemble and to petition the Government for a redress of grievances. No religious test shall ever be required as a condition of suffrage, or as a qualification to any office or public trust, in any State; and no person shall ever in any state be deprived of any of his or her rights, privileges or capacities, or disqualified for the performance of any public or private duty, or rendered incompetent to give evidence in any court of law or equity, in any consequence of any opinions he or she may hold on the subject of religion.[79]

The Index gave two reasons why "this enlargement of the First Amendment" was necessary "in order to secure to the people the full and unrestricted enjoyment of religious liberty." First, the First Amendment and Article VI, clause 3, which prohibits religious tests for office holding, applied only to acts of Congress. The Constitution contained no provision "prohibiting the several States from establishing a State religion, or requiring a religious test for office." Second, due to this limitation on the Constitution, "some of the States are, as a matter of fact, actually guilty of grave infringements on the religious liberty of their citizens," Abbot wrote. The affirmation of God and the religious test for office holding in the new Pennsylvania constitution clearly demonstrated the need for such an amendment.[80]

Other evidence convinced Abbot that the principle of church-state separation had yet to be perfected. States, which had a greater impact on the life of the average person, were limited only by the provisions of their individual constitutions which varied in their protection of civil rights. In 1875, eight of thirty-seven state constitutions required religious tests for public office holding, tests that disqualified non-Christians from office holding. Most states still imposed a requirement of a belief in God to take an oath as a witness or juror in a court proceeding. Furthermore, all of the states, with the single exception of Louisiana, had laws enforcing Sabbath practices or observances. Laws governing profane swearing and maintaining Christian features of marriage and divorce were also common.[81]

Nor were these provisions simply legal relics of the past that cluttered statute books. Sabbath laws continued to be enforced, although sporadically in cities with large immigrant populations. Uneven enforcement would encourage groups like the N.R.A., the American Sabbath Union, and the Lord's Day Alliance to push for stricter Sabbath enforcement during the 1870s and 1880s.[82] With respect to oaths, in February, 1875, the North Carolina House of Representatives used the state's religious test to expel one of its members. The incident, which attracted national attention, involved a Quaker who testified that he believed in "one living and true God" but doubted the reality of the trinity, Jesus' resurrection, or hell. His affirmation was not sufficient for his fellow legislators. The constitutional requirement of a belief in a Supreme Being, stated an approving *Raleigh News*, "must mean a God who directs human wants, who loves, and who chastises. This is the Christian's God, and this is the God meant in the constitutional disqualification." *The Christian Statesman* applauded the expulsion.[83]

Finally, Abbot and the Liberals viewed Bible reading in the public schools as a leading impediment to realizing true church-state separation and a secular society. These could never be achieved without "the secularization of the public schools by discontinuing all religious exercises in them." Curiously, even though the School Question was the most dominant church-state issue of the day, and *The Index* otherwise condemned Bible reading and religious exercises, its proposed amendment was vague on the matter. A later version of the amendment would add an express prohibition on taxing people "for the support of any sect or religious body or any number of sects or religious bodies," designed to prevent public funding of parochial schools. But the Religious Freedom Amendment would remain puzzlingly silent as to the other half of the School Question, despite the Demands of Liberalism's clear statement that Bible reading should be enjoined.[84]

This overall state of church-state relations made the Religious Freedom Amendment necessary, wrote *The Index*. "If the United States are one nation, ... if all parts of every nation must, as a condition of healthy national life, be governed by one homogeneous law, and vivified by one common spirit, then the Freedom Amendment is in some shape absolutely essential to the future greatness and happiness of our country." *The Index* asked its readers to organize associations of Liberal Leagues to support the amendment through letters and petitions to members of Congress.[85]

The initial announcement that accompanied the release of its Religious Freedom Amendment suggested that the proposal was chiefly an effort at reverse federalism—to ensure conformity between the religious liberty guarantees in the federal and state constitutions. However, in later articles and speeches, Abbot and the Liberals insisted that the proposed amendment would clarify, if not strengthen, the First Amendment itself. Indeed, the initial proposal included a clause in the first section that additionally prohibited the federal government from "favoring any particular form of religion." Efforts to acknowledge the legal primacy of Christianity necessitated such a clause.[86]

In contrast to the Christian Amendment's symbolic importance to the N.R.A., Abbot chiefly viewed his amendment as a way to realize the Demands of Liberalism. Aside from that different focus, and the obvious substantive differences between the two measures, the two amendments served similar functions for the two organizations. Both measures represented efforts by marginal groups to validate their ideological status in the culture. Both groups viewed their amendments as protecting that status as much as they advanced an ideological position. Each group insisted that its interpretation of church-state relations represented the popular, if not preferred view. Neither amendment would institute a significant change in the law, each side claimed, but simply would clarify the proper relationship between religion and government. At the same time, each group insisted its amendment was necessary to prevent America from sliding down the slope toward infidelity or theocracy, respectively. Abbot and the Liberals more willingly acknowledged that their position lacked widespread support, but that was because people did not fully understand the principle of church-state separation. Support would come when people were better educated about the principle. The aim was "to make the total separation of Church and state the *fact*, as well as the *theory*, of our national existence." Also, Abbot insisted that old attitudes, customs, and laws prevented the full realization of separation. In remarks to a meeting of Liberals, Abbot used the metaphor of an "'unfinished window' of the Constitution [that] needs now to be completed." Even though the document as it now stood established a secular government, "the imperfect guarantees of this political secularism, of this utter divorce of Church and State, need now to be perfected."[87]

The Christian Statesman responded quickly to the challenge of the Religious Freedom Amendment. The N.R.A. understood, or at least claimed for purposes of arousing audiences, that the amendment would change current church-state relations. The *Statesman* tagged the proposal "the Irreligious Amendment," which was designed "to divorce our Government from all connection with religion."

> Denying, as we do, that any wrong is done to disbelievers in the Christian religion by the existing connection of government with Christianity, we cannot admit the propriety of this designation.... So long as the nation continues [to be] predominately Christian in its population, the success of this measure would seem to us the triumph of intolerance... The 'Demands of Liberalism,' which stand beside it in the columns of *The Index*, are a frank and instructive commentary on its purpose and the effect it would have if adopted.[88]

Although the Religious Freedom Amendment was proposed in response to the Christian Amendment, it, along with the Demands of Liberalism, became the new evil the Association could point to justify its own movement. "Had the Constitution always been Christian," stated *The Christian Statesman*, the Religious Freedom Amendment would never have been proposed. "The proposal is a fresh warning that this silence should cease. There is a time to speak. We thank *The Index* for this as for many previous services to the cause of truth." Each amendment, in essence, had become the solution to the threat posed by the other.[89]

Throughout the remainder of 1874, both the N.R.A. and a growing number of Liberal Leagues worked to rally support for their respective amendments. The Association held small conventions in New York in April and in Boston in December. In early 1875, St. Louis and Columbus were sites of other rallies. "That despised movement manifests a vitality inexplicable to most people," reported *The Index*. "The last has by no means been heard of it yet."[90] The Liberals, however, were not passive. Liberal Leagues held local rallies and on October 29, the Free Religious Association held a convention in Providence, Rhode Island. By then, the F.R.A. led by Frothingham and *The Index*, edited by Abbot, were increasingly at odds over the theological drift of the journal and its militant tone. In addition to disagreeing over the secular use of the Bible in the schools, Frothingham and Abbot parted over their willingness to appeal to nontheists (Abbot, though, drew the line at atheists, arguing that one could be a freethinker, a rationalist, a non-Christian, but never an "infidel"). In early 1875, *The Index* sent out a call to form a National Liberal League, in part to unify the various local Leagues while broadening its base from spiritualists and freethinkers to include nontheistic secularists. At the same time, Abbot asked all Liberals to put aside their theological differences and work toward securing "the complete practical embodiment of the original national ideal of a purely SECULAR STATE." This was to be the "sole object" of the organization, hoping to be achieved through the passage of the Religious Freedom Amendment. For the time being, Frothingham remained an officer in the Liberal League, despite the theological stance of the journal he had helped create.[91]

The absence of national activity over the amendments for the remainder of 1874 and into 1875 did not stop *The Index* and *The Christian Statesman* from continuing their verbal battle. In February, 1874, the journals became embroiled in a dispute over the inscription of the national motto, "In God We Trust," on coins, which had been inserted during the Civil War. The motto would better read "*The* God we trust," panned *The Index*, flippantly. "These tactics are not new," responded *The Christian Statesman*. "It is an old device of the enemy to disparage the truth and value of all religious professions, as a means of their abolition."[92]

Through these exchanges, a better understanding of the underlying goals of the N.R.A. emerges. In an October 1874 editorial, *The Christian Statesman* wrote it was the duty of government to suppress "any man's teachings and efforts" if they would "weaken the foundations of law and good government." Abbot responded by asking the *Statesman* whether it favored suppressing *The Index*, since it opposed Christianity as a foundation for good government. *The Index* should be suppressed, replied the *Statesman*, if it were deemed to be blasphemous. "Is 'blasphemy,' then, the only form of speech that 'weakens the foundations of law and good government?'" asked *The Index*. Was this what the N.R.A. intends for freedom of the speech if the Christian Amendment is passed? "It strikes us that, the higher the tone and the greater the ability of an anti-Christian sheet, so much the sooner would the original declaration of the *Statesman* require it to suppress such a sheet." *The Index* asked the *Statesman* to clarify the point, but it declined to do so.[93]

A partial clarification came at a N.R.A. meeting held in Boston in December, 1874. Joseph Cummings, president of Wesleyan University, addressed the body on "The Influence of the Perversion of Truth in Regard to the Connection of Religion and State." Cummings stated that infidels claimed protection for their beliefs under the Constitution. "No man has any right to be an infidel, and no infidel or atheist has rights to protection in the expression of his sentiments," Cummings insisted. A man might be an infidel alone in the quiet of his home and might choose to blaspheme God. Even though he had no right to do so, society could not stop him. But, Cummings continued, if the man "attempted to propagate any ideas tending to subvert society—that is Christian Society—he ought to be crushed like a viper." Society should try him as a criminal.[94]

Newspapers reacted critically to Cummings' speech. "Who is to be the inquisitor that shall judge?" asked *The Independent*. "The principle would forbid and rigorously punish all inculcation of atheistically or infidel teaching." *The Index* was equally harsh. "Such sentiments need only to be put on record, as showing the real bearings of the Christian Amendment movement on freedom of speech and of the press. If the other advocates of this measure disapprove them, they must explicitly disavow them; silence will be properly construed as assent."[95] *The Christian Statesman* attempted later to disassociate the N.R.A. from Cummings' speech, but the damage had been done. The specter of extremism continued to hound the Association.[96]

Apex and Decline

The very public, private war between the N.R.A. and the Liberals came to head in 1876, as both groups organized national conventions in Philadelphia to coincide with the Centennial Exposition held in that city during the summer. Both groups were riding high. Church-state issues remained in the public eye, thanks largely to the School Question. The number of Liberal Leagues had increased from nine in 1873 to more than 40 in 1876, while the N.R.A. had used the defeat of its amendment to rally its supporters.[97] Both groups hoped to capitalize on the anticipated large audiences and press attending the Exposition. It is not clear which group announced its convention first—Abbot sent out a call at a September 1875 meeting of Liberal Leagues for a "Centennial Congress of Liberals" (as evidence of the symbiotic relationship between the two groups, the N.R.A.'s T.P. Stevenson addressed that Liberal League meeting at the invitation of Abbot). That announcement, sent to newspapers throughout the nation, described an ambitious and optimistic program. It promised an attendance of more than 500 people who would plan an agenda "to accomplish the total separation of Church and State, by repealing all laws which exempt church property from taxation, permit Bible reading and worship in the public schools, enforce a Sabbatarian observance of the Sunday, and so forth." To peak interest, the announcement stated in capital letters that delegates would consider measures for "the IMMEDIATE AND ABSOLUTE SECULARIZATION OF THE STATE." Reaction to the announcement was mixed, with some newspapers decrying the agenda as promoting atheism and immorality, but others commending the League and its goals. Whether the newspapers expressed scorn, praise, or mere curiosity, they all agreed on the timeliness of the meeting. As one Indiana newspaper editorialized about the announcement, the effort to emancipate Americans "from church extractions and tyranny, by the total severance of Church and State, is one of the most important movements of the present century."[98]

While Abbot chiefly coveted a national stage to promote his Demands of Liberalism and Religious Freedom Amendment, the N.R.A.'s motives ran beyond promoting its Christian Amendment. In the autumn of 1875, the United States Centennial Commission had announced that the summer-long Centennial Exposition would be opened seven days a week to accommodate foreign visitors and American workers. Religious groups responded quickly to the news of a Sunday opening by organizing letter-writing campaigns to the commissioners. A group of Boston Methodist ministers drafted a petition asking the Commission to "exercise your authority in closing every department, all the buildings, and as far as possible the entire grounds in your charge on . . . the Christian Sabbath." Similar appeals came from the Reformed Presbyterian Church (Covenanters) and the American Bible Society.[99] Mainstream religious periodicals, including *Zion's Herald* and *The Christian Advocate*, also supported a Sabbath ban. Noting the permissive trend in Europe, the *Advocate* asserted that Americans should "not be ashamed to hear it announced to all the world that we are a Sabbath-keeping people." Even the liberal *Christian Union* announced that a Sunday opening of the Exposition would be "discordant with both our national precedents and principles." At the same time, the *Christian Union* criticized an N.R.A. plan to erect a building at the Exposition for the purpose of holding daily prayer meetings, calling it a "nuisance." The N.R.A. sought an "opportunity for [making] utterances of patriotic sentiment sanctified by the power of religion" only to promote the Christian Amendment and its overall agenda, wrote the *Union*.[100]

Facing pressure from the religious community, the Centennial Commission reversed its initial decision opening the exposition on Sundays. This retreat elicited an opposite denunciation from secularists and labor groups. The *Nation* called on the Commission to hold to its original decision while *The Index* urged its readers to write the Commission to voice their disapproval. The Liberals viewed the decision as but another example of the government bending to the wishes of the religious majority when there was "no valid reason for closing it." Because all Americans would be taxed to support the exhibition, wrote *The Index*, it should "be open on Sundays for the accommodation of thousands of citizens who will find that day the most convenient for visiting it." Caught in the middle of a growing controversy, the Centennial Commission set a public hearing to take place on the Exposition grounds on July 6th to resolve the matter.[101]

Prior to that public hearing, the N.R.A. held its national convention in Philadelphia on June 28–30. The convention was not as well attended as in the past but enthusiasm ran high. While noting the poor attendance, the conservative *Zion's Herald* praised the Association for having made progress on behalf of "the maintenance of existing Christian features of the American government against assaults that have been made upon them."[102] The convention program focused on the need for a Christian amendment, despite the School Question being the controversy of the day. Speakers insisted that if the Constitution were Christian, the debate over religious exercises in the schools would not be occurring. Admittedly, maintaining the Bible in the common schools as "our national book" was the crucial issue of the hour. Still, the N.R.A. sought to keep that issue within a larger context, arguing that it was "not the existence of Christianity or the Bible that is a stake." Rather, it was "our national welfare, our national character, our Christian institutions of government, and our religious and civil liberties resting upon them," that were under challenge by the present controversy. Passage of the Christian Amendment was the only solution to preserving the Christian character of the public schools.[103]

The day after the N.R.A. convention concluded, the Centennial Congress of Liberals assembled in Philadelphia. Like the N.R.A. leaders, Abbot and the Liberals placed much hope on their convention, and enthusiasm ran high. Yet as with the N.R.A. convention, attendance at the Centennial Congress was disappointingly low, with approximately 200 people present out of close to 800 League members invited. Again in a mirror image to the N.R.A. convention, the Liberals made their Religious Freedom Amendment the focal point of the meeting rather than any particular item, such as resolving the School Question. The compelling issue was how to achieve the "absolute separation of church and state" through a systemic change. The delegates heard speeches about how organized religion threatened religious equality and a secular state and how unscrupulous politicians manipulated constitutional principles for political gain. The Congress passed thirty resolutions on a host of church-state issues, with one protesting the Bible's use in the schools and "the pretense of its being [declared] a non-sectarian book, as a manifest evasion of the truth, and a willful disregard of equal religious rights of people." Still, those items were the means to achieve that ultimate goal: the secularization of the state and its complete separation from religious influences.[104]

After writing about church and state matters for six years, Abbot and other secularists had little new to say about their vision for a secular America. Still, they sought to convince their audience and the press that their view of separation was not only necessary in a free society, but that it was consistent with existing constitutional principles. Building on his earlier essay, the "Unfinished Window," Abbot insisted that the legal structure for the total separation of church and state already existed in the Constitution; the republic "was founded on the idea," and the Constitution, as "framed and ordained, presuppose[d] the separation of Church and State." The nation could continue "only by virtue of this principle." The principle simply needed perfecting, which was what the Religious Freedom

Amendment was designed to do. In a sense, Liberals believed the Religious Freedom Amendment would serve as an enabling clause for the First Amendment.[105]

Abbot and the Liberals recognized, however, that identifying church-state separation as a fundamental principle was not enough; after all, groups from across the ideological spectrum professed fealty to the concept. In its closing "Patriotic Address" to the American people, the League noted that separation of church and state, as "an abstraction," had become "a stereotyped phrase of American politics, a mere truism which nobody disputes." The Address attempted to explain, in a nutshell, what the phrase truly meant:

> [The] government...is a purely secular one; that is, it confines itself strictly to the secular objects of [the Preamble to the Constitution], and remands the whole subject of religion to the people in their individual capacity. It can establish no national Church and have no national religion; it favors none, it persecutes none, it recognizes none; it deals only with the political interests of the people, and had nothing to do with their religious interests further than to maintain their religious liberties and protect their equal religious rights.[106]

This understanding church-state separation was relatively modest, containing sentiments Catholics and evangelicals could embrace: no national church; no religious preferences; protection of religious liberties. Yet in other places in the Address, and as contained in the Religious Freedom Amendment and the Demands of Liberalism, the Liberals' notion of separation went further: the government was not only forbidden from privileging religion but also from providing any financial or symbolic support for religion. Protestants agreed generally with this sentiment, but the Liberals had a broad understanding of financial or symbolic support of religion. When the government exempted church property from taxes, funded religion or promoted it in the schools, supported chaplains, enforced Sunday laws, or acknowledged religious holidays and festivals, "we unite Church and State," Abbot declared. Separation also prohibited the church from "interfere[ing] with the workings of a civil government." And, most innovative for the time, separation called for equal liberty among believers and nonbelievers and a secular state. This was what "the principle of total separation of Church and State means; and that is the general theory taken for granted in every line of our national Constitution."[107]

Despite the efforts of both groups to explain their positions and broaden their appeal, press coverage of their meetings was generally unfavorable. With two such contrasting approaches to church-state matters, press accounts frequently favored one agenda or the other, but few offered endorsements. Both groups were "made up of earnest and well-meaning men, representing two opposing tendencies," wrote the *Boston Globe*. "The one is toward a union of Church and State, and the other toward a complete severance of Church and State." While not expressing preference for the Liberals, the *Globe* criticized the N.R.A. platform, stating "it is [not] for the government to identify itself with any sect of form of religious belief." Newspapers also responded that church-state separation already existed—just not the type envisioned by the Liberals—such that tinkering with the Constitution should be avoided. Particularly painful for the Liberals were reviews by liberal Protestant journals that otherwise endorsed church-state separation. Beecher's *Christian Union* was caustic: "The 'immediate and absolute secularization of the State,' if it means anything, means the abolition of all recognition of religion from American institutions," including leaving schools without a moral basis. "To separate Church and State is one thing; to separate religion and politics is another." Even more stinging for the Liberals, the *Union* wrote that it wished that it "could bid God-speed" to the N.R.A., but it, too, found its agenda "ludicrously inadequate." Summing up its disdain for both groups, *The Independent* remarked that "[i]t remains to be seen which will outbid the other in narrowness and bigotry."[108]

The Centennial Exposition Commission held its public hearing on the Sunday closing issue two days following the conclusion of the Liberal League convention. One source of opposition to the closing came from labor groups seeking accommodations for workers to visit the exhibits on their sole day off work. George W. Biddle, representing an association of workingmen, presented a "monster petition which formed a roll quite three feet in diameter" containing 65,000 signatures against closing the grounds on Sundays. Everyone recognized that the closing was chiefly a religious issue, however, and the testimony reflected as much. Francis Abbot appeared for the Liberal League, presenting a petition gathered at the just-completed League convention. Abbot asserted that the closing preferred Sunday observers while it denied equal liberty for those who did not observe the Sabbath. The Constitution required "equal religious rights" which meant government impartiality on religious matters. "The Church has no right under the Constitution thus to impose any part of its creed on the State, or to claim for those who believe it any temporal advantage over those who dislike it." Abbot also asserted the decision discriminated against the working-class. But Abbot undercut his presentation by accusing the commissioners of hypocrisy for ignoring "the alleged sacredness of the day" by lifting the ban to allow the Emperor of Brazil to attend on a Sunday. The pugilist prevailed over the professor.[109]

T.P. Stevenson, appearing for the N.R.A., took advantage of Abbot's misstep, characterizing the Sunday closing as simply reflecting the long-standing practice of Sabbath observance. He also asserted America was a Christian nation, and the Christian community expected the Commission to uphold the Christian Sabbath, as it was the law and custom of the nation. Stevenson then launched into what the *Philadelphia Item* characterized as a "vile attack" upon liberalism. Flaunting a copy of the Demands of Liberalism, he read the commissioners selected excerpts of the League's platform. "We demand that all laws looking for the enforcement of Christian morality shall be abrogated," Stevenson read, omitting the League's call for morality based on nature and science. This was the threat that liberalism represented to society, he warned. Christians must resist all steps toward secularism. Abbot strenuously objected to Stevenson's misrepresentations, but was ruled out of order by "the religious minded portion of the Commission." After hearing other testimony the Commission reaffirmed its decision to close the Exposition on Sundays. Abbot later wrote that the episode was but the first battle between humanity and tyranny, with the latter emerging victorious. Only the passage of the Religious Freedom Amendment and the efforts of the Liberal Leagues could forestall additional ecclesiastical incursions on people's liberty.[110]

The two organizations continued to spar over their competing visions of church-state relations for the remainder of the decade. Each group worked desperately to broadcast their messages, to convince the average American that it mattered whether the nation was officially designated Christian or secular. But most people needed a concrete issue, such as the School Question, to make the broader ideological questions relevant. As discussed in the next chapter, the debate over the Blaine Amendment between 1875 and 1876 would provide that context, and both the N.R.A. and Liberals attempted to reap what ever mileage they could from that particular controversy. The irony is that the debate over the School Question was so intense, involving concrete issues about parochial school funding, Bible reading, and Catholic-Protestant infighting, that neither the N.R.A. nor the Liberal Leagues were successful in having people see the controversy from their larger perspectives. To be certain, the Blaine Amendment would lead people to think about church-state matters in broader terms, and both groups would influence that debate. But neither group was able to capitalize on those broader considerations, chiefly because their respective agendas went further than most people found necessary to resolve the School Question. With the resolution of the Blaine Amendment, widespread interest in church-state issues waned.

Decline came for the Liberal League before it did for the N.R.A. For the remainder of the 1870s, Francis Abbot and *The Index* warned all who would listen about the threats to religious freedom and republican values represented by the N.R.A. and of the need for the Religious Freedom Amendment. The League and *The Index* had had their moment, however. With the public exhausted with the School Question after 1876 and no significant church-state threat on the immediate horizon, membership in the League dropped while the number of chapters fell from the 1876 high of forty.[111]

The issue chiefly responsible for the League's decline was not Bible reading, however, but obscenity and free-love. In 1873, Anthony Comstock, an evangelical crusader against public vice, secured the enactment of a federal statute that strengthened prohibitions on the mailing of obscenity and pornography. Reputedly, Comstock had written the new law with the help of Benjamin V. Abbott, lawyer and brother of social reformer Lyman Abbott, and Supreme Court Justice William Strong. The U.S. Postmaster then appointed Comstock a special investigator, and the latter, with his organization the Society for the Suppression of Vice, mounted a campaign to cleanse American society of immorality. Targets of the new law included not only purveyors of obscene and lewd writings and pictures, but also people who distributed information through the mail about birth control, abortion, and free-love.[112]

Comstock's war on obscenity, and his overall moral crusade, was part of a larger effort to ensure America's culture remained Christian. Even though Comstock acknowledged his religious motivations, and openly associated with the N.R.A., liberals and secularists divided over how best to respond to the obscenity ban and Comstock's moral crusade. On one side, many free religionists viewed the ability to write about contraception and free-love as an extension of rights of conscience, and advocates of sexual and reproductive freedom frequently associated themselves with the freethought movement. Together, they objected to the censorship and "ecclesiastical despotism" they believed underlay the law and its enforcement. Opposition mounted after Comstock had the editor of the radical skeptical newspaper *Truth-Seeker* arrested for publishing articles on animal reproduction and one that attacked Jesus Christ. Noted agnostic orator Robert Ingersoll, a Liberal League vice president, organized a petition in 1878 containing 50,000 signatures that asked Congress to repeal the law based on its impact on freedom of conscience, freedom of the press, and personal liberty. Yet others in the liberal and secularist communities hesitated to condemn the law or call for its repeal out of fear of being labeled opponents of public morality. Francis Abbot, for one, was particularly concerned that religious conservatives would capitalize on any secularist opposition to the obscenity ban. The issue came to a head during the League's Centennial Congress, with attendees splitting over whether to oppose the obscenity crusade. Abbot resisted condemning the law, and he devoted one of the sessions to a presentation on the importance of "natural morality" as an alternative to religious-based systems. Under his guidance, the Centennial Congress passed a resolution that recognized "the absolute necessity" of "proper legislation against obscene and indecent publications" while deploring the "indefiniteness or ambiguity" in the current law and the discretionary authority possessed by Comstock. Abbot and his "moralist" allies were able to defeat a motion seeking the law's full repeal.[113]

The ability of Abbot and League moralists to control the obscenity issue was short lived. Many within the League agitated for a firmer stance, one that supported sexual freedom, free expression, and the repeal of the postal law. During the League's 1878 convention in Syracuse, New York, the growing rift broke open. The "free-love" faction took control of the convention, removing Abbot as president of the League and adopting a resolution favoring repeal. Abbot and other moralists then withdrew from the League, forming a competing organization called the National Liberal League of America, later called the American Liberal Union. But Abbot was unable to maintain the competing organization, and he eventually lost control of *The Index* to Frothingham and the Free Religious Association, the former who supported the free-love faction of the Liberal League. Having lost control of both his movement and its journal, Abbot retired from advocacy to Boston in 1880, where he wrote philosophical works about scientific theism. The old League flourished for several more years, later changing its name to the American Secular Union with Robert Ingersoll serving as president. With Abbot no longer at the helm of either *The Index* or the League, however, the movement lost its most prominent voice for secularization and against the moral crusaders for a Christian America.[114]

The overall impact of *The Index*, the Liberal League, and Abbot's work was mixed. During its heyday (1871–1876), *The Index* significantly impacted the public debate over church-state matters, engaging a much wider audience than its core supporters or actual readership. Abbot was indefatigable and unrelenting in his advocacy for secular society and the total separation of church and state, and he was the nation's leading spokesperson for that perspective. His writings and those of other contributors to *The Index* reflected an emergent questioning among intellectuals about previously accepted notions of church-state relations. While many liberal Protestants and even secularists may have disagreed with his absolutism if not his heightened rhetoric, his views represented an extension of sentiments that many people shared. His perspective, while at the margins of the debate, established one of the boundaries for the larger discussion about church-state matters. It could not be ignored.[115]

Abbot and *The Index* were most effective in exposing the machinations of the N.R.A. His greatest success came through his giant petition in opposition to the Christian Amendment; although the measure had little hope of advancing in Congress, Abbot's action effectively killed the amendment forever. On the other side, Abbot's zeal for absolute secularization made few converts, and his frequently biting articles made few friends. The Demands of Liberalism, while intended to be a positive manifesto around which liberals of many persuasions could rally, frightened moderate and liberal religionists. It only reinforced suspicions about the purported extremism of nonreligionists. For most people, Abbot's agenda was chiefly negative and threatened societal values rather than affirming core constitutional principles.

Unlike the Liberal League and *The Index*, the N.R.A. sustained itself for the reminder of the century. The Association never grew in numbers, but it found a niche as an organization promoting conservative moral reforms. The organization never abandoned its goal of securing a Christian Amendment or obtaining a formal declaration of the nation's allegiance to a Christian God. That objective, however, was put aside in favor of securing the more practical attributes of a Christian nation. Allied with an emerging cadre of moral reform organizations, the N.R.A. became a forceful advocate for stricter Sabbath law enforcement, obscenity laws, a national divorce law, prohibition, anti-polygamy laws, and devotional instruction in the public schools. With its committed and indefatigable leadership, the Association's influence far exceeded its membership.[116]

The N.R.A.'s resiliency was due in part to good timing. By the closing decades of the century, evangelical and orthodox Protestants had grown increasingly concerned over the nation's moral decline. Conservatives became alarmed not only at the secularizing trends in public education but by other threats to their ideal of a Christian republic: urbanization, industrialization, labor unrest, and a growing religious pluralism fueled by a rapidly expanding foreign immigration. These concerns were encapsulated in the 1885 best-selling book *Our Country: Its Possible Future and its Present Crisis*, where Reverend Josiah Strong listed immigration, Romanism, wealth, the city, and the School Question among eight perils facing the nation.[117] A few critics charged that Protestantism was no longer up to meeting society's challenges: the "world has, indeed, been moving very rapidly during the last generation, and theology, which used to be in the van of human thought, and in some measure to lead in human progress, has fallen to the rear, and is in imminent danger of being left altogether."[118] The challenges and criticisms represented a wake-up call for many evangelicals who were not willing to surrender. A muscular form of Protestantism was the answer. "The new and strange perils that have come upon us—socialism, anarchism, Romanism, saloonism, political corruption, and kindred evils—can be relieved only by organized, applied Christianity," asserted the *Presbyterian Quarterly* in 1888. That applied Christianity took the form of a new moral reform crusade, one that fit the N.R.A. perfectly.[119]

For conservative Protestants, the lax enforcement of Sunday laws and their flaunting by merchants and entertainment venues were troubling signs of a secularizing trend in the culture. Building on its experience in the controversy over the closing of the Centennial Exposition, the N.R.A. quickly adopted Sunday law enforcement as a chief cause. Working with the Evangelical Alliance, the Lord's Day Alliance, and the American Sabbath Union, the N.R.A. lobbied for vigorous enforcement of existing Sunday laws and enhancing statutes where they were weak. At one rally attended by President Rutherford Hayes and members of Congress, Supreme Court Justice and former N.R.A. president William Strong spoke of the "growing disregard of the Sabbath in this country." Strong charged that in immigrant neighborhoods, "Sunday differs from no other day, except by an increase in vice and disorder." Such places were "plague spots in the community, not only poisoning its morals, disturbing its good order, but depreciating its property. They are Sodoms."[120] In the mid-1880s, the N.R.A. joined a campaign with the Woman's Christian Temperance Union, the Lord's Day Alliance and the American Sabbath Union to enact a national Sunday law to prohibit Sunday mail delivery, the running of Sunday trains, and all nonessential government activity on Sundays.[121] Evangelical Senator Henry Blair held a hearing on a national Sunday law in his Committee on Education and Labor in 1888, at which representatives from moral reform organizations testified, including T. P. Stevenson of the N.R.A. Stevenson and the other evangelicals candidly acknowledged that the purpose of the new law was to ensure that Sunday activities conformed to a Christian standard. Lacking broader support, the bill died in committee.[122]

The N.R.A. continued to agitate for other moral reforms, but never lost sight of its ultimate goal of obtaining a formal recognition of God in the Constitution. That effort received a boost when in 1892 the Supreme Court of the United States issued an opinion in which it declared American to be a "Christian nation." The case, *Church of the Holy Trinity v. United States*, involved a challenge to a new immigration law by a church that had been fined for hiring a new rector from Great Britain. Writing for the Court, Justice David J. Brewer held that the law did not apply to the hiring of professionals who "toiled by the brain" and, in addition, that the government could not enforce a law that conflicted with the nation's religious heritage. Brewer's opinion cited extensively data he believed demonstrated how the nation's laws respected Christian customs and practices. Although the "Christian nation" part of the opinion constituted dicta, and did not control the Court's holding, the N.R.A. and other religious conservatives seized on the opinion as a formal declaration of nation's official Christian status.[123]

Seeking to build on the renew attention given to the issue of America's Christian nationhood, the N.R.A. had its Christian Amendment reintroduced in Congress in 1894. The Association organized a massive petition drive through its chapters and sympathetic churches, with the petitions citing *Holy Trinity* as authority for an amendment.[124] By 1896, the number of petitions had grown sufficiently large, such that Congress agreed to hear testimony on the proposed Christian Amendment. At a hearing before House Judiciary Committee on March 11, 1896, the N.R.A. renewed its arguments about the need for a formal affirmation of God in the Constitution. Justice Brewer's opinion had demonstrated the nation's religious heritage; it was time to make that connection official and indisputable. But the "Christian nation" declaration in *Holy Trinity* only undermined the amendment's chances. Congressmen replied that Brewer's opinion demonstrated that the nation was already Christian, so an amendment was unnecessary. The committee voted to table the Christian Amendment indefinitely.[125] Once again, the N.R.A. had misjudged the support for an affirmation, even among evangelicals. One evangelical scholar described the N.R.A.'s efforts as "idle and unnecessary," and appealing only to "superficial religious sentiment." The necessity of a formal legal acknowledgment of God, so important to the N.R.A., never resonated with the rank and file of evangelical Protestantism.[126]

Following the 1896 hearing, the N.R.A. slowly declined into obscurity. The Association continued to work on Christian moral legislation and publish its journal, *The Christian Statesman*, well into the twentieth century. Occasionally, it revived petition drives to Congress, but it never again received a hearing on its Christian Amendment. The N.R.A.'s greatest influence came not through its amendment drives of the 1870s and 1890s, but through lobbying for more practicable measures that reinforced the modicum of Christian morality on the culture. Even though its ultimate goal of a symbolic acknowledgment placed it on the margins, like the Liberal League and *The Index*, the N.R.A. spoke at times for a larger constituency than its core followers. Its arguments and solutions appealed to many conservative Protestants, even if they did not support the Association's overall agenda. Through its commitment to realizing America as a republic of the Bible, the N.R.A. played a significant role in the public debate over the meaning of church-state relations during the nineteenth-century.[127]

5

The Blaine Amendment

One issue that had remained central in the battles between the N.R.A. and the Liberals was the School Question. The issue had festered since the decision of the Cincinnati school board, simmering when it was not in the public spotlight. School boards in several cities followed Cincinnati's lead in abolishing religious exercises or by allowing schools in Catholic wards to conduct the exercises according to Catholic practices. The number of boards undertaking such actions was never overwhelming, but it suggested a growing trend, at least among cities in the Northeast and Midwest.[1] In the process, school boards were redefining the normative role of public education. The New York state Code of Public Instruction announced the new regime: "The object of the common-school system of this State is to afford means of secular instruction to all children. . . . For their religious training the State does not provide, and with this it does not interfere." The Code did allow for the reading of scriptures, voluntarily attended by students or with parental approval, provided it occurred before or after the school day. Even then, the Code directed that "instruction of a sectarian or religious-denominational character must be avoided; and teachers must conform themselves, during school-hours, to their legitimate and proper duties." One can question whether instruction in most public schools was now truly secular, as opposed to being nonsectarian, but the fact that the Code now identified education with the former designation indicated a significant shift was under way. Bible reading during the *secular* school day was not a legitimate function.[2]

Bible reading and religious exercises in the schools remained contentious throughout the decade, but by the early 1870s focus shifted to the funding side of the controversy: of how to preserve the public school system while ensuring that Catholic schools did not obtain a share of the school funds. By mid-decade, the funding controversy heated up, threatening to eclipse other policy issues on the national stage. The result was the introduction, and near passage, of the Blaine Amendment to the U.S. Constitution.

The Blaine Amendment is one of the more controversial proposed amendments in the history of the Constitution; in recent years it has become the most debated, and sometimes vilified, constitutional proposal concerning church-state matters. As previously described, the proposed amendment sought to apply the proscriptions of the First Amendment religion clauses to the actions of state and local governments while expressly prohibiting the appropriation of public funds to support any school under the control of a religious sect or denomination.[3] Modern-day critics have attacked the Blaine Amendment on both textual and contextual grounds. The proposed language, which would have prohibited appropriating public funds to "any religious sect," would have mandated the public financial disfranchisement of Catholic parochial and other religious schools. Even though public funding of religious education was rare by 1870, and many states already had constitutional or statutory prohibitions on funding religious schools, the Blaine Amendment would have made this prohibition universal. Second, critics allege that the choice of the word "sect," and the highly charged debate that accompanied the proposed amendment, indicate that its chief purpose was to discriminate against the Catholic Church. Because the overwhelming percentage of religious schools were Catholic, and the debate at times devolved into ethnic and religious aspersions, critics charge that the amendment and the principles it promoted were motivated chiefly by anti-Catholic animus. This is the basis for Justice Thomas' condemnation of the legal prohibition on funding pervasively sectarian institutions and for Professor Hamburger's larger critique of the no-funding rule.[4] In addition, critics maintain that because twenty-two states adopted no-funding provisions in their constitutions during the fifty years following the defeat of the Blaine Amendment, the anti-Catholic animus and bigotry that informed that latter debate are attributable to the state funding prohibitions, rendering them equally corrupt.[5]

As the previous chapters demonstrate, any such critique of the no-funding rule is incomplete. The Blaine Amendment arose during a period of heightened interest in the School Question in particular and church-state matters generally. In order to understand the Blaine Amendment, the episode must be evaluated within that context and with an appreciation for the various perspectives held by those who participated in both the specific events and the larger debate. People were not of two minds, Protestant and Catholic, in how to resolve the School Question. Like the larger debate over the no-funding rule, people approached the issues presented in the Blaine Amendment from various perspectives. They understood its significance and potential differently. Also, it is inaccurate to speak of one "Blaine Amendment" or fail to distinguish that proposal from its rivals. Multiple proposals were made during the controversy—President Grant's proposal, James Blaine's initial amendment, the House version, and the final Senate resolution—all containing distinct provisions that would have impacted church-state relations in different ways. The episode defies a simple accounting.

The "Funding Crisis" of the 1870s

Several factors came together during the first half of the 1870s to create a perfect storm of controversy over the School Question. The most direct cause of heightened tensions came from renewed Catholic efforts to secure state and local funding for Catholic schools and institutions. Since the Plenary Council of 1852, Catholic bishops had urged all parishes to create parochial schools and insisted that Catholic parents send their children to those schools if available. In conjunction with this effort, church leaders kept pressuring local officials for financial assistance, despite statutes and constitutional provisions that expressly prohibited aid to sectarian institutions or education dollars from going to schools not under public control. "We ask simply that the 'money raised by taxes'... shall be divided *pro rata*, and so, by dividing the difficulty, conquer it!" wrote the *Catholic World*. As the Catholic population grew in cities along the east coast and in the Midwest, local politicians, attune to their growing political strength, became more receptive to Catholic requests for public support for parochial schools and charitable institutions. By the late-1860s, Catholic institutions were increasingly successful in securing funds controlled by local officials and political machines such as New York's Tammany Hall, with the transactions often lacking in political transparency. One contemporary account noted that between 1869 and 1871 the Tammany-controlled city government contributed $1,125,000 to Catholic organizations, while $300,000 was given to charities controlled by Protestant, Jewish and other private entities.[6]

The chief beneficiaries of this public funding were Catholic charitable institutions—orphanages, reformatories, asylums, and hospitals—but some grants made their way to parochial schools as well. Distributions to charitable institutions were generally consistent with state law. As noted earlier, an 1850 New York law had allowed private orphan asylums to receive financial support for the care and education of its inmates from various sources, including from public school funds. In 1851, and again in 1867, the New York Supreme Court (a trial court) had interpreted that statute to allow Catholic orphan asylums to receive public monies for their operations that were not derived from the *state school fund* (though the earlier holding had appeared to bar any public financial support for essentially educational functions). Both rulings had affirmed the status quo whereby religious organizations received public monies for their charitable operations which, among Catholic orphanages, included educational functions. Still, revelations that Catholic organizations were receiving sizeable, and allegedly disproportionate, allocations led to a failed legislative effort in 1867 to prohibit grants to charities that were "religious or sectarian in character."[7]

The appropriations only increased. In a July, 1869 article entitled "Our Established Church," a guest author for *Putnam's Magazine* charged that the Catholic Church was the chief beneficiary of public political and financial largesse in New York City and in other eastern cities. In addition to decrying the number of city offices held by Irish Catholics and the value of church properties, the article charged that Catholic charities were receiving thousands of public dollars out of proportion to Protestant and Jewish entities. In a reply, the *Catholic World* acknowledged that church charities had received over $275,000, but asserted that amount was far less than comparable allocations to Protestant and public charitable institutions. The *World* denied that any public funds paid for sectarian functions, including parochial schools, though it also disputed that its activities in the orphanages and asylums could be considered sectarian. This elicited a response from *Putnam's* editors defending the original article and deriding the *World* for claiming that all grants made to non-Catholic institutions were under the control of Protestants and for their sole benefit. Neither side could see the kernel of truth in the other side's point. More than anything, the exchange indicated the growing controversy over the public funding of Catholic institutions.[8]

Wider conflict over the funding of Catholic institutions erupted in 1872 with the release of a report by the New York City Council of Political Reform on the financial corruption of Tammany Hall. Included in the report was a section on "Sectarian Appropriations of Public Money" which alleged that hundreds of thousands in public funds were paid not only to support religious charities but also to aid religious schools. In 1869, Boss William M.Tweed, in his capacity as a state senator, had hidden a provision in the city tax levy that provided grants to private schools with two hundred or more students. Of the $528,000 given to religious schools in 1869–1870, $412,000 went to Catholic institutions. Republican and Protestant leaders were able to have the law repealed in 1870, but the money from the levy continued to flow for another two years.[9] The 1872 Political Reform report highlighted the circumvention of state law and the disproportionate funding favoring Catholics, tying it to the political corruption of Tammany machine. Even with the repeal of the levy, grants to religious charities continued, with ninety percent of the funding, or approximately $640,000, going to Catholic institutions in 1871. The *Catholic World* again defended its position, claiming that many charities listed were not Catholic while objecting at the insinuation with the report's use of the word "sectarian." In the end, however, the *World* acknowledged that Catholic charities and schools received the bulk of the funds, with the journal falling back on the importance of a religious-based education. The report elicited the expected outpouring from the Protestant press. *Harper's Weekly* complained that despite a renewed legislative ban on public support for sectarian education, all Catholic agencies were interrelated, such that no one really knew how this money was being spent. The magazine also charged that at the same time as the Catholic Church was receiving the funds for its schools and charities, the Catholic archdiocese had petitioned for the removal of the Protestant Bible from New York City Schools. Giving warning to its national readership, *Harper's* asserted that such "crafty working, of which we have given sample, is going on all over the Union."[10]

A few people sought alternative solutions to the funding crisis. One possibility was to consolidate Catholic schools into the public system. The most ambitious effort took place in 1873 in Poughkeepsie, New York, where local priests placed two parochial schools under the control of public school officials. The schools were open to children of all faiths and no religious instruction took place during the school day (though a majority of the teachers remained Catholic nuns). One reporter visited the schools "expecting to find evasions of the law, and sectarian schools supported by public funds." To his surprise, he found "all provisions of the law fully complied with." The *New England Journal of Education* also commended the experiment, writing that "there has resulted a better harmony between both classes in the school," though noting that only the "merest fraction" of students remained at the schools for the voluntary religious exercises. Beecher's *Christian Union* also expressed hope that the "Poughkeepsie Plan" might serve as a model for other cities: "if it shall be found to offer a solution of the troubles between Protestants and Catholics in regard to the schools, we shall rejoice."[11] A handful of cities copied the plan, but it fell short of offering a solution to the School Question. In some places, consolidation was not done with similar trust and good faith. And consolidation drives in Buffalo and New York City fell victim to entrenched interests. Protestants remained suspicious, with *The Independent* opposing "amalgamating the parochial system with the public-school system without essentially changing the character of one or the other." Catholic leaders also condemned the actions of the two accommodating priests, with the *Freeman's Journal* characterizing the plan as "how to destroy the Catholic faith." Orestes Brownson, who twenty years earlier had recommended a similar arrangement as a means of assimilating Catholic children into American culture, also insisted that only a "thoroughly Catholic" education was valid for children.[12]

Other factors contributed to the tensions. Coinciding with the revelations over funding were reports of a convocation of bishops and other church leaders meeting in Rome in 1870. The conclave had several goals, but American newspapers highlighted two aspects particularly troubling to Protestants and secularists. A chief function of the conclave was to reassert the church's political independence and resistance to the liberalizing and modernizing trends in Europe. German Chancellor Otto von Bismarck was about to undertake his *Kulturkampf* of reforms and suppression of the Catholic Church, while Italy was finally being unified under an anti-papal republican government. The Vatican felt under siege from liberalizing movements as never before, and it sought clerical affirmation of Pope Pius IX's 1864 Syllabus of Errors against modernity and liberalism. The Syllabus, in addition to affirming the Pope's unwillingness to "reconcile himself, and come to terms with progress, liberalism and modern civilization," had condemned Protestantism, public education, freedom of conscience, and the notion of separation of church and state. Although the Syllabus was directed chiefly at the European situation and not America, the Pope now required the endorsement of the American hierarchy attending the conclave. The Protestant and secular press expressed alarm that the illiberal contents of the Syllabus contradicted American values and institutions: the Syllabus was "utterly at war with out entire theory of government, and hostile alike to human liberty, the advancement of science and learning, and the rights and dignity of man." Compounding the Syllabus, the conclave declared the infallibility of the papacy on matters of doctrine. Critics interpreted these two factors to mean that Catholic bishops would promote the church's illiberal tenets among their American parishioners, including opposing public education.[13]

The Protestant reaction was not allayed by the American Catholic press, led by an increasingly tractable Orestes Brownson, who defended both the Syllabus and papal infallibility. He embraced the criticism that "the Syllabus condemns all the distinctive features of what is called 'modern civilization.'" The church was "instituted by God himself to maintain his law in the government of men and nations," Brownson wrote. "Hence the necessity of the union of church and state; and the condemnation in the Syllabus of those who demand their total separation and the independence of the state." As for the doctrine of infallibility, it was necessary because Catholics were "beginning to go astray after so-called Catholic liberalism," which Brownson now eschewed. Only if "the American people bec[a]me truly Catholic and submissive children of the Holy Father [would] their republic [be] safe." Such statements did little to quell the growing alarm among Protestants and secularists.[14]

Responding to the Vatican conclave and other events, former New York Supreme Court judge (and future Liberal League vice president) Elisha P. Hurlbut circulated a proposed amendment to the Constitution in 1870. Like the Blaine Amendment would do, Hurlbut's measure proposed to apply the text of the First Amendment to the states. More noteworthy, his amendment contained an additional sentence: "But congress may enact such laws as it shall deem necessary to control or prevent the establishment of continuance of any foreign hierarchical power in this country, founded on principles or dogmas antagonistic to republican institutions." In an accompanying book, Hurlbut explained the amendment was necessary to prevent states from establishing or favoring any religion or otherwise infringing on religious liberty, but he directed his arguments at the threat presented by the Syllabus and a renewed Catholic aggressiveness. The proposal, he acknowledged, would authorize Congress to forbid "the exercise of any priestly office under a foreign appointment...whose organization, discipline and teachings among us, were antagonistical and dangerous to our political institutions." If anyone still doubted to whom the provision was directed, Hurlbut wrote that "[c]andor compels the admission, that this provision points to the Roman pontiff." Hurlbut's proposal attracted a fair amount of attention, despite its blatant anti-Catholic language. Brownson brushed it aside, calling it the same "old charges and calumnies" of "the very ignorant." But at a minimum, it raised the idea of addressing the growing controversy through a constitutional amendment.[15]

Other events fueled the controversy. Catholic-Protestant tensions boiled over into violence with massive rioting in New York City in July 1871. In what became known as the Orange Riot, Tammany Mayor A. Oakey Hall had denied Irish Protestants permission to march in Catholic wards to commemorate the victory of William of Orange over the Catholic King James II in the 1690 Battle of Boyne. Democratic Governor John Hoffman overrode Hall's decision and called out the state militia to protect the Orangemen in their march. Catholic crowds pelted the marchers with paving stones and rioting ensued, with the militia opening fire on the crowd. In the end, more than sixty lay dead with another one hundred wounded. The casualties were the worst since the draft riots during the Civil War, and newspapers generally blamed the tragedy on heightened tensions caused when the Tweed-controlled city government had tried to block the march due to Catholic demands. (Inconsistently, newspapers also blamed the Democratic governor for allowing the march so as to demonstrate he was not beholden to the Catholic hierarchy.) The riot had more to do with long-standing animosity and economic competition between the two Irish groups than it did with religious conflict. *Catholic World* asserted that "[i]t was, as everybody knows, an Irish riot, occasioned by an old Irish feud...not an American or a Catholic riot." Still, for most observers, the incident evinced the intractable conflict between Catholics and Protestants. The riot was instrumental in reviving nativist activity in the mid-1870s.[16]

As these revelations and events were unfolding, secular newspapers and Protestant journals continued documenting conflicts over religious exercises in the schools, tying the concessions on Bible reading to Catholic demands on the school fund. Now it appeared that the Protestant concessions had been pointless. Protestants had given up much for little gain, and Catholics, Jews and infidels were not only to blame. Moderate and liberal Protestants had surrendered their birthright by yielding willingly to minority religious concerns. This soured evangelicals even more to Catholic requests, particularly for a share of the school fund. Religious dissention over the two issues only increased throughout 1874–1875. In June, 1875, the Rochester school board banned "all religious exercises of any nature" from its schools, as did boards in other cities. "Everywhere the indications of a rising tide of Evangelical Protestant sentiment on the school question are visible," reported *The Index*. "The Chicago ministers are almost a unit in protesting against the exclusion of the Bible from the schools." Other religious leaders and educators feared that failure to bend on Bible reading would bring about a division of public funding with irreparable damage to public schooling.[17] Local grassroots groups, many with nativist leanings, sprung up to defend Bible reading and oppose the funding of Catholic schools and charities. Surveying the growing tension, the *New York Tribune* speculated that the issue was threatening "the very existence of the republic." In an 1875 article entitled "A Coming Struggle," the *Tribune* wrote that the "admission of parochial schools as part of the public school system is openly demanded. Sooner or later the broad question must be met, 'Whether popular education belongs to the State or to the churches.'"[18]

With the growing agitation over the School Question, it was only a matter of time before the issue became fully politicized. Local politicians had long manipulated the school issue for local political gain. But by 1875, the School Question was emerging as a national political issue. As early as 1871, Massachusetts Senator and Republican Party Chairman Henry Wilson had proposed that the party adopt universal education as its vanguard issue. The public was tiring of Reconstruction, and Wilson feared the Republican Party risked losing popular support unless it championed other reform causes. The party had been born "as an organization of reform and progress," Wilson wrote, and to maintain that mantel it must embrace "the living issues of the hour and march abreast with the spirit of the age." Wilson recommended that the party make it "one of its prominent and proclaimed purposes to unify and educate the people."[19] Four years later, the need for a new reform issue had become more desperate. In the 1874 election, the Republican Party lost control of the House of Representatives for the first time since the Civil War. The following year, parochial school funding and Catholic control of the state Democratic Party became leading issues in the Ohio gubernatorial election. Of note, that election featured a nomination fight between the victorious Rutherford B. Hayes and Judge Alphonso Taft in which the latter's vote in the *Minor* case became an issue (both men equally opposed funding religious schools). Finally, President Ulysses Grant's administration was racked by corruption and his political future, as well as that of the Republican Party, depended on diverting public attention away from the revelations of the Whiskey Ring. One way to counteract Democratic calls for reform was to emphasize universal public education, a cause which would distinguish the Republicans from the Democrats with their Southern conservative wing and Catholic following.[20]

A July 8, 1875 article in the Democrat-leaning *New York Tribune* confirmed this strategic move. The newspaper charged that the Republican Party was embracing "free, nonsectarian schools" in order to capitalize on the reform issue while appealing to Protestant and anti-Catholic voters. Quoting from the *St. Louis Republican*, the *Tribune* stated that all signs "indicate an intention on the part of the managers of the Republican party to institute a general war against the Catholic Church.... Some new crusading cry thus becomes a necessity of existence, and it seems to be decided that the cry of 'No Popery' is likely to prove most available." At the same time, the *Tribune* cautioned Democrats from treating the issue "as a fictitious one, manufactured by Republican demagogues." "[E]very emphatic demand for division of public school funds, recognition of parochial schools, or abolition of the system of secular education, has come from adherents of the Democratic party," the paper charged. The *Tribune* urged both parties to address the issue responsibly. Controversy over the School Question, with respect to both Bible reading and distribution of school monies, "will not die, and . . . sooner or later, the question must be met manfully, candidly, and decisively."[21]

The Proposals

In the fall of 1875, a decisive proposal came from the most manful of sources. On September 30, President Ulysses S. Grant (figure 5.1) addressed a convention of the Society of the Army of the Tennessee meeting in Des Moines, Iowa. Grant's speech touched on a host of patriotic themes, with the President asserting that one way to "preserve us as a free nation" was to "foster intelligence." To accomplish this goal, Grant urged the attendees to:

> Encourage free schools, and resolve that not one dollar, appropriated for their support, shall be appropriated to the support of any sectarian schools. Resolve that neither the State nor Nation, nor both combined shall support institutions of learning... [that teach] sectarian, pagan, or atheistical dogmas. Leave the matter of religion to the family altar, the Church, and the private school, supported entirely by private contributions. Keep the Church and State forever separate.

In his speech Grant also urged support for other important political values: guarantees for "free thought, free speech, free press, pure morals, unfettered religious sentiments, and of equal rights and privileges to all men irrespective of nationality, color, or religion." The call for universal, nonsectarian education, however, overshadowed the other aspects of the speech.[22]

The audience of veterans responded enthusiastically to Grant's speech, as did the Protestant and secular press which reprinted the remarks nationwide. The *Chicago Tribune* declared that the speech "set the nation agog," while the Methodist *Christian Advocate* described it as being "full of wisdom." The *Christian Advocate* proposed that the ends "contemplated in the well-considered words of President Grant can be reached only through an amendment to the Federal Constitution, making the maintenance of an adequate system of free schools the solemn duty of each of the States." *The Index* also commended the speech, calling it "great." The journal claimed Grant's recommendations coincided with its Religious Freedom Amendment; that "the Church and the State should be absolutely and forever separate, needs today as never before to be pressed home upon the general mind and conscience."[23] The sole voice of protest came from the Catholic Church. Vicar General John F. Brazill of Chicago sharply criticized the speech, characterizing Grant's call to guard "against every enemy threatening the prosperity of free republican institutions" as being anti-Catholic. Less accusatory but equally critical in tone, the *Catholic World* remarked that Catholics would have few complaints with the President's speech if it were true to its word. But any ban on funding "sectarian" schools must apply equally to the Protestant public schools, the *World* asserted: "'not one dollar' to our present system of schools because they are sectarian." The journal called upon Grant to free Catholics from the tax burden of supporting public schools if they could not receive their fair "pro rata" share of funds for their schools. "We ask for nothing which we are not willing to concede to all our fellow-citizens-viz., the natural right to have their children brought up according to their parents' conscientious convictions."[24]

Grant's supporters insisted that the President "spoke from the heart" in his desire to resolve the School Question and remove it from politics. The Republican-leaning *Chicago Tribune* claimed that it had been an "impromptu speech" that revealed his genuine concern for education and religious freedom, while another supporter effused that the speech "will go [down] with the last inaugural of President Lincoln."[25] But few doubted that politics were not at work. *The Index*, while embracing his sentiments, speculated that Grant hoped the speech would boost his efforts to win a third term as President. The *New York Times* and the *Nation* made similar allegations as to Grant's motives. Grant clearly understood the potential advantages of the proposal for his political future and the Republican Party. Following on the heels of the Democratic gains during the previous election, Republicans faced crucial off-year elections being held in New Jersey and Ohio. Grant's proposal was a way to identify the Republican Party with education reform while aligning it with the Protestant cause. As the Republican-leaning *New York Times* bluntly acknowledged, an "appeal to religious passions was worth twenty-five thousand votes to the Republicans." That politics might be motivating the proposal was the nation's worst kept secret.[26]

Figure 5.1 President Ulysses S. Grant. The Granger Collection, New York.

Figure 5.2 James G. Blaine. The Granger Collection, New York.

One politician with a realistic chance at securing the Republican nomination for President was James G. Blaine, the former Speaker of the House of Representatives (figure 5.2). Ousted from his position by the Democratic take-over in 1874, the loss had freed Blaine to pursue his higher political aspirations. Attune to the generally favorable reaction to Grant's proposal, Blaine released a letter he had written that fall to the chairman of the Ohio Republican Party where he had voiced his own concerns about the School Question. "The public school agitation in your late campaign is liable to break out elsewhere and occurring first in one State and then in another, may keep the whole country in a ferment for years to come," Blaine wrote. "This inevitably arouses sectarian feelings and leads to that bitterest and most deplorable of all strifes, the strife between religious denominations." Blaine implored that the controversy must "be settled in some definite and comprehensive way," but with a solution that ensured "the complete victory for nonsectarian schools."[27] One factor that stood in the way of a settlement, Blaine insisted, was that the First Amendment does not apply to the states; states "were left free to do as they pleased in regard to 'an establishment of religion,'" including the authority to tax religious minorities for the public support of religion, even if they objected. The only lasting solution was a new constitutional amendment, the text of which Blaine had conveniently prepared:

> No State shall make any law respecting an establishment of religion, or prohibiting the free exercise thereof; and no money raised by taxation in any State, for the support of the public schools or derived from any public

fund therefore, shall ever be under the control of any religious sect, nor shall any money so raised ever be divided between religious sects or denominations.[28]

This resolution, Blaine concluded, would "not interfere with any State having such a school system as its citizens may prefer, subject to the single and simple restriction that the schools not be made the arena for sectarian controversy or theological disputation." Such a solution "would be comprehensive and conclusive, and would be fair alike to Protestant and Catholic, to Jew and Gentile, leaving the religious faith and the conscience of every man free and unmolested." Obviously, the letter had been written for a wider audience.[29]

Blaine's proposed amendment shared similarities with *The Index's* Religious Freedom Amendment with its direct application of the First Amendment to the states, although the latter was broader in calling for a prohibition against religious tests by states. There is no evidence to suggest that Blaine had seen a copy of the Religious Freedom Amendment prior to writing the letter (or Judge Hurlbut's proposal either). It is also not clear why Blaine used the language of the First Amendment religious clauses when it was not necessary to resolve the school funding issue, which was addressed in a separate clause. More likely, Blaine got the idea for the amendment from two relatively unnoticed proposals earlier in the decade. In January 19, 1871, Senator Willard Warner had proposed a constitutional amendment to prohibit any governmental entity from appropriating money or property for the benefit of any religious body or sect.[30] The following session, Senator William Stewart had proposed a more specific amendment to the Constitution requiring each state and territory to maintain "a system of free and common schools; but neither the United States nor any State, Territory, county, or municipal corporation shall aid in the support of any school wherein the peculiar tenants of any religious denomination are taught." Both proposals had died in the judiciary committee without receiving a hearing.[31] Like those earlier proposals, the primary focus of Blaine's proposal was to resolve the funding controversy by prohibiting the allocation of school funds to any school "under the control of any religious sect." Noticeably absent from Blaine's proposal was the matter of Bible reading or religious exercises in the public schools.[32]

As with Grant's speech, newspapers reacted favorably to Blaine's proposal. After having commended Grant's proposal, *The Index* reacted with surprising caution to Blaine's letter, calling it an "indication of the novel and grave character of the approaching Presidential campaign." *The Index* decided to take a wait-and-see approach. *The Christian Statesman* also remained silent for the time being.[33] Still, the combination of Grant's speech and Blaine's letter broke open the floodgates of public interest in the School Question. Protestant and nativist groups held rallies in support of the twin issues of Bible reading and a ban on parochial school funding. One "immense mass meeting" took place in October at the influential Broadway Tabernacle in New York City. Organized under inter-denominational Protestant sponsorship, the sanctuary was filled "from the pulpit's edge to the outer doors, by the opponents of the measure that would banish the Bible from the public schools," reported one newspaper. Patriotic themes intermixed with the religious: the nation's flag hung over the pulpit while ushers wore ribbons of red, white, and blue. Impassioned speeches, interspersed with hymns and patriotic songs, warned that the "expulsion of the Bible is only the starting point; it means ultimately the elimination from public instruction of all that tends to the promulgation of the doctrines of true religion, or morality, and of the rights of free human worship." Speakers endorsed Grant's and Blaine's proposals, with one stating that "if there is no law or statute in the Constitution to specify what principle of religion or of faith shall be sustained, then it is necessary for the people to speak and amend the Constitution." Reporting on the rally, *The Index* criticized how speakers equated Bible reading with "our national existence and religious liberty.... [T]he bitterness of some of the speakers showed how dangerous already is the excitement of Protestant fanaticism."[34] The Broadway Tabernacle rally was not an isolated event. New grass-roots organizations also sprung up, including the "Common School League," the "Free School Guard," and the "Alpha Association," all organized to keep the Bible in the schools and opposed to dividing the school fund. Many had nativist leanings, although the Alpha Association denied reports in the *New York Tribune* of a connection to the Order of American Union, the nation's preeminent nativist organization.[35]

Despite the visible public outpouring, Protestant ranks were far from unified. Protestants concurred in opposing public funding of Catholic schools; however, they disagreed over the propriety of Bible reading and whether the character of public schools should be religious. Most Presbyterians supported existing religious exercises or even making them more devotional—Presbyterian columnist Samuel Spear being the prominent exception—while Congregational journals *The Independent* and the *Christian Union* supported removing Bible reading and religious exercises in public schools, despite a division within the church's own ranks. Northern Baptists generally agreed with the Congregationalists, with the *Baptist Quarterly* stating that there was "no good and sufficient reason why the state should furnish to all people anything more than the rudiments of education."[36] Disagreement even extended into the skeptic community. It was during this time that the editorial board of *The Index* had a falling out over whether the Bible could be used in public schools for nonreligious purposes. Some free religionists including Octavius Frothingham believed the Bible could be used to teach literature and ancient history, but Francis Abbot and others disagreed. "[S]o long as a single tax-payer believes in the Bible as the Word of God," Abbot wrote, "it ought to be totally excluded from the public schools."[37]

Divisions existed not only between liberal and orthodox bodies but within evangelical denominations themselves. During the fall of 1875, a fissure emerged within Methodism. *Zion's Herald*, a leading Methodist periodical published in Boston, reaffirmed its support for Bible reading. The journal declared it opposed sectarianism in the public schools but insisted that Bible reading was not sectarian, but Christian, and essential to teaching morals in the schools. The culprit in the controversy, according to *Zion's Herald*, was the Catholic Church. "Romanism is everywhere the same unyielding foe to the unsectarian common school. There is scarcely a public institution in the country at this moment, the harmony of whose discipline and religious instruction is not threatened by the persistent effort of the Catholic priest, not to teach in them morals and the fear of God, but Romanism, pure and simple."[38] In contrast, the *Christian Advocate*, the official organ for northern Methodists, had changed its position since the *Minor* case and now argued that Bible reading was sectarian. All religious exercises "are outside the specific designs of a public school," wrote editor Daniel Curry, and "their introduction cannot without flagrant wrong be enforced against the protest of a minority." Curry charged that Bible reading supporters held "the incorrect assumption that . . . ours is politically and organically a Christian and Protestant State." Rejecting the premise, Curry wrote that the political system, at all levels, "is simply secular, extending the same rights to all men, without respect for religious differences. It allows no discrimination between Protestants and Catholics, Christians and pagans, believers and infidels. The inexorable logic of our whole American system of non-ecclesiastical politics requires that our public schools shall be secular and not religious."[39]

Zion's Herald responded quickly to the *Christian Advocate*, writing that it was "surprised and a little mortified" by Curry's editorial. "Whether or not the reading or reciting of the Scriptures shall be positively required in common schools, it shall in no case be prohibited." The *Herald* seized on Curry's admission that he was likely "out of step and sympathy with the common Christianity of the age." "The ring of the whole article is like that of the most secular and godless press," the *Herald* charged. "To our view, nearly every position he has taken is untenable. . . . [T]o take God's Word away from a hundred children to please the blasphemous spirit often, is to punish and injure the innocent, and to do the guilty no good." Later in the spring, Curry resigned his position as editor of the *Advocate*, possibly to find a more receptive constituency.[40]

Amid this ongoing controversy, President Grant submitted his annual message to Congress on December 7, 1875. All observers expected that the message would be important, with the *Chicago Tribune* anticipating it would be "the ablest Executive document of all that he has prepared during his two terms." The message satisfied most expectations.[41]

Continuing the theme of his Des Moines speech, Grant again called for a resolution to the School Question. As in that earlier address, Grant emphasized "the greatest importance that all should be possessed of education and intelligence enough to cast a vote with a right understanding of its meaning." He then asked Congress to pass a constitutional amendment

making it the duty of each of the several States to establish and forever maintain free public schools adequate to the education of all the
children in the rudimentary branches within their respective limits,
irrespective of sex, color, birthplace, or religions; forbidding the
teaching in said schools of religious, atheistic, or pagan tenets; and
prohibiting the granting of any school funds or taxes, or any part
thereof, either by the legislative, municipal, or other authority, for the
benefit or in aid, directly or indirectly, of any religious sect or denomination, or in aid or for the benefit of any other object of any nature or
kind whatever.[42]

Grant had apparently given more thought to the matter over the previous three
months. The message went beyond his earlier remarks by calling for an end to
property tax exemptions for church properties—church sanctuaries and
cemeteries excepted—and for additional legislation banning polygamy. Also,
Grant now recommended obligating states to provide an "adequate" public
schooling for all children, regardless of race or religious affiliation. Seen in the
context of the Freedmen's Bureau schools that had operated in the South, this
implied potential federal oversight of public education, something that was an
anathema to most Democrats and many Republicans. Even though later versions of the amendment would omit language obligating universal education,
this issue remained associated with the proposed amendment and informed the
public debate.[43] These additional provisions revealed Grant's comprehensive
view of church-state matters, one closer to the sentiments of the Liberal League,
and one not limited by the School Question. He closed by imploring Congress to
"[d]eclare church and state forever separate and distinct, but each free within
their proper spheres." The focal points of the call, however, were the provisions
concerning the School Question and imposing a duty on states to operate free
public schools.[44]

Newspapers, politicians, and religious and education leaders overwhelmingly
endorsed Grant's proposal. Support was surprisingly bipartisan. Both the New
York *Times* and *Tribune* hailed Grant's call for a constitutional amendment, the
former stating that the message "will be read by the country with general satisfaction." *Harper's Weekly* observed that the speech showed a "clear perception of what
the people wish." And the *Chicago Tribune* wrote "[t]here seems to be nothing lacking in this suggestion, and it will be a boon to the country if the Democratic
Congress shall develop sufficient patriotism to act upon it in the same spirit in
which it is offered."[45] But the breadth of Grant's proposal caught some people off
guard—particularly his calls for taxing church property and forbidding religious
teaching in the schools—with evangelicals calling the latter proposal "hazardous,"
in that it might exclude nonsectarian Bible reading. Grant's recommendations
were a double-edged sword which held "about as keen an edge for the Protestant
as for the Catholic," wrote *Scribner's Monthly*.

The former will be obliged to relinquish his Bible as a school-book, while the latter will be compelled to give up his plans for getting possession of the public funds for educating his children in the interests of his Church. We hardly know which will suffer the greater grief.[46]

Following quickly on Grant's address, Blaine submitted without comment his proposed amendment in the House of Representatives on December 14. Compared to Grant's address, Blaine's proposal was relatively modest, closely tracking his earlier letter. In addition to prohibiting funding of parochial schools or the sectarian control of public schools, the proposed amendment included language making the First Amendment's religion clauses applicable to the states. Blaine's proposal omitted any provision regarding the tax exemption of church property and, more significant, any requirement that states maintain public schools in the first instance. Consistent with his earlier proposal, Blaine's amendment did not address the issue of Bible reading.[47]

Blaine's submission did not go unnoticed. "Mr. Blaine has introduced his amendment, and the chances are that he will be able to carry it," reported the Democratic-leaning *New York Tribune*. As with the response to Grant's address, secular newspapers generally viewed the amendment as a way to resolve the School Question. "Thinking men of all parties see much more to deplore than to rejoice over, in the virulent outbreak of discussions concerning the churches and the schools, and welcome any means of removing the dangerous question from politics as speedily as possible," continued the *Tribune*. "Reports from Washington indicate that the ex-Speaker is already sure of considerable Democratic support, and it would not be surprising if we should yet see his amendment passing almost by common consent."[48] The Republican-leaning *New York Times*, in contrast, was less optimistic about the amendment's prospects, stating that no one expected the measure to receive a majority of the votes in the Democratic House, let alone the necessary two-thirds.[49]

Protestant leaders again reacted favorably to the message and the proposed amendment, temporarily putting aside whatever disagreements they had over the issue of Bible reading. *Zion's Herald* called Grant's message "clear, manly, and able," while it urged support for Blaine's amendment. *The Independent*, the *Christian Union*, and the *Christian Advocate* all endorsed the proposed amendment as a solution to the School Question.[50] As expected, the Catholic Church took a different view of the message and the amendment. Without mentioning Blaine by name, the *Catholic World* criticized those "politicians who hope to ride into power by awakening the spirit of fanaticism and religious bigotry among us." The proposed amendment, the *World* continued, was "only the entrance of a wedge that, driven home, will disturb the foundations of our government [and] will create religious strife." The *American Catholic Quarterly Review* concurred, alleging that Grant's proposal would "put religion on a level with atheism," while charging that "the amendment introduced by Speaker Blaine has all the insidious cunning of the small politician." In their criticisms, Catholic journals generally did not distinguish between Grant's proposal and Blaine's amendment, despite the differences in language.[51]

Once the congratulations were over, the amendment and its sponsor came under closer scrutiny. Despite the apparent broad support for the measure, even among Democrats, few people were fooled by Blaine's motivations. Blaine was running for president, and the school amendment was chiefly a means of garnering support. Blaine was the consummate politician, and he was recognized as such by the voting public. Most observers would have concurred with the *Catholic World's* assessment that politicians were seeking to manipulate the School Question for political gain. The question was how far that manipulation would go. A cynical *Nation* retorted later that spring that "Mr. Blaine did, indeed, bring forward at the opening of Congress a Constitutional amendment directed against the Catholics, but the anti-Catholic excitement was, as every one knows now, a mere flurry; and all that Mr. Blaine means to do or can do with his amendment is, not to pass it but to use it in the campaign to catch anti-Catholic votes."[52]

The charge that the Blaine Amendment was chiefly an effort to exploit anti-Catholic sentiment has haunted the proposal. Blaine clearly appreciated the appeal of his amendment to Protestant and nativist voters; yet nothing indicates that Blaine himself was anti-Catholic or wished that to be the effect of his proposal. On the contrary, Blaine maintained that the amendment was intended to resolve the School Question and remove the divisive issue from the political arena. While this would be the expected response from a politician, there is some evidence that Blaine genuinely desired to diffuse the religious divisiveness surrounding the school issue. A comparison of Blaine's streamlined amendment to Grant's proposal reveals the absence of the latter's more religiously inflammatory provisions—Grant's call for compulsory education and the taxation of church property—both of which were popular in nativist circles. In addition, Blaine called only for a restriction on funds dedicated for public schools. This left open the possibility of continued pubic funding of religious charities. On the other hand, because Blaine's proposal was silent on the issue of Bible reading—a practice likely prohibited under Grant's proposal—it appealed more to evangelicals, a point *The Index* emphasized.[53]

That Blaine would consciously manipulate anti-Catholic sentiment is curious, as he was known for his Catholic sympathies. His mother was Catholic, and Blaine had attended Catholic religious services as a child, possibly being baptized. His daughters were educated in Catholic boarding schools with two later joining the Catholic Church, while a close cousin, Mother Angela Gillespie, was the founder of the Holy Cross Sisters. As an adult Blaine attended the Presbyterian church with his wife (his father had been a nominal Presbyterian), but nothing indicates he was very religious.[54] During the 1876 election Blaine publicly distanced himself from the way that some people were interjecting religion into the campaign. He told one acquaintance he would "never consent to make any public declaration" to arouse religious prejudices, offering two reasons:

> First, because I abhor the introduction of anything that looks like a religious test or qualification for office in a republic where perfect freedom of conscience is the birthright of every citizen; and second, because my mother was a devoted Catholic. I would not for a thousand Presidencies speak a disrespectful word of my mother's religion, and no pressure will draw me into any avowal of hostility or unfriendliness to Catholics, though I have never received, and do not expect any political support from them.[55]

Later as Secretary of State under presidents Garfield and Arthur, Blaine supported Irish home rule. In fact, once Blaine secured the nomination for President in 1884, Republicans sought to capitalize on his Irish and Catholic ancestry to attract Irish voters, particularly in New York City where Grover Cleveland was at odds with the Tammany Hall Democratic machine. One biographer noted that "the Republicans built not a little hope upon Mr. Blaine's popularly among voters of Irish blood."[56] Approved campaign biographies emphasized his Irish and Scotch-Irish backgrounds and the fact that his mother had been a life-long Catholic. During the 1884 campaign some even charged Blaine with being a "closet" Catholic himself. His Catholic sympathies led the American Protestant Association and Irish Orangemen to oppose his election. Blaine was thus an unlikely Catholic bigot.[57]

All of this suggests several alternative explanations for Blaine's motive for the amendment: that Blaine was completely unprincipled in his pro-Catholic protestations; that he was completely naïve in his assessment of popular reaction to the amendment; or that he was unrealistically hopeful that a modest proposal could garner bipartisan support and possibly diffuse the festering issue. The first two alternatives do not fit with contemporary assessments of Blaine's character and political acumen. While the third alternative is a plausible explanation, Blaine's calculations were likely to be more political than they were religious. Blaine's lack of interest in the religious aspects of his amendment is demonstrated by his total disregard for the measure once he had lost the 1876 nomination. He did not take part in any of the debates surrounding the amendment, even though he had ample opportunity to influence the measure in both chambers (Blaine was appointed to the Senate in the summer of 1876). In his 1884 campaign autobiography, *Twenty Years of Congress*, Blaine omitted any reference to the amendment. Grant's 1875 message received only a brief comment in his book, and he failed to discuss his earlier calls for nonsectarian schools and separation of church and state. In Blaine's mind, the substance of the amendment was insignificant. Rather, Blaine was concerned about the political mileage the amendment could provide. Blaine may have abhorred the way some Republicans used his amendment to stoke anti-Catholic sentiment, but he did nothing to stop such associations. After the amendment failed to secure him the nomination, it also lost all importance, even as a historical event. The lack of significance Blaine attached to the amendment is demonstrated by the fact that not one of his contemporary biographers discussed the measure.[58]

Despite the known political motivations behind the amendment, Protestants generally supported the measure. Like all good pieces of legislation, the amendment had something for everyone. Liberals applauded the proposal because it affirmed religious liberty and the separation of church and state. Conservatives endorsed it for prohibiting the transfer of public school funds while leaving other issues of education to the states. And it remained silent on the issue of Bible reading. Those Protestants in the middle, which accounted for the majority of Americans, could find things to like from both extremes.

The intensity of support among non-Catholics waivered, however, and groups continued to press concerns over the amendment and the larger School Question. The N.R.A. gave the amendment qualified support. In part, the Association was being territorial, not wanting to jeopardize its own amendment by embracing Blaine's proposal. But the latter proposal also did not go far enough. The N.R.A. wanted a specific reference to God's sovereignty, though it realized the inconsistency of such an acknowledgment with Blaine's more separationist language. The Association also wanted any amendment to guarantee religious exercises in public schools as well as in other institutions, and it began lobbying for these additions. In spite of these defects, T. P. Stevenson wrote that the Association "cordially approves of the other parts of the amendment which forbid the employment of any part of the public money for the benefit of any sect or denomination, and desires its passage in whatever form may most effectually serve that end."[59]

On the other extreme, free religionists and other liberals expressed varying degrees of enthusiasm for the amendment. Following Grant's address and Blaine's submission, the Liberal League of Philadelphia sent a congratulatory letter to President Grant, commending him for his proposal. The letter praised his call for "unsectarian public schools" and the taxation of church property. Even though the latter provision was absent from Blaine's proposal, the Philadelphia League chapter pledged its "renewed and unremitting zeal" to help accomplish the goal of "full enjoyment of religious freedom" for all American citizens.[60] Back in Boston, Francis Abbot was more ambivalent about endorsing the Blaine Amendment. *The Index* expressed guarded enthusiasm for Grant's message, describing it as "a signal advance in the right direction." It was still imperfect, however, for failing to "recommend[] explicitly that *Protestant worship* in the schools shall be discontinued." With respect to Blaine's amendment, *The Index* was less sanguine, cautioning the "necessity of avoiding all ignorant or studied ambiguity in any amendment that may be made to the Constitution." The proposal suffered from numerous defects. Like Grant's address, it failed expressly to banish Bible reading and religious exercises from the schools and public events, stated *The Index*. Abbot charged that this silence left "Protestants in undisturbed mastery of the schools themselves."

Furthermore, Blaine's amendment did not address the issue of tax exemption for religious institutions as Grant had requested. But most important, the amendment did nothing to dispel the persistent belief in a Christian America, even though Blaine was presented with the opportunity to include such a statement. Overall, the proposal just did not go far enough. "[L]et the nation be satisfied with no half-way solution," wrote *The Index*. "Nothing short of the absolute secularization of the State will now suffice."[61]

Blaine's amendment was referred to the House and Senate judiciary committees, but neither body rushed to consider the proposal. Throughout the winter and spring of 1876, other matters consumed Congress, not the least of which being the upcoming nominating conventions. Still, the School Question did not go away. One Democratic congressman, acting without the blessing of his party, tried to seize the issue from the Republicans by introducing a counter education amendment. On January 17, William J. O'Brien, a Democrat from Maryland, submitted an alternative to Blaine's amendment to the House of Representatives:

> Section 1. No State shall make any law respecting an establishment of religion or prohibiting the free exercise thereof; and no minister or preacher of the gospel or of any religious creed or denomination shall hold any office of trust or emolument under the United States or under any State; nor shall any religious test be required as a qualification for any office or public trust in any State, or under the United States.
>
> Section 2. No money received by taxation in any State for the support of Public schools, or derived from any public fund therefore, nor any public lands devoted thereto shall ever be under the control of any religious sect, nor shall any minister or preacher of the gospel or of any religious creed or denomination hold any office in connection with the public schools in and State, nor be eligible for any position of trust or emolument in connection with any institution, public or private, in any State or under the United States which shall be supported in whole or in part form any public fund.[62]

O'Brien requested that his amendment be considered immediately, but the chair found him out of order. The resolution was referred to the House Judiciary Committee, where it quietly died. No action was taken on the measure during the session.[63] O'Brien's amendment received little public attention. Both the New York *Times* and *Tribune* reported its submission without comment.[64] *The Independent* called the amendment "silly" and an unwarranted attack on ministers. The newspaper charged that Democrats were obviously concerned about the popularity of Blaine's proposal and were simply attempting to defeat the measure without appearing opposed to its principles. O'Brien's motivations may have been entirely partisan, seeking to muddy the water by proposing a related measure. But at the same time, O'Brien's proposal went further than Blaine's in several respects, prohibiting religious prerequisites for office holding—a condition that still existed in several states—while prohibiting clergy from holding any public office or being connected to a public school. With these provisions, O'Brien's proposal would have had a greater impact on church-state matters at the state level than would have occurred under Blaine's amendment if it had passed. If it was simply a way for Democrats to save face, it went further than was necessary.[65]

The Great Debate, Part Two

People debated the merits of the Blaine Amendment, and its potential impact on the School Question, throughout the winter and spring of 1876. Many participants saw the amendment as an opportunity to address not only the funding question but also broader issues about church-state relations. This aspect of the Blaine Amendment is lost in most critiques. The issue of public funding of parochial schools was the chief focus of Blaine's proposal and people's overarching concern. But few people separated that issue from the controversy over religious exercises in the schools, and then from the larger question about the nation's religious character. President Grant, if one accepts the sincerity of his proposal, perceived the controversy in broad terms, which necessitated a comprehensive remedy: require states to provide free, universal, nonreligious education to children of all races and faiths. Limit public financial support to these public institutions. Also, restrict tax exemptions for religious institutions, which would limit their wealth and power and thus reinforce a secular society. In particular, Grant believed that public schools should be free of ideologically divisive forces, which necessitated prohibiting the teaching of "religious, atheistic, or pagan tenets" in the schools. Whether by using the word "religious" rather than "sectarian" Grant was calling for a system of *secular* schools, as opposed to *nonsectarian* schools, is difficult to gauge. In most such calls, politicians, educators and religious leaders were careful to use the words "nonsectarian" or "unsectarian" rather than "nonreligious" when describing the appropriate character of public education. By asking that not simply sectarian but *religious* tenets be barred from the public schools, Grant was going beyond the status quo. With its call to "[d]eclare Church and State forever separate and distinct," Grant's address tied the School Question to the larger issue of church-state relations in America.[66]

Grant was not alone in viewing the School Question as implicating larger issues about the nation's religious character and the role of religious institutions within a republican state. Once the initial flurry of commentary on Grant's message and Blaine's amendment gave way, the debate entered a new phase. Pronouncements and rallies by militant Protestants and nativists subsided during the winter and spring of 1876. The anti-Catholic rhetoric that had accompanied much of the debate during the previous fall became less common. In its place arose a more contemplative discussion over the meaning of church-state relations in America.

As before, many participants in this debate did not view the issues through the prism of the traditional Protestant versus Catholic dispute. Four perspectives, though not accounting for all views, were most prominent: evangelical, liberal Protestant, Catholic, and secularist.

In April, 1876, Lyman H. Atwater, Princeton theologian, editor of the influential *Presbyterian Quarterly Princeton Review* and occasional supporter of the N.R.A., published a major article on "Civil Government and Religion" in the *Review*. Atwater was a religious conservative and ideological purist, and he saw inherent dangers in Blaine's amendment. Using the proposed amendment as the context, Atwater laid out a comprehensive vision of church-state relations, one based on a Calvinist understanding of national obedience to God. Atwater asserted the "impossibility of utterly divorcing civil government from religion," which he insisted underlay Grant's call. Government, as the organ of civil society, had to reflect God's authority. Yet America was a "Christian nation" only in a limited sense, Atwater declared. The nation should not be considered Christian simply because the great mass of people professed fealty to that faith. The number of professing Christians would always be much larger than the truly "spiritually regenerate," Atwater insisted. He also disputed that "Christianity [was] the law of the land" in any official sense. Yet when viewing the issue broadly, as to whether Christianity was "the faith of the great mass of the people" and had "moulded our national life, manners, institutions, and laws," then the nation was Christian in fact. The constitutions and laws found their "underlying and controlling principles in Christianity," Atwater claimed, and laws "generally, if not professedly, aim to carry out the justice, equity, and charity of the Bible."[67]

What this meant in practical terms was that the state should prosecute blasphemy and Sabbath violations because they profaned God and hindered people from honoring and worshiping God. The state could also teach Christian morality in the schools based on the Bible. "All of this is incumbent on the State primarily and essentially, because God commands it." This led Atwater to the heart of church-state relationships. If the state could not "transgress the fundamental principles of morals, religion, or Christianity," Atwater asked rhetorically, how far could it "control the church, or, the church control the State; in other words, what is the true relation and boundary between the temporal and spiritual power?" Atwater answered that though both institutions were subject to God's authority, "each is supreme and independent of the other, within its own proper sphere." At the same time, Atwater insisted that rights of conscience prohibited the state from subsidizing "the church by giving material support or aid to any one or all of its branches." It was wrong, Atwater wrote, to "compel all unbelievers to contribute for the support of what they do not believe in." Atwater extended this principle to Catholics, though he stopped short of agreeing that Catholics should be freed from paying taxes to support public schools. He argued that Catholic children should be allowed to read the Douay version in the schools or excused from attending religious exercises. But otherwise, Catholic immigrants had no ground to challenge "the genius of our institutions inbreathed into them by Protestantism."[68]

Turning to the immediate controversy, Atwater observed that Grant's recommendation and Blaine's amendment were "indicative of a deep movement in the public mind which political aspirants cannot ignore." Even though the matter called for a resolution, he could not support the specific provisions contained in the proposals. "Such a measure, in our judgment, if practicable in the nature of things, is wholly beyond the proper functions of the national government, and an unwarrantable invasion of the proper liberties and franchises of the States and the people. It not only requires that the schools be in the most absolute sense non-religious," he said, grafting Grant's broader call onto the amendment, "but that such schools be provided at public expense on a sufficient scale to supply education gratuitously to all the children.... There is no middle ground between religion, or religious principle of some sort, and atheism. Neutrality here is out of the question. Not to acknowledge God is to disown or ignore him. It is to be 'without God in the world,' and this is atheism. There is no evading this consequence." For Atwater, efforts to secularize the schools indicated a greater move to expel all "religious truth, nay, the obligations of common morality, from our civil and political institutions."[69]

Atwater spoke for many evangelicals who assailed the perceived secularizing trend in nonsectarian education. They were not willing to relinquish religious education even if it would resolve the Catholic problem. In contrast, liberal Protestants were willing to dispense with Bible reading, but not solely to solve the funding issue. The leading voice for this perspective was Samuel Spear of *The Independent*. Spear had been writing about the School Question since the Cincinnati Bible controversy, but following Grant's address Spear penned over two dozen editorials for the journal, later compiling them into a 400 page book, *Religion and the State or, The Bible and the Public Schools*. The book's title was revealing, because Spear unquestionably saw the School Question as part of a larger issue that needed to be addressed by American society. As he stated in his introductory chapter, the issues of parochial school funding and "Bible-reading and religious worship" in the public schools, "manifestly [do] not cover the whole question in controversy." They but implicated "great principles... which in their various applications bring to the surface the whole subject of Church and State, civil government and religion, in their relations to each other."[70]

Spear's fascination with the School Question and church-state matters generally had radicalized him over the years. He insisted that public schools should be "purely secular," going so far as banning the use of the Bible for literary or historical purposes. Unlike many Protestants, Spear did not embrace expelling the Bible simply as a way to placate Catholics; he understood that Catholics condemned a secular education system as much as they condemned a nonsectarian one. He understood that no bargain with Catholics over this issue was possible. Rather, Spear based his position on two ideological convictions. Bible reading was necessarily religious and inevitably sectarian in its use. Its use thus infringed on the conscience rights of Catholics and nonbelievers. Second, the state's promotion of Bible reading went beyond its authority. The practice required the state to make decisions about religious content and its universality. "What are the principles of our common Christianity upon which [all] sects are agreed?" Equally troubling for Spear was who would decide what faiths were included "within these Christian sects;" would Universalists, Quakers, Mormons be included, he asked? Any decision invited state discrimination and religious dissension.[71] But Spear also denied that the state possessed that authority in any context. The state's power over education authorized it to teach only those secular branches of knowledge and moral virtues, the latter being those habits that "are certainly good for this world, and good for citizenship, whether there be any hereafter or not." "The importance of things spiritual, as compared with things temporal, supplies no reason why the State should give its attention to the former in the public school system," Spear wrote.[72]

On the funding issue, Spear joined with evangelicals and secularists in opposing any division of school funds for parochial education. On one level, he shared the prevailing Protestant belief that Catholic education was inconsistent with the "genius and nature of our political institutions." "Ignorance and despotic control are historically the strongholds of Catholicism," Spear remarked. Not only would dividing school funds support sectarian instruction, it would undermine the financial security of public schooling. Like other common school advocates, Spear feared a pro rata distribution would invite other denominations to seek a share, ultimately leading to the dissolution of public education. The state could not "divide the school funds among the sects without destroying its own system and making itself simply a religious tax gatherer," he wrote in a later article. But Spear also criticized Protestants who insisted on maintaining control over the public schools. Much Protestant unwillingness to consider sincere Catholic complaints was "largely a matter of anti-Catholic prejudice." Spear had no sympathy or respect for "that stupid and furious Protestantism which sees nothing good in Catholicism, and brands it as evil and only evil." The public schools should be "neither a Catholic nor a Protestant machine. . . . It should be a State machine . . . supported by general taxation and conducted under the exclusive authority of the State."[73]

Spear's rejection of state authority to engage in religious matters led him to consider church-state relations generally. Spear identified a number of concepts that would be incorporated into Supreme Court doctrine one hundred years later: secularity; neutrality; and jurisdiction. The state was a secular institution, with sovereignty resting in the people, deriving no authority from God. And those who insisted that Christianity was part of the common law "are entirely mistaken."

> [I]t so happens that neither Christianity, not any other system of religion, is any part of this law, or can be, so long as the Constitution itself shall remain unchanged. . . . [The] Government is not a Christian

government in the sense of giving any legal preference to, or sanction of, Christianity, or resting its authority upon any of its doctrines. It is simply a political organization, for temporal ends, based upon the principle of popular representation, and upon nothing else, and formally and intentionally excluding religion from its scope.[74]

Not surprisingly, Spear harshly criticized the N.R.A. for attempting to place an acknowledgment of God in the Constitution. Spear no longer viewed the effort as harmless or the likely effect as merely symbolic; rather, the amendment "would fundamentally change the whole theory of the Constitution in regard to religion and, in the powers of Congress, establish a complete religious despotism."[75] But Spear also doubted that much benefit would flow from Blaine's proposed amendment. In the end, Spear believed that the mechanisms for maintaining the proper balance between church and state were already in place. The Founders had built the government "upon the principle that religion and civil government were to be kept entirely distinct." Unlike the secularists, Spear did not call for a greater legal separation of church and state, only that Americans had to be true to the existing principles. Accordingly, Spear criticized Grant's call to keep "Church and State forever separate." Such language was "altogether too general, too ambiguous, and too susceptible of diverse constructions to be of any practical service." Spear asserted that a "mere general dogma on any subject will not do for a constitutional law." And unlike Abbot and the Liberals, Spear did not call for the total secularization of society, as compared to government institutions. In fact, Spear supported Sunday laws as civil days of rest, blasphemy laws as a form of profanity enforcement, thanksgiving proclamations as recommendations, and tax exemptions for churches as reinforcing religious freedom. Yet Spear insisted that none of those actions indicated state authority over religious matters, nor should they be used to authorize religious activities in the public schools. Overall, Spear advocated a moderate separationist position, one in which the government's policies and institutions, including the public schools, were to be secular. Secularity did not mean irreligion, however, but government neutrality and impartiality toward religious matters: the "American State holds a just and impartial relation to the religion of all its citizens—just, because it does not interfere with their liberty; and impartial, because it makes no discriminations among them."[76]

If Samuel Spear was liberal Protestantism's most articulate spokesperson for secular public education, then his counterpart within the educational community was William Torrey Harris, superintendent of the St. Louis public schools (1867–1880) and later U. S. Commissioner of Education. Harris was more than an administrator or reformer; he was the nation's leading philosopher of education, "the dominating force in American public education" prior to John Dewey.[77] Like Spear, Harris wrote extensively about religion and public education and, by necessity, the role of religion in American society. Both men shared ideas about the indispensability of a *common* education and the lack of state authority over religious matters. Both men concurred that the state and its schools had to be secular to be consistent with the Constitution's promise. But whereas Spear approached his moderate separationism cautiously and from a conventional religious standpoint, Harris was more insistent that secularity led to a complete separation of the church from the state, a situation where each entity operated in their individual spheres. For Harris this meant that in civil society, the secular state was supreme.[78] As he wrote confidently in an 1876 article for the *Atlantic Monthly*, there was a "wide-spread conviction" in America

> that church and state should be kept separate; that the church should take its place side by side with secular institutions which are subordinate to the state, so far as temporal organization is concerned, but left free as regards spiritual organization and matters of faith.

Because civil government had an interest in universal education—out of "necessity of educating its citizens for the duties of self-government" and the "intelligent obedience to laws"—the secular priorities of government must control in education. Harris not only opposed all uses of the Bible and religious texts in the public schools, he believed in an utter "incompatibility between religious instruction and secular instruction." On one level, Harris held much religious-based education in disdain: religious schools were inferior educationally and often promoted "exclusiveness and distrust" of alien ideas, if not "furnishing food for fanaticism and bigotry." On a deeper level, Harris believed that inculcating religious truth and obedience was detrimental to the development of a child's intellect: "The principle of religious instruction is authority; that of secular instruction is demonstration and verification. It is obvious that two principles should not be brought into the same school, but separated as widely as possible." Because of their questioning and skeptical approach, public schools could never teach religion adequately:

> [A]s a practical fact... [public] schools tend either to cultivate habits of flippant and shallow reasoning on sacred themes, thus sapping the foundations of piety, or... on the other hand, the influence of the dogmatic tone of the religious lessons creeps into the secular recitations, and drives out critical acuteness and independent thinking from the mind of the pupil.[79]

As a result, Harris opposed all forms of nonsectarian instruction in the public schools. Breaking with Horace Mann, Henry Barnard, and the bulk of the education community, Harris insisted that it was "impossible to have any such unsectarian religion that is not regarded as sectarian by the more earnest religious denominations." This was because the "reading of the Bible, the offering of prayers, and the teaching of some simple catechism, are devices borrowed from some particular forms of Protestantism." Even an effort to identify and teach only universal religious values "amounts only to the setting up of a new religious sect, and adding one more to the many denominations of religious belief. It is impossible to make a generalization of Christianity without depriving it of something that is necessary to the form of religion, namely, an appeal to the senses and the imagination," Harris insisted. For Harris, nonsectarianism was a practical and theological impossibility.[80]

With his belief in the inferiority of religious-based education, Harris expectantly opposed the public funding of parochial schools; it would cause "a decrease of secular knowledge and a great increase of theological knowledge." But his opposition was not based on a particular disdain for Catholic doctrine or the church itself. Harris' writings were generally free of hostile statements toward Catholicism—Harris had a good relationship with the large Catholic community in St. Louis during his tenure as school superintendent, where he resisted Protestant efforts to impose religious exercises in the schools. Rather, he held a universal suspicion of religious education. Harris had additional reasons for opposing public funding of religious schooling: it would cause the state to finance the teaching of religious dogmas, in violation of rights of conscience; it would necessitate government inspection and regulation of religious schools on "standards of instruction and discipline," leading to church-state conflicts and entanglement in religious affairs; it would produce "religious animus mingling with political animus" among competing denominations; and it would result in the decline in common schools in many locations. While several of these concerns were practical in nature, Harris also understood funding of religious schools to transgress constitutional principles. "The step to a church establishment is a very short one from the endowment of church schools." One hundred years later, these same concerns would resurface in the decisions of the United States Supreme Court.[81]

In many respects, Harris's stance on the School Question placed him closer to *The Index's* Abbot than *The Independent's* Spear. Harris, in fact, was unconventional in his religious beliefs, describing himself at various times as a freethinker or a spiritualist, writing that he believed in "no God as the popular mind does." But Harris spurned Abbot's hostility toward organized religion or Christian influences in the culture. Harris was a leading student of Hegel's idealism, establishing *The Journal of Speculative Philosophy* to advance a form of ethical rationalism. While advocating a secular state and education system, Harris believed strongly in the influence of religion on the culture and state. Harris wrote numerous articles supporting moral education in the schools. He went so far as to declare that religion was "the primary foundation, not only of morality, but also of the school and even of the state itself." There was no apparent contradiction for Harris. Religious principles, though emanating from the Christian doctrines, were independent of the church, and served as the basis of civilization. There was "no freedom or independence" in the state unless it borrowed "a divine principle revealed in religion for [its] organic form"—that being "justice." "When the state is organized on justice, the principle of freedom, it has adopted from religion one of the divine attributes, and not only may but *must* be separated from the church as an institution." In essence, the state could not perform its necessary function of ensuring freedom and justice, and providing for the temporal needs of people, including their education, until it was emancipated from the church and became a "free realization[] of some divine form." For Harris, this demonstrated "the inherent necessity of the separation of church and state in order that the former may become perfect spiritually, and that the latter may make political and civil freedom possible." Thus while Harris believed the state was "the supreme secular institution," that secularity could not fulfill its promise of achieving universal freedom "until it adopts from religion a divine attribute." Understandably, Harris emphasis on church-state separation and a secular state and school was at times mistaken for being anti-religious and, with respect to the public schools, anti-Bible. But upon closer inspection, Harris' philosophy was far removed from atheism or Abbot's free religion. Harris insisted that "the religious and secular realms do not conflict, but mutually complement each other." He even claimed that the "religious world is the divine itself, [and] the secular world is the manifestation or reflection of it." That could not occur unless church and state were completely separate.[82]

Harris' writings on public education and church-state relations extended over a forty-year period, so they were not tied particularly to the events surrounding the Blaine Amendment. Harris' decision to publish his *Atlantic Monthly* article in the midst of that controversy demonstrates that he and the publishers appreciated that the School Question was part of a larger debate over the religious character of the nation and its institutions. The funding of parochial schools might be the "main question," but its resolution depended on "the settlement of a variety of social and political questions," Harris insisted. Although Harris' views did not necessarily represent those of the larger education community, he was at the forefront of a movement to fully secularize American public education, and he was indisputably the most influential educator of the last quarter of the century.[83]

One point upon which Catholics agreed with the above commentators was that the School Question implicated the larger issue about the nation's spiritual character. Agreement generally ended there. Unlike those perspectives, Catholic commentary on church-state matters commonly took place within the prism of Protestant-Catholic competition. This is understandable as American Catholics were a religious minority responding to the dominant Protestant culture. For Catholics, Protestant Bible reading in the schools was only the most visible manifestation of a Protestant ethos that permeated American culture and its institutions. Protestant educators and school boards controlled the public schools, and children read from Protestant oriented texts that often denigrated Catholicism. Even more serious, the common schools were used to assimilate Catholic children into a culture saturated with Protestant values, causing children to renounce their faith and cultural heritage. The public schools were the chief perpetuators of a Protestant hegemony and an impediment to Catholics obtaining full religious equality and respect.[84]

Throughout the winter and spring of 1876, Catholic leaders and journals continued their effort to explain the Catholic position on the School Question. The Catholic position had essentially been set since the 1852 Plenary Council, and the arguments reflected that consistency: Catholics opposed education separated from Catholicity; education was generally the duty of the church, not the state; neither nonsectarian nor secular-based education systems could ever satisfy Catholic objections to the public schools, and neither would removing Bible reading and other religious exercises; Catholic schools should receive a pro rata share of school funds for children attending parochial schools; neither Catholics nor Protestants should be taxed to support the other's schools.[85]

While these points constituted the bulk of Catholic commentary during the debate over the Blaine Amendment, a handful of Catholic writers sought to offer a more systematic perspective on church-state relations. Orestes Brownson, who died in early 1876, had argued for a schema not that dissimilar from that advocated by the orthodox Presbyterian Lyman Atwater: all authority, temporal and spiritual, came from God, and both the church and the state were bound to follow God's laws; however, each entity operated in their respective separate spheres, with the state exercising no authority over religious matters or doctrines. This situation, while promoting an institutional separation, rejected any further separation that suggested a secular state free of religious obligations. Brownson had also asserted that the School Question implicated a larger question of religious inclusion in a democratic society. The non-Catholic majority had "the false notion that the country belongs to them," he wrote in one of his final articles. "They no more own the country than we do; it belongs to the whole American people, and all American citizens, whatever their religious beliefs or no-religious beliefs, are politically and civilly equal." No Catholic had done more to explain the Catholic position in America than Brownson. In a closing statement in one of his last articles, an ill Brownson brought that experience back to one issue. "The great question for us Catholics, and the great question even for our country, is the school question."[86]

Building on the foundation laid by Brownson, the *Catholic World* published two articles early in 1876 which discussed more practical applications of the Catholic position to the American experience.[87] The *World* embraced the religious freedom guarantees in the federal and state constitutions. For Catholics, those provisions were most important for protecting Catholic conscience rights not to be taxed for Protestant schools and providing for civil, political and religious equality. The *World* considered the existing constitutional guarantees to be sufficient—structural changes, such as those urged by the N.R.A. and Liberal League, were not necessary. Instead, Catholics called merely for the fair application of existing principles; the *World* asserted that "[w]e ask nothing to which every citizen has not a right."

> Under the Constitution, and according to the spirit of our government, all men are equal. Under the present system of common schools, and, according to the spirit of those who uphold them, men are not equal, and there is no such thing as regard for conscience; but every majority had a right to enforce upon any minority . . . the question of religion itself.

For Catholics, the purpose of the religious clauses in the constitutions was not to maintain a Christian nation but to protect minority religious rights, ensuring that they were not subjected to majority will. Complementing that function, Catholics asserted the state lacked authority over spiritual matters, an interpretation of the Constitution that coincided with Catholic theology. "Having no spiritual or theological competency, [the state] has no right to undertake to say what shall or shall not be the religion of its citizens; it must accept, protect, and aid the religion its citizens see proper to adopt, and without partiality for the religion of the majority any more that the religion of the minority." Yet religious equality and protection for minority rights had their limits. Conscience rights should not be afforded to unbelievers; while the infidel had civil and political rights, he deserved no protection for his beliefs. "He cannot plead conscience in its behalf for conscience supposes religion."[88]

The *World* also claimed that American Catholics professed fealty to the principle of separation of church and state, a concept that Orestes Brownson had refuted later in life. Here again, separation did not mean a secular state but a means of ensuring that each entity operated in its respective sphere without interference from the other entity. A separation was necessary to protect church doctrines and institutions from control by the government. One such threat to religious autonomy, the *World* asserted, existed with Grant's call to tax church property. While it did not claim that religious exemptions were required by free exercise principles, it insisted that taxation would encroach on the separate functions and institutional independence of the church. But primarily, the *World* viewed Grant's call as a crass political move designed to raise more public opprobrium against the church. The *World* warned that if the proposal were adopted, there could be no discrimination in its application as the church stood "before the law as do all other religious denominations." It was a suicidal idea for those Protestants motivated by hatred of the Catholic Church, and would cause "irreparable mischief to their own church or churches."[89]

Complementing the overall debate was the perspective of secularists, primarily free religionists and atheists, the former represented by the Free Religion Association and the Liberal League. More than any other faction, the secularists perceived the interconnectedness of the School Question with the larger issue of church-state relations. Their practical goals, as represented in the Demands of Liberalism and examined in the pervious chapter, need not be repeated here. But Abbot and other secularists continued to advance their views, appreciating that the public attention given the School Question represented an opportunity to present their vision of the "total separation of Church and State."[90]

These various perspectives, as well as that of the N.R.A., demonstrate how the School Question served as a catalyst for a more robust consideration of church-state relations in America. The views were diverse and multifaceted, and people appreciated the significance of resolving the School Question for constitutional doctrine and republican polity. The public debate continued throughout the spring of 1876. Although heightened interest in the School Question waned as the summer approached, that controversy, and the larger issue of church-state relations were never far below the surface. Ongoing tensions over religious exercises in public schools persisted, while the controversy over the Sunday closings of the Philadelphia Centennial Exposition and the pending conventions of the N.R.A. and Liberal League, as discussed earlier, kept matters in the news.[91]

The Vote

By summer, public attention turned to nominating conventions of the Democratic and Republican parties. Members of Congress delayed considering important legislation, including Blaine's school amendment, until after the selection of the nominees. The Republican Party held its convention first, meeting in Cincinnati in mid-June. During the spring, Blaine had emerged as the clear favorite. Entering into the convention, he held a plurality of the delegates but not enough to win the nomination. Blaine was opposed by Roscoe Conkling, senator from New York. With neither man able to secure the necessary two-thirds majority for the nomination and the convention deadlocked, the party settled on Rutherford B. Hayes, the tee-totaling Ohio governor whose recent reelection campaign had been marred by anti-Catholic rhetoric.[92]

Hayes's nomination presented a stark contrast from the prospect of having selected Blaine. Blaine's own nominal religious commitments and ambivalence about advancing the nation's Protestant identity was evidenced by his selection of Robert Ingersoll, the famous freethinker, to give a nominating speech. During his speech on behalf of Blaine, Ingersoll made only an oblique reference to the School Question: "[Republicans] demand a man who believes in the eternal separation and divorcement of Church and School."[93] Otherwise, the issue was not a theme of the speech or the campaign. In contrast to Blaine, Hayes's own commitment to evangelical Protestantism, and to resolving the school issue in a way consistent with those beliefs, could not have been more different. In a speech during the 1875 Ohio election, Hayes defended Bible reading in the public schools. The goal of education was to promote "religion, morality, and knowledge," Hayes declared, which was the equivalent of "good government," quoting from the Ohio Constitution. "Now the proposition to banish the Bible from the schools is a blow at this end [and] really discards the end, so far as 'religion and morality' are concerned, while the means—the schools—are maintained. It is idle to urge that there will be 'religion and morality' without the Bible." Hayes parted even from the narrow interpretation of the *Minor* decision that it merely authorized communities to decide whether to have Bible reading. "As a citizen, I have a right to insist that that basis and pledge shall be respected and preserved. All that is asked is that the Bible may be read in the schools."[94]

Recognizing that the die had been cast with the selection of Hayes, the Republicans approved a platform calling for preserving the nation's public school system and prohibiting using public funds to benefit "any school or institution under sectarian control."[95] According to the *New York Times*, upon hearing the above provision the convention erupted into "great cheering [that] continued for several minutes." The response was so great that the delegates called on the moderator, General Joseph Hawley, to read the section a second time, the only part of the plank to be so repeated. The audience again broke into cheering. As the *Times* editorial continued, "[a]mong the most notable points in the platform is its declaration in favor of an amendment to the Federal Constitution forbidding appropriations for sectarian schools. This was naturally received with great satisfaction by the Convention. It expresses a conviction profoundly cherished by a very large part of the American people."[96]

The Index was one of the few newspapers to criticize this part of the Republican platform. Even though the Liberal League opposed funding sectarian schools, *The Index* charged the provision was simply politically motivated. "For 'sectarian,' read 'Catholic,' and you have the full meaning of that ambiguous seventh plank, which is so worded as to catch, if possible, the Evangelical and the Liberal votes at the same time," wrote *The Index*. "We do not propose to ride on any elephant whose trunk cannot be distinguished from its tail. We intend to know in which direction the animal will move, before we take our seat on its back." Abbot and *The Index* were distancing themselves even more from the proposed amendment.[97]

The Democrats held their national convention in St. Louis from June 26 to 29. The Democratic nomination was less in doubt, with New York Governor Samuel J. Tilden easily capturing the party's banner on the first ballot. The selection of Tilden, with his connections to the New York Catholic hierarchy, provided a stark choice for many people. The Democrats criticized the Republican platform, charging their opponents with seeking to create a "false issue" over the School Question, claiming it "would enkindle sectarian strife in respect to the public schools, of which the establishment and support belong exclusively to the several States, and which the Democratic party has cherished from their foundation." Still, the Democrats were unwilling to be outdone by the Republicans, and they included their own church-state provision in their platform. The provision was purposefully vague, simply stating that the party was in favor of maintaining "the two-fold separation of church and state, for the sake alike of civil and religious freedom." Yet the platform also called for maintaining public schools "without partiality or preference for any class, sect or creed, and without contributions from the treasury to any."[98] By including a call to prohibit funding of religious schools, the Democrats risked alienating their Catholic constituents. The

Democrats' support for separation of church and state demonstrates the wide appeal for the concept, however one defined it. It may also suggest that the concept was not necessarily identified in partisan, anti-Catholic terms. Few people read party platforms, however, and the provisions simply confirmed, rather than directed, the strategies of the respective parties. Democrats did not want to appear to oppose public education by advocating a division of school funds, though no one was about to confuse the commitment of the two parties about the School Question. Even with its inclusion in the platforms, the School Question was a second-tier issue for Republicans and Democrats when compared to Reconstruction, political corruption, hard-money currency policies, tariffs, and the distribution of western government lands.[99]

With the political conventions over and the Republican Party's stance on the school issue established, congressional attention turned back to the Blaine Amendment. Democrats were divided over the amendment, with party members attempting to walk a tightrope between Catholic voters and public support for the issue. In early June the Democrat-controlled House Judiciary Committee voted along party lines not to report the measure before the end of the session, thereby hoping to delay the vote until after the November elections. Following the national conventions, the House Democratic leadership realized that public interest in the school issue made it impossible to remain silent indefinitely. The *New York Times* reported that Governor Tilden desired immediate action on the amendment so as to "take the Catholic question out of politics."[100] Since the Democrats controlled the House and the amendment's fate, the Judiciary Committee decided to weaken the measure and then pass it on to the Republican Senate for its consideration. On August 4, the Committee reported the resolution to the full House with an amendment. Attached to the end of Blaine's proposal was the added proviso: "This article shall not vest, enlarge, or diminish legislative power in the Congress." According to the committee report, the amendment to the resolution was unanimously adopted. "While there may be a difference of opinion as to the necessity of such a constitutional amendment, all agree that the underlying principles are right and in accordance with the spirit of the age."[101]

On the House floor, Representative George McCrary (R-Iowa) objected to the addendum as amounting to a nullifying clause. The resolution, McCrary stated, "amends the Constitution and denies to Congress the power to legislate for enforcing the amendment after you have made it. . . . [I]f the people of the country, desire the Constitution of the United States to be amended in this particular, then it follows it ought to be so amended that the legislative body that makes laws for the National Government shall have power to enforce it by proper legislation." Otherwise, the amendment was superfluous.[102] McCrary, of course, was stating the very reason the resolution had been amended: to eliminate whatever authority existed in its wording and to make it a statement of general principles. The Democrats from the Judiciary Committee freely admitted that the new amendment gave Congress no power to enforce its provisions, particularly any authority to obligate states to operate public schools. But, Representative Scott Lord (D-NY) insisted, this is what Blaine intended. "[T]he gentleman who introduced the amendment—and I know his views upon the question, for he stated them to me more than once—never contended that such amendment to the Constitution, which was drawn by him, conferred any legislative power on Congress whatever, and he never intended that it should.... [T]his additional clause does not in any manner change the preceding part of the proposed article. It is simply declaratory; more than this, if Congress had any power over the question before, it is thoroughly and absolutely reserved."[103]

The Democrats' argument was immensely appealing. The resolution, as amended, would not empower Congress to ensure the amendment carried any weight. But, Democrats argued, the amendment was never intended to be more than a declaration of principles in the first place. And since the addendum also provided that Congress' power was not diminished by the amendment, Congress still had the same authority to do whatever it could have done before the amendment. Or, as Lord put it, "if the Congress has any power now, under any possible view, over the subject-matter of the proposed amendment, such power remains in full force and vigor. The words of limitation only apply to the proposed article." Lord's convoluted logic was too tempting to pass up, for it offered something for everyone. The amended resolution passed by an overwhelming vote of 180 to 7. The Blaine Amendment had received its first level of approval.[104]

The resolution went immediately over to the Senate. It was here that Blaine's relatively modest amendment underwent significant modification, with the final product that emerged being more partisan and sectarian in tone. On August 7, the President pro tem of the Senate announced receiving the House version of the amendment. Even before he could refer it to the Judiciary Committee, several Republican senators objected to the House version. Leading the charge was evangelical Senator Frederick Frelinghuysen (R-NJ), who called the House resolution "brutum falmen;" it had no sanction and there was no way to enforce it. Frelinghuysen also objected that the House version barred only appropriations to religious schools from designated funds while leaving open the possibility of state funding of other religious institutions, such as theological seminaries, reformatories, monasteries and nunneries, from other sources. To address this problem, Frelinghuysen proposed his own version of the amendment:

> Section 1. No State shall make any law respecting the establishment of religion or prohibiting the free exercise thereof; and no public property and no money raised by taxation in any state, Territory, or District, or derived from public lands or other public source, shall be appropriated to any school, educational or other institution, that is under the control of any religious sect or denomination; and no such appropriation shall be made to any religious sect or denomination or to promote its interests;

nor shall any public money, land, or property be divided between religious sects or denominations.

    Section 2. The Congress shall have power to enforce by appropriate
legislation the provisions of this article.[105]

Frelinghuysen insisted that Congress would be derelict to pass an unenforceable
measure, and he urged the removal of the nullifying clause.

> But, more importantly, the House version contained an inherent incon-
> sistency. The resolution applied only to indirect appropriations from
> school funds to sectarian schools. It did not cover direct grants from
> state treasuries or appropriations to other religious institutions, such as
> to seminaries or reformatories. It was incongruous to pass a resolution
> that prohibited indirect support of religious schools, "but leaves the
> States full power to commit the same wrong whenever they choose to do
> it directly."[106]

Senator Isaac Christiancy (R-MI) agreed with Frelinghuysen's substitution, particularly with broadening the prohibition on the source of public funding.
Christiancy also thought that if the Senate was going to amend the House version, it should be as thorough as possible. He proposed changing the second
clause of Frelinghuysen's substitution to include acts of the federal government
and specifically to prohibit teaching any religion or religious belief as a course of
study in a public or tax supported school. "This substitute, as I have said, covers
the entire ground. It takes up the poisonous tree by the root, while the resolution sent us by the House cuts off but a minor and unimportant branch."
Christiancy moved that his substitution also be considered by the Judiciary
Committee.[107]

    Before the resolution and substitutions could be referred to the committee,
Senator Aaron Sargent (R-CA) proposed his own substitution:

> There shall be maintained in each state and Territory a system of free
> common schools; but neither the United States nor any state, or Territory,
> county or municipal corporation shall aid in support of any school
> wherein the peculiar tenets of any religious denomination are taught.[108]

Sargent offered his substitution without comment. His proposal was similar to
Senator Stewart's 1872 amendment which had died in committee. Sargent's
substitution, along with those of Frelinghuysen and Christiancy, and the House
version were all referred to the Judiciary Committee for consideration. With
Frelinghuysen and Christiancy's substitutions, the complexion of the Blaine
Amendment had already shifted. Not only were its prohibitions being broadened,
its tone was becoming more sectarian.

The Index reacted immediately to the substitutions, calling Frelinghuysen and Christiancy's proposals "the event of the week." The substitutions with their expanded prohibitions were more than Liberals could have hoped for. Whereas only a month earlier the Liberal League had called for the defeat of the school amendment, now *The Index* urged the immediate adoption of Christiancy's version: "We do not see but that the above amendment covers the entire ground of the Religious Freedom Amendment, proposed as a substitute for the first amendment to the United States Constitution, which has stood for some time in the columns of *The Index*," Abbot wrote.[109]

Abbot's endorsement was premature, for once again he had misjudged the resolve of his opponents and the whims of politicians. On August 11, the Judiciary Committee issued its report on the school amendment. The committee report proposed the following wording for the amendment:

> No state shall make any law respecting an establishment of religion, or prohibiting the free exercise thereof; and no religious test shall be required as a qualification to any office or public trust under any State. No public property and no public revenue, nor any loan of credit by or under the authority of the United States, or any state, Territory, District, or municipal corporation, shall be appropriated to or made or used for the support of any school, educational or other institution under the control of any religious or anti-religious sect, organization, or denomination, or wherein the particular creeds or tenets shall be taught. And no such particular creed or tenets shall be read or taught in any school or institution supported in whole or in part by such revenue or loan of credit; and no such appropriation or loan of credit shall be made to any religious or anti-religious sect, organization, or denomination or to promote its interests or tenets. *This article shall not be construed to prohibit the reading of the Bible in any school or institution, and it shall not have the effect to impair the rights of property already vested.*[110]

The Senate resolution was comprehensive, to say the least. The committee used parts of Frelinghuysen and Christiancy's substitutions by prohibiting appropriations to all religious institutions, not simply parochial schools. The resolution also prohibited appropriations to religious institutions from all sources of public revenue, whether from the federal or state governments, a provision Christiancy and other Republicans wanted included. Finally, the report went beyond any of the substitutions to include a prohibition on religious tests for state office holding, a provision called for in the Religious Freedom Amendment. The Senate resolution was far broader than Blaine's amendment, or even Grant's recommendation.

One other provision distinguished the Senate version from Blaine or Grant's proposals, and particularly from the Religious Freedom Amendment. The committee had attached to the end of the resolution a provision requiring that nothing in the amendment could be "construed to prohibit the reading of the Bible in any [public] school or institution." The sentence had apparently been inserted as a result of the lobbying efforts of the N.R.A. Back in the winter, the Association had unsuccessfully urged Blaine to add an identical provision in his original proposition. Now with the amendment in the hands of the Senate, the Association had decided to try again.[111]

While the amendment was in committee, T. P. Stevenson sent letters to all members of Congress suggesting the phrase as a compromise. "The clause proposed will introduce no new feature into our education," Stevenson wrote. "It will not require the reading of the Bible. It will not forbid or prevent the discontinuance of Bible-reading by the decision of the Legislatures, or of the school authorities. It simply provides that this amendment, which contemplates mainly another question, shall not be construed to declare illegal the existing usage of our schools." Apparently, Republican members of the committee were impressed with the argument that the clause would maintain the status quo regarding Bible reading, however each member interpreted that status. But, as Stevenson knew, by inserting the clause in the amendment, the Constitution would be sanctioning the Bible and, by implication, the Christian religion. For the N.R.A. and other religious conservatives, this would be an important step toward ensuring America's Christian character.[112]

Critiques of the Blaine Amendment frequently fail to distinguish Blaine's proposal from the ultimate Senate version as amended by the Republicans and their evangelical allies. Participants at the time understood that the Senate resolution differed from Blaine's original proposal in several ways, that it was more partisan and pro-Protestant than earlier versions. Leading Democrats, in fact, announced they were willing to support a measure similar to Blaine's original amendment. Theodore Randolph (D-NJ) noted that Blaine's proposal "had received no alteration" since its introduction and "had been the text of praise and approval from one end of the country to the other." He claimed he had "labored hard" to secure "an amendment passed substantially like that sent to us from the House." But the Senate version was an "altogether different affair" from the amendment the people had supported, Randolph stated. "It opens, if adopted, many grave questions, good enough for the welfare of the legal profession, but bad enough for the body-politic."[113] Democratic New York Senator Francis Kernan, a Catholic, declared he too was "willing to vote for the Blaine amendment," even though "it is against the principles I believe to be wise." Kernan's support was pragmatic—to resolve a contentious issue:

> Inasmuch as there was danger that sectarian dissensions would arise in regard to the common-school moneys, inasmuch as it was asserted that efforts were being made to divide these moneys between the religious denominations, and there was great danger that the subject of common

schools would be made a political question and sectarian prejudices aroused as an element in political contests, I was willing to adopt the Blaine amendment, in the hope and belief that it would quiet these groundless fears as to the common schools and avert the evils which spring from religious prejudices.

But Kernan, like Randolph, "consider[ed] the proposed amendment now before the Senate as going far beyond that proposed by Mr. Blaine." Rather than "allaying strife and dissension," Kernan remarked, "it will increase them and bring evil to our schools, to our institutions, and to the people of our country." It is likely that Randolph and Kernan's support for Blaine's original amendment was a strategic move to appear centrist while emphasizing the excesses of the Senate version. Still, like the House Democrats who realized their party had more to lose over the controversy than to gain, the senators seemed prepared to support a scaled-down version of the measure to remove the School Question as a political issue. And Kernan was already on record opposing a division of school funds, having given a speech supporting common schools before a Catholic audience at New York's Tammany Hall the previous November. As Kernan and other Democrats indicated, a proposal limited to restricting appropriations from school funds, while leaving open grants to religious charities, would likely have received bipartisan support. This was essentially Blaine's proposal.[114]

Debate over the Senate resolution focused on three issues: the authority of states to control education; the partisan nature of the Senate version, including charges the version was anti-Catholic; and the Bible reading clause. The first issue was of greatest concern to the senators and consumed the bulk of the debate. Democrats, and some Republicans, were troubled by the breadth of the Senate proposal, less by its church-state provisions than by the specter of federal interference with state-run education. Even though the Senate resolution lacked a clause obligating states to maintain public schools as Grant had proposed, it contained language authorizing Congress to enforce its provisions. As a result, Democrats pilloried the measure with states' rights arguments, charging there was "no duty devolving upon the Federal Government, by reason of any provision in the Constitution, to directly care for the education of its citizens." The "power is not in the Federal Government," Kentucky's John Stevenson declared. "Kentucky does not want New England and other States to dictate to her what her schools shall be or what her taxes shall be, and least of all what her religion shall be." Education was "a home right," Kernan echoed. "The founders of the Federal Government had the wisdom to perceive the advantage of leaving to the people of each State the control and management of their local State matters."[115] Republicans lacked a good response to the charge of federal interference; with Reconstruction winding down, Republicans understood the public's weariness with federal involvement in local affairs. Instead, they resorted to affirming the importance of public education and the threat presented by a division of school funds. Despite insisting that the "public schools of this country are dear to the hearts of almost all American citizens," as Vermont's George Edmunds asserted, the argument carried little weight against the charge of federal interference.[116]

In addition to the states' rights issue, debate focused on the partisan nature of the Senate resolution. Republicans claimed, as Grant and Blaine had insisted earlier, that an amendment was necessary so that "the question is taken out of politics." Although Democrats had more to gain by diffusing religious prejudice in the political arena, they asserted the Republican proposal would only exacerbate matters. And the claim fell apart once Republicans attacked Democrats for lacking commitment to public education while supporting Catholic schooling. Senate Democrats fired back. The Senate resolution was "a cloak for the most unworthy partisan motives," Missouri Senator Lewis Bogy charged; the Republicans were replacing the "bloody shirt" with unfounded fears of an imperial papacy. Rather than seeking to diffuse religious tensions, the measure sought "to arouse feeling against the democratic party, and make it appear that it is dependent upon the support of the Catholics for success." Stating the obvious, Connecticut's William Eaton claimed the "whole matter is brought up as an election dodge" to attract evangelical voters while diverting attention away from other matters.[117]

The issue of anti-Catholic partisanship has surrounded the Blaine Amendment for years. It needs to be considered on two levels. First, all participants understood that the amendment, like all forms of legislation, was designed to appeal to particular constituencies, which the Republicans hoped would translate into electoral support. The chief constituency was evangelical Protestants who overwhelmingly supported public schooling. The acknowledged political reality was that Protestants more naturally aligned themselves with the Republicans, as Catholics did with the Democrats. Throughout American history political parties have attempted to tie the opposing party to the presumed negatives of their constituencies, whether they are labor unions or corporations, Protestants or Catholics. Although Protestants represented a natural voting block, Republicans needed to invigorate those evangelicals who might otherwise be repulsed by the political corruptions of the day. A school amendment appealed to Protestant support for public education and played on latent suspicions about Catholic challenges to the financial and ideological basis of public schooling. The newly added Bible reading clause made the resolution only that much more sectarian (pro-Protestant) and partisan. Most of the Senate debate took place on this level, with senators discussing Protestant and Catholic perspectives on schooling and whether the measure advantaged Protestants or disadvantaged Catholics. Despite the claim of Indiana Republican Oliver Morton that the amendment was "no more for Protestants than it is for Catholics," all participants understood the measure would negatively impact Catholics and their schools. This was simply the political lay-of-the-land.[118]

Rarely did the rhetoric of the Senate debate enter a different level, one that was distinctly anti-Catholic in tone. The most overt exchange occurred between

Republican William Edmunds and Democrat Lewis Bogy, the latter being a Catholic. Edmonds charged that Catholics opposed not only public education but principles of republican government and freedom of conscience. He read into the record excerpts from the 1864 Papal Syllabus which condemned liberty of worship and church-state separation. Bogy, in response, defended the Catholic position. He agreed that Catholics opposed public schools, but for "the reason they were sectarian. Even the very Bible which was used in the schools was a sectarian book." Catholics also opposed being taxed to support schools where such religion was taught, Bogy stated; these positions were well known. Bogy in turn charged that Republicans were not truly interested in public education but were using the amendment to stir up anti-Catholic sentiment. "I think I know the motive and the animus which have prompted all this thing." Republicans did not support the amendment "because of a great devotion to the principle of religious liberty," he asserted. "That great idea which is now moving the modern world is used merely as a cloak for the most unworthy of partisan motives." Rather, it was "the old Pope of Rome . . . that we are all to attack."[119] Aside from these exchanges, however, the debate was relatively free of religious dispersions, possibly reflecting that each side's positions and constituencies were already known. All participants understood that the immediate effect of the amendment would be to protect the economic position of public schools to the disadvantage of Catholic schools. That aspects of the debate played on religious prejudices is true, but more commonly the debate reflected the realities of the divisions between the parties and their constituencies.

The issues of state's rights and Republican opportunism consumed the bulk of the Senate debate, indicating that the senators viewed the proposal primarily in partisan terms. Only occasionally did the debate turn to the underlying church-state issues at stake. Unlike the public debate that took place outside the halls of Congress, the Senate discussion of church-state theories was neither extensive nor profound.

One of the few substantive discussions took place between New York's Catholic Democratic senator, Francis Kernan, and Republican Oliver Morton. Kernan objected to the first sentence of the amendment which would have applied the religious liberty and disestablishment provisions of the First Amendment (and the prohibition against religious tests in Article VI) to the states. That matter had been "discussed in the convention that made the Constitution," Kernan asserted, "and it was not thought wise to put in any such provision, but leave it to the states." In his statement, Kernan was not expressing any view over whether the Fourteenth Amendment had subsequently incorporated the Bill of Rights (which would become an issue in the 1940s), as that issue had recently been settled in two Supreme Court decisions ruling against incorporation. Rather, Kernan merely objected to increasing federal authority at the expense of state power to regulate religious matters. Imposing federal authority "would be an insult to the people of every State of the Union" by insinuating that "there was a danger that they would begin now to establish a State religion, or begin to prohibit its exercise, or make religious belief a test or qualification for holding office." In making this claim, Kernan did not elaborate on what constituted a state religious establishment other than to assert that none existed.[120] Oliver Morton responded to Kernan's remarks with an interpretation of the religion clauses that transcended the federalism question. Morton claimed that "an essential principle of American liberty...upon which the perpetuity of our Government depends" was that "we shall have perfect freedom of religious worship, that there shall be no established church, no religion established by law." Applying those values to the School Question, Morton asserted that the "support of a school by public taxation is the same thing in principle as an established church."

> This is not a new idea. The idea of free schools not denominational but general, the idea of a free church not supported...or maintained by the government is an original one in American liberty. It has always prevailed in this country.

Thus for Morton, the First Amendment stood for the voluntary support of religious institutions, whether they be houses of worship or schools, which in turn enhanced religious freedom. This was why applying the First Amendment to the states was crucial: "so far as states being left free to establish a church if they see proper or to establish denominational schools at public expense, I believe that the safety of this nation in the far future depends on their being deprived of any such power." Morton also tied his understanding of nonestablishment to notions of religious conscience. Americans could not have "perfect freedom of religious opinion" or "prefect [religious] equality" except "on the condition that religion shall not be maintained at public expense." Morton did not respond to Bogy's earlier claim that public schools failed this very principle because of their Protestant character. But his statements that schools should be "general in character" rather than religious, suggest he supported a moderate version of nonsectarian curriculum for teaching morals. He disputed claims that "our public schools in which religion is not taught are infidel and wicked." It was those people who "utterly oppose...any [common] school that does not teach religion," that Catholics should fear, he warned Kernan.[121]

The other substantive church-state discussion involved the Bible reading clause. Morton's criticism of a religious-based curriculum represented a subtle rebuke of the resolution's Bible reading provision. He was not the only senator to see the inconsistency, as Democrats also attacked the clause. The resolution prohibited the teaching of any particular creeds or tenets in the schools but then guaranteed that the Bible shall not be prohibited. "Is not this a flat contradiction; or is the Bible a nonreligious book?" Theodore Randolph asked. "Which edition shall it be, if the state assumes to designate one according to its 'consciences?'"[122]

Republicans generally avoided discussing the Bible reading clause. Only Frederick Frelinghuysen of New Jersey, scion of a notable evangelical family, eagerly defended the provision. In contrast to Morton's interpretation, he insisted the provision prohibited only the teaching of "sectarian creeds." There was "nothing in it that prohibits religion as distinguished from the particular creed or tenets of religious and anti-religious sects and denominations being taught anywhere." In so doing, Frelinghuysen embraced an older view of nonsectarianism, insisting the Bible "is a religious and not a sectarian book."

> [W]here shall we go for public morals? If you must exclude the Bible you must banish all our literature or expurgate it, for it would be the height of folly to say that it is lawful to drink from the conduits which human hands had made, but not from the pure fountain.... No sir; the people of this country want that book let alone. The Constitution must not touch it. It is to be forced upon no one and the constitution is to make it unlawful to read it nowhere.[123]

Frelinghuysen's perspective on the School Question also informed his views on church-state matters generally, and again he diverged from Morton. The idea of "pure and undefiled religion which appertains to the relationship and responsibility of man to God" was integrated into the nation's institutions and integral for its survival, he asserted. It was that religion "which permeates all our laws, which is recognized in every sentence against crime and immorality, which is invoked in every oath, which is reverentially deferred to every morning at that desk and on like occasions at the capitol of every State of the Union;... that religion which is our history, which is our unwritten as well as our written law, and which sustains the pillars of our liberty." As a result, Frelinghuysen did not view the First Amendment as banning government support of Christianity generally, and the resolution, he assured his colleagues, "places no unhallowed touch upon that religion."[124] No other Republican defended the Bible reading clause on religious grounds; the only other comments were that the provision maintained the status quo. Oliver Morton alone came close to disputing his colleague's remarks by asserting that public schools were not irreligious simply because religion was not taught. The views of the other senators on Bible reading are not known.[125]

Senate debate over the Blaine Amendment covered more than twenty three pages in the *Congressional Record*. In the end, the debate had little impact on the outcome of the resolution. The Senate split 28 to 16 in favor of the amendment, with Republicans and Democrats voting along party lines. The final result was four votes short of the two-thirds necessary for passage, though a defection of two Democrats would have carried the measure. Twenty-seven Senators were absent from the vote, including Simon Cameron of Pennsylvania and John Sherman of Ohio, both Republicans and N.R.A. supporters. Both men would likely have voted for the amendment, which would have brought it close to passage. The most obvious absence was that of James G. Blaine, who had been appointed to the Senate a month earlier. Blaine, who was recovering from his unsuccessful campaign for President, failed to show up to vote on the amendment that bore his name. His presence alone may have been sufficient to have influenced reticent Democrats and carry the day.[126]

The Senate resolution, of course, differed significantly from the House version, so even if it had passed it would not have been submitted to the states for ratification. It is unlikely the Democratic House would have assented to the Senate version in a conference committee. There the measure may have died, or at least languished until after the election when it would have lost its political usefulness. It is also possible that a version similar to that introduced by James Blaine could have passed both chambers. Senators Randolph and Kernan, among other Democrats, had expressed support for the original version of the amendment. Had the Republicans left the House version intact or even omitted the House's nullifying clause, the amendment may have passed.

Had it passed, the Blaine Amendment would have significantly impacted the development of separation of church and state in America, chiefly because it would have made incorporation unnecessary seventy years later. Even though the amendment would merely have nationalized the accepted rule against funding religious schools, it would have obviated any future questions whether the Establishment Clause accomplished as much. Yet even though the religion clauses hung in the balance, the debate over the measure revealed little concern for its implications. Aside from the brief exchanges between Frelinghuysen, Randolph, Kernan, and Morton, most senators showed little interest in interpretations of the First Amendment. Rather, the amendment became embroiled in questions about federal interference in state-run education and in the partisan nature of the measure. The Bible reading clause, which had been important to assuage evangelical concerns, had not been a crucial issue, though it had provided Democrats with an additional reason to vote against the measure.[127]

That said, the N.R.A. had come much closer to pulling off a victory with the Bible reading clause than it ever had with its Christian Amendment. While the clause fell short of the Association's ultimate goal, it would have acknowledged the primacy of the Bible and ensured that future interpretations of the Constitution's religion clauses were favorable to Christianity. This would have significantly impacted church-state jurisprudence. The Liberal League appreciated the significance of the vote and how close it had come to losing not only an important battle but the entire war. *The Index*, which a week earlier had announced its support for Christiancy's version of the amendment, expressed frustration over the final turn of events. Rather than achieving the goal of church-state separation, the amendment had been contorted into a measure that would have all but recognized Christianity as the national religion. *The Index* knew where to lay the blame. "The origin of that concluding clause of the first section—its evil purpose being cloaked with such preternatural cunning and plausibility—could not have been in the Judiciary Committee: the toad at Eve's ear in Paradise was no more Satan in disguise than was the Christian Amendment emissary who evidently suggested to one member of that Committee the insertion of this seemingly harmless clause."[128] The Index pointed to an August 12 editorial in The Christian Statesman that took credit for the clause as proof of the Association's culpability. "The baleful political influence and power of the Christian Amendment party are proved beyond the possibility of cavil by the fact that, although Mr. Blaine apparently resisted its approaches, the Judiciary Committee succumbed to its plausible representations at once. We have been ridiculed again and again for attributing vitality to this Christianizing fanaticism; but, we confess, we were thunderstruck at such an evidence of the vast strides towards ultimate success which it has already made."[129]

The Index ended its editorial by raising a call of alarm for the future. "No words of ours could paint the magnitude of the disaster which the nation has so narrowly escaped. . . . Will any man after this be so idiotic as to despise the Christian Amendment movement or underrate its craftily hidden power? It has proved its power; it has almost succeeded; it will renew its accursed attempt."[130] The N.R.A. did renew its attempt, but it would never get as close to realizing its goal as it did in 1876. When Congress reconvened in December, it faced the far more pressing matter of choosing a President. Not until March 1877, did the nation know that Rutherford B. Hayes would be the next President. By then, most people had forgotten the Blaine Amendment. Its political usefulness ended with the election, and few people were interested in reviving the issue, especially since many states were enacting their own measures to limit the funding of parochial schools. Despite The Index's warnings, the Christian Amendment was dead, as were all efforts to amend the religious content of the Constitution for another generation. In contrast, the Blaine Amendment came close to passing, and a modified version may have succeeded, forever altering the First Amendment.

With the defeat of the Blaine Amendment, the School Question faded as a political issue, at least temporarily. Local conflicts over the School Question also subsided for a while, with people seemingly exhausted from the events of the previous years. Ironically, even though the Blaine Amendment did not pass, it appeared to achieve one of its desired goals. With the Senate vote, Cincinnati Archbishop Purcell published a pronunciamento on behalf of the America bishops addressed to "the people of the United States." The address sought, on one level, to diffuse recent tensions that had arisen out of the School Question, but its language revealed the alienation many Catholics felt from the public schools. Purcell wrote that the Catholic Church had no "intention whatever to interfere with your public school system." Catholics, he insisted, would cease criticizing public education and "leave yourselves the care of your own children." Purcell asked only that Catholics be given the same right to educate their children as they wished. This last point was key. In addition to signaling a truce on the School Question, the address was designed to counteract a movement in the states toward requiring compulsory education, a reform called for in Grant's address. But the pronunciamento also had an element of capitulation. The document reasserted that

Catholics deserved an exemption from school taxation or a proportional share of school funds for operating Catholic schools. But, Purcell concluded, "even this claim we are disposed to waive in your favor." The statement caught Protestant journals by surprise. Did this mean the church would give up on future claims for public support for its schools? *The Independent* doubted that the church would abide by this "new departure," if it was one. The Catholic *Tablet*, however, confirmed Purcell's statement: "we are content to be taxed, unjust, as it is, for the schools we cannot use; [and] we will not even require our just share of the school funds for the support of our own schools." [131]

The Catholic statement, of course, did not signal an end to the School Question. Controversies over funding and religious exercises would arise throughout the remainder of the century and into the next. But the Blaine Amendment did close a particularly divisive chapter in the overall development of public education in America. And despite its divisiveness, the period was also one of significant constitutional development, one that would serve as the crucible of future church-state doctrine.

6

The Legacy of the School Question

The debate over the School Question was the closest that Americans have ever come to having a national conversation about the meaning of the religion clauses of the Constitution. As is often the case with public discussions of religion and politics, the conversation was not always civil or profound. Much was at stake, considering that most people viewed public schooling to be the "nursery of the Republic"—the institution responsible for instilling civic and moral values in each new generation of Americans. Also, the School Question served as a proxy for how the nation would address a host of other challenges—immigration, religious pluralism, labor and economic competition—so the debate and accompanying rhetoric played on a host of hopes, fears, and prejudices. Yet some people seized the opportunity to have a serious discussion about the role of religion in American public life. The arguments of Horace Mann, Alphonso Taft, Orestes Brownson, Henry Ward Beecher, Francis Abbot, Samuel Spear, and William Torrey Harris, among others, may not have convinced the majority of listeners, but they invited Americans to reevaluate their positions. More significant, their arguments—and not those of the inciters—laid the foundation for the legal theories that the United States Supreme Court would adopt a century later. The religious hyperbole surrounding the School Question could not obscure this more significant debate over constitutional principles.[1]

The School Question was not the only church-state controversy of the day—the Mormon Question forced Americans to ponder whether a religious body could exercise temporal authority in a republic and whether the government could suppress a religious practice that outraged public sensibilities. Other church-state controversies that arose during the century, such as Sunday law enforcement, also garnered significant public attention. The federal policy of "Christianizing" Native Americans by funding religious missions was, disappointingly, less controversial. But Mormons and Native Americans were outliers, and so those issues were, to the vast majority of Americans, less consequential. The School Question was mainstream and went to the heart of what it meant to be an American and how communities should instill moral and republican values. It challenged truncated understandings of religious pluralism and equality. And more than any other controversy, the School Question impacted a significant number of people across the nation.

Most important for our purposes, the debate over the School Question set the stage for modern religion clause jurisprudence. The legal standards that emerged after 1947 to govern church-state doctrine arose out of similar controversies over religion and education. Although those legal tests owe their origins to the Court's modern cases, the rationales for those standards are directly traceable to the events of 1869–1876.[2] To be sure, the School Question controversy was not limited to the decade following the Civil War. Issues of whether public schools should transmit religious values or whether the state should financially assist religious schools predated the creation of American public education and remain unresolved to this day.[3] Even so, the period between 1869 and 1876 became the fulcrum of the controversy, which raised larger issues about the role of religion in an increasingly pluralistic society. That this debate occurred at a time of competing religious and secularizing forces only heightened the interconnectedness of the School Question with the overarching issues of church-state relationships generally. It was during this period that the arguments and rationales governing the two issues congealed, ordaining the legal and policy discussions of the twentieth century. The Cincinnati Bible case, Grant's Des Moines speech, and the Blaine Amendment have been touchstones for legal briefs and court decisions since the 1940s.[4]

The emergent legal doctrine of the latter nineteenth century did not arise in an intellectual vacuum but was impacted by the diversity of perspectives about the role of religion in education and in the culture. Was America a "Republic of the Bible" that deferred to its Protestant heritage, or was it a secular nation governed by constitutional norms that emphasized religious equality and pluralism (or was it possible to embrace both perspectives)? If it was the latter, did that mean the government should remain neutral in conflicts between religion and nonreligion, or could it privilege secular values? These issues remain unresolved. As they do today, people holding various religious perspectives struggled with those issues 150 years ago. And as today, that debate was not two-dimensional—Protestant versus Catholic. Protestant perspectives were fractured among evangelicals, moderates, and liberals, and Catholics (traditionalists and liberals), Jews and secularists also entered the discussion. Educators also disagreed over the role of religion in public education, as the divisions among Horace Mann, Rev. Mathew Smith, and William Torrey Harris demonstrated. Participants in the debate held contrasting views about the above questions and, in their own ways, advanced positions they considered principled. Even many nativists, particularly the rank-and-file, believed they were protecting ideals and values that were essential for the perpetuation of republican society. It is this aspect of the debate that should not be overlooked.

The legacy of the "great church-state debate" that culminated with the Blaine Amendment was extensive, impacting legal doctrine and educational policy well into the twentieth century. One result of that debate was that in the future, the connections between Bible reading and religious school funding were frayed. The secularization of public education continued, while Catholics—who had never been the main source of the secularizing pressure—focused on expanding parochial schools. And following the Blaine Amendment, frontal assaults by Catholics on state school funds all but vanished. The two issues, so seemingly interrelated, disengaged. How those issues evolved over the ensuing seventy years would impact how the Supreme Court would finally engage the School Question in the late 1940s.

The Funding Question

The Blaine Amendment holds a strange status in the development of church-state doctrine. It served as the capstone in the evolution of the no-funding rule and, even though it was not enacted, it set the tone of constitutional development for the next generation. Despite this legacy, the amendment was more significant as a political event than as a constitutional one. To be sure, the proposal represented the closest that the nation has come to altering the First Amendment. Yet the majority of the politicians involved in the debate, including its namesake, expressed little interest in the substantive principles embodied in the proposed amendment. For them the amendment was chiefly a partisan device, and they exhibited few reservations about rewriting the First Amendment for political gain. Only a handful of politicians—Grant, Frelinghuysen, Morton—expressed a real interest in the underlying constitutional principles, though their commitment to those ideals was likely overshadowed by political considerations. For many others, though—Samuel Spear, Francis Abbot, Lyman Atwater, William Torrey Harris, and the members of the N.R.A. and Liberal Leagues—the substantive principles mattered greatly.

Despite the efforts of the N.R.A. and Liberal Leagues to seize the moment, few people believed the Blaine Amendment would refine or expand on existing constitutional principles. By 1876, the no-funding rule was the accepted legal doctrine in the states, one that had been developing since the 1820s. All participants in the debate recognized this fact. Senator Frelinghuysen, the floor manager of the amendment, declared that the measure affirmed long-standing principles of freedom of conscience, including that "people should not be taxed for sectarian purposes." Frelinghuysen believed that these principles were not new; indeed, "[t]he whole history of our country, from its origin to the present day, establishes and fortifies these positions." A Democratic senator concurred that the proposal "founds no new principle. . . . It recognizes the fact that a system known as the common-school system has obtained in almost every State, has the sanction directly or indirectly of most State governments [and] has the generous support of most taxpayers." The amendment would nationalize an existing principle rather than create a new one.[5]

Seventy years later, critics of the Supreme Court's holdings in the *Everson* and *McCollum* cases would raise two arguments about the significance of the Blaine Amendment. First, they argued that the amendment undermined the emergent Incorporation Doctrine. They claimed that language in the amendment imposing the religion clauses on the states demonstrated that the members of the Forty-Fourth Congress did not consider the Due Process Clause of the Fourteenth Amendment to have accomplished that task. In essence, because several members of that Congress had been representatives in 1866–1868, they would not have supported language prohibiting states from establishing a religion if they had though that due process liberty already imposed that burden on the states. This argument, attractive in its simplicity, overlooked two crucial factors, one general and the other specific. As discussed in the previous chapter, the overriding focus of the debate over the Blaine Amendment was on resolving the School Question or on using it for political gain. Absent brief statements by Senator Morton, the Fourteenth Amendment was not discussed in a meaningful way in either House. The First Amendment received similar short shrift. More significant was Morton's reference to the recent *Slaughter-House* and *Cruikshank* decisions, where the Court had severely restricted the scope of the Fourteenth Amendment's due process and privileges and immunities clauses. Morton believed that the Blaine Amendment was now needed because the Fourteenth Amendment, "which we supposed to be broad, ample, and specific," had he "fear[ed], been very much impaired by [judicial] construction." For Morton, the Blaine Amendment would not have introduced a new idea of incorporation but corrected an erroneous judicial interpretation that prevented it from occurring through the Fourteenth Amendment.[6]

The second argument about the Blaine Amendment is related to the substantive meaning of the Establishment Clause. During the 1940s and 1950s, critics of the no-funding rule argued that because the proposal included an express provision prohibiting public funding of religious institutions, Blaine and his supporters could not have believed the Establishment Clause prohibited the same. Attention centered on remarks by Senator Christiancy, who criticized the House version of the amendment for restricting only funding by the states. The proposal "simply prohibits the States from doing these things; it does not prohibit the United States," Christiancy said. "[U]nder the Constitution of the United States, as it now stands, it is entirely competent to devote lands or impose taxes and appropriate money for sectarian purposes." In essence, critics argued, Christiancy's statement revealed that legislators interpreted the Establishment Clause as not prohibiting the neutral funding of religion, thus necessitating the additional provision. Critics also insisted that Congress confirmed this narrow view of the clause's proscriptions by defeating the Blaine Amendment and later similar proposals.[7] Christiancy's statement must be seen within context, however. He was responding to the just-passed House version which prohibited only appropriations from funds designated for school support. Following Senator Frelinghuysen's criticism of the same, Christiancy urged that the prohibition should extend to public monies from any source, flowing through direct and indirect channels. Fearing the negative inference in the House version, both men sought to clarify that the no-funding principle applied to federal appropriations as well. This reflected the prevailing attitude among Republicans, and most Democrats, that the no-funding principle was already constitutionally required—that the amendment "founds no new principle," according to Frelinghuysen—and merely needed emphasizing.[8]

This interpretation is consistent with the limited statements about the constitutional basis for the no-funding rule. Indiana Republican Senator Oliver Morton was one of the few senators to discuss the substantive aspects of the proposed amendment and their relation to the First Amendment. He too asserted that the amendment merely reaffirmed the status quo:

> The idea of free schools not denominational but general, the idea of a free church not supported by the government or maintained by the government is an original one in American liberty. It has always prevailed in this country. Now it is proposed to give it form and put it in the Constitution. [But] [i]t has been in the minds of our people for one hundred years. . . .[9]

Understandably, this claim required Morton and the Republicans to justify the need for the amendment. They responded that an amendment would prevent further erosion of existing principles. Morton asserted that "circumstances ha[d] occurred in the last fifteen or twenty years proving that there is danger and that the time has come when this idea which has been somewhat nebulous in its character should receive distinct form and enunciation and go into the fundamental law."[10] That "danger," of course, came from the Catholic claim on public school funds, a point on which all participants concurred. On one hand, Morton's assertion that the Blaine Amendment would not impact the constitutional equation was self-serving, and should be viewed with skepticism, as he was seeking to allay concerns of reticent Democrats. Democrats and Republicans alike knew that the amendment, if enacted, would be an additional impediment to the state funding of religious schools. But Morton was correct that the amendment would have established no new legal principle by enforcing the no-funding rule in those states with lax enforcement or that lacked express statutory or constitutional provisions. As he remarked in one of the few statements that put the no-funding principle in constitutional terms:

> I believe that the example of one State establishing a religion, or doing what amounts to the same thing in principle, establishing denominational schools to be supported at public expense, endangers the perpetuity of the nation. The support of a school by public taxation is the same thing in principle as an established church.[11]

The Blaine Amendment, if it had been enacted, would have reaffirmed this principle, not created it. No doubt, Catholics disagreed with both of Morton's propositions—that support for parochial schools equaled a religious establishment and that public funding of their schools would endanger the nation. But the former proposition was not a novel constitutional principle in 1876.[12]

Accordingly, the Blaine Amendment would have nationalized the legal status quo. The public and legislative debate over the Amendment merely gave the controversy a public platform. In the end, the Blaine Amendment added little to understandings of the no-funding principle.[13]

This makes the legacy of the Blaine Amendment difficult to assess. Despite the measure's failure on the national stage, it has widely been credited as the basis for later state no-funding provisions. This connection has led critics to charge that the anti-Catholicism associated with the Blaine Amendment can also be attributed to the various state provisions. Few could doubt that the Blaine Amendment inspired several state legislatures to adopt express no-funding provisions in their own constitutions. Less certain is whether the Blaine Amendment caused or served as the primary model for these subsequent state measures. Equally unclear is whether the Blaine Amendment perpetuated a climate of anti-Catholicism that is allegedly responsible for these state no-funding provisions.[14]

One indisputable fact is that twenty-one states adopted express provisions prohibiting the public funding of religious schools in the half-century following the Blaine Amendment. Yet the constitutions of seventeen other states contained express no-funding provisions that pre-dated that event. No-funding provisions had been evolving since the 1830s, with many of them arising absent anti-Catholic activity. Not only was the Blaine Amendment not responsible for these earlier provisions; just as important, the no-funding provisions in these seventeen state constitutions could have served as models for the post-Blaine provisions.[15] The common practice at the time was for states to borrow provisions from sister states. In one example, the Washington Constitutional Convention of 1889 modeled many of its provisions on the 1857 Oregon Constitution, which in turn borrowed language from the Iowa and Indiana constitutions. Many later state no-funding provisions contain language that parrots that found in earlier state constitutions.[16]

An additional consideration is whether state provisions arose through the drafting of entire constitutions—such as with reconstructed or newly admitted states—or from instances of states simply adding a no-funding provision. Twelve of the twenty-one states enacting no-funding provisions after 1876 did so as part of comprehensive constitutional drafting. Following the usual practice, state conventions commonly looked to the constitutions of other states, freely borrowing language and phrasing. Creating a public education system and securing its financial footing became a chief concern of states in the post-Civil War era. The addition of a no-funding provision as part of wholesale constitution drafting would raise fewer inferences that it was added pursuant to an anti-Catholic agenda. While this point is debatable, greater inference of hostile motives can be drawn from efforts to shore-up existing (or nonexistent) no-funding rules rather than from provisions that were included as part of comprehensive constitution making that used existing models.[17]

For some critics of the no-funding rule, attaching controlling significance to the Blaine Amendment obscures the point that many state no-funding amendments arose in the same climate of religious bigotry that fueled the Blaine Amendment. According to this argument, it is not important whether the Blaine Amendment served as a cause of the later state enactments but whether the same prejudice that motivated congressmen to support the no-funding principle on the national stage was shared by those state legislators who were successful in their endeavors.[18]

There are several responses to this argument. First, drawing particular attention to the Blaine Amendment may be undeserved, but it has been the center of criticism. Critics of the no-funding provisions in the various state constitutions have focused almost exclusively on the national amendment. This is likely due to the substantial historical record surrounding the Blaine Amendment, which contains damning rhetoric, and the lack of corresponding state legislative histories. Critics have sought to taint the state provisions with material connected to the national effort, sometimes to the extent of inaccurately attributing anti-Catholic animus to James Blaine, as if his alleged bigotry transfers through his amendment down to the state measures. In the recent debate over the propriety of the state no-funding provisions, the Blaine Amendment *has* mattered.[19]

Stepping back from the particulars of the Blaine Amendment, it is difficult to draw more than vague parallels to the national amendment. Although the Blaine Amendment gave the School Question a national platform, it was essentially a state or local issue. As such, one would need to examine the degree of Protestant-Catholic animosity from locale to locale. The bigotry exhibited in part of the debate over the Blaine Amendment was not unique to that measure, but was also tied to Republican manipulation of the issue to exploit anti-Catholicism for political gain.[20] This dynamic cannot automatically be transferred to the states. Undoubtedly, supporters of each state provision were aware that it impacted Catholic schooling while it protected nonsectarian public schooling. But an awareness that enacting a no-funding provision would disadvantage Catholic schooling cannot be equated with anti-Catholic animus. New York's Catholic senator, Francis Kernan, for one, opposed the public funding of religious schools. Many people considered the late-century resolution of the School Question—encompassing the integrated issues of religious observances and school funding—as a compromise. The same variety of reasons that drew people to support the Blaine Amendment on a national level also led them to support a resolution of the School Question at the state and local levels.

As with the national proposal, state legislators may have been motivated by concerns about ensuring the stability of still nascent public schools, preserving the integrity of public school funds, avoiding religious competition and dissention, and adhering to a principle of nonestablishment. Legislators could understandably have viewed the public funding of parochial schools as a threat to these principles without devolving into anti-Catholicism.[21] If the anti-Catholic animus associated with the national debate is transferable to the various state enactments, so too are the legitimate impulses that informed the national debate. This then leads one back to the same conclusion that anti-Catholicism was a factor in the public debate over the Blaine Amendment and the larger School Question, but it was not the only factor.[22]

There may be one place to see the direct legacy of the Blaine Amendment. At the close of the century, four new states—Washington, Montana, North and South Dakota—included no-funding provisions in their constitutions pursuant to a congressional mandate. The Enabling Act of 1889 required the state constitutional conventions to include a provision "for the establishment and maintenance of a system of public schools, which shall be open to all the children...and free from sectarian control." Later admitted states faced similar requirements. Thus, unlike the no-funding enactments in other states, the impetus for these state provisions came from Congress.[23] Further suggesting a connection between the Blaine Amendment and the Enabling Act are the nativist comments of one senator, Republican Henry William Blair of New Hampshire. Blair had been a member of the House of Representatives in 1875–1876, and was elected to the Senate in 1879. An evangelical Methodist, Blair supported the Blaine Amendment and later introduced a series of bills designed to prohibit the funding of religious schooling while guaranteeing the reading of the Bible in the public schools. While in Congress, Blair closely aligned himself with conservative Protestant groups, including the N.R.A.; at their urging, he once sought to enact a national Sunday observance law.[24] During the Senate debate over the Enabling Act, Blair remarked the law would prohibit funding sectarian schools while ensuring that public schools could educate children in "virtue, morality, and the principles of the Christian religion," likely code words for Protestant nonsectarainism.[25] In other remarks, Blair attacked the Catholic Church and Jesuits in particular, claiming that the latter sought "to secure the control of this continent by destroying the public school system of America." He also tied the present legislative efforts to the Blaine Amendment of twelve years earlier.[26]

Whether Blair's motivations and interpretations reflected those of other senators is impossible to assess. Although no senator objected to Blair's comments about the purpose behind the Enabling Act, no senator concurred. Silence alone cannot be interpreted as consent or agreement.[27] Blair had his own religious agenda, one aspect being to increase the religious character of public schooling; yet his own understanding of "nonsectarian" education—which included devotional instruction—was no longer the norm in most public schools by 1889, much to his chagrin. As we will see below, his legislative effort to ensure Protestant Bible reading went down to defeat. His sentiments with respect to the Enabling

Act thus cannot be attributed to other members of Congress. Even if Blair's anti-Catholicism can be attached to the Enabling Act, those motives cannot be transferred to the delegates to the state conventions who wrote no-funding provisions that federal law required them to include. The Washington Convention of 1889 reveals no evidence of anti-Catholic animus during the debates, even though several religious matters were considered by the convention. Critics of the Blaine Amendment have been unable to point to anti-Catholic animus in the debates for the other three state constitutions.[28]

In sum, many of the state no-funding provisions would likely have been enacted regardless of the failed Blaine Amendment. No doubt the federal measure inspired several of the state provisions, but it was not necessary for those enactments. The best case for a connection between the Blaine Amendment and state no-funding provisions are those of the states governed by the Enabling Act. But it is also likely that those states would have followed other states by enacting a no-funding provision absent the Enabling Act. Overall, it is impossible without more evidence from the twenty-one states to claim that the anti-Catholicism that surrounded the Blaine Amendment was the chief motive behind each of these state measures. As on the national stage, too many factors were in play.[29]

One state where anti-Catholicism may have played a role in the enactment of a no-funding provision is New York, the site of so many church-state conflicts throughout the century. In spring 1894, delegates met in Albany for a constitutional convention to undertake wholesale revision of the state's 1777 constitution. An impetus for the convention, which was controlled by Republicans, was to institute political reforms in light of ongoing government corruption. As part of this reform drive, the delegates included in the new constitution a provision prohibiting the funding of any school under "the control or direction of any religious denomination or in which any denominational tenet or doctrine is taught." The group most responsible for the provision was the National League for the Preservation of American Institutions (NLPAI), an influential organization supported by the state's leading Protestant ministers and business figures, including J. P. Morgan, John D. Rockefeller, Cyrus W. Field, and Cornelius Vanderbilt. The NLPAI drafted the proposal for the no-funding provision, and League lobbyists and delegates worked with the convention's Republican leadership to hammer out the language. (The organization also proposed an amendment to the national constitution to apply the religion clauses to the states while prohibiting them from appropriating money or property to "any church, religious denomination or religious society, or any institution...under sectarian or ecclesiastical control.") As its name suggested, the NLPAI promoted "American" values and institutions, chiefly by defending public education and opposing funding of sectarian institutions. The organization denied having nativist leanings, though its officers, attorney John Jay and Methodist pastor James King, regularly used anti-Catholic rhetoric in their missives and public addresses. The impetus for the amendments was not any new Protestant-Catholic conflict over Bible reading or school funding. Rather, the NLPAI was caught up in ongoing tensions over immigration, which fueled a revival of organized nativism led nationally by the American Protective Association. The rise in anti-Catholic sentiment in the 1890s "was due more to fertile non-Catholic imaginations that to any real Catholic threat."[30]

Even within this context, anti-Catholicism may have played a small role in the enactment of the New York no-funding provision. With the ongoing allegations of Democratic corruption involving financial dealings with Catholic Church officials, everyone understood that the Republican-controlled convention would seek an enhanced prohibition on sectarian appropriations. Early on, Catholic officials announced that they made no claim for pubic support of parochial schools and would not oppose a funding prohibition. While the NLPAI identified the Catholic Church as the primary threat to the school fund and public schooling generally, it publicly disassociated itself from efforts of the A.P.A. to inflame the debate. To the disappointment of the NLPAI, Republican leaders rejected its request for a comprehensive prohibition that would have defunded religious charities as well as schools. As a compromise, the convention enacted a provision that authorized state aid for the "care, support, maintenance, and secular education" of children in private orphan asylums and reformatory institutions. The compromise had the support of the Catholic Church, and the final vote on both the education and charities provisions cut across party lines.[31]

The compromise reached by the delegates to the 1894 New York convention reaffirmed the distinction between schools and charities that had existed within the state for forty years. Still, a philosophical tension existed between the two constitutional provisions, one that courts acknowledged in a 1901 lawsuit that challenged an appropriation from Rochester city funds to pay for teacher salaries at a Catholic orphan asylum. Both the trial court and the Court of Appeals rejected the plaintiff's argument that the appropriation violated the prohibition against giving public aid to "any school or institution of learning under the control of any religious denomination or in which any denominational tenets are taught." Even though the appropriation paid for teacher salaries and the asylum was in all practical senses an "institution of learning," the courts had to reconcile the two provisions. The judges fell back on the earlier dichotomy, noting that "[a]n orphan asylum is organized mainly as a shelter" and the "instruction given is incidental to [its] main purpose." Still, the judges seemed unsure about the distinction and the possibly broader command of the new no-aid provision, so they emphasized additional distinguishing facts: the salaries were not paid out of the common school fund (though the 1894 Constitution had abolished this factor); and that denominational tenets were not taught in the asylum during the school hours. The "money was raised for the secular education of the inmates of the orphan asylum." With their confidence bolstered, the judges put their stamp of approval on the compromise of 1894.[32]

New York was unique with its competing constitutional provisions. Without similar constitutional safe-harbors for charities in other states, courts declined to distinguish between instruction and care, with most holding that religious orphanages were sectarian institutions ineligible to receive public monies, regardless of the funding source. Commonly, judges interpreted the no-funding rule to be a comprehensive principle that required consistent application. The Nevada Supreme Court wrote in 1882 that the purpose of the funding ban was not only "to keep all sectarian instruction from the schools," but also to prohibit using public funds for any sectarian purpose. The rule was a "wise and needful measure," one designed "to avoid a possible recurrence of the evils borne in the past." In a similar case, the Illinois Supreme Court banned an appropriation for tuition, maintenance, and clothing for two Catholic asylums in Chicago. Noting that the state constitution prohibited any appropriation "in aid of any church or [for a] sectarian purpose," the court held that "[a] constitutional mandate cannot be circumvented by indirect methods" such as the funding of religious asylums. Even though the institutions were orphanages, "[i]f the instruction is of a sectarian character," the court wrote, "the school is sectarian." However, twenty years later the Illinois court reversed course after the legislature enacted a law that required judges to place adjudicated juveniles in orphanages "holding the same religious belief as the parents of said child." Pursuant to this new law, the Illinois Supreme Court upheld an appropriation to the same Catholic orphanages for clothing, board, and tuition. Conscious of the tension between the law and the no-funding rule, the court explained that the per capita appropriations amounted only to half of the institutions' expenses for care. Any cost of providing religious instruction was made up by private donations, the court remarked.[33]

Public appropriations for charitable uses, including the education and care of children in religious orphanages, presented the only quandary for courts when interpreting laws against funding religious institutions. Otherwise, they uniformly enforced constitutional and legislative bans on appropriations to religious schools from the late 1870s into the early decades of the twentieth century. In so doing, judges commonly relied on express constitutional prohibitions on funding sectarian institutions where available. As frequently, however, judges understood the principles as emanating also from no-establishment or no-compelled support clauses, or simply from general constitutional principles. In striking a law to provide textbooks and other educational supplies to private schools, the New York Supreme Court in 1922 referenced three constitutional provisions, not solely the no-aid clause. Identifying even broader, unifying themes, the court wrote that "[a]t no time has it been the intent of government in our republic to permit the union of secular and religious education.... The state may not join religious instruction with secular education, but a church may.... [I]n that respect, the state may not interfere, but it may not assist in aid of any distinct religious tenet."[34] Although the no-funding rule was most clearly enunciated in express educational provisions, courts also interpreted the rule against funding religious institutions as arising from broader, more foundational understandings of church-state separation.

Bible Reading in the Schools

The events of 1869–1876 did not settle the issue of Bible reading or religious instruction in the schools. Yet the die had been cast. Although religious exercises remained the dominant practice in the schools, the norm was Bible reading without note or comment. Increasingly, readings were a pro forma part of daily opening ceremonies and justified on nonreligious grounds. At the same time, a growing number of urban school districts, chiefly in the Northeast and Midwest, abolished religious exercises or made them optional. The practices that remained did little to halt the secularizing trend in American public education.

The trend was spurred by an eagerness to defuse religious complaints over religious exercises, along with professionalization, standardization, and desire to make public schooling more religiously inclusive. Public opposition to the Cincinnati Bible case and to repeals by other school boards did little to blunt the trend. Writing in 1881, Rochester Catholic Bishop Benjamin J. McQuaid quipped sarcastically that New York had made "great progress in the eliminating of every shade and semblance of religious instruction and usages from its common schools." As for those public schools where the Bible was still being read, it was done "in a very perfunctory way," McQuaid noted.[35] McQuaid was not alone in his view, as there was a growing perception that Bible reading was in rapid retreat.[36]

How far religious exercises truly declined during the final quarter of the nineteenth century is difficult to gauge. Newspapers reported repeals by school boards and outbreaks of religious conflict, but places where Bible reading continued without controversy was not a news story. Education remained chiefly under the control of local authorities, and religious exercises varied widely from one community to another. In many smaller cities and religiously homogeneous communities, distinctly Protestant exercises persisted under the guise of nonsectarianism. No doubt, some remained highly devotional, but the clear trend was toward unmediated Bible reading with objecting students being dismissed from the classrooms or at least being excused from participating in the exercises.[37] And as Bishop McQuaid bemoaned, these practices were increasingly perfunctory or done chiefly for symbolic reasons. A survey conducted by the Woman's Christian Temperance Union in 1887 confirmed that perception, revealing that the Bible was not being read in schools in 175 counties out of 254 reporting. In those counties where the exercises persisted, Bible reading frequently was "not so generally read as formally." A report by the N.R.A. substantiated those findings, noting that in Chicago, St. Louis, San Francisco, Rochester, Cincinnati, and "in a multitude of smaller places, the reading of the Bible and all religious exercises have been prohibited." The implications of the trend were too serious to be ignored: "unless the apparent tendency can be arrested, the secular or atheistic theory of education will yet triumph in all parts of the land." Whether the status of Bible reading in the closing decades of the century was so dire, the perception of decline was as important as the reality.[38]

The decline in religious exercises did not mean that the controversy over Bible reading died away. On the contrary, the secularizing of education created a concern shared by Protestants and Catholics alike. "It is certainly gratifying to Catholics to know that Protestants, in reality, agree with them regarding the necessity of religious teachings and observances in children's schools," Bishop McQuaid wrote. Conservative Protestants remained committed to nonsectarian *religious* instruction, agreeing with Reverend O. A. Kingsbury in 1885 that "you cannot teach morality without teaching religion." They were unwilling to give up on the idea that there were "great fundamental religious principles which are tacitly admitted by all Christian people, Romanists as well as Protestants." They believed such principles could still be taught without devolving into divisive sectarianism.[39]

Alarmed at the trend, religious conservatives in 1888 approached their ally in Washington, Senator Henry Blair. Beginning in 1881, Blair had introduced a series of bills that would have provided federal funding to states to maintain public schools where nonsectarian instruction would take place. Now, at the urging of the Woman's Christian Temperance Union and the N.R.A., Blair proposed a constitutional amendment that borrowed from his funding bills and the Blaine Amendment. Like the latter, the measure prohibited state and federal funding of schools or institutions that were controlled by any denomination or instructed in the doctrines, tenets or beliefs particular to any sect. Blair's proposal went further than its predecessor, however, by including a provision requiring each state to "establish and maintain a system of free public schools" where children between six and sixteen would be taught the "common branches of knowledge, and in virtue, morality, and the principles of the Christian religion." To placate critics of this last provision, Blair's proposal prohibited teaching "particular doctrines, tenets, belief[s], ceremonials, or observances" in any public school. Yet this provision, when read with the requirement that schools teach "virtue, morality, and the principles of the Christian religion," left no doubt that nonsectarian religious instruction, not simply rote Bible reading, would be the national standard.[40]

Blair held hearings on his education amendment in February 1889, and the religious conservatives who dominated the testimony all attested to the dire state of public education. Witnesses condemned the secularizing trend, pointing to the Cincinnati Bible case and the abolishing of Bible readings by city school boards as justifications for the amendment. Most were unwilling to accede to Bible reading without note or comment, however. Rather, they urged that the exercises had to be devotional in purpose and content. Not only should the Bible be read in the public schools, N.R.A.'s T.P. Stevenson urged, but Christian teachers "should inculcate the general [Christian] principles which have been regarded in the framework of our Government. If there is any sense in which we are a Christian nation, and which this is a Christian Government, in the same sense and to the same extent our schools ought to be Christian." To blunt criticism, the witnesses insisted they were not seeking to turn back the clock but were only defending the practice of nonsectarianism, which was under attack. The "Bible has been read and the general principles of morality and of the Christian religion have been inculcated in the American common school from the beginning of its history," Stevenson insisted. "In this respect we are seeking no change. We are resisting a change which amounts to a revolution." Stevenson and other witnesses claimed their position had overwhelming public support, but their statements revealed a sense of defensiveness and desperation. They railed against the secular public schools, atheistic incursions, and the persistent Catholic threats to public education and American values.[41] In the end, Blair's education amendment suffered the same fate as his national Sunday law, dying in committee. A more temperate proposal to protect unmediated Bible reading may have attracted greater legislative support. But Blair's measure would have gone beyond preserving existing nonsectarian practices to constitutionalizing religious activities that predated Horace Mann's innovations. Witnesses and observers alike understood the proposal for what it was: an effort not simply to forestall the secularization of public education but to reverse it.[42]

Other Protestants, along with sympathetic educators, proposed less drastic solutions to stem the decline in Bible reading and moral education. One alternative was to use the Bible to teach history or literature, as some had suggested previously, but to prohibit its use for moral instruction. Others advocated its scientific study, usually meaning a mild form of biblical criticism. "The literary and historical study of the Bible is universally coming to be taught purely from the standpoint of objective science," boasted one advocate. "Bible as literature" or "as history" courses increased after the turn of the century, but they remained controversial among Protestant clergy and many religious scholars. "The biblical books are indeed masterpieces of literature," wrote one critic, "but they have a much more important service to render to the world. The Bible is first of all for religious and moral instruction." Critics charged the "literary, historical, and moral truths of the Bible cannot be truly taught without involving the teaching of its religious truths," while others simply condemned the entire enterprise. University of Chicago theologian Shailer Mathews insisted in 1906 that to teach the Bible "merely as a piece of literature . . . is worse than not teaching it at all."[43]

Another alternative to Bible reading, promoted by the Chicago Woman's Educational Union, was to use a reader that comprised moral extracts from the Bible. The idea was that a book containing excerpts from the Bible, but being one step removed from the scriptures itself, would be unobjectionable. In a pamphlet promoting the book, *Readings from the Bible*, Union president Elizabeth Blanchard Cook held back little in her esteem for the Bible as a source of inspiration, stating that she saw no valid reason for excluding its use in the schools, particularly when it was read without note or comment. But circumstances being what they were—that "1 or 2 percent" of people objected to the practices—necessitated a readings book containing the Bible's essential moral teachings. Cook claimed that a wide spectrum of religious leaders endorsed her readings book, including several

Catholic bishops.[44] *Readings from the Bible* received judicial sanction in 1898 from the Michigan Supreme Court, which upheld its use in the Detroit public schools. The court acknowledged that *Readings from the Bible* was composed "almost entirely of extracts from the Bible, emphasizing the moral precepts of the Ten Commandments." But because the book excluded sectarian passages and was used "merely to inculcate good morals" and a sense of citizenship among students, the court majority held the readings were permissible. One justice dissented, however, arguing that the book was still religious and being used for a religious purpose: "So far as religious teaching is concerned, the attitude of the schools should be that of neutrality."[45]

The third alternative Protestants offered in lieu of Bible reading was for schools to permit religious instruction to be conducted in classrooms during noninstructional hours. This arrangement, later termed "released time," had been part of the Poughkeepsie Plan for consolidated schools, in which Catholic priests conducted instruction and catechisms at the end of the school day. Protestants now picked up on the idea. In 1895 Lyman Abbott encouraged educators "to find a method by which out of school hours, either in the school-rooms or in other adjoining rooms, distinctly catechetical, theoretical, and denominational instruction may be given, not by or under the public school authorities," but by local religious leaders or associations. Communities across the nation adopted similar arrangements, based on a model developed in Gary, Indiana in 1914, and released time programs gained popularity throughout the first half of the twentieth century. To a degree, all three alternatives experienced success over the succeeding years. But for many purists, they were compromises in which Protestants had given up on the Bible's central role in American education. All three alternatives confirmed that a break now existed between common schooling and religious instruction, which only reinforced the idea that public education was becoming secularized.[46]

Despite the trend, no court had followed the lead of the Ohio Supreme Court in the seventeen years following the *Minor* decision. After *Minor*, school board actions repealing religious exercises were not challenged in courts. But the *Minor* decision, and the voluntary repeals, encouraged people to challenge nonsectarian exercises where they persisted. Challenges arose in Illinois (1880), Iowa (1884), and Pennsylvania (1885), all resulting in courts upholding the practices. The type of "nonsectarian" exercises varied from reading extracts of the King James Bible in the Illinois case to Bible reading, Protestant hymn singing, and the recitation of the Lord's Prayer in Iowa and Pennsylvania. In all cases the judges deferred to the school boards' assurances that the practices were nonsectarian and intended solely for the purpose of inculcating morals. As the judge remarked in the Pennsylvania case, there was no evidence "to warrant the conclusion that the King James' version of the Bible is sectarian.... [Nothing] could be inferred that [the practices] tend to teach the distinctive doctrine of one religious sect or to condemn that of another." The judges also appeared swayed by the fact that objecting students were excused from participating in the exercises, even though such requirements worked against claims that the practices promoted only universal principles.[47]

Finally, in 1890, a second state court struck down nonsectarian exercises in the public schools, this time in Wisconsin. In *Weiss v. District Board of School District No. 8*, Catholic parents challenged daily readings from the King James Bible conducted without note or comment. The parents lost at trial, but a unanimous Wisconsin Supreme Court reversed, throwing out the practice of Bible reading. The holding was more sweeping than the *Minor* decision, which had essentially upheld the authority of school boards to abolish Bible reading (although Justice Welch had suggested Bible reading was inconsistent with constitutional principles). In *Weiss*, the Wisconsin court went further by expressly holding that Bible reading was inherently sectarian and unconstitutional under the state Bill of Rights. Unlike in earlier cases, the *Weiss* court scrutinized the manner in which the Bible was used in the schools rather than deferring to school authorities who claimed that the practices were nonsectarian and inoffensive. "[W]e cannot doubt," Justice William Penn Lyon wrote for the court, "that the use of the Bible as a text-book in the public schools, and the stated reading thereof in such schools, without restriction, 'has a tendency to inculcate sectarian ideas.'" This, the court held, violated mandates of religious equality and no-preference found in the state constitution; the religious practices "tend[ed] to destroy the equality of the pupils which the constitution seeks to establish and protect."[48]

The *Weiss* holding confirmed that the secularizing trend in public schooling would continue. As the justices had done in *Minor*, the *Weiss* court refuted the concept of nonsectarian religious instruction. The nation's growing religious diversity made it impossible to identify common religious principles upon which all people could agree. But more significant, the court rejected the secular justifications for Bible reading that had been developing since mid-century.[49] Evangelicals generally condemned the holding, but the public reaction overall had a sense of resignation. The *New York Times* defended the Wisconsin holding, insisting that people had nothing to fear from a secular education system. "To say that a 'godless' instruction in those branches of knowledge, or in any other that are properly within the province of the public schools, is 'necessarily immoral,' is to make a perfectly meaningless assertion." The *Times* asserted the Wisconsin decision represented the inevitable direction for pubic education, particularly if "the common school system [wishes to] maintain...its integrity." Increasingly, people were reconciling themselves with a system of secular public education.[50]

In the forty years following *Weiss*, state courts would rule on fifteen challenges to nonsectarian Bible reading in the schools, with judges upholding the practices in ten of the cases. That record belied the significance of the holdings, however. In the 1898 Michigan case upholding the use of *Readings from the Bible*, the court clarified that its decision did not authorize religious instruction. Moreover, school boards were not obligated to teach religious values simply because the state constitution stated that one purpose of public education was to further "religion, morality and knowledge." Rather, that clause simply meant, for the members of the court, that school officials could not "exclude wholly from the school all reference to the Bible" when they taught morality.[51] Other court decisions upholding religious exercises followed this pattern, deemphasizing their religious significance by noting the value of the Bible reading for its moral, literary, and historical qualities. "If all religious instruction were prohibited," exclaimed the Colorado Supreme Court in 1927, "no history could be taught." All of the courts declared the unmediated readings, with excusals for objectors, to be nonsectarian in nature. Only the Texas Supreme Court affirmed a religious purpose for Bible reading, writing that because Christianity was interwoven with the "web and woof of the state government," to prohibit prayer and Bible reading would border on "moral anarchy."[52] In contrast to those decisions, supreme courts in Nebraska, Illinois, Louisiana, Washington, and South Dakota followed *Minor* and *Weiss* by holding that unmediated Bible reading was inherently sectarian and unconstitutional. The public school, "like the government, is simply a civil institution," declared the Illinois court. "It is secular, and not religious, in its purposes."[53]

By the early twentieth century, unmediated Bible reading remained legal in the majority of states, though based on the theory that the practices were conducted for nonreligious purposes. The Bible could be used to teach morality or for the purpose of "quieting" students, as one court held, but not to instill religious devotion or instruct in religious tenets, even where the latter were assumed to be universally held. In this way, unmediated Bible reading was consistent with a system of secular public schooling. The practices were generally constitutional, but at a cost to their integrity.[54]

Outside of the courts, public schools continued to deemphasize the religious nature of nonsectarian exercises or abolish the practices entirely. U.S. Commissioner of Education William Torrey Harris documented this phenomenon in a series of annual reports between 1888 and 1898. The reports indicated that not only was religious instruction in decline, but so too was the use of the Bible as textbook for teaching morals or literature. Even the amount of time schools devoted to character and moral instruction had declined considerably. In his 1895 government report, Harris summarized that:

> [outside] New England there is no considerable area where [the Bible's] use can be said to be uniform. This condition has come about as much by indifference as by opposition.... There has been a change in public sentiment gradually growing toward complete secularization of the Government and its institutions.... Secularization of the schools is accepted or urged by many devout people who deem that safer than to trust others with the interpretation of the laws of conscience.[55]

Harris, who was a long-time advocate for secular education and abolishing Bible reading, may have been editorializing. His own reports, based on informal surveys of state education officials, indicated that a majority of schools still used the Bible in some manner, although practices varied greatly by region. In larger cities and in the West, Bible reading was increasingly uncommon. Where it remained, the true nature of its use was impossible to assess, as the reports commonly described the activities as nonsectarian and conducted for the purposes of instilling morals and character development. Devotional exercises likely remained common in rural areas or in religiously homogeneous communities with small or politically power-less immigrant populations. Still, the reports indicated that a significant number of school districts had restricted the religious exercises or discontinued them in their entirety.[56]

A report conducted by Columbia Teachers College in 1912 confirmed this, con-cluding that for "over a century there has been going on in the United States a gradual but widespread elimination of religious and church influences from public education." In every state, "civic and industrial aims [were] dominant," while "reli-gious instruction [was] either entirely eliminated or else reduced to the barest and most formal elements." The report attributed this transformation to two factors. The first was a "conviction that a republic can securely rest only on an educated citizenship." The second was "a sacred regard by the state for the religious opinion of the individual citizen." The report noted that "non-religious elements" had fre-quently promoted the secularization of education, but they were not the controlling factor.

> Differences of religious belief and a sound regard on the part of the state for individual freedom in religious matters, coupled with the necessity for centralization and uniformity, rather than hostility toward religion as such, lie as the bottom of the movement toward a secular school.[57]

This transformation did not spell the end of Bible reading and religious exercises in the nation's public schools. The perception that Bible reading was in decline spurred a revival of interest in the practice during the early twentieth century. Several state legislatures, responding to an upsurge in religious piety related to the rise of Protestant fundamentalism and Pentecostalism, enacted laws to ensure that Bible reading remained the practice in the schools. By the late 1920s, one survey of legislation reported that "the legal status of Bible reading in the public schools has undergone a change since 1900." The trend was "very definitely in the direction of giving Bible reading more place in the public schools."[58] All in all, by 1930 eleven states required nonsectarian Bible reading in public schools, with another six states authorizing religious exercises. On its own, the upswing in leg-islation indicates little about any increase in the incidence of Bible reading. In many instances, the legislation simply confirmed preexisting practice. While it is likely that Bible reading increased in those states that now mandated the exer-cises, practices in states with no statutory authorization or judicial prohibition varied between unmediated readings as part of opening exercises to using the

Bible in literature and history courses. Increasingly popular were the released time programs for religious instruction during noninstructional periods or held at neighboring churches.[59]

By 1930, the legislative reaction to the secularization of schooling had stalled. Bible reading and other religious exercises would persist in many parts of the nation, particularly in the South and Northeast, until the decisions of the U.S. Supreme Court in 1962 and 1963. But the renewed attention given Bible reading during the first third of the century was unable to forestall the overall decline in the practice. By 1962, only 40 percent of the nation's public schools conducted religious exercises in any form. Before then, however, the issues of religious instruction and of public support for religious schooling would come to a head in two Supreme Court cases: *Everson v. Board of Education* (1947); and *McCollum v. Board of Education* (1948). In these two watershed cases, the Supreme Court would for the first time apply the Establishment Clause of the U.S. Constitution to mediate state controversies over religious school funding and religious instruction. Despite criticism in some circles that the decisions broke with long-standing traditions and constitutional norms, both holdings, as well as the prayer and Bible reading decisions some fifteen years later, rested on the foundation laid seventy years earlier.[60]

Affirming the Legacy

The Supreme Court's foray into the controversy over the public funding of religious education involved a relatively insignificant issue: state reimbursements for transportation expenses of children attending Catholic schools. Upon closer consideration, the issue was a likely mechanism for the high court to first explore the constitutional proscriptions on religious school funding. With various state constitutions and laws prohibiting public aid for sectarian schools, a challenge involving a large-scale appropriation for tuition costs or facility maintenance for parochial schools seemed unlikely. Facing these comprehensive bans, Catholic officials had lobbied legislatures and city councils for more discrete forms of financial assistance. By the mid-1930s, the most common types of aid were loans of textbooks and reimbursements for transportation costs. The expenditures under individual programs were never large, but the growing number of arrangements suggested a trend; one report indicated that in 1937, 370 Catholic schools nationwide benefited from such appropriations. It was on these issues that the Supreme Court would cut its Establishment Clause teeth. All observers understood, however, that the legality of these modest aid programs would serve as a proxy for the constitutionality of more substantial forms of public funding for religious schools. Still, Orestes Brownson and Samuel Spear would have appreciated the irony that the weightiness of a principle might turn on such trivial matters.[61]

The *Everson* case involved a challenge to a New Jersey law authorizing reimbursements for bus fares for children attending private, not-for-profit schools. The New Jersey legislature had followed the lead of New York. There, the legislature had enacted a transportation reimbursement law in 1936 at the behest of Catholic school officials. Taxpayers challenged the statute, and in 1938 the New York Court of Appeals held that the law violated the no-funding provision of the state constitution, with the judges affirming that "in all civil affairs there has been a complete separation of Church and State jealously guarded and unflinchingly maintained." Following that decision, New York voters approved an amendment to the constitution authorizing the legislature to provide for transportation of children "to and from any school or institution of learning." The amendment was supported by both political parties and passed by a comfortable margin, indicating that many people considered the assistance to be relatively uncontroversial. In 1941, the New Jersey legislature followed suit, enacting a reimbursement law, also with bi-partisan support.[62]

One group that had opposed the reimbursement law was the New Jersey Taxpayers Association. Its executive director, Arch R. Everson, filed a taxpayers' suit in state court challenging the law under the state constitution, adding a Fourteenth Amendment takings claim as an afterthought. Prevailing at trial but losing on appeal, Everson sought review by the U.S. Supreme Court. There, for the first time, Everson's lawyer alleged that the reimbursement for expenses associated with religious schooling violated the Establishment Clause of the Constitution.[63] The parties knew that the case would test of the constitutionality of the no-funding principle, and each side's supporters appreciated that as well. Everson received amicus curiae support from education groups, the Seventh-Day Adventists and Baptists, and the American Civil Liberties Union. Legal representation for Everson came from the Junior Order of United American Machinists (JOUAM), of which he was also a member. The JOUAM had been a nativist organization during the nineteenth century but had drifted from its anti-Catholic roots following the First World War; now, it was a patriotic and fraternal organization running a benefit life insurance program. Still, the organization remained committed to protecting the financial integrity of public education. On the other side, the school board received legal support from Catholic organizations, with Cardinals Francis Spellman and Samuel Stritch reputedly urging counsel to raise the federal claims as a means of testing the waters of the First Amendment. With these alignments, the case evoked the funding controversies of the nineteenth century.[64]

Despite those similarities, the briefs of the parties and their amici all but ignored the earlier episode. Of more immediate concern for Everson and his allies was to distinguish a 1930 U.S. Supreme Court decision in which the justices had upheld a Louisiana law that provided free textbooks to children attending private religious schools. In *Cochran v. Louisiana State Board of Education*, taxpayers had challenged the law as a taking of property for a private purpose, so the case had not been analyzed under the Establishment Clause. Still, in upholding the appropriation the Supreme Court had identified two theories that implicated the religion clause: that providing for the education of children in private schools was a public purpose; and that the textbooks benefitted the children, not the religious schools.[65] Everson and his amici focused on rebutting those two arguments, asserting that religious schools could not serve a public purpose when they were under the control of a religious organization not accountable to the public. Here, themes from the nineteenth century debate resonated in the arguments, particularly where counsel distinguished the purposes of public and private schools. Americans had committed "our nation's progress" to a common education, insisted the JOUAM's brief, and funding private sectarian schools "could not fail to weaken our public school system." As for the "child benefit" theory, Everson's amici characterized the principle as "unsound and devious," and then, misapplied in this case. The A.C.L.U. asserted that unlike the identifiably secular character of the textbooks, the reimbursement subsidized the parents in their choice to send their children to religious schools. But the amici argued that, more fundamentally, the theory would authorize almost any type of appropriation for religious education; there was "no logical stopping point," wrote the JOUAM. The A.C.L.U. concurred that if the theory were carried to its logical conclusion, it "would enable any one leading sect to control the schools."[66]

All in all, Everson and his amici offered no novel theories but proceeded on several assumptions: that there was no distinction between religious schools and churches; that the no-funding rule was firmly established as a constitutional principle; and that principle was enshrined in the Establishment Clause. Their arguments were tautological, not explaining the constitutional wrong associated with funding, relying instead on assertions such as "*financial aid* to sectarian schools from public funds ... [is] contrary to our conception of absolute separation of church and state." Although the briefs did not refer directly to the events of the nineteenth century, they reflected a belief in the conclusiveness of principles derived from that era. If there was one principle "well settled in the policies and purposes of the American people as a whole," wrote the Seventh-Day Adventists and Baptists, it was "the fixed and unalterable determination that there shall be an absolute and unequivocal separation of church and state, and that our public school system ... shall not be used directly or indirectly for religious instruction."[67]

Little contrast existed in the briefs of the board of education and its amici, the states of New York and Massachusetts. Proceeding cautiously, they sought to place the reimbursement program within the two *Cochran* safe-harbors of public purpose and child benefit. As a result, the briefs agreed that church-state separation was a settled principle, that it was represented by the Establishment Clause, and that it otherwise prohibited public subsidization of sectarian education. But all cooperation was not prohibited, particularly where it involved children's health and welfare: "The approach must be realistic." Like the filings on behalf of the appellant, the briefs did not elaborate on the purposes and commands of the Establishment Clause. They too assumed that the grand outlines of the clause had already been settled; the instant controversy was over how those principles applied along the margins.[68]

Only one brief explored the underlying purpose of the Establishment Clause and its relationship to the no-funding principle: the amicus brief on behalf of the Catholic Church. Cardinals Spellman and Stritch, in conjunction with the National Catholic Welfare Conference, organized an amicus brief written chiefly by theologian John Courtney Murray and filed on behalf of the National Councils of Catholic Men and Catholic Women. Murray was an influential church moderate and a leading commentator on American church-state matters who reflected the influence of Orestes Brownson. In the brief, Murray strove for balance: he articulated the Catholic theological position on church-state matters while setting a nonconfrontational tone that affirmed republican principles and American institutions. Initially addressing the practical claims, Murray argued strongly that Catholic schools fulfilled a public purpose. Careful to use the term "non-profit private schools" rather than "parochial schools," he emphasized how Catholic schools benefitted the commonweal, arguing that the religious character of the program was immaterial. In these schools "the child is prepared for his civic status and responsibility." Ever-cautious, Murray did not emphasize the injustice of taxing Catholic parents for schooling for which they did not benefit. Murray's discussion of church-state theory also reflected his moderate approach. Responding to a reference in the A.C.L.U. brief, he acknowledged that the "Jeffersonian metaphor of a 'wall of separation' between Church and State has validity." That wall should not be transformed, however, into "an illegitimate 'iron curtain' separating areas between which there should be free passage." Murray insisted the purpose of church-state separation was to secure distinct spheres of authority, and then to protect the independence of the church as it fulfilled its divine mission. Citizens, however, operated in both spheres, and the state could not use its authority "to compel the believer and nonbeliever in matters regarding his religious belief." As a result, full citizenship, and the benefits afforded thereto, could not turn on one's religious faith. This brought Murray back to the issue before the Court: under the principle of separation, the state should not disadvantage Catholic parents, as citizens, from exercising their religious choices over educating their children. Murray's understanding of an "establishment of religion" was considerably narrower than that of his opponents. Murray argued that the First Amendment was not violated "unless the State singled out one particular church for special public recognition and at the same time denied equal juridical status to other existing churches." And Murray's brief was the only one to address the Blaine Amendment. He insisted that the amendment had been proposed to provide a constitutional basis for the no-funding rule and, in the absence that provision, the Establishment Clause did not prohibit aid to religious schools. Overall, Murray's argument was comprehensive and lucid, seeking to place the Catholic position on church and state within a boarder constitutional tradition. It reflected many of the arguments that Orestes Brownson had promoted some eighty years earlier.[69]

In February 1947, the Supreme Court upheld the program by a 5–4 margin, finding that the reimbursements did not violate the Establishment Clause. The majority opinion, written by Justice Hugo Black, embraced parts of the Catholic argument, holding that the Constitution could not be interpreted to disable members of any faith, "because of their faith, or lack of it, from receiving the benefits of public welfare legislation." Out of a duty to guard against "state-established churches," Black wrote, the Court must be careful "not [to] inadvertently prohibit New Jersey from extending its general State law benefits to all citizens without regard to their religious belief."[70]

But running throughout Black's opinion was the theme that the Establishment Clause required a rigorous form of church-state separation, one that otherwise prohibited public funding of religious institutions. Black described a long tradition against public support of religion, emphasizing the disestablishment experience in revolutionary Virginia and the writings of Thomas Jefferson and James Madison. Nonestablishment meant that government could not "aid one religion, aid all religions, or prefer one religion over another." Contained within this mandate was the no-funding principle, which meant that "No tax in any amount, large or small, can be levied to support any religious activities or institutions." Black ended his litany by embracing Jefferson's metaphor of "a wall of separation between Church and State." But because the state had done "no more than provide a general program to help parents get their children, regardless of their religion, safely and expeditiously to and from accredited schools," it had "not breached [the wall] here."[71]

The pronouncements in Black's opinion "seem[ed] utterly discordant with its conclusion," Justice Robert Jackson wrote in dissent. The reason for the inconsistent opinion was clear: Black was responding to the concerns of the dissenters while attempting to hold onto his tenuous majority. The conference notes reflect that all of the justices accepted a strong understanding of church-state separation. All were either critical of the child benefit theory or saw the need to confine its application. Justice Wiley Rutledge, who led the opposition to the program in conference, expressed the concern of the justices in both camps that "[t]his is not...just a little case over bus fares." Both Rutledge and Jackson issued blistering dissents, charging that the holding contravened long-standing understandings of church-state separation. To bolster his case, Rutledge pointed to the example of the founding period—generously referencing a new biography of Madison by his friend Irving Brant, which drew strong separationist conclusions—but he also found support from Grant's 1875 Annual Message. The dispute between Black and the dissenters was not over competing principles, however; the justices concurred on the centrality of the no-funding principle to constitutional law. They disagreed only over its application in this instance, which Black claimed amounted to an "indirect benefit" to religion, similar to police and fire protection, albeit a benefit that approached "the verge of state support for a religious sect." After the vote, Black reputedly told an acquaintance that he intended to make his opinion "as tight" as possible in order to forestall any greater amount of aid flowing to parochial schools.[72]

The *Everson* decision drew heavy criticism, chiefly for Black's erratic opinion. Protestants, secularists, and the press generally applauded the Court's strong embrace of separationism, splitting over the appropriateness of the ruling. Some commentators viewed Black's distinction as sensible, while others argued that the public purpose and child benefit theories were exceptions that threatened to swallow the rule; it was a "thin edge of the wedge which would ultimately crack open the Constitution," wrote the editor of *Christian Century*, Charles Clayton Morrison. Baptists called *Everson* an "ominous decision," and along with an odd coalition of secularists and evangelicals, formed Protestants and Other Americans United for Separation of Church and State to lobby against all forms of "parochi-aid." Despite having prevailed in *Everson*, Catholic officials condemned the opinion, with John Courtney Murray remarking that "We have won on bussing but lost on the First Amendment." In the academy, legal scholars and historians were also divided. Several harshly criticized Black's selective use of history and his exclusive reliance on the writings of Jefferson and Madison. Most scholars endorsed Court's embrace of separationism and its interpretation of the no-funding rule, though some questioned whether the logical extension of the principle would preclude tax exemptions for churches and chaplains in the military. A smaller, but notable group of scholars condemned the opinions, arguing that the Establishment Clause prohibited only preferential aid to a particular religion while others criticized the incorporation of the Establishment Clause under the Due Process Clause of the Fourteenth Amendment.[73]

Generally absent from the critiques at the time was the charge that the justices' embrace of separationism reflected an anti-Catholic bias. This claim arose chiefly in later years. Historians have noted that the case was argued at a time of renewed Protestant-Catholic tensions in which conservative Protestants and liberal intellectuals expressed open disdain for Catholicism and Catholic institutions. Some commentators have alleged that this perspective motivated the *Everson* justices in their decision-making. Criticism has centered chiefly on Justice Black who, early in his political career, had been a member of the Ku Klux Klan. Black disputed that he had been a committed Klan member, but he had a life-long aversion to religious autocracy and occasionally made statements critical of the power of the Catholic Church. Later, in a dissent to case upholding the provision of textbooks to children attending religious schools, Black would characterize advocates of parochial school aid as "powerful sectarian religious propagandists...looking toward complete domination and supremacy of their particular brand of religion." Other justices apparently shared a suspicion of Catholic institutions and a belief that the church promoted an agenda at tension with democratic values. In his *Everson* dissent, Justice Jackson intimated the church was hostile toward individualism, noting that Catholic schools relied on "early and indelible indoctrination in the faith." Public schools, he wrote, were "more consistent with [Protestantism] than with the Catholic culture and scheme of values." Understood in this context, *Everson's* constitutional pronouncements appear of dubious legitimacy.[74]

This critique of *Everson* and the modern Court's embrace of the no-funding rule cannot be dismissed out-of-hand; after all, the no-funding rule developed in large part out of the competition between public and Catholic schooling in the 1800s. Concerns over such competition reemerged in the mid-twentieth century, fueled by renewed efforts by Catholic officials to seek public funding and a 1938 report by a presidential advisory commission recommending federal aid for public and private educational institutions.[75] Yet while parallels exist between the nineteenth century and the post-war years, the dynamics of the two eras were quite different. Catholic scholars Andrew Greeley, John McGreevy, and Thomas Berg have traced the complexity of American attitudes toward the Catholic Church during the mid-twentieth century. The church's conservative stance on social and cultural matters put it increasingly at odds with the emerging liberalism of the era. Liberals and intellectuals pointed to the church's support of fascists during the Spanish Civil War, the demagoguery and anti-Semitism of the populist lecturer Father Charles Coughlin, and the alleged passivity of church authorities in the face of the actions of fascist Italy and Germany. Domestically, the American church and its institutions still fostered a pervasive sense of separatism, one closer to the approach of Bishop Hughes a century earlier than to the stance that would emerge only twenty years later with Vatican II. Liberals also perceived the church's lobbying for censorship of films, books, and information about birth control demonstrated an intolerance of individual freedoms. These attitudes toward the church were held not only by members of the Court but by figures such as John Dewey, Eleanor Roosevelt, and Reinhold Niebuhr. The "threat" to American institutions that many saw lurking in the church's illiberal policies and practices was clearly exaggerated; Protestants and liberals failed to appreciate the diversity within Catholicism demonstrated by "Americanists" such as Cardinal James Gibbons of Baltimore and John Courtney Murray. But concerns over "Catholic power" fit with a larger perspective during the post-war era that eschewed illiberal attitudes and practices. Historian John McGreevy has written that:

> Discussions of Catholicism, along with criticism of racial segregation and opposition to fascism and communism, helped define the terms of post-war American liberalism. These terms included the insistence that religion, as an entirely private matter, must be separated from the state, and that religious loyalties must not threaten intellectual autonomy or national unity.

This is not to suggest that suspicions of the Catholic Church did not enter into the justices' embrace of church-state separation. But critics of *Everson* are generally unable to demonstrate that animosity toward the Catholic Church directed the Court's justices to adopt a corrupt theory of church-state relations. All of the parties and amici in *Everson* endorsed the concept of church-state separation, and all, with the exception of the Catholic brief, agreed that that principle, as embodied in the Establishment Clause, included some restriction on the public funding of religious schools. By the time of *Everson*, those principles were widely accepted and relatively uncontroversial.[76]

Before the ink was dry on the *Everson* opinions, briefing was under way on the Court's next church-state case, *McCollum v. Board of Education*. In *McCollum*, the impact of the nineteenth century School Question was even more evident than in *Everson*. In late 1947, the Court heard arguments in a challenge to an Illinois statute that authorized public schools to release children to attend religious instruction in school classrooms conducted by private religious teachers. As discussed above, "released time" had arisen in the early 1900s in response to the decline in Bible reading occasioned by hostile judicial decisions and voluntary actions by school administrators. Supporters promoted released time as an alternative to school-run exercises, insisting that it avoided pitfalls about state promotion of religion and coercion of children while it offered a meaningful religious experience compared to the rote Bible reading common in many schools. The popularity of released and "dismissed" time instruction—the latter taking place off school campuses—had grown dramatically, from programs operating in approximately 200 communities in 1930 to more than 2,200 communities involving 2,000,000 children by 1947. In the Illinois lawsuit, however, the plaintiff mother, an avowed atheist, charged that school officials were facilitating sectarian instruction while the program singled out her son for derision for not participating in the exercises. Relying on the strong language contained in the *Everson* majority and dissenting opinions, she claimed that all such programs violated the Establishment Clause.[77]

Like the controversy over bus reimbursements in *Everson*, released time was a side issue to the more central question of classroom prayer and Bible reading. Observers recognized, however, that if the Court held released time programs unconstitutional, then public school Bible reading was likely doomed as well. *McCollum*'s brief and those of her amici emphasized the connection, relying on the authority of those state court decisions holding Bible reading to be unconstitutional. The A.C.L.U. argued that because the Bible was inherently sectarian, as the Wisconsin and Illinois supreme courts in *Weiss* and *Ring* had held, released time, as facilitated by school officials, also promoted sectarianism. The program was only another example of the "commingling and unification of sectarian and secular education in the public schools," A.C.L.U. asserted. The briefs of McCollum and her amici also claimed that the program violated the Establishment Clause by providing financial and symbolic assistance to religious groups. Highlighting the interconnectedness of religious instruction and religious funding, the briefs insisted that these "two great questions...of separating Church and State" were but sides of one coin that implicated the same constitutional principle.[78]

The legacy of the School Question was more evident in the board of education's brief defending the program. The board faced the immediate task of reconciling the program with the broad pronouncements in the *Everson* opinions. Rather than minimizing any conflict between the released time program and those statements, the brief attacked *Everson* directly. The board's attorneys filed a massive brief—167 pages in length—tracing church-state relations since the founding era and challenging the justices' reading of history. Like John Courtney Murray's brief in *Everson*, the board argued that nonpreferential aid to religion was consistent with nonestablishment; the clause prohibited only an official religion or one "sect [being] favored by law over other religions or sects." More central to its argument, however, was the board's interpretation of the events of the 1870s, the Blaine Amendment in particular. The board insisted the debate over the amendment demonstrated two things. First, language in the proposal applying the religion clauses to the states indicated that neither President Grant nor members of Congress understood the Fourteenth Amendment to incorporate any of the Bill of Rights, particularly the Establishment Clause. At a minimum, the brief argued, due process of law protected *liberties*, and "the establishment of religion clause does not directly involve personal freedoms." But even more crucial, the Blaine Amendment's express provision preventing the payment of public monies to support religious education indicated a prevailing view that the Establishment Clause, on its own, did not prohibit nonpreferential funding of religious institutions, including schools. Here, the board built on an argument raised in Murray's *Everson* brief: that Grant and the Congress believed that "a constitutional amendment was considered necessary in order to supply a constitutional basis" for the no-funding rule. Because Congress rejected that attempt, and subsequent similar proposals, the board argued, the Court should not read such a prohibition into the Establishment Clause. The board's argument was only tangentially related to the issue of released time, seeking to rebut the appellant's claim that tax-supported schools aided in religious instruction. But the board knew that the Court's broad pronouncements in *Everson* regarding church-state separation affected not only school funding issues but religious instruction as well. For the board, that meant arguing that the events of the 1870s—or at least its interpretation of those events—should control the Court's understanding of the Establishment Clause.[79]

With this interpretation squarely before the Court, the significance of the Court's holding in *McCollum* and its debt to the nineteenth-century School Question becomes clear. In an opinion written by Justice Black, the Court held the released time program violated the Establishment Clause by utilizing a "tax-supported public school system to aid religious groups to spread their faith." Black summarily rejected the board's claims that the clause prevented only government aid for one religion over another and that its prohibitions did not apply against the states. By so holding, the Court implicitly refuted the board's interpretation of the Blaine Amendment's significance, reaffirming that the no-funding rule was based on broad constitutional principles rather than on specific prohibitory language. Black's treatment of the board's argument was curt, however, not even mentioning the Blaine Amendment by name. His chief focus was to respond to the *Everson* dissenters and other critics by demonstrating the continuity between the *McCollum* ruling and his pronouncements in *Everson*.[80]

It fell to the four dissenters in *Everson* to enunciate the connection to the School Question. Still miffed over the misapplication of the law in that decision, the four justices filed a separate concurring opinion in *McCollum*. Written by Justice Felix Frankfurter, the opinion refrained from criticizing *Everson's* holding, emphasizing instead the "absolute" nature of the principle of church-state separation. Frankfurter's discussion of the facts revealed the extent to which the events of the nineteenth century had influenced the Court's decisions in *Everson* and *McCollum*. Frankfurter related the rise of nonsectarian education in America and the efforts of Horace Mann to diffuse denominational conflicts in public schools by barring all sectarian teachings. He reaffirmed the role of public schools in educating children while teaching common democratic values. "The public school is at once the symbol of our democracy and the most pervasive means of promoting our common destiny." Frankfurter, who was himself an immigrant, also praised how public schools assimilated schoolchildren into the American experience, noting that common schooling was "the most powerful agency for promoting cohesion among a heterogeneous democratic people." For Frankfurter, the development of nonsectarian public education should be commended as among the nation's greatest achievements. Finally, Frankfurter directly challenged the board's narrow interpretation of the Blaine Amendment. Rejecting claims the amendment revealed a deficiency in the proscriptions of the Establishment Clause, Frankfurter insisted that Grant's speech and annual message, and the amendment itself, indicated a widely shared commitment to church-state separation. Not only was the proscription "comprehensive," Frankfurter wrote, "by 1875 the separation of public education from Church entanglements, of the State from the teaching of religion, was firmly established in the consciousness of the nation." Thus the proponents not only did not see a deficiency in the Establishment Clause, "[s]o strong was this conviction," that they decided to insert into the Constitution "particular elaborations, including a specific prohibition against the use of public funds for sectarian education." Frankfurter clearly overstated the consensus on church-state relations at that time, particularly over the issue of religious instruction. His rationale for Blaine Amendment was also incorrect, as the prevailing justification for the amendment had been that the principle of church-state separation was being undermined. Where Frankfurter's historical analysis came closest to the mark was in identifying that the amendment's no-funding language would not have introduced a novel constitutional principle. As had evolved by the mid-1800s, nonestablishment was equated with separation of church and state, and the principle forbade financial aid for religious schooling and public encouragement of religious instruction. The supporters of the Blaine Amendment believed that the proposal would ebb any erosion to an existing constitutional principle. Based on that legacy, separation was "a spacious conception," Frankfurter remarked, not to be interpreted narrowly. More than any other opinion, Frankfurter's concurrence indicated the debt the justices owed to the developments of mid-nineteenth century.[81]

With the *Everson* and *McCollum* decisions, the link between the constitutional developments of the mid-nineteenth century and the modern interpretation of the Establishment Clause was complete. The "separationist" position announced in those decisions would guide the Court's church-state jurisprudence for the next forty years. The unyielding terms contained in the various *McCollum* opinions— "eternal separation," "complete separation," a "high and impregnable" wall— opened the justices to another round of criticism that the Court's language went further than was necessary. John Courtney Murray charged the Court had succumbed to a "horror of absolutes," embracing an "an absolute separation of church and state as an absolute principle." Conservative Protestants—the dominant group utilizing released time—condemned the ruling, as did the Catholic Bishops, who issued a statement that "the term 'separation of Church and State'...has become the shibboleth of doctrinaire secularism." For many, the Court's banning of released time, which seemed a sensible alternative to school-run religious instruction, indicated a hostility toward religion.[82]

Criticism that the *McCollum* decision had thrown "the whole weight of the public school system...against the child's religious conscience," led the Court to reconsider its ruling four years later in a "dismissed time" case arising out of New York, *Zorach v. Clauson*. There, in what many interpreted as a retreat, a majority of justices upheld the program, distinguishing it from the one in *McCollum* on the grounds that it "involve[d] neither religious instruction in public school classrooms nor the expenditure of public funds." The crucial fact was that religious instruction took place *off* school campuses, wrote Justice William O. Douglas, so "classrooms were [not] turned over to religious instructors." Additionally, the Court found no evidence that schoolchildren were coerced to participate in the program: "the force of the public school was [not] used to promote [religious] instruction." By accommodating the religious practices, the Court seemed to be backing away from its separationist stance in *Everson* and *McCollum*. Douglas's opinion only added to the uncertainty by affirming that "separation must be complete and unequivocal," while declaring that "state encourage[ment of] religious instruction...follow[ed] the best of our traditions." Justice Black, in a dissent, charged that the majority had succumbed to the public criticism, a claim widely repeated by pundits. However, conference notes in *McCollum* indicate that several justices had reserved judgment at the time about the New York program and viewed it as distinct.[83]

The *McCollum* decision still controlled religious instruction conducted within public school buildings. But the breadth of the *McCollum* ruling remained unsettled. Because participating students had been released to attend classes particular to their individual faith, the instruction had been presumed to be sectarian in its content. As a result, the holding did not speak directly to nonsectarian religious exercises conducted by school employees, such as rote prayer and Bible reading. Most observers believed that *McCollum* provided the answer, but after *Zorach*, questions remained whether public schools could accommodate children's "spiritual needs" through nonsectarian exercises. When the Court finally addressed the issue of nonsectarian prayer and Bible reading in 1962 and 1963, such practices were still common, though far less so than earlier in the century. In striking down the nonsectarian exercises, the Court made clear that its separationist pronouncements in *Everson* and *McCollum* represented the controlling law.[84]

The first case, *Engel v. Vitale*, involved a prayer approved by the New York Board of Regents that public school students repeated at the beginning of each school day as part of the opening exercises. The defendant school district argued that the prayer—"Almighty God, we acknowledge our dependence upon Thee, and we beg Thy blessings upon us, our parents, our teachers and our Country"—was "clearly nonsectarian in language" and that participation in the prayer was "not compulsory." The constitutionality of nonsectarianism was thus squarely before the Court. Its answer was unequivocal. Writing for himself and seven other justices, Justice Black claimed that prayer was inherently religious activity. "It is a solemn avowal of divine faith and supplication for the blessings of the Almighty. The nature of such a prayer has always been religious," he asserted. Black also refuted the central premise of nonsectariansim: that the practices affirmed only universal religious values while student participation was not compulsory. That "the prayer may be denominationally neutral" or "that its observance on the part of students is voluntary" could not "free it from the limitations of the Establishment Clause," he wrote. In so holding, Black embraced a rationale that Horace Mann, Alphonso Taft, and Samuel Spear had advanced: the state lacked authority or jurisdiction over religious matters. Government was "without power to prescribe by law any particular form of prayer which is to be used as an official prayer in carrying on any program," Black wrote. It was "neither sacrilegious nor antireligious" for government to "stay out of the business of writing or sanctioning official prayers." And finally, seeking to clear up possible confusion caused by the *Zorach* decision, Black reaffirmed that the proper jurisprudential paradigm was one of church-state separation. Opting for less uncompromising language than before, however, he asserted that the "most immediate purpose" of the Establishment Clause was to prevent "a union of government and religion" which tended "to destroy government and to degrade religion." Though more circumspect in its language, the *Engel* holding was path breaking. With it, the Court finally settled the 150 year old debate over the constitutionality of nonsectarian education.[85]

Reaction to the Court's ruling was swift and chiefly negative. The press sensationalized the holding by reporting that the Court had thrown God and religion out of the public schools; even responsible newspapers were "completely swept off their feet by the tide of emotionalism," wrote a restrained *New York Herald Tribune*.

Public reaction mirrored the reporting. Evangelist Billy Graham charged the decision was but "another step toward the secularism of the United States" and lamented "God pity our country when we can no longer appeal to God for help." Many mainstream Protestants criticized the holding, with Episcopal Bishop James A. Pike stating that the Court had "deconsecrated the nation." More surprising for many was that Catholic leaders overwhelmingly condemned the holding. In a statement filled with irony, Cardinal Francis Spellman declared that the decision struck "at the very heart of the Godly tradition in which America's children have for so long been raised." Despite its historical lapse, Spellman's statement revealed how Catholic officials had reconciled themselves to nonsectarian religious practices over the years and now saw them as a check on a growing secularism. And, not surprising, political figures rushed to condemn the ruling. Senator Sam Ervin, a reputed constitutional expert, declared that "the Supreme Court had made God unconstitutional," while Senator Herman Talmadge charged the Court had "given aid to the disciples and followers of atheism." The day following the *Engel* decision, Republican Congressman Frank Becker introduced a proposed constitutional amendment to permit religious exercises in the public schools.[86]

Reaction to the prayer decision was not all one-sided, however. While the assemblage of secularists, Jews, and liberal Protestants endorsed the holding, support came from an unlikely source. After the dust had settled, several leading evangelicals came out in favor of the ruling. A point of concern was that the prayer had been drafted by a state agency; another was that the prayer was so nonsectarian, and nonoffensive, that it was devoid of religious meaning. Carl McIntire, president of the International Council of Christian Churches, the fundamentalist response to the mainstream National Council of Churches, insisted that the *Engel* decision was "sound," as the prayer was "offensive to Bible-believing Christians because it was not made in the name of Jesus Christ." The National Association of Evangelicals, while reading the holding narrowly to prohibit only a prayer "written and sanctioned by an official government body," also commended the Court for "uphold[ing] the constitutional stipulation that church and state must be kept separate." The leading evangelical journal, *Christianity Today*, also called for restraint. In part, the evangelical response reflected a disdain over how nonsectarian exercises had become secularized. But evangelicals were picking their battles, too, as they knew the Court was considering the constitutionality of practices even closer to the heart of nonsectarianism: Bible reading and recitation of the Lord's Prayer.[87]

As expected, in *Abington School District v. Schempp*, the Court struck down nonsectarian Bible reading and the recitation of the Lord's Prayer in the nation's schools. By an 8–1 margin, the justices reaffirmed the principles identified in *Engel*, turning aside the parties' efforts to distinguish the practices by the lack of a government author. The exercises were religious, Justice Tom Clark noted, and "held in the school buildings under the supervision and with the participation of teachers employed in those schools." Clark agreed with the plaintiffs that reading from the King James Bible "was sectarian." Even if the purpose behind the exercises was "not strictly religious, it is sought to be accomplished through readings, without comment, from the Bible." In essence, the Court held, the "pervading religious character of the ceremony [was] evident."[88]

More than had been the case in *Engel*, the legacy of the School Question dominated the *Schempp* decision. The school district had argued that the practices should be upheld because of their long-standing pedigree. Citing Horace Mann and the handful of state court decisions upholding unmediated Bible reading, the attorneys maintained that Bible reading had developed "as an aid to moral training, and not for the purpose of introducing religion or sectarian instruction into public education." Clark's response was revealing, though his choice of authority may have been unfamiliar to uninformed readers. Rather than citing to Jefferson or Madison, Clark began his discussion with a quotation from Judge Alphonso Taft's opinion in the *Minor* case: the Constitution required "'absolute equality before the law of all religious opinions and sects.'" Bible reading, even when conducted without note or comment and solely for the purpose of promoting moral values, was still religious, and hence violated the Constitution's mandate of government neutrality toward religion. By choosing to rely on *Minor*, the Court demonstrated that it understood, and endorsed, the evolution that had taken place in nonsectarian instruction over the previous century. Justice William Brennan's concurring opinion also confirmed the significance of the School Question on the Court's deliberations. He related how the Bible controversy in Cincinnati and the debate over the Blaine Amendment had laid the foundation for the Court's holding. Like the majority, he, too, affirmed that Taft's principle of neutrality toward religion formed the basis for the Court's holding.[89]

Together, the *Engel* and *Schempp* decisions settled any remaining questions about the legality of nonsectarian religious exercises. Nonsectarianism, which had been so instrumental in the development of public education, and so intertwined in its operation for much of its existence, was dead. The process of secularization of American education that had begun with Horace Mann's innovations, and had been accelerated by the events of 1869–1876, was completed.

Conclusion

With the decisions of *Everson*, *McCollum*, *Engel* and *Schempp*, nonsectarianism ended its rule as a legal concept. Those decisions, of course, did not settle the public debate over prayer and Bible reading in the public schools or the public funding of religious schools. A second wave of criticism to the Court's rulings followed the *Schempp* decision and reinvigorated efforts to amend the Constitution to allow for voluntary prayer and Bible reading in the nation's schools. Congress held hearings on a proposed "school prayer" amendment in 1964, and again in

1971, but the matter died in committee, in part due to ambivalence about the idea among mainstream Protestants and even some evangelicals. Legislative efforts in later years also failed. The goal of amending the Constitution to protect Bible reading, as many had embraced during the 1870s, seemed within reach in the early 1980s after President Ronald Reagan announced his support for a school prayer amendment. But momentum on the "Reagan Prayer Amendment" was forestalled by the 1984 passage of an "equal access" law authorizing public school students to organize noncurricular "Bible clubs" to meet during noninstructional times. Afterward, the popularity of a constitutional amendment to allow for Bible reading and prayer in the public schools waned, but it has never died. In all instances, proponents have justified the measures as a means to combat the perceived secularization in America's schools, not realizing that that transformation had begun long before the Court's 1962 and 1963 decisions.[90]

Despite the ongoing public controversy over Bible reading and prayer in the nation's public schools, the Supreme Court has not waivered from its holdings in *McCollum*, *Engel*, and *Schempp* that school directed or promoted religious exercises violate the Establishment Clause. In later rulings the justices struck down "moments of silence" for prayer, prayers at graduation ceremonies, the teaching of creationism, and the posting of the Ten Commandments in public school classrooms. As recently as 2000 the Court turned aside a practice of student-led prayers at athletic events. With the issue of public funding of religious schools, the Court's later holdings have been less consistent, reflecting the mixed ruling in *Everson* which identified separation and neutrality as complementary, if not competing, principles. Throughout the 1970s and 1980s the Court struck down most funding programs, but in the mid-1980s the justices began to distinguish between direct and indirect funding mechanisms, the latter represented by tuition vouchers. In 2002, a divided Court upheld the use of vouchers for children attending religious schools. Within the ongoing debate over the public funding of religious education, the legacy of the School Question remains dominant.[91]

Modern church-state doctrine, regardless of its evolution in recent years, reflects the commanding impact of the events of the nineteenth century. The constitutional rationales for secular public schooling and a broader understanding of separation of church and state came together during that crucial period. During that time, nonsectariansm, which had developed as a means to preserve the Protestant character of public education and teach a common religious devotion, was transformed into a shell of its original self. That transition did not happen suddenly, but incrementally, as educators, clergy, and jurists struggled to reconcile the evolving goals of public schooling with a growing religious pluralism and emergent constitutional principles. It was the transformative era in American church-state law, the one in which America ceased to be a Republic of the Bible.

NOTES

Introduction

1. *Abington School District v. Schempp*, 374 U.S. 203 (1963); *Engel v. Vitale*, 370 U.S. 421 (1962); William M. Beaney and Edward N. Beiser, "Prayer and Politics: The Impact of Engel and Schempp on the Political Process," *Journal of Public Law* (1964): 475, 478; Steven K. Green, "Evangelicals and the Becker Amendment," *Journal of Church and State* 33 (Summer 1991): 541–67.
2. Green, "Evangelicals and the Becker Amendment," 555–6.
3. CBS Reports, "Storm Over the Supreme Court," March 13, 1963, transcript 66–7; *Christianity Today*, April 12, 1963, 699; statement of Carl T. McIntire, Hearings on School Prayers before the Committee on the Judiciary, House of Representatives, 88th Cong., 2d Sess. (1964), 1299; *Christian Crusade* (May 1964), 24; Green, "Evangelicals and the Becker Amendment," 555–64; *Santa Fe Independent School District v. Doe*, 530 U.S. 290 (2000); *Wallace v. Jaffree*, 472 U.S. 38 (1985).
4. *Schempp*, 374 U.S., 214–15; ibid., 257, 272–3.
5. *Everson v. Board of Education*, 330 U.S. 1 (1947); *McCollum v. Board of Education*, 333 U.S. 203, 211 (1948).
6. *Lemon v. Kurtzman*, 403 U.S. 602 (1971).
7. *Stone v. Graham*, 449 U.S. 39 (1980); *Epperson v. Arkansas*, 393 U.S. 97 (1968); *Edwards v. Aguillard*, 482 U.S. 578 (1987); *Lemon*, supra; *Meek v. Pittenger*, 421 U.S. 349 (1975); *Grand Rapids School District v. Ball*, 473 U.S. 373 (1985).
8. Richard John Neuhaus, *The Naked Public Square: Religion and Democracy in America* (Grand Rapids, MI: William B. Eerdmans Pub., 1984); Stephen L. Carter, *The Culture of Disbelief: How American Law and Politics Trivialize Religious Devotion* (New York: Basic Books, 1993).
9. *Board of Education of Westside Community Schools v. Mergens*, 496 U.S. 226 (1990); *Good News Club v. Milford Central School*, 553 U.S. 98, 116, 119–20 (2001).
10. *Mitchell v. Helms*, 530 U.S. 793 (2000).
11. Ibid., 826–9.
12. Madison wrote in 1785 that the authority to "force a citizen to contribute three pence only of his property for the support of any one establishment, may force him to conform to any other establishment in all cases whatsoever." Memorial and Remonstrance (1785), in Philip Kurland, *The Founders' Constitution* (Chicago: University of Chicago Press, 1987), 5: 82–4.
13. Philip Hamburger, *Separation of Church and State* (Cambridge, MA: Harvard University Press, 2002).
14. Samuel T. Spear, *Religion and the State or, the Bible and the Public Schools* (New York: Dodd, Mead & Co., 1876), 18, 24.
15. Steven K. Green, *The Second Disestablishment: Church and State in Nineteenth-Century America* (New York: Oxford University Press, 2010), chapters 8 and 9.

Chapter 1

1. Elwood P. Cubberley, *Public Education in the United States*, rev. ed. (Boston: Houghton Mifflin Co., 1934, 1962), 222–30; Bernard Bailyn, *Education in the Forming of American Society* (Chapel Hill: University of North Carolina Press, 1960), 10–11; Carl Kaestle, *Pillars of the Republic: Common Schools and American Society* (New York: Hill and Wang, 1983), ix.

2. Michael Katz, *The Irony of Early School Reform* (Cambridge: Harvard University Press, 1968), initiated the reappraisal of the standard account. More recent critiques include: Joseph P. Viteritti, *Choosing Equality: School Choice, the Constitution, and Civil Society* (Washington: Brookings Institution Press, 1999), 145–51; Charles L. Glenn, *The Myth of the Common School* (Amherst: The University of Massachusetts Press, 1988), 63–83; Lloyd P. Jorgenson, *The State and the Non-Public School* (Columbia, MO: University of Missouri Press, 1987), 20–68.

3. Lawrence A. Cremin, *The American Common School: A Historic Conception* (New York: Teachers College, Columbia University, 1951), 67.

4. Joseph P. Viteritti, "Blaine's Wake: School Choice, the First Amendment, and State Constitutional Law," *Harvard Journal of Law and Public Policy* 21 (1998): 657–718, 667 (1998) ("One cannot separate the founding of the American common school and the strong nativist movement that had its origins at the Protestant pulpit."); Jorgenson, *State and Non-Public School*, 20–30.

5. A thorough and balanced analysis of nonsectarianism is Noah Feldman, "Non-Sectarianism Reconsidered," *Journal of Law & Politics* 18 (2002): 65–117.

6. B.J. McQuaid, "Religion in the Schools," *North American Review* 132 (April 1881): 332, 337 (criticizing the secularizing trend of the previous decade and the "perfunctory" use of the Bible); R. Laurence Moore, "Bible Reading and Nonsectarian Schooling: The Failure of Religious Instruction in Nineteenth-Century Public Education," *Journal of American History* 86 (2000): 1581, 1594–9. One could argue that a fourth phase occurred in nonsectarian education at the end of the nineteenth century through a reaction to secularization which occasioned a re-emphasis of Bible reading in the early twentieth century. Jerome K. Jackson and Constance F. Malmberg, *Religious Education and the State* (Garden City, NY: Doubleday, Doran & Co., 1928), 1 (discussing a post-1900 "trend very definitely in the direction of giving Bible reading more place in the public schools.").

7. Kastle, *Pillars of the Republic*, 13–29; David Nasaw, *Schooled to Order: A Social History of Public Schooling in the United States* (New York: Oxford University Press, 1979), 30, 34; Timothy L. Smith, "Parochial Education and American Culture," in *History and Education*, ed., Paul Nash (New York: Random House, 1970), 192–4.

8. Frederick Rudolph, ed., *Essays on Education in the Early Republic* (1965), xvi–xvii; Ellwood P. Cubberely, ed., *Readings in Public Education in the United States* (Boston: Houghton, Mifflin & Co.,1934), 47–55, 75–140; Kastle, *Pillars of the Republic*, 3–4; Jorgenson, *The State and the Non-Public School*, 4–7.

9. Elmer Ellsworth Brown, *The Making of Our Middle Schools* (New York: Longmans, Green & Co., 1926), 31–58, 60–6, 72–7, 80–93; Bernard Bailyn, *Education in the Forming of American Society* (Chapel Hill: University of North Carolina Press, 1960), 11.

10. Jefferson quote reprinted in David Tyack, Thomas James and Aaron Benavot, *Law and the Shaping of Public Education, 1785–1954* (Madison: University of Wisconsin Press, 1987), 23. Adams quote reprinted in Peter S. Onuf, "State Politics and Republican Virtue," in Paul Finkelman and Stephen E. Gottlieg, eds., *Toward a Usable Past: Liberty Under State Constitutions* (Athens: University of Georgia Press, 1991), 101.

11. Nasaw, *Schooled to Order*, 40; Onuf, "State Politics and Republican Virtue," 102–7; Cremin, *The American Common School*, 33–44; "Popular Education vs. Sectarianism," *Hours at Home: A Popular Monthly of Instruction and Recreation* (May 1870), 5.

12. Noah Webster, "On Education of Youth in America," (1790), in Frederick Rudolph, ed., *Essays on Education in the Early Republic* (Cambridge: Belknap Press, 1965) 65–6; Benjamin Rush, "Thoughts upon the Mode of Education proper in a Republic," (1786), ibid., 17;

Lawrence A. Cremin, *American Education: The National Experience, 1783–1876* (New York: Harper & Row, 1980), 107–21.

13. Carl F. Kaestle, *The Evolution of an Urban School System: New York City, 1750–1850* (Cambridge: Harvard University Press, 1973), 112–13.

14. Henry Barnard, *Report on the Use of the Bible in Common Schools* (Providence: Knowles, Vose & Co., 1838), 11.

15. "Our Schools," *New York Times*, May 8, 1875, 4; William T. Harris, "The Church, the State, and the School," *North American Review* 133 (Sept. 1881), 215, 220 ("the forms for the political life of a representative self-government have never been created nor needed before in world-history.").

16. Ellwood P. Cubberley, ed., *Readings in Public Education in the United States* (Boston: Houghton, Mifflin Co., 1934), 47–51, 55; John H. Westerhoff, III, *McGuffey and His Readers: Piety, Morality, and Education in Nineteenth-Century America* (Nashville: Abington Press, 1978); Ruth Miller Elson, *Guardians of Tradition: American Schoolbooks of the Nineteenth Century* (Lincoln: University of Nebraska Press, 1964).

17. Jefferson, "A Bill for the More General Diffusion of Knowledge," in Martin A. Larson, ed., *The Essence of Jefferson* (Greenwich, CT: Devin-Adair, 1984), 150.

18. V.T. Thayer, *Religion in Public Education* (New York: Viking Press, 1947), 28–31; Rush, "Thoughts upon the Mode of Education," 10; Webster, "On Education of Youth in America," 50–1, 64–7; Elson, *Guardians of Tradition*, 41–2.

19. Samuel Knox, "An Essay on the Best System of Liberal Education Adapted to the Genius of the Government of the United States," in Rudolph, *Essays on Education*, 332–4.

20. Ibid.

21. William Oland Bourne, *History of the Public School Society of the City of New York* (New York: William Wood & Co., 1870); John Webb Pratt, *Religion, Politics, and Diversity: The Church-State Theme in New York History* (Ithaca, NY: Cornell University Press, 1967), 158–203; Diane Ravitch, *The Great School Wars: New York City, 1805–1973* (New York: Basic Books, 1974), 3–76.

22. Kaestle, *Evolution of an Urban School System*, 41–74; Kaestle, *Pillars of the Republic*, 30–40.

23. Bourne, *Public School Society*, 9, 38, 641; Kaestle, *Pillars of the Republic*, 30–40; Nasaw, *Schooled to Order*, 18–21.

24. Bourne, *Public School Society*, 30–5; Kaestle, *Evolution of an Urban School System*, 80–4; Kaestle, *Pillars of the Republic*, 40–1; Nasaw, *Schooled to Order*, 20–2.

25. Bourne, *Public School Society*, 6–7, 636–44.

26. Ibid., 640, 642–6.

27. Elson, *Guardians of Tradition*, 41.

28. Bourne, *Public School Society*, 164–77; Vincent P. Lannie, *Public Money and Parochial Education* (Cleveland: The Press of Case Western Reserve University, 1968), 4.

29. Bourne, *Public School Society*, 7; Cubberely, *Public Education*, 121–3; Kaestle, *Pillars of the Republic*, 34, 44–7; Kaestle, *Evolution of an Urban School System*, 120–6; Nasaw, *Schooled to Order*, 23–4; Jorgenson, *State and Non-Public School*, 11–15.

30. Bourne, *Public School Society*, 7, 37, 636–41.

31. "1839 Report," in ibid., 641.

32. Cubberely, *Readings*, 54–6; Ravitch, *Great School Wars*, 18–19.

33. Kaestle, *Pillars of the Republic*, 75–103; Cremin, *The American Common School*, 67.

34. Bourne, *Public School Society*, 37–8, 7.

35. Ronald H. Baylor and Timothy J. Meager, *The New York Irish* (Baltimore: The Johns Hopkins University Press, 1996), 51; Gerald Shaughnessy, *Has the Immigrant Kept the Faith? A Study of Immigration and Catholic Growth in the United States 1790–1920* (New York: MacMillan Co., 1925), 117.

36. Noah Feldman, "Non-Sectarianism," 67, 66.

37. Smith, "Protestant Schooling," 682; William Kailer Dunn, *What Happened to Religious Education? The Decline of Religious Teaching in the Public Elementary School 1776–1861* (Baltimore: Johns Hopkins University Press, 1958), 116–29 (Mann was responding to the

disestablishment controversy in Massachusetts between Congregationalists, Baptists and Unitarians); Feldman, "Nonsectarian Reconsidered," 73–4.

38. *Report of the Minority of the Committee on By-Laws, Rules and Regulations of the Board of Education, Against the Adoption of By-Laws Compelling the Reading of the Bible in the Public Schools* (New York: Wynkoop, Hallenbeck & Thomas, 1859); Cremin, *The American Common School*, 46–7.

39. Timothy L. Smith, "Protestant Schooling and American Nationality, 1800–1850," *Journal of American History* 53 (1966–67): 679, 680.

40. Stephen Macedo, *Diversity and Distrust* (Cambridge: Harvard University Press, 2000), 54–9.

41. Bourne, *Public School Society*, 85–95, 93–101; Nasaw, *Schooled to Order*, 29–34, Kaestle, *Evolution of an Urban School System*, 85–8.

42. Kaestle, *Pillars of the Republic*, 13–29; Nasaw, *Schooled to Order*, 29–34.

43. Kaestle, *Pillars of the Republic*, 56–61; Cubberely, *Public Education*, 128–37, 189–98; Cremin, *American Common School*, 83–118.

44. Feldman, "Non-Sectarianism," 79.

45. Horace Mann, *Twelfth Annual Report of the Board of Education, Covering the Year 1848* (Boston: Dutton & Wentworth, 1849), 113; Dunn, *What Happened to Religious Education*, 98–116, 129–31; Neil Gerard McCluskey, *Public Schools and Moral Education* (New York: Columbia University Press, 1958), 14–16; Feldman, "Non-Sectarianism," 79 ("In Boston, the drive for broadly available public education that culminated with [Horace] Mann's appointment was not, to begin with, expressed in rhetoric of concern with Catholic immigration.... Civilizing Catholics was eventually to become a goal of the common school movement, but it was not yet a major goal when non-sectarianism developed as a solution to the problem of teaching morality in the common schools.").

46. Mann, *Twelfth Annual Report*, 113.

47. Horace Mann, *The Common School Journal* 1 (November 1838): 14.

48. Mann, *Twelfth Annual Report*, 116–17.

49. Horace Mann, *Lectures and Annual Reports* (1867), Lecture IV, 289–90; Mann, *The Common School Journal* 1 (November 1838): 14.

50. Horace Mann, *Eighth Annual Report of the Board of Education, Covering the Year 1844* (Boston: Dutton & Wentworth, 1845), 75–6; Mann, *Twelfth Annual Report*, 117–18.

51. Horace Mann, *Go Forth and Teach, An Oration Delivered Before the Authorities of the City of Boston, July 4, 1842*, (reprint 1937), 44–5.

52. Mann, *First Annual Report*, 62; *Twelfth Annual Report*, 90–8; McCluskey, *Public Schools and Moral Education*, 43.

53. Mann, *The Common School Journal* 1 (November 1838): 14.

54. Feldman, "Non-Sectarianism," 80–1.

55. "Moral Education – The Bible in Schools," *Connecticut Common School Journal* (January 1, 1841), 70; Calvin E. Stowe, *The Religious Element in Education* (Boston: William D. Ticknor & Co., 1844), 20–34; "The Bible Essential in Education," *New York Evangelist* (May 17, 1842), 44.

56. Sidney E. Mead, *The Lively Experiment* (New York: Harper & Row, 1963), 67; Cubberely, *Readings in Public Education*, 202–12; Speech of Bishop John Hughes, in Bourne, *Public School Society*, 436.

57. Mann to Packard, March 18, 1838, reprinted in "Appendix A," in Raymond B. Culver, *Horace Mann and Religion in the Massachusetts Public Schools* (New Haven: Yale University Press, 1929), 241–3.

58. Packard to Mann, Sept. 11, 1838, in ibid., 270, 281.

59. Matthew Hale Smith to Mann (no date), in Cubberely, *Readings in Public Education*, 207; Culver, *Horace Mann and Religion*, 180–213; Dunn, *What Happened to Religious Education*, 155–79.

60. "Remarks on the Seventh Annual Report of the Hon. Horace Mann, Secretary of the Board of Education," *Brownson's Quarterly Review* (October 1844), 547; Second Annual Report of the Board of Education, *Boston Quarterly Review* (October 1839) 405–6; James

M. McDonnell, *Orestes A. Brownson and Nineteenth-Century Catholic Education* (New York: Garland Pub., 1988), 31–56; Arthur M. Schlesinger, *A Pilgrim's Progress: Orestes A. Brownson* (Boston: Little, Brown & Co., 1966).

61. Mann, *First, Second, Eighth, Ninth* and *Twelfth Annual Reports.*

62. Mann to Reverend Matthew Hale Smith, Oct. 19, 1846, in Cubberely, *Readings in Public Education*, 205–6.

63. Mann, *Twelfth Annual Report*, 113, 125.

64. Mann, *Twelfth Annual Report*, 110–11, 119; Mann to Packard, July 22, 1838, in Culver, *Horace Mann and Religion*, 260–1; Mann, *Sequel to the So-Called Correspondence between the Rev. M.H. Smith and Horace Mann* (1847), reprinted in Cubberely, *Readings*, 207–9.

65. Mann, *Twelfth Annual Report*, 98–144.

66. Ibid., 105.

67. Madison, Memorial and Remonstrance (1785), reprinted in Kurland, *The Founders' Constitution*, 5: 82–4. Jefferson also used similar language in his Act for Establishing Religious Freedom (1779, 1786): "the opinions of men are not the object of civil governments, not under its jurisdiction." Ibid., 84.

68. Mann, *Twelfth Annual Report*, 119–20.

69. Ibid., 98–9.

70. Ibid., 105–6, 117, 113.

71. Ibid., 111.

72. Massachusetts Constitution, Declaration of Rights, Art. III.

73. Mann, *Twelfth Annual Report*, 111–12.

74. Ibid., 117–18.

75. Ibid., 118.

76. "The School Question," *Catholic World* (April 1870): 91–106.

77. Horace Bushnell, "Christianity and the Common Schools," *Connecticut Common School Journal* 2 (1839): 102.

78. B. P. Aydelott, *Report on the Study of the Bible in Common Schools* (Cincinnati: S. S. Johnson, Printer, 1837), 3.

79. D. Bethune Duffield, "Education: A State Duty," *American Journal of Education* 3 (1857), 97.

80. Horace Bushnell, "Common Schools" (1853), in *Building Eras in Religion* (New York: Charles Scribner's Sons, 1903), 76, 90–1.

81. "Sectarianism of the Bible," *New York Observer*, May 2, 1840, 70; John Dowling, *The History of Romanism* (New York: Edward Walker, Pub., 1846), 612–13; Aydelott, *Report on the Study of the Bible*, 5.

82. George Burgess, "Thoughts on Religion and Public Schools," *American Journal of Education* 2 (1856), 562, 567.

83. Charles Brooks, "Moral Education," *American Journal of Education* 1 (1856): 340, 338–9.

84. Elson, *Guardians of Tradition*, 41–55.

85. Henry Barnard, *Report on the Use of the Bible in Common Schools* (Providence: Knowles, Vose & Co., 1838), 3–4, 9, 11–13.

86. Vincent P. Lannie and Bernard C. Diethorn, "For the Honor and Glory of God: The Philadelphia Bible Riots of 1840," *History of Education Quarterly* 8 (Sept. 1968): 47–8; Nancy R. Hamant, "Religion in the Cincinnati Schools 1830–1900," *Bulletin of the Historical and Philosophical Society of Ohio* 21 (October 1963): 239, 240.

87. *Catholic Herald*, January 30, 1834, reprinted in Lannie and Diethorn, "For the Honor and Glory of God," 48.

88. Jorgenson, *The State and the Non-Public School*, 73.

89. Elson, *Guardians of Tradition*, 47–53; F. Michael Perko, *A Time to Favor Zion: The Ecology of Religion and School Development on the Urban Frontier, Cincinnati, 1830–1870* (Chicago: Educational Studies Press, 1988), 33–43.

90. Peter Guilday, ed., *The National Pastorals of the American Hierarchy (1792–1919)* (Washington: National Catholic Welfare League, 1923), 27–8. See also "Pastoral Letter of 1840," in ibid., 134; *Catholic Telegraph*, February 2, 1837, 67.

91. Reprinted in F. Michael Perko, "The Building Up of Zion: Religion and Education in Nineteenth Century Cincinnati," *The Cincinnati Historical Society Bulletin* 38 (Summer 1980): 96, 99.

92. Stowe, *Religious Element in Education*, 29–30.

93. *The Reports of the Committee of the Board of Education of the City of Detroit, on the Petition for the Admission of the Bible into the Public Schools of the City* (Detroit: Harsha & Wilcox, 1844), 4, 7.

94. Ibid., 7–8; Jorgenson, *The State and the Non-Public School*, 101–2.

95. "The Bible Burning in New York," *New York Observer*, January 14, 1843, 6.

96. Ray Allen Billington, *The Protestant Crusade 1800–1860* (New York: MacMillan Co., 1938), 220–34; Michael Feldberg, *The Philadelphia Riots of 1844: A Study of Ethnic Conflict* (Westport, CT: Greenwood Press, 1975); Lannie and Diethorn, "For the Honor and Glory of God," 44–106.

97. *Donahoe v. Richards*, 38 Me. 379, 381, 385–90 (1854).

98. Ibid.

99. Ibid., 377, 383; *The Bible in Schools. Arguments of Richard H. Dana, Jr., Esq.,* (Boston: Massachusetts Sabbath School Society, 1855), 16, 18, 19; "The Right of the People to Have the Bible in Public Schools," *New York Observer*, August 31, 1854, 274–5.

100. *The Bible in Schools*, 20–1, 32.

101. *Donahoe v. Richards*, 38 Me. 398–414.

102. Ibid., 398–401.

103. Ibid., 413.

104. Ibid., 409–10.

105. *Commonwealth v. Cooke*, 7 Am. Law Register 417 (Ma. Police Ct. 1859). Background in the incident is found in Robert H. Lord, et al., *History of the Archdiocese of Boston* (New York: Sheed and Ward, 1944), 2: 585–601, 683–703; John T. McGreevy, *Catholicism and American Freedom* (New York: W.W. Norton & Co., 2003), 7–11.

106. *Boston Daily Evening Telegraph*, March 15, 1859, 2, 4; March 16, 1859, 2; *New York Times*, March 16, 1859, 1; *New York Observer*, March 24, 1859, 91.

107. *Boston Daily Evening Telegraph*, March 15, 1859, 2.

108. *Boston Daily Evening Telegraph*, March 18, 1859, 2; March 19, 1859, 2, 4; *Cooke*, 7 Am. Law Reg., 418.

109. *Boston Daily Evening Telegraph*, March 18, 1859, 2; March 21, 1859, 2; March 22, 1859, 2, 4; March 24, 1859, 4; March 25, 1859, 2; McGreevy, *Catholicism and American Freedom*, 7–11, 19–26.

110. Henry F. Durant, *The Arguments in the Case of the Eliot School Rebellion* (Boston: Hubbard W. Swett & Co., 1859), 1–14.

111. Ibid., 6, 9.

112. Ibid., 12–13.

113. Ibid., 20.

114. *Cooke*, 7 Am. Law Reg., 423, 426 (internal quotation marks omitted).

115. Ibid., 423.

116. *New York Times*, July 11, 1859, 3; *Report of the Minority of the Committee on By-Laws*, 17, 20.

117. "Pastoral Letter of 1852," in Guilday, *National Pastorals*, 190.

118. George B. Cheever, *The Right of the Bible in Our Public Schools* (New York: Robert Carter & Bros., 1854), xi.

119. *Spiller v. Inhabitants of Woburn*, 94 Mass. 127, 129 (1866).

120. Samuel T. Spear, *The Bible in Public Schools: A Sermon* (New York: William C. Martin, Printer, 1870).

121. "Our Schools," *Harper's New Monthly Magazine* (March 1860), 550, 554.

Chapter 2

1. Kaestle, *Pillars of the Republic*, 13–61; "Editor's Table," *Harper's New Monthly Magazine* 7 (July 1853), 269.

2. William T. Harris, "The Division of School Funds for Religious Purposes," *The Atlantic Monthly* 38 (August 1876), 171–84.

3. Kaestle, *Pillars of the Republic*, 10–12; Cremin, *American Common School*, 86–94.

4. Kaestle, *Evolution of an Urban School System*, 41–60, 64–71; Ravitch, *The Great School Wars*, 6–7; Pratt, *Religion, Politics, and Diversity*, 161–3.

5. Bourne, *Public School Society*, 85–9; Kaestle, *Evolution of an Urban School System*, 84–5.

6. Ravitch, *The Great School Wars*, 23–4.

7. Pratt, *Religion, Politics and Diversity*, 165–7; Bourne, *Public School Society*, 49–50.

8. Bourne, *Public School Society*, 52–3; Cremin, *American Common School*, 151–6; see *Hunt v. McNair*, 413 U.S. 734 (1973).

9. The Society's initial request was modest: that Bethel Baptist Church should be excluded from receiving surplus state funds while its share of tuition funds be restricted to pay for only those students whose parents attended Bethel Baptist Church. Bourne, *Public School Society*, 52–5, 67. As a result, several Presbyterian, Dutch Reformed, Methodist and even Baptist churches with charity schools supported the Society's memorial. Bourne, *Public School Society*, 71.

10. Ibid., 52–5, 88; Pratt, *Religion, Politics and Diversity*, 167.

11. Bourne, *Public School Society*, 64–7.

12. Ibid., 70–2.

13. Ibid., 72–5, 90–4, 101; Pratt, *Religion, Politics and Diversity*, 167.

14. Bourne, *Public School Society*, 51, 64–7.

15. Ibid., 66. See "The Bible in the Schools," *Report to the Board of Education of the City of New York* (1859) (declaring that the word "sectarian," as used in an 1842 state law, "was intended to be applied to the various denominations into which the people of the state are divided.").

16. Bourne, *Public School Society*, 218.

17. Ibid., 125–9, 142–5.

18. Ibid., 133–8.

19. Ibid., 139.

20. Ibid.

21. Ibid., 140.

22. Ibid., 148.

23. Ibid., 145, 148; Cremin, *American Common School*, 163–4.

24. Pratt, *Religion, Politics and Diversity*, 204–24; *People ex. rel. the Roman Catholic Orphan Asylum Society v. Board of Education*, 13 Barb. 400 (N.Y. Supreme Court, 1851).

25. Kaestle, *Evolution of an Urban School System*, 120–9; Billington, *Protestant Crusade*, 143.

26. Kaestle, *Evolution of an Urban School System*, 146–7.

27. Ibid., 147–8.

28. Guilday, *Pastorals*, 26–8, 78, 134, 74.

29. Vincent P. Lannie, *Public Money and Parochial Education: Bishop Hughes, Governor Seward, and the New York School Controversy* (Cleveland: The Press of Case Western Reserve University, 1968), 11–12; Andrew M. Greeley, *The Catholic Experience* (New York: Doubleday, 1967), 101–25; Billington, *Protestant Crusade*, 146, 290–2; Kaestle, *Evolution of an Urban School System*, 151; Pratt, *Religion, Politics, and Diversity*, 177–8; Ravitch, *Great School Wars*, 36; Glyndon G. Van Deusen, "Seward and the School Question Reconsidered," *Journal of American History* 52 (September 1965): 313, 318.

30. Ravitch, *Great School Wars*, 35–6; Greeley, *The Catholic Experience*, 101–25; McGreevy, *Catholicism and American Freedom*, 37–42; Lannie, *Public Money*, 8–9.

31. Lannie, *Public Money*, 12.

32. David J. O'Brien, "American Catholics and the Diaspora," *Cross Currents* (Summer 1966), 307–23; Greeley, *The Catholic Experience*, 13, 123–6; Billington, *Protestant Crusade*, 290–1.

33. Lannie, *Public Money*, 11–12; Pratt, *Religion, Politics, and Diversity*, 177–8.

34. Allan Nevins and Milton H. Thomas, eds., *The Diary of George Templeton Strong* (New York: The Macmillan Co., 1952), 1: 94.

35. Pratt, *Religion, Politics and Diversity*, 173–6; John W. Pratt, "Religious Conflict in the Development of the New York City Public School System," *History of Education Quarterly* 5 (June 1965): 110–20.

36. Reprinted in Pratt, "Religious Conflict," 112; Bourne, *Public School Society*, 179.

37. Vincent Peter Lannie, "William Seward and Common School Education," *History of Education Quarterly* 4 (September 1964): 181–92; Lannie, *Public Money*, 12–28.

38. John W. Pratt, "Governor Seward and the New York City School Controversy, 1840-2," *New York History* 42 (October 1961): 351–64, 357.

39. Lannie, *Public Money*, 29–44; Bourne, *Public School Society*, 179.

40. Bourne, *Public School Society*, 180–1. The Society submitted an additional statement in March that was more critical of Catholic motivations, noting that the Catholic complaint was not over the content of the instruction in the Society's schools but "because the peculiar doctrines of the Church of Rome are not taught therein." The statement also warned that the funding of parochial schools would lead to an "unholy alliance between Church and State." Ibid., 181–6.

41. Lannie, *Public Money*, 47.

42. Ibid., 47–9; Pratt, *Religion, Politics and Diversity*, 177.

43. *New York Observer*, May 2, 1840, 70; Lannie, *Public Money*, 51–74.

44. *New York Observer*, May 2, 1840, 70; September 5, 1840, 142; August 1, 1840, 122.

45. Bourne, *Public School Society*, 189–95; *Catholic Telegraph*, October 24, 1840, 337.

46. *Complete Works of the Most Rev. John Hughes, D.D., Archbishop of New York*, ed., Lawrence Kehoe (New York: Lawrence Kehoe, 1866), 1: 125–83; Bourne, *Public School Society*, 202–24.

47. Hughes, *Complete Works*, 125–83; Bourne, *Public School Society*, 202–24; Lannie, *Public Money*, 76–9; *New York Observer*, November 7, 1840, 178.

48. Bourne, *Public School Society*, 239–49; Lannie, *Public Money*, 82–5; Greeley, *The Catholic Experience*, 116.

49. Bourne, *Public School Society*, 229–30.

50. Ibid., 224–39; Lannie, *Public Money*, 79–82.

51. Hughes, *Complete Works*, 125–83; Bourne, *Public School Society*, 262, 253–318; Lannie, *Public Money*, 86–98.

52. Bourne, *Public School Society*, 241.

53. Ibid., 317–18.

54. Ibid., 319.

55. Ibid., 323.

56. Billington, *Protestant Crusade*, 148–50.

57. Lannie, *Public Money*, 101.

58. Bourne, *Public School Society*, 322; Lannie, *Public Money*, 101.

59. *New York Observer*, January 16, 1841, 10.

60. Lannie, *Public Money*, 119–23; Pratt, *Religion, Politics and Diversity*, 179–81; *New York Observer*, February 20, 1841.

61. Reprinted in Bourne, *Public School Society*, 353–6; Van Deusen, "Seward and the School Question Reconsidered," 317; Lannie, *Public Money*, 123–4.

62. Bourne, *Public School Society*, 353–6; Van Deusen, "Seward and the School Question Reconsidered," 317–18; Pratt, "Religious Conflict," 113; Lannie, *Public Money*, 123–4.

63. Van Deusen, "Seward and the School Question Reconsidered," 317–18.

64. "Report of the Secretary of State upon Memorials from the City of New York, Respecting the Distribution of the Common School Moneys in That City, Referred to Him by the Senate," Document No. 86, *Documents of the Senate*, April 26, 1841, reprinted in Bourne, *Public School Society*, 356–73; Lannie, *Public Money*, 132–4.

65. See *Zelman v. Simmons-Harris*, 536 U.S. 639 (2002).

66. Bourne, *Public School Society*, 356–73; Pratt, "Religious Conflict," 113; Pratt, *Religion, Politics and Diversity*, 182–3; Lannie, *Public Money*, 130–6.

67. Pratt, *Religion, Politics and Diversity*, 183–4.

68. Bourne, *Public School Society*, 373–402; Lannie, *Public Money*, 137–40.
69. Hughes, *Complete Works*, 242–84; Lannie, *Public Money*, 170–83; Greeley, *The Catholic Experience*, 114.
70. "The 'Church and State' Party," *Christian Reflector* (March 3, 1841), 33; "Agitations of Romanists in New York," *Christian Observer* (March 5, 1841), 38; Lannie, *Public Money*, 170–83; Pratt, *Religion, Politics and Diversity*, 183–5.
71. Bourne, *Public School Society*, 501–23; Pratt, *Religion, Politics and Diversity*, 187–8; Lannie, *Public Money*, 188–237; Ravitch, *Great School Wars*, 58–76.
72. Lannie, *Public Money*, 188–237.
73. O'Brien, "American Catholics and the Diaspora," 307–23; Greeley, *The Catholic Experience*, 114–18.
74. Pratt, *Religion, Politics and Diversity*, 189–90.
75. *People ex rel. Roman Catholic Orphan Asylum v. Board of Education*, 13 Barb. 400 (N.Y. Sup. 1851).
76. Ibid., 410–12; accord *St. Mary's Industrial School v. Brown*, 45 Md. 310 (1876) (parochial training school not a "public" school and ineligible for public funds).
77. See, for example, James W. Sanders, *The Education of an Urban Minority: Catholics in Chicago, 1833–965* (New York: Oxford University Press, 1977), 3–25; Cremin, *American Education*, 163–78.
78. Kaestle, *Pillars of the Republic*, 166–7.
79. See Art II, Declaration of Rights, Pennsylvania Constitution of 1776, Francis Newton Thorpe, The *Federal and State Constitutions, Colonial Charters, and Other Organic Laws of the…United States of America* (Washington, DC: Government Printing Office, 1909), 5:3082 ("And that no man ought or of rights can be compelled to attend any religious worship, or erect or support any place of worship, or maintain any ministry, contrary to, or against, his own free will and consent."); Frank R. Kemerer, "State Constitutions and School Vouchers," *Education Law Reporter* 120 (October 1997), 1.
80. Massachusetts (1827), St. 1826, ch. 143, § 7 (March 10, 1827).
81. *Twelfth Annual Report*, 117–18.
82. Mich. Const. of 1835, Art. I, sec. 5, Thorpe, *Federal and State Constitutions*, 4:1931; Thomas M. Cooley, *Michigan: A History of Governments*, 8th ed. (Boston: Houghton, Mifflin & Co., 1897), 306–29.
83. Thorpe, *Federal and State Constitutions*, 2:1074 (Indiana); 4:1993 (Minnesota); 5:2925 (Ohio); 7:4078–9 (Wisconsin).
84. Kansas Const. Art VII, § 5; Oregon Const. Art. I, § 5.
85. *Scofield v. Eighth School District*, 27 Conn. 499 (1858).
86. *Jenkins v. Inhabitants of Andover*, 103 Mass. 94, 101–2 (1869).
87. *St. Patrick's Orphan Asylum v. Board of Education of the City of Rochester*, 34 How. Pr. 227, 230 (N.Y. Sup. 1867).
88. Billington, *Protestant Crusade*; John Higham, *Strangers in the Land: Patterns of American Nativism 1860–925* (New York: Atheneum, 1955, 1974); Dale T. Knobel, *"America for the Americans" The Nativist Movement in the United States* (New York: Twayne Publishers, 1996).
89. Jorgenson, *State and the Non-Public School*, 28, 69; Viteritti, "Blaine's Wake," 667.
90. *Mitchell v. Helms*, 530 U.S. 793, 829 (2000) (plurality opinion).
91. Hamburger, *Separation of Church and State*, 481–3. "[T]he idea of separation did not become popular until the mid-nineteenth century, when opponents of Catholicism—many of them nativists – depicted it as a principle of government evident in most American constitutions." Ibid., 10.
92. Higham, *Strangers in the Land*, 3; Knobel, *"America for Americans,"* xxiii–xxviii.
93. "A Few Words on Native Americanism," *Brownson's Quarterly Review* (July 1854): 328–34; George M. Stephenson, "Nativism in the Forties and Fifties, with Special Reference to the Mississippi Valley," *Mississippi Valley Historical Review* 9 (December 1922): 185, 190.
94. Jean Baker, *Ambivalent Americans: The Know-Nothing Party in Maryland* (Baltimore: The Johns Hopkins University Press, 1977), 153; Higham, *Strangers in the Land*, 3–4.

95. Billington, *Protestant Crusade*, 1, 36. Not until chapter 13 does Billington explore other "social, political and economic" factors that may have attracted people to the nativist impulse. Ibid., 322.

96. Hamburger, *Separation of Church and State*, 193–251; Jorgenson, *The State and the Non-Public School*, 28–30, 69–110.

97. Michael Feldberg, *The Philadelphia Riots of 1844: A Study of Ethnic Conflict* (Westport, CT: Greenwood Press, 1975), 41; Higham, *Strangers in the Land*, 7–11; Knobel, *"America for Americans,"* 1–39.

98. Higham, *Strangers in the Land*, 7–11; Knobel, *"America for Americans,"* 1–39; Baker, *Ambivalent Americans*, 6–7, 49; Feldberg, *Philadelphia Riots*, 41–73.

99. Higham, *Strangers in the Land*, 3–11; Knobel, *"America for Americans,"* xxvi–39; David Brion Davis, "Some Themes of Counter-Subversion: An Analysis of Anti-Masonic, Anti-Catholic, and Anti-Mormon Literature," *Mississippi Valley Historical Review* 47 (September 1960): 205–24; Michael F. Holt, "The Politics of Impatience: The Origins of Know Nothings," *Journal of American History* 60 (September 1973): 309–31.

100. This discussion relies on Knobel, *"America for Americans,"* 2–26.

101. Ibid; Dale T. Knobel, *Paddy and the Republic: Ethnicity and Nationality in Antebellum America* (Middleton, CT: Wesleyan University Press, 1986), 39–42.

102. Davis, "Themes of Counter-Subversion," 211–12.

103. Holt, "The Politics of Impatience," 309–31; Ronald P. Formisano, *For the People: American Populist Movements from the Revolution to the 1850s* (Chapel Hill: University of North Carolina Press, 2008), 202–3.

104. Knobel, *"America for Americans,"* 2–17; Davis, "Some Themes of Counter-Subversion," 209.

105. Feldberg, *Philadelphia Riots*, 49, 83.

106. Knobel, *"America for Americans,"* 102–3; Feldberg, *Philadelphia Riots*, 49–50, 83–4.

107. *The Diary of George Templeton Strong*, 1:94.

108. Knobel, *"America for Americans,"* 46–7; Knobel, *Paddy and the Republic*, 44–5; Billington, *Protestant Crusade*, 34–6; Baker, *Ambivalent Americans*, 16–17.

109. Billington, *Protestant Crusade*, 34–6, 194–5.

110. Knobel, *Paddy and the Republic*, 133.

111. Billington, *Protestant Crusade*, 23; Higham, *Strangers in the Land*, 7–9; Knobel, *Paddy and the Republic*, 25–6, 66.

112. Michael Feldberg, *The Turbulent Era: Riot & Disorder in Jacksonian America* (New York: Oxford University Press, 1980), 13–14.

113. "Know-Nothingism," *Brownson's Quarterly Review* (October 1854), 449; "A Few Words on Native Americanism," *Brownson's Quarterly Review* (July 1854), 336.

114. Theodore Parker, "The Dangers Which Threaten the Rights of Man," July 2, 1854, in *Additional Speeches, Addresses, and Occasional Sermons* (Boston: Little Brown & Co., 1855), 241; Billington, *Protestant Crusade*, 1–25; Higham, *Strangers in the Land*, 5–6; Knobel, *"America for Americans,"* 31.

115. Hamburger, *Separation of Church and State*, 202.

116. Parker, "The Dangers Which Threaten the Rights of Man," 244–5; Higham, *Strangers in the Land*, 6.

117. Knobel, *"America for Americans,"* 122–4; Samuel F. B. Morse, *Foreign Conspiracy Against the Liberties of the Unites States* (New York: Leavitt, Lord & Co., 1835); Morse, *Imminent Dangers to the Free Institutions of the United States Through Foreign Immigration* (New York: E. B. Clayton, Printer, 1835); Lyman Beecher, *Plea for the West* (Cincinnati: Truman and Smith, 1835).

118. Morse, *Foreign Conspiracy*, 48; McGreevey, *Catholicism and American Freedom*, 29.

119. Morse, *Foreign Conspiracy*, 57, 47; Beecher, *Plea for the West*, 60; Parker, "The Dangers Which Threaten the Rights of Man," 242–3.

120. Davis, "Some Themes of Counter-Subversion," 207.

121. Morse, *Foreign Conspiracy*, 57.

122. Holt, "The Politics of Impatience," 323.

123. Beecher, *Plea for the West*, 118, 60.

124. Baker, *Ambivalent Americans*, 6, referring to the "muscular Protestantism" of the time. Michael F. Holt, *The Rise and Fall of the American Whig Party* (New York: Oxford University Press, 1999), 190.

125. Jenny Franchot, *Roads to Rome: The Antebellum Protestant Encounter with Catholicism* (Berkeley: University of California Press, 1994), 106.

126. *The Catholic Telegraph*, August 29, 1834, 316; Knobel, *Paddy and the Republic*, 45.

127. Baker, *Ambivalent Americans*, 7; Knobel, *Paddy and the Republic*, 45; Knobel, "America for Americans," 30–8.

128. Feldberg, *Philadelphia Riots*, 33–4; Feldberg, *The Turbulent Era*, 9–32.

129. Lannie and Diethorn, "For the Honor and Glory of God," 46–50; Feldberg, *Philadelphia Riots*, 89–92.

130. Lannie and Diethorn, "For the Honor and Glory of God," 55–7.

131. Reprinted in ibid., 57; *New York Observer*, January 28, 1843, 15.

132. Walter Colton, "The Bible in Public Schools," *The Quarterly Review of the American Protestant Association* 1 (January 1844), 11.

133. Lannie and Diethorn, "For the Honor and Glory of God," 59–63.

134. Lannie and Diethorn, "For the Honor and Glory of God," 62–3; Billington, *Protestant Crusade*, 220–3; Feldberg, *Philadelphia Riots*, 94–5.

135. William H. Furness, *A Discourse, Delivered on the Lord's Day, March 17, 1844, in the First Congregational Unitarian Church* (Philadelphia, 1844), 11–12.

136. Ibid., 13, 12.

137. George B. Cheever, *Right of the Bible in Our Public Schools* (New York: Robert Carter & Bros., 1854), 60.

138. Lannie and Diethorn, "For the Honor and Glory of God," 72–8; Feldberg, *Philadelphia Riots*, 99–116; Billington, *Protestant Crusade*, 222–6.

139. Feldberg, *Philadelphia Riots*, 120–40; Lannie and Diethorn, "For the Honor and Glory of God," 78–81.

140. Lannie and Diethorn, "For the Honor and Glory of God," 83–8; Feldberg, *Philadelphia Riots*, 143–59; Billington, *Protestant Crusade*, 227–31.

141. Feldberg, *Philadelphia Riots*, 78–86.

142. *Address of the General Executive Committee of the American Republican Party of the City of New York* (1845): 9–10, reprinted in Hamburger, *Separation of Church and State*, 228–9.

143. Ibid.

144. Billington, *Protestant Crusade*, 238–40.

145. Ronald P. Formisano, *The Birth of Mass Political Parties: Michigan, 1827–61* (Princeton: Princeton University Press, 1971), 217–65; Formisano, *For the People*, 202–3; Michael F. Holt, *The Political Crisis of the 1850s* (New York: John Wiley & Sons, 1978), 101–81; Knobel, "America for Americans," 88–115; John R. Mulkern, *The Know-Nothing Party in Massachusetts: The Rise and Fall of a People's Movement* (Boston: Northeastern University Press, 1990), 61–6.

146. Holt, "The Politics of Impatience," 324; Knobel, "America for Americans," 88–124; Knobel, *Paddy and the Republic*, 129–64.

147. Merle Curti, "The Impact of the Revolutions of 1848 on American Thought," *Proceedings of the American Philosophical Society* 93 (July 1949): 209–15; McGreevy, *Catholicism and American Freedom*, 21–5; Peter Steinfels, "The Failed Encounter: the Catholic Church and Liberalism in the Nineteenth Century," in *Catholicism and Liberalism*, eds., R. Bruce Douglass and David Hollenbach (New York: Cambridge University Press, 1994), 19–44.

148. "The Decline of Protestantism and its Cause," *Brownson's Quarterly Review* (January 1, 1851), 97–117; Greeley, *Catholic Experience*, 106–8; Billington, *Protestant Crusade*, 289–93.

149. Guilday, *National Pastorals*, 191; Billington, *Protestant Crusade*, 292–3; Kaestle, *Pillars of the Republic*, 168–70; Jorgenson, *The State and the Non-Public School*, 93–104; Bushnell, "Common Schools," 72–3.

150. Guilday, *National Pastorals*, 184–6; "Cincinnati—The Pope's Nuncio—Police Riots," *Christian Watchman and Reflector* (February 2, 1854), 18; "The Pope's Nuncio, Bedini," *National Era*

(January 5, 1854), 2; "Catholic Insubordination," *New York Evangelist* (November 3, 1853), 174; Billington, *Protestant Crusade*, 295–314; Michael F. Holt, *Political Parties and American Political Development from the Age of Jackson to the Age of Lincoln* (Baton Rouge: Louisiana State University Press, 1992), 118–19, 282.

151. Mulkern, *The Know-Nothing Party in Massachusetts*, 102–3; Formisano, *For the People*, 198–212.

152. The Kansas Constitution of 1858 is representative. Article I, section 7 provided in part that "No person shall be compelled to attend, erect, or support any place of worship, or maintain any form of worship against his consent." Article VII, the education article, contained two additional provisions restricting funding of private religious education. Section 3 provided that "The income of the school-fund shall be devoted exclusively to the support of [free] schools," while section 5 provided that "No religious sect or sects shall ever have any right to, or control of, any part of the school-funds of this State." Thorpe, *Federal and State Constitutions*, 2:1223, 1232; Jorgenson, *The State and the Non-Public School*, 100–7.

153. Cooley, *Michigan: A History of Governments*, 306–29; Billington, *Protestant Crusade*, 130.

154. "The Bible in Common Schools," *The Reports of the Committee of the Board of Education* (Detroit: Harsha & Wilcox, 1844), 7–8; Formisano, *The Birth of Mass Political Parties*, 220–2; Jorgenson, *The State and the Non-Public School*, 101–2.

155. Thorpe, *Federal and State Constitutions*, 4:1931, 1950; "The Bible in Common Schools," 7–8; Jorgenson, *The State and the Non-Public School*, 101–2.

156. Formisano, *The Birth of Mass Political Parties*, 217–35, 256–7.

157. Alice E. Smith, *The History of Wisconsin* (Madison: The State Historical Society of Wisconsin, 1985), I: 588–9, 593; Richard N. Current, *The History of Wisconsin*, (Madison: The State Historical Society of Wisconsin, 1976), II:162–9; Joseph A. Ranney, "'Absolute Common Ground': The Four Eras of Assimilation in Wisconsin Education Law," *Wisconsin Law Review* (1998): 791, 793–3, 796–7 (placing the development of the parochial school systems after the enactment of the 1848 Constitution); Jorgenson, *The Founding of Public Education in Wisconsin* (Madison: State Historical Society of Wisconsin, 1956), 68–93; Glen, *The Myth of the Common School*, 73–8.

158. Barclay Thomas Johnson, "Credit Crisis to Education Emergency: The Constitutionality of Model Student Voucher Programs Under the Indiana Constitution," *Indiana Law Review* 35 (2001): 173, 200–3.

159. *The Oregon Constitution and Proceedings and Debates of the Constitutional Convention of 1857* (Charles Henry Clay, ed., 1926), 296–308.

160. Ibid., 305 (Statement by Mr. Williams).

161. Ibid., 302–3 (Statement by Mr. Grover). "The late constitutions of the western states have, step by step, tended to a more distinct separation of church and state, until the great state of Indiana, whose new constitution has been most recently framed, embracing very nearly the principle contained in this section, as reported, now under consideration."

162. Jorgenson, *The State and the Non-Public School*, 85–93, 99–104.

163. Mulkern, *The Know-Nothing Party in Massachusetts*, 76, 94–103; Ronald P. Formisano, *The Transformation of Popular Culture: Massachusetts Parties, 1790s-1840s* (New York: Oxford University Press, 1983), 332–3; Billington, *Protestant Crusade*, 412–17; Baker, *Ambivalent Americans*, 47; Oscar Handlin, *Boston's Immigrants* (Cambridge: Belknap Press of Harvard University Press, 1959), 202–3.

164. Mulkern, *The Know-Nothing Party in Massachusetts*, 41–59.

165. Ibid., 102–3; Jorgenson, *The State and the Non-Public School*, 88–9; Formisano, *The Transformation of Popular Culture*, 332–4; Handlin, *Boston's Immigrants*, 211.

166. Mulkern, *The Know-Nothing Party in Massachusetts*, 76, 94–103; Formisano, *For the People*, 199; Formisano, *The Transformation of Popular Culture*, 332–3; Handlin, *Boston's Immigrants*, 202–3.

167. Mulkern, *The Know-Nothing Party in Massachusetts*, 104.

Chapter 3

1. *Board of Education v. Minor*, 23 Ohio St. 211 (1873).

2. F. Michael Perko, "The Building Up of Zion: Religion and Education in Nineteenth Century Cincinnati," *Cincinnati Historical Society Bulletin* 38 (Summer 1980): 96–114; F. Michael Perko, *A Time to Favor Zion: The Ecology of Religion and School Development on the Urban Frontier, Cincinnati, 1830–1870* (Chicago: Educational Studies Press, 1980), 40–50; Robert Michaelsen, "Common School, Common Religion? A Case Study in Church-State Relations, Cincinnati, 1869–70," *Church History* 38 (1969): 202–3.

3. Perko, *A Time to Favor Zion*, 16–53.

4. George M. Stephenson, "Nativism in the Forties and Fifties, with Special Reference to the Mississippi Valley," *The Mississippi Valley Historical Review* 9 (December 1922): 185–202; Lyman Beecher, *A Plea for the West* (Cincinnati: Truman and Smith, 1835), 11, 48, 60, 66, 68, 108–9; Perko, *A Time to Favor Zion*, 51–2; Tracy Fessenden, "The Nineteenth-Century Bible Wars and the Separation of Church and State," *Church History* 74 (December 2005): 784–811.

5. Perko, *A Time to Favor Zion*, 56–65; Nancy R. Hamant, "Religion in the Cincinnati Schools 1830–1900," *Bulletin of the Historical and Philosophical Society of Ohio* 21 (October 1963): 239–40; Margaret DePalma, "Religion in the Classroom: The Great Bible Wars in Nineteenth Century Cincinnati," *Ohio Valley History* (Fall 2003): 18–22.

6. *Catholic Telegraph*, May 16, 1834, n.p.; Stowe, *The Religious Element of Education*, 25; Perko, *A Time to Favor Zion*, 88–9.

7. *Catholic Telegraph*, September 5, 1840, 288.

8. Hamant, "Religion in the Cincinnati Schools," 240–2; Perko, "The Building Up of Zion," 99–103; DePalma, "Religion in the Classroom," 22–4.

9. "Conspiracy Against the School System," *Christian Advocate*, November 25, 1869, 372; Perko, *A Time to Favor Zion*, 154–8.

10. "Religion in the Cincinnati Schools," *Old and New* (January 1870), 122–4; Robert G. McCloskey, ed., *The Bible in the Public Schools: Arguments in the Case of John D. Minor, et al. versus The Board of Education of the City of Cincinnati, et al.* (Cincinnati: Robert Clarke & Co., 1870) (New York: De Capo Press, 1964), x–xi; *The Bible in the Public Schools. Proceedings and Addresses at the Mass Meeting, Pike's Music Hall, Cincinnati, Tuesday Evening, September 28, 1869; with a Sketch of the Anti-Bible Movement* (Cincinnati: Gazette Steam Book and Job Printing House, 1869), 1–2; Hamant, "Religion in the Cincinnati Schools," 242–4; Michaelsen, "Common School, Common Religion," 203–5; DePalma, "Religion in the Classroom," 28.

11. *Cincinnati Gazette*, August 27, 1869; "Conspiracy Against the School System," *Christian Advocate*, (November 25, 1869), 372.

12. *Proceedings and Addresses*, 3–6; Hamant, "Religion in the Cincinnati Schools," 244–5; Perko, *A Time to Favor Zion*, 168–71.

13. Amory D. Mayo, *Religion in the Common Schools: Three Lectures Delivered in the City of Cincinnati, in October, 1869* (Cincinnati: Robert Clarke & Co., 1869), 4, 12.

14. Ibid., 37–9.

15. Ibid., 20–8, 35, 36. See Syllabus of Errors (1864), http://www.papalencyclicals.net/Pius09/p9syll.htm.

16. "Conspiracy Against the School System," *Christian Advocate*, November 25, 1869, 372; "The Common School War," *Christian Advocate*, December 2, 1869, 380.

17. "School Troubles in Cincinnati," *New York Times*, September 27, 1869, 5; Walter P. Herz, "Influence Transcending Mere Numbers: The Unitarians in Nineteenth Century Cincinnati," *Queen City Heritage* 51 (Winter 1993): 11; *The Bible in the Public Schools: Opinions of Individuals and of the Press, and Judicial Decisions* (New York: J.W. Schermerhorn & Co., 1870), 58–71; Michaelsen, "Common School, Common Religion," 206; DePalma, "Religion in the Classroom," 29–30.

18. *The Bible in the Public Schools. Proceedings*, 8–9; *New York Times*, September 29, 1869, 5.

19. *The Bible in the Public Schools. Proceedings*, 21.

20. Ibid., 14–38.

21. Ibid.

22. McCloskey, *Bible in the Public Schools*, xi; Perko, *A Time to Favor Zion*, 176; Michaelsen, "Common School, Common Religion," 207.

23. Helfman, "The Cincinnati Bible War," 380–1; Michaelsen, "Common School, Common Religion," 207.

24. "The Common School War," *Christian Advocate*, December 3, 1869, 380; "Shall the Bible or the Pope be Schoolmaster!" *Zion's Herald*, December 16, 1876, 590.

25. "The Bible in Schools," *Christian Advocate*, November 18, 1869, 364; "Conspiracy Against the School System," *Christian Advocate*, November 25, 1869, 372; *The Bible in the Public Schools. Proceedings*, 8–9.

26. "The Common School," *The Bible in the Public Schools: Opinions*, 8–9, 12; "Has the State a Right to Establish Common Schools?" ibid., 22–4; "The School Question," ibid., 17–18; "Henry Ward Beecher on the School Question," *New York Tribune*, December 3, 1869, 5.

27. "Sectarian Legislation," *New York Times*, February 7, 1870, 5; "The Bible in Our Public Schools," *The Independent*, November 11, 1869, 1.

28. *Living Church*, n.d., in *Bible in the Public Schools: Opinions*, 83–90; *American Churchman*, December 16, 1869, ibid., 77–83; *Utica Herald*, December 1869, ibid., 90–1. See also materials in "The Bible in the Schools," *The Christian World* 21 (February 1870).

29. Samuel T. Spear, *The Bible in the Schools: A Sermon Preached . . . in the South Presbyterian Church of Brooklyn, April 24, 1870* (New York: Wm G. Martin, Pub., 1870); "Reviews and Literary Notices," *Atlantic Monthly* 25 (May 1870), 638–9; "The Battle of the Schools," *Harper's Weekly*, December 18, 1869, 802.

30. *Harper's Weekly*, December 18, 1869, 802.

31. McCloskey, *Bible in the Public Schools*, xii–xiii; Helfman, "Cincinnati Bible War," 381–2; Perko, *A Time to Favor Zion*, 180–1; Michaelsen, "Common School, Common Religion," 210.

32. McCloskey, *Bible in the Public Schools*, xi–xii; Perko, *A Time to Favor Zion*, 179–80; Helfman, "Cincinnati Bible War," 381–2; Herz, "Influence Transcending Mere Numbers," 7–8, 10.

33. McCloskey, *Bible in the Public Schools*, passim.

34. Ohio Const. Art. 1, Section 7, Article VI, Section 2; *Bloom v. Richards*, 2 Ohio St. 387 (1853); *McGatrick v. Wason*, 4 Ohio St. 566 (1855).

35. McCloskey, *Bible in the Public Schools*, 50–1, 48.

36. Ibid., 326, 347.

37. Green, *The Second Disestablishment*, 149–247; *Bloom v. Richards*, 2 Ohio St. 387 (1853); *McGatrick v. Wason*, 4 Ohio St. 566 (1855).

38. McCloskey, *Bible in the Public Schools*, 324–7.

39. Ibid., 152–6, 51.

40. Ibid., 53, 122, 161–2, 211.

41. Ibid., 53, 182.

42. Ibid., 121.

43. Ibid., 253–4, 256.

44. Ibid., 121–2, 65–7, 255–7.

45. Ibid., 256.

46. Ibid., 77–96.

47. Ibid., 253–7.

48. Ibid., 151, 160.

49. Ibid., 265.

50. "Bible in the Schools," *Christian Advocate*, November 18, 1869, 34; "The Coming Fight," *New York Observer*, December 16, 1869, 398; "The Bible in School," *New York Times*, December 3, 1869, 1; "Current Events," *Putnam's Magazine*, January, 1870, 134.

51. McCloskey, *Bible in the Public Schools*, 351; *New York Times*, February 16, 1870, 5.

52. McCloskey, *Bible in the Public Schools*, 358–64.

53. Ibid., 363–71.

54. Ibid., 379–80.

55. Ibid., 379–83.

56. Ibid., 392, 394–6, 403.

57. Ibid., 406, 411–16.

58. Ibid., 414–15.

59. Ibid., 407–8, 392.

60. Ibid., 408–15.

61. *School District of Abington Township v. Schempp*, 374 U.S. 203, 214–15 (1963).

62. *New York Tribune*, February 16, 1870, 4, 8; *Christian Advocate*, March 10, 1870, 73; *Zion's Herald*, March 3, 1870, 103; Ward M. McAfee, *Religion, Race, and Reconstruction* (Albany: State University of New York Press, 1998), 31.

63. *New York Tribune*, February 17, 1870, 4; *New York Times*, March 17, 1870, 4.

64. *The New York Observer*, December 16, 1869, 303; *The Independent*, February 20, 1870, 4.

65. "Current Events," *Putman's Magazine*, January 1870, 134; *New York Times*, June 12, 1872, 5, April 15, 1873, 8; *Christian Advocate*, March 10, 1870, 73; *New York Times*, February 16, 1872, 4; *Atlantic Monthly* 25 (May 1870), 638; "A Wise Decision," *Christian Union*, June 30, 1875, 551.

66. "The Complex Question of the Day," *New York Evangelist*, April 14, 1870, 4. See "The Bible in Schools," *Circular*, December 6, 1869, 301(discussing various perspectives); "Plain Talk on the School Question, *Christian Union*, October 11, 1871, 228 (same); *Bible in the Public Schools, Opinions*, passim.

67. "Current Events," *Putman's Magazine*, January 1870, 134; Samuel T. Spear, *Religion and the State, or The Bible and the Public Schools* (New York: Dodd, Mead & Co., 1876), 24.

68. "The Bible in Common Schools," *Mercersburg Review* (January 1870), 352; *The Bible in the Public Schools: Opinions*, 91–8; Andrew P. Peabody, "The Bible in the Public Schools," *Massachusetts Bible Society* (1870).

69. George N. Webber, "The Bible and the Public Schools: A Sermon Preached at the Congregational Church, in Middlebury, Vt." (April 15, 1870), 8.

70. Rev. W. H. Boole, *A Discourse on the Bible in the Schools and State* (Brooklyn: L. Darbee & Sons, 1870), 11; "How to Establish the Catholic Church," *New York Evangelist*, March 31, 1870, 6; Rev. Daniel Rice, *The Bible in the Public Schools. A Sabbath Evening Discourse* (Lafayette, IN: Rosser, Spring & Co., 1869), 12–13; George R. Rudd, "A Sermon, Preached before the Presbytery of Lyons, N.Y., September 13, 1870," 8.

71. Peabody, *The Bible in the Public Schools*, 7, 14; Rudd, "A Sermon," 7–8.

72. Webber, "The Bible and the Public Schools," 10; Warren H. Cudworth, *The Bible in our Public Schools. Has it any Right There?* (Boston: Alfred Mudge & Son, 1870), 14; "How to Establish the Catholic Church," *New York Evangelist*, March 31, 1870, 6.

73. Peabody, *The Bible in the Public Schools*, 21; Rudd, "A Sermon," 6; "Meeting of the American Institute of Instruction," *Massachusetts Teacher and Journal of Home and School Education* (October 1870), 366.

74. Tayler Lewis, "Education and Religion," in *The Bible in the Public Schools: Opinions*, 24–32; Tayler Lewis, in "The Bible in the Schools," *The Christian World* (February, 1870), 48–50; J. H. Seelye, ibid., 45–8; Lyman Atwater, "Recent Publications on the School Question," *Presbyterian Quarterly and Princeton Review* 42 (April 1870): 313–25; Paul Carter, *The Spiritual Crisis of the Gilded Age* (DeKalb, IL: Northern Illinois University Press, 1971).

75. See sources in previous endnote.

76. Seelye, "Bible in the Schools," 45–7; Lewis, "Education and Religion," 32.

77. Lewis, "Education and Religion," 32; Atwater, "Recent Publications," 324–5.

78. "What does the Bible Represent in the American Common School?" *The Universalist Quarterly and General Review* (July 1874), 265; A. E. Rankin, "Report to the Vermont Board of Education" (September 1868), in "The Bible in the Schools," *The Christian World*, 41–5.

79. Beecher, "The Common School as an Element of National Unity," in *The Bible in the Public Schools: Opinions*, 3–14; Beecher, "The School Question," *The Christian Union*, January 8, 1870, in ibid., 14–19; *New York Tribune*, December 3, 1869, 5; "Foolish Protestants," *Christian Union*, January 15, 1870, 40.

80. Samuel T. Spear, "The Bible and the Public Schools," in *The Bible in the Public Schools: Opinions*, 33–41; Spear, *A Sermon*, 11–14, 17, 22.

81. Spear, *A Sermon*, 20; Beecher, "Our Common Schools," *Christian Union*, December 5, 1875, 476.

82. Spear, *A Sermon*, 23–4.

83. Ibid., 17–19; Spear, *Religion and the State*, 78–86.

84. H. L. Wayland, "The Compulsory Use of the Bible in Schools" (June 1871), 14; Nathaniel Seaver, Jr., *The Bible in the Public Schools* (Davenport, IA: Globe Steam Book and Commercial Print, 1872), 5–6; G. W. Collings, *Bible Reading and Prayer in the Public Schools* (Rockville, IN: Patriot Printing House, 1875), 7–8.

85. Reprinted in "The Bible in the Schools," *The Christian World*, 39–40; reprinted in *The Bible in the Public Schools: Opinions*, 90–1. See also R.P. Stebbins, "Peril and Vindication of our Free Public Schools," *Monthly Review and Religious Magazine* (March 1870), 236–47.

86. "The Bible and the Public Schools," *Jewish Times*, January 28, 1870, reprinted in *The Bible in the Public Schools: Opinions*, 58–62. See Benny Kraut, "Judaism Triumphant: Isaac Mayer Wise on Unitarianism and Liberal Christianity," *Association for Jewish Studies Review* 7/8 (1982/1983): 179-230.

87. Damon Y. Kilgore, *The Bible in Public Schools. [An] Address... Delivered Before the Liberal League of Philadelphia* (Philadelphia: Henry S. Volkmar, Printer, 1875), 6, 11, 16.

88. *Atlantic Monthly* 25 (May 1870): 638–9.

89. Sydney E. Ahlstrom and Robert Bruce Mullin, *The Scientific Theist: A Life of Francis Ellingwood Abbot* (Macon, GA: Mercer University Press, 1987), 72–5, 88–92; William R. Hutchinson, *The Modernist Impulse in American Protestantism* (New York: Oxford University Press, 1976), 29–37; James Turner, *Without God, Without Creed: The Origins of Unbelief in America* (Baltimore: The Johns Hopkins University Press, 1985), 148–9; Hamburger, *Separation of Church and State*, 288–9.

90. *The Index*, June 24, 1875, 294.

91. Ibid., September 30, 1875, 463.

92. Reprinted in "The Bible in the Schools," *The Christian World*, 34.

93. Reprinted in *The Bible in the Public Schools: Opinions*, 57–8; *New York Times*, March 21, 1870, 4.

94. "The School Question," *Catholic World* (April 1870): 91–106. Although the article is unsigned, Bownson's correspondence verified authorship. McDonald, *Orestes Brownson*, 162.

95. "The School Question," *Catholic World*, 98–9; Kaestle, *Pillars of the Republic*, 168–9. Brownson's earlier writings are found in *Brownson's Quarterly Review*, July 1854, 354; October 1, 1858, 425; July 1859, 324.

96. "The School Question," *Catholic World*, 97–102.

97. Ibid., 101–2.

98. "Church and State," *Catholic World* (May 1870): 145–6.

99. Ibid., 146–8, 152.

100. Ibid., 149.

101. Ibid., 147, 155–6.

102. *Board of Education v. Minor*, 23 Ohio St. 211 (1873).

103. Ibid., 243–7.

104. Ibid., 249, 253.

105. Ibid., 248–50, 253–4.

106. Ibid, 250–1.

107. *Christian Statesman*, February 28, 1874, 35; *Christian Advocate*, July 17, 1873, 228.

108. 23 Ohio St. at 221–38.

Chapter 4

1. *The Independent*, February 19, 1874, 4; *The Christian Statesman*, July 15, 1868, 169.

2. Report on the General Conference of the Methodist Episcopal Church, *The Christian Advocate and Journal*, June 2, 1864, 173.

3. Horace Bushnell, *Reverses Needed: A Discourse delivered on the Sunday after the Disaster of Bull Run* (Hartford, CT: L.E. Hunt, 1861), 25–6; Morton Borden, "The Christian Amendment,"

Civil War History 25 (1979): 156–67; Morton Borden, *Jews, Turks and Infidels* (Chapel Hill: University of North Carolina Press, 1984), 61.

4. *The Independent*, September 26, 1861, reprinted in *Proceedings of the National Convention to Secure the Religious Amendment of the Constitution of the United States* (Philadelphia: Christian Statesmen Association, 1874), 53–4.

5. *The Index*, October 28, 1871, 338; "Relation of the Church and State," *Presbyterian Quarterly and Princeton Review* 35 (October, 1863): 689–90; Gary Scott Smith, *The Seeds of Secularization: Calvinism, Culture, and Pluralism in America 1870–1915* (Grand Rapids, MI: Christian University Press, 1985), 53–8.

6. B. F. Morris, *Christian Life and Character of the Civil Institutions of the United States* (Philadelphia: George W. Childs, Pub., 1864), 760–3; Edward L. Pierce, *Memoir and Letters of Charles Sumner, 1860–1874* (Boston: Roberts Brothers, 1898), 4:174.

7. John Alexander, *History of the National Reform Movement* (Pittsburg: Shaw Brothers, 1893), 6–11; David McAllister, "Brief History of the National Reform Movement," *National Reform Documents* (Allegheny, PA: National Reform Association, 1900), 5–6; David McAllister, *Christian Civil Government in America* (Pittsburgh: National Reform Association, 1927), 20–1.

8. McAllister, *Christian Civil Government*, 23; Borden, *Jews, Turks, and Infidels*, 62.

9. *Constitution and Addresses of the National Association for the Amendment of the Constitution of the United States* (Philadelphia: James B. Rodgers, Pub., 1864); McAllister, *Christian Civil Government*, 23.

10. Smith, *Seeds of Secularization*, 15–16; Morris, *Christian Life and Character*, 765–7; "Minutes of the General Assembly of the Presbyterian Church in the U.S.A." (1864), 315; *The Christian Advocate and Journal*, June 2, 1864, 173.

11. *New York Times*, February 2, 1864, 4; *The Independent*, March 17, 1864, 1; "Memorial to the Voting Citizens of the United States" (1866), 7.

12. *The Independent*, February 4, 1864, 4; Borden, *Jews, Turks and Infidels*, 68–9; McAllister, *Christian Civil Government*, 24; Alexander, *History of the National Reform Movement*, 24.

13. Horace Bushnell, "Our Obligations to the Dead" (1865), and "Popular Government by Divine Right" (1864), in Horace Bushnell, *Building Eras in Religion* (New York: Charles Scribner's Sons, 1903), 286–340; Paul C. Nagel, *This Sacred Trust, American Nationality 1798–1898* (New York: Oxford University Press, 1971), 130.

14. Pierce, *Memoir and Letters of Charles Sumner*, 174–5; Borden, *Jews, Turks and Infidels*, 68; Joseph Bradley, Letter to Rev. David McAllister, December 7, 1871, *Miscellaneous Writings*, 357–8; *The Independent*, March 9, 1865, 3; *Proceedings of the National Convention*, 55.

15. The Congressional Globe, 38th Congress, 2nd Session, March 2, 1865, 1272; *New York Tribune*, March 3, 1865, 4.

16. McLoughlin, *The American Evangelicals, 1800–1900* (Gloucester, MA: Peter Smith, 1976), 21.

17. J. H. M'Ilvaine, "Our National Obligations to Acknowledge God in the Constitution of the United States," *Christian Statesman Tracts No. 2* (1868), emphasizing the nation's moral character and its sinfulness for failing to acknowledge God.

18. Alexander, "Opening Address," *Constitution and Addresses*, 11–12; *The Christian Statesman*, October 1, 1867, 18, February 28, 1874, 35; McAllister, *Christian Civil Government*, 23.

19. Stevenson, "The Ends We Seek," *Proceedings of the National Convention*, 26–30; Gaines M. Foster, *Moral Reconstruction: Christian Lobbyists and the Federal Legislation for Morality, 1865–1920* (Chapel Hill: University of North Carolina Press, 2002), 82–3, 101–2, 107–9. Foster places the N.R.A.'s change in strategy as coming after its 1870 drive for an amendment.

20. Daniel G. Strong, "Supreme Court Justice William Strong, 1808–1895: Jurisprudence, Christianity and Reform" (Ph.D. diss., Kent State University, 1985); Charles Fairman, *Mr. Justice Miller and the Supreme Court, 1862–1890* (Cambridge: Harvard University Press, 1939), 167–8; Jon C. Teaford, "Toward a Christian Nation: Religion, Law and Justice Strong," *Journal of Presbyterian History* (Winter 1976), 424–5; *Sparhawk v. Union Passenger Railroad Co.*, 54 Pa. 401 (1867).

21. Address attributed to William Strong, in *Constitution and Addresses*, 9–10; *Proceedings of the National Convention* (1874), 33.

22. William Strong, *Two Lectures Upon the Relations of Civil Law to Church Polity, Discipline, and Property* (New York: Dodd & Mead, Pub., 1875), 31, 35–6.

23. *Proceedings of the National Convention* (1873), xi–xii; "Memorial to the Voting Citizens of the United States, and to All Thoughtful Persons Who Love Their Country," (1866), 6–7.

24. *Proceedings of the National Convention* (1873), xii; *New York Times*, October 30, 1871, 8.

25. *The Christian Statesman*, December 15, 1868, 61; January 15, 1869, 78.

26. Congressional Globe, 40th Congress, Second Session, 2623; ibid., 40th Congress, 3rd Session, 1158 and 1201.

27. Ibid., 1158, 1201.

28. Ibid., 974, 1028.

29. Ibid., 974; Congressional Globe, 41st Congress, 3rd Session, 391–2.

30. *New York Times*, February 13, 1869, 4.

31. *The Christian Statesman*, March 1, 1869, 104.

32. Congressional Globe, 41st Congress, 3rd Session, 1029; Boren, *Jews, Turks and Infidels*, 70.

33. The Congressional Globe, 41st Congress, 3rd Session, 391–2.

34. Ibid.

35. Borden, *Jews, Turks, and Infidels*, 71–2.

36. *New York Times*, January 10, 1871, 4; Spear, *Religion and the State*, 220.

37. *New York Times*, May 29, 1869, 1; "Modern Principles: A Synopsis of Free Religion," *The Index*, January 7, 1871, 1; Ahlstrom and Mullin, *The Scientific Theist*, 74–5; William R. Hutchinson, *The Modernist Impulse in American Protestantism* (New York: Oxford University Press, 1976), 33–7.

38. Ahlstrom and Mullin, *The Scientific Theist*, 88–9; *The Index*, January 21, 1871, 20.

39. Spear, *Religion and the State*, 215.

40. "Is Our Movement Practical?" *The Christian Statesman*, December 15, 1868, 60.

41. *The Index*, January 6, 1872, 1–2; Call for the Centennial Congress of Liberals (1875), in *"Equal Rights in Religion:" Report of the Centennial Congress of Liberals* (Boston: National Liberal League, 1876), 30–1.

42. *The Index*, January 7, 1871, 1; March 12, 1874, 126; April 2, 1874, 162; November 19, 1874, 558; October 14, 1875, 486; "The Practical Separation of Church and State," *Equal Rights in Religion*, 99; Francis E. Abbot, "The Catholic Peril in America," *The Eclectic Magazine of Foreign Literature* (May 1876): 553–69; Ahlstrom and Mullin, *The Scientific Theist*, 95, 101–2,128.

43. "What does the Bible Represent in the American Common School?" *Universalist Quarterly and General Review* (July 1874), 273; "Free Religion," *Catholic World*, November 1, 1869, 195–206.

44. *Chicago Tribune*, January 5, 1872.

45. *The Index*, January 4, 1873, 1; "Nine Demands of Liberalism," in *Cornerstones of Religious Freedom in America*, ed., Joseph L. Blau (Boston: Beacon Press, 1950), 208–9.

46. Ahlstrom and Mullin, *The Scientific Theist*, 102–3; *Proceedings of the National Convention* (1874), 27–8.

47. "Recent Publications on the School Question," *Presbyterian Quarterly and Princeton Review* (April 1870), 319–20, "Christianizing the Constitution," *New York Observer*, February 28, 1872, 42.

48. *The Index*, January 6, 1872, 5.

49. Congressional Globe, 42nd Congress, 2nd Session, 1254, 2630.

50. *The Index*, April 27, 1872, 130.

51. *Board of Education v. Minor*, 23 Ohio St. at 248.

52. *New York Times*, December 9, 1872, 8; *Christian Statesman*, February 28, 1874, 35.

53. *New York Times*, January 20, 1873, 8.

54. *The Index*, March 8, 1873, 119.

55. Ibid., March 15, 1873, 128.

56. *New York Times*, January 28, 1873, 8.

57. *The Christian Advocate* (New York), March 6, 1873, 76.
58. Franklin B. Hough, *American Constitutions* (Albany: Weed, Parsons & Co., 1872), 2:224; John Alexander, *Addresses in Behalf of the Proposed Religious Acknowledgements in the Pennsylvania Constitution* (Philadelphia: Jas. B. Rodgers Co., 1873), 2.
59. Alexander, *Addresses*, 2.
60. Ibid., 4–10.
61. *Purdon's Pennsylvania Statutes Annotated-Constitution* (St. Paul, MN: West Publishing Co., 1930), Preamble, Article I, Sections 3 & 4; *The Index*, January 1, 1874, 8.
62. *The Index*, January 1, 1874, 6. *The Independent* also criticized the constitution's retention of the qualification for public office as "virtually a religious test (which) may be used to exclude those who do not believe in the being of God." *The Independent*, January 8, 1874, 17.
63. *The Christian Statesman*, December 20, 1873, 124–5.
64. *The Index*, January 1, 1874, 8; *The Debates and Proceedings of the Constitutional Convention of the State of Michigan* (Lansing: John A. Kerr & Co., 1867), 1:92, 585, 2:854, 931–5.
65. *The Index*, March 8, 1873, 114; The Congressional Record, 43rd Congress, 1st Session, p. 432; *Boston Globe*, January 8, 1974, 1; *The Index*, January 15, 1874, 30.
66. House Miscellaneous Reports, Vol. 1623, No. 143, 43rd Congress, 1st Session, 1873–1874.
67. *The Christian Statesman*, February 28, 1874, 197.
68. Ibid.
69. Ibid.
70. See generally McAllister, *Christian Civil Government*; Cong. Record, 44th Cong., 1st Sess., 3653 (June 7, 1876).
71. *Church of the Holy Trinity v. United States*, 143 U.S. 457 (1892); Foster, *Moral Reconstruction*, 81–4; 93–117.
72. *The Index*, February 19, 1874, 90.
73. *The Index*, June 15, 1876, 277.
74. *New York Times*, February 5, 1874, 5; *Pittsburgh Dispatch*, February 6, 1874; *The Index*, February 26, 1874, 99–100.
75. *The Independent*, February 19, 1874, 4; February 26, 1874, 18.
76. Ibid.; *The Index*, February 12, 1874, 76. Supporters included leading Professors A. A. Hodge and William Henry Green of Princeton, Professor J. H. Seelye of Amherst, Reverend Stephen H. Tyng, and the presidents of Syracuse, Emory, Indiana State, Wesleyan and the University of North Carolina.
77. *Proceedings of the National Convention* (1874), 27, 33, 75, and passim.
78. Ibid., 26–9.
79. *The Index*, January 1, 1874, 6.
80. Ibid., 6–7.
81. Hough, *American Constitutions*, passim; Blakely, *American State Papers*, passim. The District of Columbia also had Sabbath laws during this period.
82. Borden, *Jews, Turks, and Infidels*, 107–28; Foster, *Moral Reconstruction*, 93–117.
83. *The Chicago Tribune*, February 27, 1875, 2; *The Index*, March 11, 1875, 109; April 1, 1875, 148; *Raleigh News*, February 23, 1875, reprinted in *The Index*, March 25, 1875, 131.
84. *The Index*, January 1, 1874, 6–7; October 14, 1875, 486.
85. Ibid., January 1, 1874, 7.
86. Ibid., 6–7; ibid., January 6, 1876, 6–7.
87. *Report of the Centennial Congress*, 37, 70–1, 163–9; *The Index*, January 6, 1876, 6–7; October 14, 1875, 486.
88. Reprinted in *The Index*, February 12, 1874, 76.
89. Ibid.
90. Ibid., May 7, 1874, 222; December 10, 1874, 589; February 25, 1875, 85; March 18, 1875, 121; *The Independent*, May 14, 1874, 17: December 24, 1874, 15.
91. *The Index*, November 19, 1874, 555; October 14, 1875, 486; Ahlstrom and Mullin, *The Scientific Theist*, 97, 128.
92. Ibid., February 26, 1874, 99.

93. Ibid., November 19, 1874, 558–9; *The Christian Statesman*, October 10, 1874.

94. *Boston Journal*, December 17, 1874, and *Boston Daily Advertiser*, December 17, 1874, reprinted in *The Index*, December 24, 1874, 618.

95. *The Independent*, January 7, 1875, 18; *The Index*, December 24, 1874, 618.

96. *The Index*, January 21, 1875, 30.

97. *Report of the Centennial Congress*, 11; Ahlstrom and Mullin, *The Scientific Theist*, 103.

98. "The Liberal League Convention," *The Index*, September 30, 1875, 462–3; "Opinions of the Press," ibid., July 27, 1876, 350–3, 356–7.

99. *Zion's Herald*, October 14, 1875, 323; *New York Tribune*, October 28, 1875, 5; *The Index*, February 24, 1876, 85.

100. *Zion's Herald*, October 14, 1875, 323; *Christian Advocate*, June 1, 1876, 172; *Christian Union*, May 10, 1876, 366; *The Index*, October 7, 1875.

101. *The Index*, February 10, 1876, 61.

102. *Zion's Herald*, August 10, 1876, 255.

103. "Call for a National Reform Association National Centennial Convention," *The Index*, June 22, 1876, 292.

104. *The Index*, July 13, 1876, 327–8; *Report of the Centennial Congress*, 5 and passim; Ahlstrom and Mullin, *The Scientific Theist*, 106–7; Hamburger, *Separation of Church and State*, 296–302.

105. "Reply," *Report of the Centennial Congress*, 37; "Patriotic Address of the National Liberal League," ibid., 164–5.

106. "Patriotic Address," *Report of the Centennial Congress*, 163–9; *The Index*, July 13, 1876, 327.

107. *The Index*, July 13, 1876, 327–8.

108. Reprinted in *The Index*, July 27, 1876, 350, 357; *Christian Union*, June 28, 1876, 530.

109. *Philadelphia Item*, July 6 and 7, 1876, reprinted in *The Index*, July 20, 1876, 339–40.

110. *The Index*, July 13, 1876, 331; July 20, 1876, 339–40; August 3, 1876, 336–7.

111. Atwood, *Report on the Centennial Congress*, 11; Ahlstrom and Mullin, *The Scientific Theist*, 104–11.

112. Ahlstrom and Mullin, *The Scientific Theist*, 112–15; Foster, *Moral Reconstruction*, 48–54.

113. *Report of the Centennial Congress*, 143–50, 157–62, 170–1; Ahlstrom and Mullin, *The Scientific Theist*, 114–18; Foster, *Moral Reconstruction*, 48–54; George E. McDonald, *Fifty Years of Freethought* (New York: The Truth Seeker, 1929), 190–3.

114. A.F. Beard, "The National Liberal League Congress," *Christian Union*, November 6, 1878, 378; "The National Liberal League," *New York Evangelist*, September 30, 1880, 1; Ahlstrom and Mullin, *The Scientific Theist*, 118–35; McDonald, *Fifty Years of Freethought*, 281–3.

115. "Opinions of the Press," *The Index*, July 27, 1876, 350.

116. Foster, *Moral Reconstruction*, 73–117; Smith, *Seeds of Secularization*, 56–73.

117. Josiah Strong, *Our Country: Its Possible Future and its Present Crisis* (New York: The Baker and Taylor Co., 1885, 1891), 184–7.

118. T. Jackson Lears, *No Place of Grace: Antimodernism and the Transformation of American Culture, 1880–1920* (New York: Pantheon Books, 1981), 42; "Church Attendance," *The North American Review* 137 (1883): 76.

119. Mason W. Pressly, "The 'Personal Liberty' Movement," *The Presbyterian Quarterly* 1 (January 1888): 544; Foster, *Moral Reconstruction*, passim.

120. *The Right of the People to the Sunday Rest* (New York: New York Sabbath Committee, 1880), 5–7; *New York Times*, May 17, 1880, 5.

121. *New York Times*, December 6, 1888, 2; Alonzo T. Jones, *The Two Republics, or Rome and the United States of America* (Battle Creek, MI: Review and Herald Pub. Co., 1891), 820–6; Alonzo T. Jones, *Civil Government and Religion, or Christianity and the American Constitution* (Chicago: American Sentinel, 1889), 65–77; Eric Syme, *A History of SDA Church-State Relations in the United States* (Mountain View, CA: Pacific Press Publishing Assoc., 1973), 29–31.

122. "Senate Rest Bill," Notes of a Hearing before the Committee on Education and Labor, United States Senate, Thursday, December 13, 1888, 50th Cong., 2nd Sess., Mis. Doc. 43; Foster, *Moral Reconstruction*, 96–101.

123. *Church of the Holy Trinity v. United States*, 143 U.S. 457, 471 (1892). See Steven K. Green, "Justice David Josiah Brewer and the 'Christian Nation' Maxim," *Albany Law Review* 63 (1999): 427–76.

124. 26 Congressional Record 1374, 1430 (January 25, 1894).

"We the people of the United States, devoutly acknowledging the supreme authority and just government of Almighty God in all the affairs of men and nations, grateful to Him for our civil and religious liberty, and encouraged by the assurances of His Word to invoke His guidance as a Christian nation, according to His appointed was, through Jesus Christ, in order to form a more perfect union…"

See generally, J. M. Foster, *Christ the King* (Boston: James H. Earle, Pub., 1894); "Hearings Before the House Committee on the Judiciary on H. Res 28, Proposing an Amendment to the Constitution of the United States" (March 11, 1896).

125. Testimony and memorials in support of the amendment came from the N.R.A., the American Sabbath Union, the Christian Endeavor, the Woman's Christian Temperance Union, and the Y.M.C.A. "Hearings on H. Res. 28," 3, 5, 21–3, 32, 38; *Washington Post*, March 12, 1896, 4.

126. Sanford H. Cobb, *The Rise of Religious Liberty in America* (New York: Cooper Square Pub., 1902), 524–5, 527.

127. See generally, McAllister, *Christian Civil Government*; Borden, "The Christian Amendment," 165–7; Smith, *Seeds of Secularization*, 56–73; Borden, *Jews, Turks, and Infidels*, 72–4.

Chapter 5

1. "The Bible in the Schools," *New York Times*, June 12, 1872, 5; "The Bible in Schools," ibid., December 9, 1872, 8; "A Wise Decision," *Christian Union*, June 30, 1875, 551.

2. Reprinted in Joseph P. Thompson, *Church and State in the United States, with an Appendix on the German Population* (Boston: James R. Osgood & Co., 1873), 131–3.

3. See Steven K. Green, "The Blaine Amendment Reconsidered," *Journal of Legal History* 36 (1992): 38–69; Steven K. Green, "'Blaming Blaine': Understanding the Blaine Amendment and the 'No-Funding' Principle," *First Amendment Law Review* 2 (Winter 2003): 107–152. The full text of the original Blaine Amendment follows:

No State shall make any law respecting an establishment of religion, or prohibiting the free exercise thereof; and no money raised by taxation in any State for the support of public schools, or derived from any public fund thereof, nor any public lands devoted thereto, shall ever be under the control of any religious sect; nor shall any money so raised or lands so devoted be divided between religious sects or denominations."

4 Congressional Record, 5453 (1876).

4. *Mitchell v. Helms*, 530 U.S. 793, 828–9 (2000) (plurality opinion). See Hamburger, *Separation of Church and State*, 14, 193–251, 324–6; Jorgenson, *The State and the Non-Public School*, 216–17; J. Viteritti, *Choosing Equality: School Choice, the Constitution, and Civil Society*, 18, 152–4; Note, "School Choice and State Constitutions," *Virginia Law Review* 86 (2000): 117, 134–40.

5. Frank R. Kemerer, "State Constitutions and School Vouchers," *Educational Law Reporter* 120 (1997), 1. A sampling of critical articles includes: Michael J. Dailey, "Blaine's Bigotry: Preventing School Vouchers in Oklahoma…Temporarily," *Tulsa Law Review* 39 (2003): 207–35; Kyle Duncan, "Secularism's Laws: State Blaine Amendments and Religious Persecution," *Fordham Law Review* 72 (2003): 493–593; Robert William Gall, "The Past Should Not Shackle the Present: The Revival of a Legacy of Religious Bigotry by Opponents of School Choice," *N.Y.U. Annual Survey of American Law* 59 (2003): 413–37; Brandi Richardson, "Eradicating Blaine's Legacy of Hate: Removing the Barrier to State Funding of Religious Education," *Catholic University Law Review* 52 (2003): 1041–79; Mark Edward DeForrest, "An Overview and Evaluation of State Blaine Amendments," *Harvard Journal of Law and Public Policy* 26 (Spring 2003): 551–626.

6. "Our Established Church," *Catholic World* 9 (August 1869): 577–87; Pratt, *Religion, Politics and Diversity*, 212–18.

7. *People ex rel. Roman Catholic Orphan Asylum Society v. Board of Education*, 13 Barb. 400 (N.Y. 1851); *St. Patrick's Orphan Asylum v. Board of Education*, 34 How. Prac. 227 (N.Y. Sup. 1867); Pratt, *Religion, Politics, and Diversity*, 209–17.

8. "Our Established Church," *Putnam's Magazine* (July 1869): 39–52; "Our Established Church," *Catholic World*, 577–87; "The Unestablished Church," *Putnam's Magazine* (December 1869): 698–711.

9. "Sectarian Schools," *New York Times*, February 16, 1872, 4–5; "The Sectarian Faucet," *Christian Union*, February 5, 1870, 88; "Apportionment of the Sectarian School Fund," *Christian Union*, September 7, 1870, 283; "Romanism and the Common School System," *Methodist Quarterly Review* (April 1870), 211–12; Pratt, *Religion, Politics, and Diversity*, 196–9.

10. "Sectarian Schools," *New York Times*, February 16, 1872, 4–5; "Are Our Public Schools Free? *Catholic World* (October 1873): 1–9; *Harper's Weekly*, January 1, 1876, reprinted in *The Index*, January 13, 1876, 16.

11. Wolcott Calkins, "The Poughkeepsie Plan," *Christian Union*, May 26, 1875, 436; "The School Question," ibid., March 31, 1875, 267; Pratt, *Religion, Politics, and Diversity*, 199–200, 226–7.

12. "Iowa Politics," *New York Times*, October 11, 1875, 5; "Parochial Free Schools," *The Independent*, March 25, 1875, 16; "The School Question in Buffalo," ibid., April 8, 1875, 14; "Roman Catholics and the Public Schools," *Christian Advocate*, March 25, 1875, 93; "The School Problem," *Christian Union*, April 28, 1875, 354; "Education in Relation to the Stability of the Republic," *Brownson's Quarterly Review*, January 1, 1874, 37–54.

13. Syllabus of Errors (1864), at http://www.papalencyclicals.net/Pius09/p9syll.htm; Elisha P. Hurlbut, *A Secular View of Religion in the State* (Albany, NY: Joel Munsell, 1870), 16–21; "The Common School War," *Christian Advocate*, December 2, 1869, 380 ("The 'Syllabus' equally denies the essential doctrines of American liberty – of out very constitutional law. It denounces liberty of conscience and of worship, of the State's independence of the Church, [and the] toleration of all religions."); ibid., January 13, 1870, 12; James H. Smylie, "American Protestants Interpret Vatican Council I," *Church History* 38 (December 1969): 459–74; Steinfels, "The Failed Encounter: the Catholic Church and Liberalism in the Nineteenth Century," 19–23.

14. "Introduction to the Last Series," *Brownson's Quarterly Review*, January 1, 1873, 1; "The Papacy and the Republic," ibid., January 1, 1873, 12.

15. Hurlbut, *Religion in the State*, 5–6, 16; Brownson, "The Secular not Supreme," *Catholic World* (August 1871), 685–701.

16. "A Fatal Riot," *New York Times*, July 13, 1871, 1; "The Orange Procession," *Christian Union*, July 12, 1871, 24; "The Riot of the Twelfth," *Catholic World* (October 1871): 117–26; Michael A. Gordon, *The Orange Riots* (Ithaca: Cornell University Press, 1993).

17. "Our Public School System," *New York Times*, July 25, 1873, 2; *The Index*, June 24, 1875, 295; November 11, 1875, 517.

18. *New York Tribune*, July 8, 1875, 4; December 24, 1875, 5; *The Index*, August 5, 1875, 365; December 30, 1875, 613.

19. McAfee, *Race, Religion, and Reconstruction*, 192–7; Henry Wilson, "New Departure of the Republican Party," *The Atlantic Monthly* 27 (January 1871): 104–20.

20. "Ohio Politics," *New York Times*, June 2, 1875, 10; "The Campaign in Ohio," *New York Times*, August 2, 1875, 2; "Catholics and the Schools," *Christian Union*, September 8, 1875, 198; William H. Hesseltine, *Ulysses S. Grant, Politician* (New York: Dodd, Mead & Co., 1935), 390; McAfee, *Race, Religion, and Reconstruction*, 190–2; *New York Tribune*, October 1, 1875, 4.

21. "The Coming Struggle," *New York Tribune*, July 8, 1875, 4.

22. *New York Tribune*, October 1, 1875, reprinted in *The Index*, October 28, 1875, 513; "The President's Speech at Des Moines," *Catholic World* (January 1876): 434–5.

23. *The Index*, October 28, 1875, 513; *Chicago Tribune*, October 1, 1875, 3; *New York Tribune*, October 1, 1875, 4; *Christian Advocate*, October 7, 1875, 316; *The Index*, November 4, 1875, 522.

24. *Chicago Tribune*, October 1, 1875, 2; "The President's Speech at Des Moines," *Catholic World*, 433–43.

25. Reprinted in *The Index*, October 28, 1875, 513.

26. *The Index*, October 7, 1875, 469; "The Campaign in Ohio," *New York Times*, August 2, 1875, 2; ibid., October 22, 1875, 1; McAfee, *Race, Religion, and Reconstruction*, 177–81; Higham, *Strangers in the Land*, 28–9.

27. James P. Boyd, *Life and Public Services of Hon. James G. Blaine* (Philadelphia: Publishers' Union, 1893), 351–3; "Letter from Mr. Blaine," *Maine Farmer*, December 4, 1875, 3.

28. Boyd, *Life and Public Services*, 353.

29. Ibid.; *The Index*, December 2, 1875, 570; *Chicago Tribune*, December 8, 1875, 4.

30. The Congressional Globe, 41st Congress, 3rd Session, 592.

31. Ibid., 42nd Congress, 1st Session, 730; ibid., 42nd Congress, 2nd Session, 206, 3892.

32. It is impossible to know whether Blaine had read Hurlbut's anti-Catholic proposal, but the latter lacked a no-funding provision, while Blaine's lacked an attack on any "foreign hierarchical power." Hurlburt, *Religion in the State*, 5.

33. *The Index*, December 2, 1875, 570.

34. *The Index*, November 4, 1875, 517.

35. *New York Tribune*, December 24, 1875, 5; January 20, 1876, 25; February 10, 1876, 61; *The Index*, December 30, 1875, 613.

36. *Presbyterian Quarterly and Princeton Review* (April 1870), 313, 319–20; *Chicago Tribune*, November 11, 1875, 4; "Religious Instruction in the Schools," *The Independent*, May 20, 1875, 4; *Christian Union*, February 2, 1876, 1; "The State and Religion," *The Baptist Quarterly*, January 1874, 77.

37. "The Bible as a School Book," *The Index*, June 24, 1875, 294.

38. *Zion's Herald*, January 13, 1876, 1; April 1, 1875, 100.

39. "The Public Schools and the Churches," *Christian Advocate*, December 2, 1875, 380.

40. *Zion's Herald*, January 13, 1876, 1.

41. *Chicago Tribune*, December 8, 1875, 4.

42. "Seventh Annual Message," in *Ulysses S. Grant, 1822–1885*, ed., Philip P. Moran (Dobbs Ferry, NY: Oceana Pub., 1968), 92; *Chicago Tribune*, December 8, 1875, 4; *The Index*, December 16, 1875, 593.

43. McAfee, *Race, Religion, and Reconstruction*, 192–7; Spear, *Religion and the State*, 21; 4 Cong. Rec. 5190, 5453–6; 5580–95 (1876).

44. "Seventh Annual Message," *Ulysses S. Grant*, 92, 94; *The Index*, December 16, 1875, 593.

45. *New York Times*, December 8, 1875, 6; *New York Tribune*, December 8, 1875, 6; *Harper's Weekly*, January 1, 1876, reprinted in *The Index*, January 13, 1876, 15; *Chicago Tribune*, December 8, 1875, 4; *Scribner's Monthly* (February 1876), 579–80; *Christian Union*, December 15, 1875, 498–9.

46. *New York Evangelist*, quoted in *Christian Union*, December 22, 1875, 519; "The School Question," *Scribner's Monthly* (February 1876), 579.

47. 4 Congressional Record, 5453 (1876).

48. *New York Tribune*, December 15, 1875, 4.

49. *New York Times*, December 15, 1875, 6.

50. *Zion's Herald*, December 16, 1875, 4; December 23, 1875, 4; *Christian Advocate*, February 10, 1876, 4; Spear, *Religion and the State*, passim.

51. "The President's Message," *Catholic World*, February 1876, 707, 711; "The Catholic Church in American History," *American Catholic Quarterly Review* (January 1876), 170.

52. *The Nation*, reprinted in *The Index*, April 27, 1876, 193.

53. "Letter from Mr. Blaine," *Maine Farmer*, December 4, 1875, 3; Abbot, "Catholic Peril in America," 563.

54. "Blaine's Religious Faith," *New York Times*, March 31, 1884, 2; Marie Carolyn Klinkhamer, "The Blaine Amendment of 1875: Private Motives for Political Action," *Catholic Historical Review* 42 (1955): 15–49, 29–34.

55. "Ex-Secretary Blaine's Religion," *New York Times*, March 15, 1884, 5; Theron Clark Crawford, *James G. Blaine* (Philadelphia: Edgewood Pub. Co., 1893), 49–50; Klinkhamer, "The Blaine Amendment," 30.

56. See David Saville Muzzy, *James G. Blaine, Political Idol of Other Days* (New York: Dodd & Mead Co., 1934), 308 ("Republicans were confident of winning thousands of recruits from the ranks of the Irish Americans. Blaine was played up as the great champion of the Irishmen claiming American citizenship who were imprisoned under the Coercion Acts."); Edward Stanwood, *James Gillespie Blaine* (New York: Houghton, Mifflin & Co., 1905), 285. Accord George Brown Tindall, *America: A Narrative History* (New York: W. W. Norton & Co.,1984), 2: 837 (noting Blaine's popularity among Irish Americans).

57. Russell Herman Conwell, *The Life and Public Services of James G. Blaine* (Augusta, ME: E. C. Allen & Co., 1884), 52–3; Thomas Valentine Cooper, *Campaign of '84* (San Francisco: J. Dewing & Co., 1884), 8; Benjamin Perley Poore, *Life and Public Services of Hon. James G. Blaine* (1884), 220–2; "To Vote Against Blaine," *New York Times*, August 24, 1884, 7; "Orangemen Opposing Blaine," ibid., June 10, 1884, 1.

58. James G. Blaine, *Twenty Years of Congress*, 1861–1881 (Norwich, CT: Henry Bill Pub. Co., 1884), 570 and passim. See James Perry Boyd, *Life and Public Services of Hon. James G. Blaine* (Philadelphia: Publisher's Union, 1893) (no mention); Henry Davenport Northrop, *Life and Public Services of Hon. James G. Blaine, "The Plumed Knight"* (Chicago: National Pub. Co., 1893), 104; Crawford, *James G. Blaine* (no mention); Gail Hamilton, *Biography of James G. Blaine* (Norwich, CT: The Henry Brill Pub. Co., 1895) (no mention); Walter Raleigh Houghton, *Early Life and Public Career of Hon. James G. Blaine* (Syracuse: Alvard Bros., 1884) (no mention); Muzzey, *James G. Blaine* (no mention);Willis Flethcher Johnson, *Life of James G. Blaine, "The Plumed Knight"* (Philadelphia: The Atlantic Pub. Co., 1893) (no mention); Henry J. Ramsdell, *Life of Hon. James G. Blaine* (Philadelphia: Hubbard Bros., 1888) (no mention); John Clark Ridpath, et al., *Life and Work of James G. Blaine* (San Francisco: Occidental Pub., 1893) (no mention); Charles Edward Russell, *Blaine of Maine: His Life and Times* (New York: Cosmopolitan Book Co., 1931) (no mention).

59. T. P. Stevenson, "An Open Letter to Members of Congress," *The Christian Statesman*, August 12, 1876.

60. "Congratulatory Letter to the President," *The Index*, January 13, 1876, 19.

61. "The President's Message," *The Index*, December 16, 1875, 594; "The Unfinished Window," ibid., January 6, 1876, 6; Abbot, "Catholic Peril in America," 563.

62. Congressional Record, 44th Congress, First Session, January 17, 1876, 440–1.

63. Ibid., 441.

64. *New York Times*, January 18, 1876, 2; January 18, 1876, 2.

65. *The Independent*, January 20, 1876, 17; see also *Christian Union*, February 9, 1876, 1.

66. "Seventh Annual Message," *Ulysses S. Grant*, 92. Many contest Grant's motives were sincere, based on his past nativist associations. See Tyler Anbiner, "Ulysses S. Grant, Nativist," *Civil War History* 43 (June 1997): 119–41.

67. "Civil Government and Religion," *Presbyterian Quarterly and Princeton Review* (April 1876), 195–236, 205, 224.

68. Ibid., 201, 207–8, 213, 229.

69. Ibid., 232–3.

70. Samuel T. Spear, *Religion and the State or, the Bible and the Public Schools* (New York: Dodd, Mead & Co., 1876), 18, 24.

71. Ibid., 65, 77–87.

72. Ibid., 57–9, 63.

73. Ibid., 28–31, 45–6; Samuel Spear, "The Bible and the Public School," *Princeton Review* (March 1878): 361–94, 390.

74. *Religion and the State*, 212.

75. Ibid., 217.

76. Ibid., 16–24, 276–332; "The Bible and the Public School," 388.

77. McCloskey, *Public Schools and Moral Education*, 99–173; Nicholas Murray Butler, "The Changes of a Quarter Century," in Cubberley, *Readings in Public Education*, 391.

78. McCloskey, *Public Schools and Moral Education*, 99–173; Harris, "Division of School Funds," 171–84.

79. Harris, "Division of School Funds," 176, 180–2; Harris, "The Separation of the Church from the Tax-supported School," *Education Review* 26 (October 1903), 224.

80. McCluskey, *Public Schools and Moral Education*, 145–53; Harris, "The Separation of the Church from the Tax-supported School," 226–7.

81. Harris, "Division of School Funds," 172–5.

82. Ibid., 173, 179; Harris, "The Church, the State, and the School," *North American Review* 133 (September 1881): 215–27; McCloskey, *Public Schools and Moral Education*, 99–173.

83. Harris, "Division of School Funds," 177; McCloskey, *Public Schools and Moral Education*, 145–73; Cubberly, *Readings in Public Education*, 389–92.

84. "The School Question," *Catholic World* (April 1870), 91–106.

85. Bishop B. J. McQuaid, "The Public School Question, as Viewed by a Catholic American Citizen," *The Index*, February 24 and March 2, 1876, 86–9, 98–100; "The School Question," *Catholic World*, 94–9.

86. Brownson, "Church and State," *Catholic World* (May 1870): 145–60; "Our Public Schools," *Brownson's Quarterly Review*, October 1, 1875, 518, 536.

87. "The President's Speech at Des Moines," *Catholic World* (January 1876), 433–43; "The President's Message," *Catholic World* (February 1876), 707–11.

88. "The President's Speech," 436, 438; "The School Question," 101, 105.

89. "The President's Speech," 440; "The President's Message," 708.

90. "The Unfinished Window," *The Index*, January 6, 1876, 6–7. While Jewish leaders, particularly Rabbis Max Lilienthal and Isaac Mayer Wise, publically opposed the N.R.A.'s Christian Amendment and religious exercises in the public schools, they mostly stayed out of the debate over the Blaine Amendment, in part due to Grant's earlier reputation for anti-Semitism. Anbiner, "Ulysses S. Grant, Nativist," 123–127; Borden, *Jews, Turks, and Infidels*, 63–66.

91. "Call for a National Reform Association National Centennial Convention," *The Index*, June 22, 1876, 292; *Equal Rights in Religion. Report of the Centennial Congress of Liberals and Organization of the National Liberal League at Philadelphia* (Boston: National Liberal League, 1876).

92. Higham, *Strangers in the Land*, 28–9.

93. Reprinted in Northrop, *Life and Public Services of Hon. James G. Blaine*, 190.

94. *The Index*, September 7, 1876, 426.

95. Donald Bruce Johnson, *National Party Platforms* (Urbana: University of Illinois Press, 1978), 1:53–4.

96. *New York Times*, June 16, 1876, 2, 4; *New York Tribune*, June 16, 1876, 1.

97. *The Index*, September 7, 1876, 426.

98. Johnson, *National Party Platforms*, 49, 51.

99. Ibid., 49; Tindall, *America*, 2: 702–3.

100. *The Index*, June 29, 1876, 301; *New York Times*, August 5, 1876, 5.

101. Congressional Record, 44th Congress, First Session, August 4, 1876, 5189.

102. Ibid., 5190.

103. Ibid., 5191.

104. Ibid.

105. Ibid., 5245.

106. Ibid., 5245–6.

107. Ibid., 5246.

108. Ibid., 5245.

109. *The Index*, August 17, 1876, 391.

110. 4 Congressional Record, 5453.
111. "An Open Letter," *Christian Statesman*, August 12, 1876, reprinted in *The Index*, August 31, 1876, 411, 414; *The Index*, August 24, 1876, 402.
112. Ibid.
113. 4 Congressional Record, 5454.
114. Ibid., 5580–3; "Our Catholic Senator and the School Question," *Christian Union*, November 3, 1875, 366–7.
115. 4 Congressional Record, 5455, 5589, 5580.
116. Ibid., 5587.
117. Ibid., 5589, 5590, 5592.
118. See statement of Senator Randolph, ibid., 5454–5; ibid., 5585.
119. Ibid., 5587–9, 5590–1.
120. Ibid., 5581; *Slaughter-House Cases*, 83 U.S. 36 (1873); *United States v. Cruikshank*, 92 U.S. 542 (1875).
121. 4 Congressional Record, 5584–5.
122. Ibid., 5456.
123. Ibid., 5562.
124. Ibid.
125. Ibid., 5585.
126. Ibid., 5595.
127. Ibid.
128. "The Defeated Constitutional Amendment," *The Index*, August 24, 1876, 402.
129. Ibid., August 31, 1876, 414.
130. Ibid., August 24, 1876, 403.
131. "Archbishop Purcell's Declaration," *The Independent*, August 17, 1876, 16; "Roman Catholics and the Public Schools," *New York Evangelist*, September 7, 1876, 4; "A New Aspect of the Common school Question," *Christian Advocate*, October 26, 1876, 340.

Chapter 6

1. "Our Schools," *New York Times*, May 8, 1875, 4.
2. *Abington School District v. Schempp*, 374 U.S. 203, 214–15 (1963); *Lemon v. Kurtzman*, 403 U.S. 602 (1971).
3. See *Zelman v. Simmons-Harris*, 536 U.S. 639 (2002); *Santa Fe Independent School District v. Doe*, 530 U.S. 290 (2000).
4. *McCollum v. Board of Education*, 333 U.S. 203, 218 (1948); *Abington School District*, 374 U.S. at 214–15, 272–3; *Mitchell v. Helms*, 530 U.S. 793, 826–9 (2000).
5. 4 Congressional Record 5561 (1876) (statement of Sen. Frelinghuysen); ibid., 5454 (statement of Sen. Randolph). Senator Randolph, a Democrat from New Jersey, made the remark in reference to the House version of the Amendment, which more closely tracked Blaine's proposal, in opposition to the final expanded version proposed by the Republican-controlled Senate.
6. Alfred W. Meyer, "The Blaine Amendment and the Bill of Rights," *Harvard Law Review* 64 (April 1951): 939–45; James M. O'Neill, *Religion and Education Under the Constitution* (New York: Harper & Brothers, 1949), 153–62; F. William O'Brien, "The Blaine Amendment 1875–1876," *University of Detroit Law Journal* 41 (1963): 137–205; Green, "Blaine Amendment Reconsidered," 38–69; Curtis, *No State Shall Abridge*, 169–70.
7. O'Neill, *Religion and Education*, 122–4; Lynford A. Lardner, "How Far Does the Constitution Separate Church and State?" *American Political Science Review* 45 (March 1951): 110–32.
8. 4 Congressional Record 5245–46 (1876).
9. Ibid., 5585 (statement of Sen. Morton).
10. Ibid.
11. Ibid.

12. See Bourne, *Public School Society*, 139 (quoting the Report of the Committee on Laws and Applications to the Legislature, 1831: "Your committee cannot, however, perceive any marked difference in principle, whether a fund be raised for the support of a particular church, or whether it be raised for the support of a school in which the doctrines of that church are taught as a part of the system of education.").

13. The vast majority of court cases during this period involved challenges to public funding of religious orphanages rather than religious schools, the latter being presumed to be ineligible for funding. See *People v. McAdams*, 82 Ill. 356 (1876); *St. Mary's Indus. Sch. v. Brown*, 45 Md. 310 (1876); *Jenkins v. Inhabitants of Andover*, 103 Mass. 94 (1869); *Nevada ex rel. Nev. Orphan Asylum v. Hallock*, 16 Nev. 373 (1882); *People v. Bd. of Educ.*, 13 Barb. 400 (N.Y. 1851); *St. Patrick's Orphan Asylum v. Bd. of Educ.*, 34 How. Pr. 227 (N.Y. 1867).

14. Steven K. Green, "The Insignificance of the Blaine Amendment," *Brigham Young University Law Review* (2008): 295–333.

15. Jill Goldenziel, "Blaine's Name in Vain?: State Constitutions, School Choice, and Charitable Choice," *Denver University Law Review* 83 (2005): 57, 66–70.

16. Arthur S. Beardsley, *Notes on the Sources of the Constitution of the State of Washington 1889–1939* (1939). *See also* Robert F. Utter & Hugh D. Spitzer, *The Washington State Constitution: A Reference Guide* (Westport, CT; Greenwood Press, 2002), 9 (stating that the Washington Declaration of Rights drew from a model drafted by W. Lair Hill, which was based on the Oregon Constitution).

17. Arizona, Florida, Idaho, Kentucky, Montana, New Mexico, North Dakota, Oklahoma, South Dakota, Utah, Washington, Wyoming. Thorpe, *Federal and State Constitutions*, passim.

18. Viteritti, "Blaine's Wake," 670–5; Duncan, "Secularism's Laws," 507–23; DeForrest, "An Overview and Evaluation of State Blaine Amendments," 555–76.

19. See *Mitchell v. Helms*, 530 U.S. at 828–9, and sources in previous note.

20. McAfee, *Religion, Race, and Reconstruction*, 175–202.

21. Marc Stern, "Blaine Amendments, Anti-Catholicism, and Catholic Dogma," *First Amendment Law Review* 2 (Winter 2003):153–78, 176 ("[T]he Blaine Amendments were legitimate attempts to protect a conception of religious liberty different than that endorsed by the Catholic Church...."); Stephen Macedo, *Diversity and Distrust* (Cambridge: Harvard University Press, 2000), 63 ("It was not unreasonable for Americans to worry about the fragility of their experiment in self-government. There were also civic, secular reasons for fearing that an education in orthodox Catholicism could be hostile to republican attitudes and aspirations.").

22. Feldman, "Non-Sectarianism Reconsidered," 111–13 (discussing the "very broad appeal" of the non-sectarian ideology that transcended anti-Catholicism).

23. See Enabling Act, ch. 180, § 4, 25 Stat. 677 (1889). Wyoming and Idaho also wrote constitutions with no-funding provisions in 1889 and 1890, respectively, but were not controlled by the same Enabling Act.

24. Foster, *Moral Reconstruction*, 39–42 (discussing Blair's religious background and his ties to religious reform groups); Anson Phelps Stokes & Leo Pfeffer, *Church and State in the United States* (New York: Harper & Row, 1964), 566 (discussing Blair's association with ultraconservative religious causes).

25. S. 86, 50th Cong., 1st Sess. § 2 (1888); see Robert F. Utter & Edward J. Larson, "Church and State on the Frontier: The History of the Establishment Clauses in the Washington State Constitution," *Hastings Constitutional Law Quarterly* 15 (1988): 451–67.

26. 19 Congressional Record 1218 (1888) (statement of Sen. Blair).

27. See 20 Congressional Record 2100–101 (1889); *United States v. O'Brien*, 391 U.S. 367, 384 (1968) ("What motivates one legislator to make a speech about a statute is not necessarily what motivates scores of others to enact it....").

28. See *Pucket v. Rounds*, Civ. No. 03-5033, 2006 WL 120223 (U.S. Dist. Ct. for South Dakota) (challenging the no-funding provisions of the South Dakota Constitution, Article VI, section 3 and Article VIII, section 16).

29. Feldman, "Non-Sectarianism Reconsidered," 113–14 ("From the beginning of the last quarter of the nineteenth century, states uniformly—even where no state Blaine existed—declined to fund religious education directly, instead restricting direct funding to the public schools.").

30. "The Sectarian Principle," *The Independent*, September 13, 1894, 14–15; "Sectarian Schools Barred," *New York Times*, September 5, 1894; Alfred Young, "Christian and Patriotic Education in the United States," *Catholic World* (July 1894): 444–53; Pratt, *Religion, Politics and Diversity*, 225–56; "Another Proposed Sixteenth Amendment to the Federal Constitution," *American Law Review* 26 (1892): 427–8, 789–93.

31. See N.Y. Const., article 9, section 4; ibid., article 8, section 14; "A Question of Church and State," *The Independent*, June 28, 1894, 10; "Not Modeled After A.P.A.," *New York Times*, June 2, 1894, n.p.; "Sectarian Schools Barred," *New York Times*, September 6, 1894; "Action of the New York State Constitutional Convention," *Christian Advocate*, October 11, 1894, 654; Pratt, *Religion, Politics and Diversity*, 244–56.

32. *Sargent v. Board of Education*, 71 N.Y. Supp. 954–7 (Sup. 1902), aff'd, 69 N.E. 722–5 (N.Y. 1904); Pratt, *Religion, Politics and Diversity*, 268–9.

33. *Nevada v. Hallock*, 16 Nev. 373, 379, 387 (1882); *St. Mary's Industrial School v. Brown*, 45 Md. 310 (1876); *Cook County v. Chicago Industrial School for Girls*, 18 N.E. 183, 193 (Ill. 1888); *Dunn v. Chicago Industrial School for Girls*, 117 N.E. 735 (Ill. 1917).

34. *Smith v. Donahue*, 195 N.Y. Supp. 715, 718 (Sup. Ct. 1922). See also *Jenkins v. Inhabitants of Andover*, 103 Mass. 94 (1869); *People v. McAdams*, 82 Ill. 356 (1876); *Otken v. Lankin*, 56 Miss. 758 (1879); *Millard v. Board of Education*, 10 N.E. 669 (Ill. 1887); *Synod of South Dakota v. State*, 50 N.W. 632 (S.D. 1891); *Atchison, Topeka and Santa Fe Railway v. City of Atchison*, 28 P. 1000 (Kan. 1892); *Sargent v. Board of Education*, 69 N.E. 722 (N.Y. 1904); *Williams v. Board of Trustees*, 191 S.W. 507 (Ky. 1917); *Knowlton v. Baumhover*, 166 N.W. 202 (Iowa 1918); *Bennett v. City of La Grange*, 112 S.E. 482 (Ga. 1922).

35. Benjamin J. McQuaid, "Religion in Schools," *North American Review* 132 (April 1881): 332–44; William T. Harris, "Recent Progress in the Public Schools," *Harper's New Monthly Magazine* 90 (April 1895): 789–95 (discussing professionalization); Samuel Windsor Brown, *The Secularization of American Education* (New York: Teachers College, Columbia University, 1912), 1; R. Laurence Moore, "Bible Reading and Nonsectarian Schooling: The Failure of Religious Instruction in Nineteenth-Century Public Education," *Journal of American History* 86 (March 2000):1581–99.

36. Samuel T. Spear, "The Bible and the Public School," *Princeton Review* (March 1878): 361–94; McQuaid, "Religion in Schools," 332–8; Oliver Johnson, "Morality in the Public Schools," *Atlantic Monthly* 51 (June 1883): 748–57; O. A. Kingsbury, "The Roman Catholics and the Public Schools," *New Englander and Yale Review* (September 8, 1885): 620–34; Lyman Abbott, "Religious Teaching in the Public Schools," *The Century* 49 (April 1895): 943–8.

37. William T. Harris, *Report of the Commissioner of Education for the Year 1896–1897* (Washington, DC: Government Printing Office, 1898), 2189–91.

38. "Respecting Establishments of Religion and Free Public Schools," *In Defense of the Public Schools* (Philadelphia: Aldine Press Co., 1888), 95.

39. McQuaid, "Religion in Schools," 336; "Catholics and Protestants Agreeing on the School Question," *Catholic World* (February 1881), 700–5; Kingsbury, "The Roman Catholics and the Public Schools," 627–8, 632.

40. "Religion and Schools," Notes of Hearings before the Committee on Education and Labor, United States Senate, on Joint Resolution S.R. 86, February 15, 1889, 3.

41. Ibid., 10–13, and passim.

42. John Whitney Evans, "Catholics and the Blair Education Bill," *Catholic Historical Review* 46 (October 1960): 273–98.

43. "The Bible and the Common Schools," *The Biblical World* 20 (October 1902): 243–7; "The Use of the Bible in Public Schools: A Symposium," *The Biblical World* 27 (January 1906): 48–62.

44. Elizabeth Blanchard Cook, *The Nation's Book in the Nation's Schools* (Chicago: The Chicago Woman's Education Union, 1898).

45. *Pfeiffer v. Board of Education*, 77 N.W. 250, 252, 259 (Mich. 1898).

46. Lyman Abbott, "Religious Teaching in the Public Schools," *The Century* 49 (April 1895), 948; Alvin W. Johnson, *The Legal Status of Church-State Relationships in the United States* (Minneapolis: University of Minnesota Press, 1934), 129–36; Stokes and Pfeffer, *Church and State in the United States*, 363–71.

47. *McCormick v. Burt*, 95 Ill. 263, 265 (1880); *Moore v. Monroe*, 20 N.W. 475 (Ia. 1884); *Hart v. School District of Sharpsville*, 2 Lanc. 346, 351–5 (Pa. Com. Pl. 1885).

48. *State ex rel. Weiss v. District Board of School Dist. No. 8*, 44 N.W. 967, 973 (Wis. 1890).

49. Ibid.

50. "A Report on Schools: The Conference Opposes the Secular Idea," *New York Times*, April 8, 1890, 8; "The Bible in Schools," March 19, 1890, 1; March 20, 1890, 4.

51. *Pfeiffer v. Board of Education*, 77 N.W. 250, 252 (Mich. 1898).

52. *Nessle v. Hum*, 1 Oh. N.P. Rpts 140, 142 (1894); *Curran v. White*, 22 Pa. Cty Rpts 201 (1898); *Stevenson v. Hanyon*, 7 Pa. Dist. 585 (1898); *Billard v. Board of Education*, 76 P. 422, 433 (Kan. 1904); *Hackett v. Brooksville Graded Sch. Dist.*, 87 S.W. 792, 794 (Ky. 1905); *Church v. Bullock*, 109 S.W. 115, 118 (Tex. 1908); *Wilkerson v. City of Rome*, 110 S.E. 895 (Ga. 1922); *Kaplan v. Independent School District*, 214 N.W. 18 (Minn. 1927); *People ex rel. Vollmar v. Stanley*, 255 P. 610, 616 (Col. 1927).

53. *State ex rel. Freeman v. Scheve*, 91 N.W. 846, 847 (Neb. 1902); *State ex rel. Freeman v. Scheve*, 93 N.W. 169 (Neb. 1903); *People ex rel. Ring v. Board of Education*, 92 N.E. 251, 254–6 (Ill. 1910); *Herold v. Parish Board of School Directors*, 68 So. 116 (La. 1915); *State ex rel. Dearle v. Frazier*, 173 P. 35 (Wash. 1918); *State ex rel. Finger v. Weedman*, 226 N.W. 348 (S.D. 1929).

54. *Billard*, 76 P. at 433.

55. William T. Harris, *Report of the Commissioner of Education for the Year 1894–1895* (Washington, DC: Government Printing Office, 1896), 2: 1656; Moore, "Bible Reading and Nonsectarian Schooling," 1585–86.

56. Harris, *Report of the Commissioner* (1897–1898), 1539–63; ibid. (1896–1897), 2189–91; ibid. (1888–1889), 622–34.

57. Brown, *Secularization of American Education*, 1–4.

58. Jerome K. Jackson and Constance F. Malmberg, *Religious Education and the State* (Garden City, NY: Doubleday, Doran & Co., 1928), 1.

59. Ibid., 2–5; "Religious Education," *Biblical World* (October 1917), 250–52; Donald E. Boles, *The Bible, Religion, and the Public Schools* (Ames, IO: Iowa State University Press, 1965), 48–53; Richard B. Dierenfield, *Religion in American Public Schools* (Washington, DC: Public Affairs Press, 1962).

60. Boles, *The Bible, Religion, and the Public Schools*, 48–53; Dierenfield, *Religion in American Public Schools*, 39–61; *Everson*, 330 U.S. 1; *McCollum*, 333 U.S. 203; *Engel*, 370 U.S. 421; *Abington School District*, 374 U.S. 203; Edward S. Corwin, "The Supreme Court as a National School Board," *Law and Contemporary Problems* 14 (1949): 3–22; Lynford A. Lardner, "How Far Does the Constitution Separate Church and State?" *American Political Science Review* 45 (March 1951):110–32; Mark deWolf Howe, *The Garden and the Wilderness* (Chicago: University of Chicago Press, 1965), 1–14.

61. Note, "Catholic Schools and Public Money," *Yale Law Journal* 50 (1941): 917–27.

62. Pratt, *Religion, Politics and Diversity*, 282–8; *Judd v. Board of Education*, 278 N.Y. 200, 210 (1938); Daryl R. Fair, "The *Everson* Case in the Context of New Jersey Politics," in *Everson Revisited: Religion, Education, and Law at the Crossroads*, ed. Jo Renee Formicola and Hubert Morken (Lantham, MD: Rowan & Littlefield, 1998), 1–21.

63. *Everson v. Board of Education*, 44 A.2d 333 (N.J. 1945); Brief of Appellant, 5.

64. Fair, "The *Everson* Case," 3–4, 7, 13–14; Higham, *Strangers in the Land*, 57, 173–4; Jo Renee Formicola, "Everson Revisited: 'This is Not . . . Just a Little Case Over Bus Fares,'" *Polity* 28 (Fall 1995): 49–66.

65. *Cochran v. Louisiana State Board of Education*, 281 U.S. 370, 374–5 (1930).

66. Brief of Appellant, 19; Brief of the State Council of the Junior Order of United American Mechanics, 6, 12; Brief of American Civil Liberties Union, 23.

67. Brief of Appellant, 19; Brief of the General Conference of Seventh-Day Adventists, et al., 18.

68. Brief of Appellees, 28–30; Brief of New York, 7–8; Brief of Massachusetts, 11.

69. Brief of the National Council of Catholic Men and the National Council of Catholic Women, passim; Formicola, "Everson Revisited," 51–2.

70. *Everson*, 330 U.S. at 16.

71. Ibid., 11–16; ibid.,19 (Jackson, J., dissenting).

72. Ibid., 57, 61 n.56; J. Woodford Howard, Jr., "On the Fluidity of Judicial Choice," *American Political Science Review* 62 (March 1968), 54; John M. Ferren, *Salt of the Earth, Conscience of the Court: The Story of Justice Wiley Rutledge* (Chapel Hill, University of North Carolina Press, 2004), 264–6; Roger K. Newman, *Hugo Black* (New York; Pantheon Books, 1994), 361–4.

73. "Edge of the Wedge?" *Time*, March 3, 1947, 94; "Now Will Protestants Awake," *Christian Century*, 64 (1947): 262; Stokes and Pfeffer, *Church and State in the United States*, 427–30; Milton R. Konvitz, "Separation of Church and State: The First Freedom," *Law and Contemporary Problems* 14 (1949): 44–60; Wilber G. Katz, "Freedom of Religion and State Neutrality," *University of Chicago Law Review* 20 (Spring 1953): 426–40; Corwin, "The Supreme Court as a National School Board," 3–22; Lardner, "How Far Does the Constitution Separate Church and State?" 110–32; James E. Zucker, "Better a Catholic than a Communist," *Virginia Law Review* 93 (December 2007): 2069–86.

74. *Board of Education v. Allen*, 392 U.S. 236, 251 (1968) (Black, J., dissenting); Gerald T. Dunne, *Hugo Black and the Judicial Revolution* (New York: Touchstone Books, 1977), 109–24; Thomas C. Berg, "Anti-Catholicism and Modern Church-State Relations," *Loyola University Chicago Law Journal* (2001): 121–72; McGarvey, "Thinking on One's Own," 121–24; Hamburger, *Separation of Church and State*, 422–34, 462–63. Much attention has been given to a statement by Black's son that his father was attracted to the Klan because of its anti-Catholicism and that he "used to read all of Paul Blanchard's books exposing power abuse in the Catholic Church." Hugo Black, Jr., *My Father: A Remembrance* (New York: Random House, 1975), 104. Blanchard was the author of hyperbolic books in 1949 and 1951 that critiqued the political machinations of an autocratic Catholic Church. See *American Freedom and Catholic Power* (Boston: Beacon Press, 1949), and *Communism, Democracy, and Catholic Power* (Boston: Beacon Press, 1951).

75. "Catholic Schools and Public Money," 919–23.

76. Andrew M. Greeley, *The Catholic Experience* (New York: Doubleday, 1967); McGarvey, "Thinking on One's Own," 104–21; McGarvey, *American Freedom*, 168; Berg, "Anti-Catholicism and Modern Church-State Relations," 133–42; Mark Massa, "Catholic-Protestant Tensions in Post-War America," *Harvard Theological Review* 95 (July 2002): 319–39; Ferren, *Salt of the Earth*, 267.

77. Dierenfield, *Religion in American Public Schools*, 75–82; "Religion Growth Held Gaining in U.S.," *New York Times*, September 21, 1947, 22; Brief of Appellant, 16–32.

78. Brief of Appellant, 16–32; Brief of A.C.L.U., 15, 9; Brief of the Synagogue Council of America, 36; Appellant's Supplemental Brief, 11.

79. Appellees' Brief, 19, 12, 101–4; Brief of the National Council of Catholic Men and the National Council of Catholic Women in Everson, 19–20. According to Leo Pfeffer, the Board's brief was based on an early manuscript of James M. O'Neill's book, *Religion and Education Under the Constitution*, which Pfeffer claimed represented the official position of the Catholic Church. Pfeffer, "Church and State: Something Less than Separation," *University of Chicago Law Review* 19 (Autumn 1951): 1–29.

80. *McCollum*, 333 U.S. at 211.

81. Ibid., 215–20, 231 (Frankfurter, J., concurring).

82. Murray, "Law or Prepossessions?" *Law and Contemporary Problems* 14 (1949), 23, 39; "Catholic Bishops Hit Supreme Court," *New York Times*, November 21, 1948, 1, 63; Agnes E. Meyer, "The School, the State, and the Church," *Atlantic Monthly* (November 1948): 45–50.

83. *Zorach v. Clauson*, 343 U.S. 306, 308–9, 311, 314 (1952); Note (Samuel Alito), "The 'Released Time' Cases Revisited," *Yale Law Journal* 83 (May 1974): 1202–36.

84. *Zorach*, 343 U.S. at 314; Dierenfield, *Religion in American Public Schools*, 51–2.

85. Brief of Respondents, 10; *Engel*, 370 U.S. at 424–5, 430–2.

86. "Tempest Over School Prayer Ban," *Christianity Today*, July 20, 1962, 46; "Repercussions of Supreme Court Prayer Ruling," ibid., August 3, 1962, 25; *New York Herald Tribune*, July 5, 1962, 18; "Storm Over the Supreme Court," *CBS Reports*, March 13, 1963, transcript 66–7; William E. Boles and Edward N. Beiser, "Prayer and Politics: The Impact of Engel and Schempp on the Political Process," *Journal of Public Law* (1964): 475–503; Philip B. Kurland, "The Regents' Prayer Case: 'Full of Sound and Fury, Signifying…'" *Supreme Court Review* (1962): 1–33.

87. "Tempest Over School Prayer Ban," 46; "Repercussions of Supreme Court Prayer Ruling," 25; Green, "Evangelicals and the Becker Amendment," 541–67.

88. Brief of Appellants in School District of Abington Township, 16–19; *Abington School District*, 374 U.S. at 223.

89. Brief of Appellants in School District of Abington Township, 16–19; *Abington School District*, 374 U.S. at 214–15, 223; ibid., at 257–8, 272–3 (Brennan, J., concurring).

90. Green, "Evangelicals and the Becker Amendment," 557–7; Boles and Beiser, "Prayer and Politics," 483–503; Joan DelFattore, *The Fourth R: Conflicts Over Religion in America's Public Schools* (New Haven: Yale University Press, 2004), 130–44, 191–7; 205–16.

91. *Wallace v. Jaffree*, 472 U.S. 38 (1985); *Lee v. Weisman*, 505 U.S. 577 (1992); *Edwards v. Aguillard*, 482 U.S. 578 (1987); *Stone v. Graham*, 449 U.S. 39 (1980); *Santa Fe Independent School District v. Doe*, 530 U.S. 290 (2000); *Lemon v. Kurtzman*, 403 U.S. 602 (1971); *Meek v. Pittenger*, 421 U.S. 349 (1975); *Grand Rapids School District v. Ball*, 473 U.S. 373 (1985); *Mueller v. Allen*, 463 U.S. 388 (1983); *Witters v. Washington Department of Services for the Blind*, 474 U.S. 481 (1986); *Zelman v. Simmons-Harris*, 536 U.S. 639 (2002).

INDEX